The
RenderMan™ Companion
A Programmer's Guide to Realistic Computer Graphics

Steve Upstill
Pixar

ADDISON–WESLEY

Boston • San Francisco • New York • Toronto • Montreal
London • Munich • Paris • Madrid
Capetown • Sydney • Tokyo • Singapore • Mexico City

Library of Congress Cataloging-in-Publication Data

Upstill, Steve.
  The RenderMan companion / Steve Upstill.
    p.   cm.
  Bibliography: p.
  Includes index.
  ISBN 0-201-50868-0
  1. Computer graphics.   I. Title.
T385.U67 1990
006.6—dc20   89-33853
                                                CIP

Reprinted with corrections July, 1992

Text printed on recycled and acid-free paper.

ISBN 0201508680

13 1415161718 MA   04 03 02 01

13th Printing   August 2001

Preface

Computers and humans have been struggling for almost thirty years to forge a new tool for visual creation. The ambitions of computer graphics practitioners have hurtled along with stunning improvements in imaging methods to the point today that realistic three-dimensional image synthesis is ready to take its place as a legitimate, rich medium for artistic expression. The worldwide computer graphics research community has brought forth a host of powerful techniques all across the field, yielding a quality of realism that would have been too much to hope for twenty, or even ten, years ago. Increases in computer power have brought the machines to within the reach of ordinary mortals, and the quality of software for generating images has improved in parallel. A field that began as a laboratory novelty and luxury is now ready to hand visual artists a mature technology for creating stunning three-dimensional images.

The major remaining problem is familiar from other computing technologies: tying it all together and making it accessible to people. The RenderMan Interface provides that access. It is a method for describing the content of an image to a computer program in the kind of detail required to reach realistic levels of complexity and quality. The two key characteristics of the interface are its conceptual simplicity and its completeness. RenderMan is about access to realism, and this book is about access to RenderMan. Cover to cover, every image in this book was rendered by a computer using the RenderMan Interface.

The capabilities provided by RenderMan span much of present-day computer graphics. It is not practical to cover that topic from the ground up in one book. The ideal reader brings the equivalent of an undergraduate course in computer graphics. He or she should, however, be able to survive armed only with a feeling for three-dimensional geometry, an intuition into the nature of light reflection and enough experience with computers to read a program. Each discussion includes enough background to use the corresponding features, leaving out non-essential information. There are also suggested readings for anyone who wants more background.

Those who will benefit most from the book are programmers who can generate computer models in enough detail to produce interesting imagery. The RenderMan Interface is meant to be challenged, to expand the limits of what can be imagined with a computer.

Structure of This Book

This book is divided into four parts. The first part is intended mainly to define terms and break ground for the remainder. Chapter 1 discusses the roots of synthetic imagery in the behavior of light, and how RenderMan in particular reflects that process. A series of example programs in Chapter 2 step the reader through a basic RenderMan program, introducing specific aspects of the interface as they arise. After these examples, the key concepts of the interface can be drawn in more detail in Chapter 3.

After this introductory material, Parts II and III should be self-sufficient. They separately address the topics of shape and shading. Part II covers shape, the description of geometric content in three dimensions, as well as the process of viewing that content in an image.

The ability to create interesting variations in shading is introduced in Part III: lighting scenes as a whole, and controlling the reflective properties of objects in a scene. The fourth part describes the RenderMan facilities that are important for achieving the most powerful shading effects: the RenderMan

Shading Language. The shading language challenges the user's imagination by providing nearly complete control over the ultimate appearance of an image.

The goal of this book is to help the reader make pictures. In the beginning, we set out the conceptual structures and terms embodied in the interface so that the actual routines and standard methods make sense. That exposition begins with the broad discussions of the introductory chapters and culminates in the Glossary of Technical Terms found at the end. Every term is highlighted in **boldface** when first discussed or significantly expanded, and is summarized in the Glossary.

To flesh out the conceptual material, there are program examples at each point of discussion, beginning with the simplest. The examples should be useful for learning the interface and should serve as a model for writing other programs.

Once the concepts are mastered and the examples assimilated, the book should serve as a useful reference to the functionality of the interface, so that the programmer can look back and quickly extract the information necessary for actually using a particular routine. Two features are provided for that purpose. When a given procedure is first discussed, its definition is set off in a box along with a terse description of the procedure's parameters and, if appropriate, a figure illustrating their meanings. At the end of the book, Appendix D declares all procedures in alphabetical order, together with the page where the boxed declaration appears.

Appendixes A and C are also useful references; Appendix A summarizes the structure of RenderMan for determining what routines are appropriate at which point in a program, and Appendix C reproduces a C header file, *ri.h*, which declares all RenderMan types, routines and constants. Almost any RenderMan renderer will have a similar *ri.h*.

Since this is a book about computer images, they are often used to illustrate points and concepts. All of the raster imagery found in the book was computer-generated, sometimes with line art added using Adobe Illustrator. All the synthetic imagery used the RenderMan Interface.

Acknowledgments

I would never have had the opportunity to write this book without the support of Pixar. It took a great leap of faith to put a work of this complexity into the hands of a first-time author, and a great deal of patience to remain calm as the scope of it actually dawned on him. In particular, the manager of RenderMan, Mickey Mantle, was a steady, cheerful pillar in the face of inflating schedules and authorial stress.

A book like this is like an enormous, open-book take-home quiz consisting of one essay question, in which the only acceptable score is Perfect. Sooner or later you realize that there is no alternative but to cheat by calling on the help of others. My warmest thanks and heartiest gratitude go to those who stepped in to contribute major pieces of this work:

Thanks to: my Alpha readers (Ken Fishkin, Rick Sayre, Alvy Ray Smith, Flip Phillips, Dana Batali) for their tolerance for half-baked prose; my technical reviewers (Tony Derose, Lincoln Hu, Andy Hertzfeld and Andries Van Dam) for their tact; my Beta readers (Ed Catmull, Alvy Ray Smith, Tom Porter, Pat Hanrahan, Darwyn Peachey, Tony Apodaca and Jim Lawson at Pixar, and Peter Shieh and Ann Eldredge at Autodesk) for their thoroughness and immunity to repeated readings; Craig Good for the use of his Venice photograph; and of course to Krys, Andrea and Kimberly for understanding my frequent absences from home to work.

The images rendered here would have had to await the second edition without the tools of the Animation Production Group at Pixar. In particular, Eben Ostby provided handholding and bug fixes with a cheerful, unflappable patience, and Don Conway worked weekends scanning color plates.

Tom Deering and Fred Bunting bore the brunt of turning a large body of text into a finished book: Tom's line art graces every chapter, and Fred had to condense hundreds of technical terms into the Glossary. The two of them skillfully worked a pile of touchy software to great effect, and Tom's twins spent many Dadless weekends as a result. Nancy Tague's consultation on typography and layout was equally essential. Without the sense of craft brought by Nancy, Tom and Fred, the finish on this project would have been much the worse.

Tom Porter spent many weeks with Pat Hanrahan on diplomatic forays gathering industry input on the RenderMan Interface. Tom's contribution didn't stop there, however. He was already available to pick up thankless tasks like managing the production of the color section and correcting images. His desk has for years borne a worn, cracked, chipped bowling pin labelled "The Complexity of Reality." He made that complexity a reality for the cover image, dubbed "Textbook Strike," assembling the power of RenderMan to make what I believe to be the second most convincing synthetic image ever produced. The greatest of thanks to him and to Flip Phillips, who animated the bowling pins.

The entire RenderMan team at Pixar contributed to this book either directly, by pitching in, or indirectly, by clearing space for others to help out. This is the first publicly available fruit of their effort, and I only hope it is a faithful reflection of their capability and dedication.

The RenderMan Mafia, Tony Apodaca, Darwyn Peachey and Jim Lawson, took their microscopes to a whole series of penultimate drafts of the manuscript, ferreting out errors and taking the time in the midst of hectic implementation to nail down dozens of details at the fringes of the specification. They also responded immediately to bug reports when the images were in production.

Mike Malione shouldered the job of collecting a set of useful, pedagogically interesting shaders and making them presentable in Chapter 16. The results are a credit to his care and skill.

Malcolm Blanchard developed the shaders for the office scene, pencils and guitar in the color plates, and he was always available and cheerful to pick up pieces of work, render pictures, instantly read one more penultimate draft or make a program useful, correct or interesting.

Finally, I am in many ways only a ghost writer for the architect of the RenderMan Interface, Pat Hanrahan. Not only did he sally forth on dozens of missions to hammer out a coherent design. Not only did he bring his own clarity of thought and sense of purpose to maintaining order in the face of potential chaos. Not only did he read more drafts of this book than anyone else, and in more exhaustive detail. Not only did his comments clarify the text consistently. But his determination to make this a useful, cogent, accessible description of RenderMan kept me going two drafts after my own motivation had worn to the nub. Those two drafts made all the difference in the finished product.

This book is affectionately dedicated to Pat. His contribution to Pixar will long be felt.

Further Reading

For playing catch-up before beginning this book, there are two widely-used general texts in the computer graphics field. Newman and Sproull's *Principles of Interactive Computer Graphics* [NEWMAN79] has been a standard for almost fifteen years. It covers much more than three-dimensional raster graphics, and as a result its coverage of that topic may be too broad for the current reader. Foley & Van Dam's *Fundamentals of Interactive Computer Graphics* [FOLEY82] is more recent, and has concomitantly more emphasis on raster graphics. The upcoming second edition promises to be exhaustive. Either of these texts would be useful to readers who skip around intelligently. Less well-known, but no less useful, is Roger's *Procedural Elements of Computer Graphics* [ROGERS85].

At a more sophisticated level, computer graphics is a fast-moving field, and a substantial amount of its work is found in academic papers. The yearly proceedings of the Association for Computing Machinery's Special Interest Group in Computer Graphics (SIGGRAPH) are the venue of choice for leading research, along with the ACM's Transactions on Graphics. They form a rich source of advanced information. A good collection of papers from SIGGRAPH and other sources is John Beatty and Kelly Booth's "Tutorial: Computer Graphics" [BEATTY82], published by the Institute of Electrical and Electronic Engineers.

Table of Contents

Foreword

The quest for realism in computer graphics has had an exciting history. We have seen an evolution from crude pictures made on expensive research machines to compelling images made on desktop computers. This quest has been one of the focal points of my professional life. It has been a fun and rewarding twenty years.

Back in the early days of computer graphics we were happy to get any pictures at all. The objects had jagged edges and looked like they were made out of plastic, but we were full of ideas that could make them look better. Our goal was to make the images look real.

Most of the early developments were at the University of Utah, where Dave Evans and Ivan Sutherland started a remarkable computer graphics program that attracted people from all over. In addition, Utah had a notable image processing group led by Tom Stockham. The first major task was to develop algorithms for determining what was visible in a scene, which led to the famous paper analyzing hidden-surface algorithms by Ivan Sutherland, Bob Sproull, and Bob Schumacher. My own contribution here was the development of the Z buffer.

Better shading was the next major problem. Henri Gouraud discovered that he could substantially reduce the faceted appearance of objects by linearly interpolating the values at the vertices of the polygons. Bui T. Phong took it a step further by interpolating the surface normals to get a smoother appearance as well as highlights. I made a contribution by developing texture mapping and the display of cubic patches. It was only at this point that I felt pictures were starting to look realistic. Jim Blinn went on to extend texture mapping to include perturbation of surface normals, producing stunning pictures of oranges and strawberries. We had reached the point where the calculations required to shade became greater than those required to determine visibility.

As computer graphics developed, major advances began to come from other places. I left Utah to become the director of the Computer Graphics Lab at the New York Institute of Technology, where researchers from all over the country came to develop realistic images and animation. During the late 70's Cornell grew to be a major computer graphics institution under the direction of Don Greenberg. It was there that Rob Cook discovered that the lighting model everyone used best approximated plastic. He proposed a different model that let us simulate other surfaces such as metals.

By the early 80's realism fever began to catch hold. Turner Whitted made ray tracing popular and thus started a cavalcade of advances in ray tracing. At first the pictures took extraordinarily long to produce—sometimes days. But again new algorithms were developed that made ray tracing more efficient. Around the same time SIGGRAPH became a phenomenon. Each year the proceedings had some great new pictures: fractals, plants, radiosity, cloth, and so on. Some criticized the emphasis on "pretty pictures," but the excitement was undeniable. Every time someone made a new discovery it would be shown to colleagues, resulting in raves and applause, and causing others to redouble their efforts to do even better.

In 1979 Alvy Ray Smith and I had joined Lucasfilm to start the Computer Division, which later became Pixar. Some of the best people from the above institutions gathered to try to make images so realistic that they could be used in live-action motion pictures.

We decided to throw the book out and start all over again in defining a system for creating extremely complex pictures with a high degree of realism. We had a phenomenal team—both Loren Carpenter and Rob Cook were amazingly productive and creative. Rodney Stock suggested dithered sampling and Tom Porter suggested spreading the samples over time. Rob generalized the shading formulas to "shade trees;" Pat Hanrahan and Jim Lawson generalized this to a shading language.

The pictures were starting to look amazingly good.

And just as important, we now understood what it meant to *describe* an image. This opened the door to the definition of an interface that could be independent of algorithms, hardware, and speed of execution. Pat Hanrahan put all that we knew about geometry, lighting models, ray tracing, antialiasing, motion blur, and shade trees into a compact interface, which he named RenderMan.

Our goal wasn't just to make photorealistic pictures; it was also to make the tools and systems that would let thousands of people create pictures of whatever they chose to design. Two more things were needed. Mickey Mantle, Tony Apodaca, Darwyn Peachey, and Jim Lawson took research code and made software that met the RenderMan specification. Finally, Steve Upstill took responsibility for explaining it all in this book.

The quest for better pictures will continue, of course, but we have reached a new era. I am proud to be associated with the team that has made the results of twenty years of research available to everybody.

Ed Catmull
May 1989

The RenderMan interface is meant to be the PostScript of 3-D graphics. Just as PostScript allows a desktop publishing system to pass page representations to a printer, RenderMan allows three-dimensional modeling systems to pass scene descriptions to a renderer. The design of the RenderMan interface has been the result of a great deal of experience designing and implementing rendering systems.

In 1981 Loren Carpenter wrote the first rendering system at Lucasfilm. He named it REYES, which stood for *Renders Every-*

thing You Ever Saw. After its use for the Genesis effect of *Star Trek II, the Wrath of Khan*, Rob Cook and Ed Catmull set out with Loren to redesign it to produce film resolution pictures of typical naturally occurring scenes. They estimated that a model of a natural scene would require 80,000,000 polygons, a level of complexity far beyond the capabilities or even aspirations of existing systems. This goal forced them to rethink every aspect of the rendering process.

Another fundamental goal of the Lucasfilm group was to avoid digital artifacts in image production. The most troublesome were those due to spatial aliasing (jaggies), but they came to realize that temporal aliasing was responsible for strobing artifacts during animation. A practical motion blur algorithm was therefore needed. A friendly competition among Ed, Loren and Rob culminated in Rob's discovery of stochastic sampling, which led to practical solutions for spatial antialiasing, motion blur, depth of field and a variety of other effects. One of the most challenging aspects of the RenderMan design was the goal to allow control over these effects, and image quality in general.

During this period Rob also invented shade trees, which Jim Lawson and I have enhanced to be a complete shading language. The observation that modeling the optical properties of real materials requires the full generality of a programming language is perhaps the most important aspect of RenderMan, and one which distinguishes it from other graphics interfaces, which are usually based on a single large parameterized shading model.

It was painfully obvious that to routinely generate pictures containing 80,000,000 polygons in a reasonable amount of time would require special-purpose hardware. Tom Porter, Adam Levinthal, Mark Leather and Jeff Mock set out to design a large-scale machine, named the REYES machine, to render these types of pictures. The prospect of the REYES machine led to the need for a standard interface between the scenes being produced by a modeling system and accepted by the rendering system. This interface is RenderMan.

Bill Reeves and I designed the first version of RenderMan. Most notable was the fact that the interface was built around curved-surface primitives. It was thought crucial that the modeling program not convert these into polygons, because this would lead to geometric artifacts (polygonal silhouettes) and shading artifacts (Mach bands) in the final images. In fact, rendering curved surfaces had always been an active area of research at Lucasfilm and Pixar, beginning with Tom Duff's quadric and Loren Carpenter's bicubic patch rendering algorithms. Of course, the process of choosing the exact set of primitives caused many heated arguments. In the end, we allowed for primitives that rendering systems could be expected to handle directly, without decomposition.

Our initial specification was then circulated internally for an extensive design review. Tony Apodaca, Loren Carpenter, Ed Catmull, Rob Cook, Charlie Gunn, Paul Heckbert, Jim Lawson, Sam Leffler, Mickey Mantle, Eben Ostby, Darwyn Peachey, Tom Porter, Bill Reeves, and Alvy Ray Smith all participated in these sessions at Pixar. During these discussions the style and content of the interface was largely decided.

During this time we also began a joint project with Silicon Graphics to work on a three-dimensional graphics library usable for both interactive graphics and high-quality rendering. Jim Clark contributed his thoughts on a simple graphics library and Dan Baum, Paul Haeberli, Allen Leinwand, and Rob Myers at SGI contributed to the design. A major goal of this joint collaboration was to insure that the interface was compatible with emerging trends in real-time graphics workstation hardware.

This version was then circulated to approximately 20 companies for critical review. Included among these were companies specializing in architectural and mechanical CAD, animation production, and graphics workstations. Tom Porter and I personally met with graphics researchers at many of these companies and collected their thoughts and criticisms. Particularly helpful comments came from Andy Van Dam, David Laidlaw, and Jeff MacMann at Stellar; from Peter Schoeler and Gavin Miller at Alias; Kevin Hunter at Symbolics; Roy Hall at Wavefront; Doug Kay, George Joblove, and Lincoln Hu at Industrial Light & Magic; Michael Schantz, Lewis Knapp and Eileen McGinnis at Sun; and from Larry Gelberg and Tom Stephenson at TASC.

I was the chief architect and was responsible for incorporating the comments of the above individuals. During the final design period Tony Apodaca was always available to discuss various design alternatives. It was very difficult to pass a bad idea by him, but if I did, I alone am to blame.

Pat Hanrahan
May 1989

CHAPTER 1

The Image-Rendering World

An astronomer recording images of distant galaxies with an hours-long time exposure. A fashion photographer snapping models in his cunningly lit studio. An Ansel Adams or Elliot Porter capturing the essence of natural grandeur on film. A proud father trying to get his whole squirming family together in the view finder of his camera. These people are all creating images: putting a camera in front of some scene, providing or waiting for appropriate lighting, then focusing that light on film.

Computers mimic that process to make synthetic images. The key parts of the process are defining, arranging and illuminating a set of objects, and employing a viewing device to convert the three-dimensional scene into two dimensions. The difference is that all of these steps take place entirely inside a computer.

This chapter discusses the parallels between the natural and the simulated worlds. The first section is a summary of how pictures come into being in the real world of physics and geometrical optics, and the second discusses how rendering programs simulate that process. The third section draws a distinction between modeling and rendering, and defines the role of the RenderMan Interface between them. Next there is a discussion of the technology RenderMan is designed to harness. The final section describes how the computer process of image synthesis is driven by the interface. The idea is to assemble a global view of the RenderMan methodology and provide a context for the rest of the book.

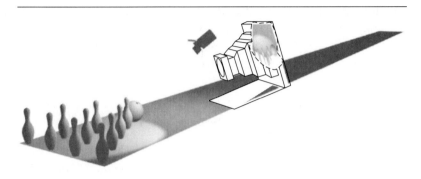

Figure 1.1 *Light interacting with objects and being seen by a viewer*

Making Pictures in the Real World

Taking pictures in nature is a physical process that centers around light: its emission, transmission, reflection and refraction. It ends when the light passes through the lens of an imaging device such as a camera or an eye and finally falls on a recording surface.

Figure 1.1 depicts the basic model of three-dimensional computer graphics. The process features three main elements. **Light** leaves a light source and travels in a straight line through space. It strikes, reflects from and (possibly) passes through **objects**, and ultimately arrives at a **viewer**, a term that includes both the eye and all varieties of camera.

Secondary elements are the objects' **surface**s, where light and object interact; and an **atmosphere**, which may alter the light's direction between objects or modify it as it moves toward the viewer.

Emission

Light pours out from light sources into the world in a straight path until it reaches the surface of an object.

Reflection and refraction

When it reaches a surface, light is partially absorbed, partially reflected and, sometimes, partially transmitted. The surface usually imparts a **color** different from the arriving light by absorbing certain wavelengths more than others. Calculating the direction and color of the outgoing light is a complex problem in geometrical optics, but it can be simplified by some fairly faithful approximations.

Light may be reflected in different ways. Two simple cases represent opposite extremes. A **mirror** reflection leaves the surface in one direction (called, appropriately enough, the **mirror direction**). Mirror reflections are only visible from viewpoints lying in the mirror direction; this specificity provides the coherence of objects seen in a mirror. A **diffuse** reflection, on the other hand, **scatters** light from the point struck, making the surface appear equally bright from all viewpoints. Most surfaces have neither completely mirror nor completely diffuse reflection but are graded somewhere in between. A reflection concentrated near but not confined to the mirror direction is termed a **specular** reflection, or **highlight**. A specular reflection is brightest when seen from viewpoints along or near the mirror direction, and becomes much dimmer away from that direction.

If an object is partially **transparent**, then part of the light passes through it, perhaps with a slight **refraction**, or change of direction.

Hiding

If light leaves a point on a surface toward the viewer, it may strike another object before it gets there. If the second object is opaque, the point on the first object will be hidden from view and will not appear in the image. A surface is in shadow when it is hidden from a light source.

Atmospheric effects

Any light ray traveling between surfaces passes through the atmosphere. Materials like dust and smoke suspended therein may introduce **atmospheric effects** that affect the resulting image. Common atmospheric effects include haze and fog, which make the light seem whiter, and pollution, which gives it a different, usually unpleasant, color. These kinds of atmospheric effects are important to realism partially because they can provide **depth cues**, clues to the relative distances of objects.

Projection

After bouncing around in the world, some light winds up headed toward a viewer consisting of a **viewing device**, such as a camera or eye, which includes a **viewing surface** like film or a retina. The purpose of the viewing device is to organize, or **project**, the light as a coherent **image** onto the viewing surface. The image is simply a two-dimensional representation of a three-dimensional scene.

Viewing devices have an **optical system**, either a set of **lenses** or a **pinhole**, for assembling the image either by bending the light appropriately with a lens or by forcing it to pass through a pinhole. The process of arranging the image on the viewing surface usually has side effects on the content of the image, rendering some objects sharply and throwing others out of focus, bringing some objects nearer or showing them from a wider **field of view**.

Cameras and retinas

Finally, light strikes the viewing surface. In the real world, the most common viewing surfaces are **film**, **print media**, **photosensitive cathodes** (TV tubes) and the **retinas** in the eyes of living organisms. The viewing surface may be flat or curved, and oriented at various angles with respect to the incoming light, thus becoming part of the projection process. But every viewing surface has two key characteristics. First, it is two dimensional. This makes the viewing process one of projection, in the mathematical sense, from a three- to a two-dimensional world. Secondly, each viewing surface has **granularity**: it is divided into physical sensors (grains of emulsion in film, halftone screen in print, photoreceptors in eyes, etc.), the density of which limits how much detail the visual system can extract from the image.

Visual artifacts

In addition to the processes above, certain artifacts can materially affect the final image. If the image of a moving object is exposed over time, it contains **motion blur**: the object appears "smeared." A lens used as a projection device has a characteristic known as **depth of field**: objects over a certain range of depth appear in sharp focus, while others outside that range appear blurred. The extent of that effect depends on the actual size of the opening (the **aperture**) that admits light, as well as on the focus of the camera.

Completeness caveat

This quick sketch minimizes or ignores a number of significant effects of real-world physics: relativistic effects such as bending due to gravity or the curvature of the universe, diffraction, fluorescence, variations in the speed of light, quantum effects, optical chromatic aberration, atmospheric scatter, holography, etc. These are ignored here (and in most of computer graphics) because they have comparatively little impact on images.

Synthetic Rendering: How Computers Do It

The real-world processes described above are reflected in the digital realm by the process of **rendering**. This section sketches the parallels between the two.

Instead of objects, lights and cameras, the rendering process works on an **internal representation** of an imaginary scene in the world. The passage of light through the world, its interaction with surfaces and its projection onto the viewing surface, are simulated by algorithms that operate on this internal representation. One principal job of the RenderMan Interface is to communicate scene descriptions to renderers, giving them enough information to form this internal representation.

Calculating light travel

While there is no reason to dwell on the exact processes that simulate light in the world, there is one important difference between the real world and this computer model. Whereas in physics light pours out into the world, and only some of it arrives at a viewing surface, computers cannot afford to simulate light that is never seen. An alternative model begins with the viewing surface and traces rays back through the projection process into the world. The former asks, "Light is heading out; where does it go?"; the latter "Where did the light hitting the viewing surface come from?" Fortunately, optical processes are mostly reversible, so the question can be answered. Virtually all rendering systems use this tactic.

Hidden surface elimination

The visibility of objects in a scene relative to a viewer is calculated in the process of **hidden-surface elimination**. It is one of the most venerable topics in computer graphics, since it is both tricky to implement and computationally expensive. In fact, renderers are commonly distinguished primarily by the hidden-surface technique they use.

Shading

The **shading** portion of the rendering process calculates the appearance of an object in a scene under a set of light sources. The shading process calculates the light leaving a surface as a function of the light striking the surface. Some of the factors most important to this process are the following:

Colors of the surface and the light source(s). Their interaction is critical; a surface which appears blue under white light will normally appear black under a red one. The color of most real objects (a piece of wood, for example) changes from one point on its surface to another, giving it what is perhaps inappropriately termed **texture** in computer graphics parlance. The meaning of "light source" should be flexible: a mirror or other particularly shiny object might use the whole world, its **environment**, as a "light source."

Position and orientation of the surface relative to the light. The greater the distance between a surface and a light source, or the more the surface faces away from the light, the darker the surface appears. In many cases, the **orientation** of a surface varies from point to point on the surface. The surface of an orange shows how much visual interest can arise solely from a variation in orientation. For some materials, the reflected *color* even varies with orientation.

Roughness of the surface. The **roughness** of a surface refers to how light is scattered when reflected. A surface from which most outbound rays leave near the mirror direction will appear shiny; one with a great deal of scatter will appear rough even though the individual variations are too small to be resolved. A shiny material like metal appears very unmirror-like if its surface is roughened to a matte finish.

Computing the outgoing color and direction of the light striking a surface can be complicated and expensive, requiring clever simplifications and approximations to make it tractable. Both the physics of shading and the problem of finding adequate approximations to it have held considerable attention in computer graphics in recent years, with more progress still to be made. On the positive side, control over shading exerts the most powerful and subtle influence over the ultimate appearance of an image. There is probably more room for creativity and innovation in the shading process than in any other aspect of rendering.

A good rendering system helps users cope with the complexity of shading in three ways: by predefining powerful procedures to hide its complexity behind a few intuitive parameters, by making it possible to write specialized extensions, and by making it easy to incorporate improvements developed by others. The later parts of this book will demonstrate how the RenderMan Interface satisfies all three.

Atmospheric effects

A few rendering systems modify light on the way from surface to viewer. These effects usually depend on the color of the light and the properties of the intervening atmosphere, including its color, moisture content and density. Their effects are usually more profound the greater the distance between viewer and object.

Camera model

The camera model typically used in computer graphics is a simple pinhole. Computationally, this is a very easy approach, since one can calculate a color at a given point on the

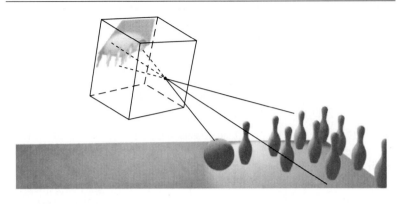

Figure 1.2 *Pinhole viewer*

viewing screen by projecting a line back from that point through the pinhole and out into the world (see Figure 1.2).

A pinhole camera is a simple example of **perspective projection** from world to screen, a term which indicates that objects near the viewpoint appear larger than farther objects of similar size. It is also possible to use an **orthographic projection**, which is like an infinitely long telephoto lens: all objects appear to be the same size regardless of their distance.

These simple projections produce images in which every object is in perfect focus. A more complicated technique is to model a camera complete with a lens and non-infinitesimal **aperture**, or opening. Then, depending on the size of the aperture, and the focal length and focus of the lens, it becomes possible to introduce **depth of field** artifacts: objects within a certain range in depth appear in focus, and those outside that range appear blurred. Advanced renderers may also be capable of blurring the image of a moving object.

Viewing surface

One constant among realistic computer-graphic camera models is a rectangular viewing screen divided into thousands of picture elements, or **pixels**. Each pixel represents the color of the image at a point, typically (but not necessarily) as three smaller dots of red, green and blue. Taken together, the three parts of a pixel can represent a wide variety of colors as independent variations of those three primaries.

Since the pixels are arranged on a regular grid, the **resolution** of the viewing screen can be specified as the number of rows and columns of pixels that make up the screen. An image in the graphics sense is such a two-dimensional rectangular array, or **raster**, of pixels. There are two contrasting, but useful, ways to view the notion of a pixel.

Pixels as screen dots

One view is that the pixels of an image may be used to drive a **display**, a full-color monitor, to see the image of the scene. In this view, each pixel in the image represents the color of one dot on the screen. The resolution of the screen determines the power of the resulting image to resolve details of the world when viewed.

Pixels as samples

In the second view, that of the rendering process, a pixel represents a **sample** in time and space, the color of a part of the world as projected onto the viewing surface during the exposure of the image. Since a pixel on a viewing surface is finite (though small) in size, it represents a view of all the surfaces within some slender pyramidal volume of space. An image retains no notion of the surfaces and geometry involved, and must content itself with a single color at each pixel. This is calculated by **filtering** the scene data projected near a pixel into a single color.

In the real world, each viewing surface contains sensors (grains of film, rods and cones of the eye, etc.) at the pixel locations. The filtering characteristics of the viewing surface then become a function of the sensor's response, the optical system projecting onto the sensor and the influence exerted by neighboring sensors.

Importance of filtering

Given the small size of a pixel, filtering sounds like a very straightforward process, but in fact there are many different ways to filter an image. The choice of filtering technique can

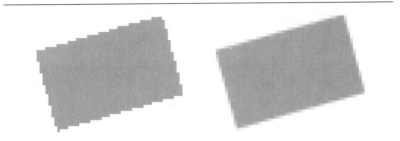

Figure 1.3 *Jaggies: left, an unfiltered image; right, a filtered version*

have pronounced effects on the ultimate quality of the image. Bad or nonexistent filtering results in **aliasing**, the most common example of which is **jaggies**: if each pixel represents the light hitting the screen from one precise, infinitesimal direction, then each pixel will be colored entirely by exactly one point on one surface. If some object has a straight edge inclined slightly with respect to the rows or columns of pixels, and it contrasts strongly with its background, the result is a staircase effect (see Figure 1.3), which is especially pronounced in images of thin lines. It is particularly annoying when objects are animated, their edges crawling with jaggies.

The optical systems of the real world do a fairly good job of eliminating aliasing by their nature. Computer models require filtering to be added as a separate, potentially expensive, process. However, it is essential to truly high-quality realistic imagery.

Quantization

One final problem in the computerized sampling process concerns **quantization**, the process of reducing a sample pixel value to one of a number of fixed values. While pixel values as computed may be arbitrarily precise, digital displays can display pixels at only a small number of discrete levels. If the dynamic range of a display is divided evenly among those levels, and the number of levels is too small, then abrupt changes (**false contours**) appear where the image intensity changes from one level to another.

Modeling vs. Rendering

Making pictures involves two basic concerns. One is subject to creative control, and the other is not. The photographer, or the image synthesist, works to arrange a scene and organize it for a camera. He has great control over lighting, composition, and framing, all elements that vary from picture to picture. However, all pictures are created in the context of a physical universe, whether real or simulated, which is the same from picture to picture: light emission, reflection and transmission; the projection of light through lenses onto film; the photosensitivity of film, etc., do not vary.

The first sections of this chapter described the latter elements in detail. Embodying those elements in a rendering program requires enormous amounts of computing power and programming sophistication for every spot in the image, independent of the actual image content. However, once that program is written — once the universe is formed — creating a synthetic image becomes a matter of setting up those elements that make each image unique, of arranging objects and light sources, placing a camera, and so on.

RenderMan exists at the boundary between the two. The process of setting up a scene goes by the name **modeling**; the scene is turned into an image via the physical simulation called **rendering**. One of the tenets of RenderMan is that it is important and useful to recognize the distinction between the two.

Rendering is a very difficult problem, but it is relatively stable. Since it is based on physical reality, a user's demands in the rendering domain are not likely to change. Modeling, on the other hand, is not so stable in terms of systems designed to support it. An architect's modeler, for example, looks very different from a mechanical-parts design system. As there is no end to the need for new modelers, it makes sense to separate the rendering part of making pictures and provide all modelers access to the same rendering solution. If the interface between these modelers and the renderer is sufficiently general, any modeler can use any renderer driven by that interface.

The overriding goal of the RenderMan Interface is to meet the needs of diverse modelers in accessing the power of a variety of renderers.

What is RenderMan?

RenderMan is first of all a **scene description** methodology: a comprehensive way to describe objects, scenes, lights and cameras so that a computer can create images from them. A user of the RenderMan Interface writes, compiles and runs a program in a conventional programming language, calling a set of special procedures to describe a scene. Some procedures specify the color and placement of objects, while others control the camera viewing the scene and the lights that illuminate the objects.

But while RenderMan's scene description facilities are complete, its true power lies in its facilities for describing the *appearance* of objects. The visual interest of much of the world comes not from **shape**, the geometric configuration of objects, but from **shading**. A typical room environment includes objects of relatively simple shape (the most geometrically complex object in an office, for example, is often the telephone), but wildly varying surface qualities: the paint on the wall may vary from matte to glossy; the underlying surface may be smooth, pebbly or anything in between; metal appears shiny or burnished; practically every kind of plastic has its own idiosyncratic texture; finished wood varies across its surface not only in color but also in shininess. Natural environments are even more diverse. The visual complexity, or detail, seen in these environments arises much more from these surface variations than from the surfaces' overall geometry.

The second purpose of RenderMan is to bring this kind of surface variety to synthetic imagery. The key is flexibility in shading the surfaces in the scene. Geometry is described using RenderMan procedures, and the expectation is that any reasonable scene can be configured using them. Appearance, on the other hand, is governed by a special programming language for describing how light sources emit light, surfaces reflect and transmit it, and the atmosphere affects it. Procedures written in this **shading language** are associated with individual surfaces and called during rendering so that the shading can vary with position on the surface, angle of view, time, etc. The power of this approach can be seen in the color plates later in the book: the geometry is identical for each of the light bulbs there; only the shading procedures vary.

The closest that most current computer graphics systems come to this level of flexibility is the ability to apply images, or **texture maps**, to surfaces in the manner of a decal. A wood-grain texture can be obtained, for example, by using a photograph of wood as a texture map. The shading language, on the other hand, subsumes this approach: not only an image, but *any* function of position on the surface can be used to modulate the surface's appearance. Even better, a texture map can be used as input to a shading language routine and so the shader can operate not just on position, but on any function of position. For example, an inlaid tabletop can be rendered by using a texture map to determine what material to apply where.

The key idea behind RenderMan is the separation between the modeling and the rendering domains. The development of a modeling system no longer requires concurrent development of a renderer. A modeling system using the RenderMan Interface has immediate access to the full power of all features of RenderMan, including the shading language. The modeler can also choose a renderer on any basis that seems appropriate: cost, efficiency, speed or image quality. This selection of renderer may even change during the development of a single model. Designs often proceed from "roughing out" with crude object placement, to "fine-tuning" attributes of lighting and shading.

There are a variety of reasons to use a well-defined standard interface between modeling and rendering:

- It becomes feasible to compare a variety of solutions to the rendering problem, not only for efficiency but for capability. The set of capabilities defined in the interface provides a comprehensive checklist of features for software supporting that interface.

- It becomes possible to choose an appropriate renderer for different stages of the modeling process with different requirements for speed and quality.

- The nature of the output device need no longer be a concern of the modeler.

- Renderers can continue to evolve and improve with a minimum of attention from modelers.

- A flexible interface can be used in novel ways simply by loosening the definition of "rendering." For example, a three-dimensional scene could be represented as line drawings in a book by "rendering" scene data with PostScript commands.

What RenderMan Offers

Later chapters address writing programs with the RenderMan Interface. The remainder of this one relates the facilities provided by the interface to the synthetic rendering model discussed earlier.

Here is a summary of the features RenderMan includes:

- **A small, powerful set of primitive surface types.** The types of geometric primitive included in the interface are basic: they do not readily reduce to simpler primitives without sacrificing either efficiency or information useful in rendering.

- **Hierarchical modeling.** Surface primitives may be grouped together and treated as a single composite object with common properties.

- **Constructive Solid Geometry.** Objects may be defined by taking the union, intersection or difference of other objects.

- **Hierarchical geometry.** RenderMan supports a stacked geometric transformation environment.

- **Camera model.** The RenderMan Interface provides a low-level camera model and the ability to specify an arbitrary geometric transformation in projecting a scene into an image. Real camera attributes like motion blur and depth of field can be specified.

- **Shading attributes.** An advanced renderer should be able to get any information it needs to produce its pictures. Since any such information can be ignored by more primitive renderers, RenderMan supports a wide variety of shading attributes.

- **Extensibility.** User definitions and procedures can be included in the RenderMan Interface at many key points, including object definitions, geometric transformations, appearance attributes and shading.

- **Generalized shading model.** The method by which object and light positions and colors are transformed into image colors is generalized by RenderMan: shading models can be expressed by the user as a procedure in the RenderMan Shading Language.

There are other potential features of a rendering interface that are left out of RenderMan, either because they compromise its conceptual simplicity, or because it is better to do one thing well than several things poorly. Accordingly, the RenderMan world leaves out the following:

- **Abstractions peculiar to modelers.** In the interest of simplicity and generality, RenderMan avoids encroaching on the modeling realm. High-level objects can be reduced to RenderMan's basic surface types. The same philosophy is applied to camera characteristics: a variety of useful parameters is built into the system, sufficient for expressing more human-oriented controls.

- **Implementation details.** As part of its role as a standard, the RenderMan Interface should not care about the nature of any renderer for which it serves as a front end. Any implementation-dependent information can be communicated using one of the "back-door" methods included in the interface.

- **Editable display list.** The models built up by the interface are write-once: it is not possible to modify a single object or transformation from one image to the next. Scenes must be specified in their entirety for each image. However, it *is* possible to define invariant parts of a model, then efficiently create instances of them at each frame.

- **Database capabilities.** RenderMan is not a database system. Descriptions of models may only be passed into the interface. There is no mechanism for reading back the descriptions. Database issues are so important that to include them in RenderMan would have complicated the rendering interface and probably would not have produced a good database system either.

CHAPTER 2

Getting Started

This chapter and the next are complementary parts of a first discussion of RenderMan. This chapter is "bottom-up," starting with a simple example program and progressing to more elaborate ones, introducing concepts and principles as they arise. In the next chapter, a more "top-down" approach groups those concepts and principles according to function and provides more detail. Taken together, the two chapters should provide the groundwork for specifics laid out in later chapters.

The programs here introduce the basics of creating an image with the RenderMan Interface: creating and viewing a simple object, replicating it to make a more interesting object, coloring objects using the graphics environment, and creating an animation by modifying a scene over time. The examples are deliberately simplified. The goal is not to create mind-boggling graphics, but to set out some key concepts in the context of specific code. The elaborations of later chapters introduce more interesting object, lighting, shading and viewing procedures.

A Basic Program

The first example program, shown in Listing 2.1, does everything necessary to produce an image: initialize the interface and create a scene by describing an object to be rendered.

The most obvious characteristic of the program is that it is written in the C language, as are all the examples in this book. The RenderMan Interface is *not* limited to C. Its procedure

```
#include <ri.h>
RtPoint Square[4] = { {.5,.5,.5}, {.5,-.5,.5}, {-.5,-.5,.5}, {-.5,.5,.5}
};

main()
{
    RiBegin(RI_NULL);   /* Start the renderer */
        RiWorldBegin();
            RiSurface( "constant", RI_NULL);
            RiPolygon( 4,          /* Declare the square */
                RI_P, (RtPointer) Square, RI_NULL);
        RiWorldEnd();
    RiEnd();              /* Clean up */
}
```

Listing 2.1 *A minimal program using RenderMan*

calls may be transported to other languages, even an interpreted command language. For the time being, though, C is the most convenient explanatory medium.

Initializing the environment

The first line of the program, the call to **RiBegin**(), initializes the RenderMan Interface. These initialization tasks are essential: *Any program using the RenderMan Interface must first call **RiBegin**() and eventually call **RiEnd**().*

Describing the world

The second line is a call to **RiWorldBegin**(), matched later with a call to **RiWorldEnd**(). The former signals that the application is about to begin describing a specific scene by passing geometric data across the interface. The latter indicates that the scene is complete.

Appearance

After **RiWorldBegin**() there is a call to **RiSurface**(). The character string "constant" passed as a parameter to **RiSurface**() indicates that surfaces in the scene will be rendered with a constant color. That fact explains how this scene can be seen without a light source.

Specifying an object

Only one object appears in this scene: a square declared by the call to **RiPolygon**(). The information necessary to define the square is contained in *Square*, an array of four **RtPoint**s. Each **RtPoint** is a floating-point triple specifying a point in three-dimensional space. When passed to **RiPolygon**() this way, each **RtPoint** represents a **vertex**, the *x*, *y* and *z* locations of a corner of the polygon. The vertices are connected by line segments in the order the triplets appear in *Square*; those line segments define the boundary of the polygon.

The first argument to **RiPolygon**() gives the number of vertices in the polygon. The next two arguments constitute a **token-value pair**: the first is a character string, passed as an **RtToken**, and the second is an array passed as an **RtPointer**. The character string indicates the type of data in the array. Here, the predefined string RI_P denotes an array of points giving positions in three-dimensional space. The **RiPolygon**() routine interprets them as the polygon's vertices, *and assumes that they are given in clockwise order*. **RiPolygon**() allows for any number of token-value pairs, so that a variety of values may be attached to the vertices of a polygon. Other possibilities will be discussed in later chapters.

Both **RiSurface**() and **RiPolygon**() have RI_NULL as the last argument. It is used here as a terminating token, since there is no other way for the procedure being called to know exactly how many token-value pairs are being passed to it.

Result

The program in Listing 2.1 is austere, but complete as far as RenderMan is concerned. When compiled and run, it should create an image with a square in its middle. This might seem peculiar, considering that there is no mention of display anywhere in the program. There are defaults for much of the behavior controlled by RenderMan, and in this case the default is to produce an image file named *ri.pic*.

Why does the square appear in the middle of the image? The default view is an orthographic projection aimed along the *z* axis so that the screen includes every point which is in positive *z* with an *x* and *y* value within the range –1 to +1. The *x* (*y*) values of −.5 and +.5 therefore describe points one-quarter and three-quarters of the way across (up) the screen.

Controlling the Picture

The next job is to view the square from a more interesting, or at least different, angle. The program in Listing 2.2 also shows how to give it a different color, provide a light source, and use a perspective projection.

```
#include <ri.h>

RtPoint Square[4] = { {.5,.5,0}, {.5,-.5,0}, {-.5,-.5,0}, {-.5,.5,0} };

static RtColor Color = { .2, .4, .6 };

main()
{
        RiBegin(RI_NULL);        /* Start the renderer */

                RiLightSource( "distantlight", RI_NULL);

                RiProjection( "perspective", RI_NULL);
                RiTranslate(0.0, 0.0, 1.0);
                RiRotate(40.0, -1.0, 1.0, 0.0);

                RiWorldBegin();

                        RiSurface( "matte", RI_NULL);
                        RiColor(Color);          /* Declare the color */
                        RiPolygon( 4,            /* Declare the square */
                                RI_P, (RtPointer) Square, RI_NULL);

                RiWorldEnd();

        RiEnd();                  /* Clean up after the renderer */
}
```

Listing 2.2 *Control over viewer and color*

Preparing a light source

The first call after **RiBegin**() is to **RiLightSource**(), passing it the character string "distantlight". A distant light source functions like the sun: its brightness does not vary with distance, and its rays are essentially parallel. Although other configurations are possible (as we'll see in Chapter 11), the default distant light points along the positive z axis.

Perspective projection

Listing 2.2 then declares a perspective projection by calling **RiProjection**() with the character string "perspective". Now the image will include any object with a positive z value, but only if the z value is greater than the absloute value of either x or y. In other words, the perspective image captures objects inside a pyramid whose peak is at the origin opening along z.

The effect of a perspective projection can be compared by running the program both with and without the **RiProjection**() call. When the perspective is applied, one corner of the square looms large, and the other is foreshortened with distance. In an orthographic projection the rotated square is symmetric.

Changing the viewer

After the light source and projection are declared, two routine calls in Listing 2.2 redefine the viewing parameters of the scene. The first, **RiTranslate**(0.0, 0.0, 1.0), is a **geometric transformation** specifying that all subsequent surfaces should be spatially transformed for viewing. The three parameters to **RiTranslate**() specify motion along the x, y and z axes, respectively. This call causes objects in the scene to be **translated** by 1.0 along the z axis. Since the viewpoint is at the origin pointing along the positive z axis, the entire scene is moved away from the viewer.

The **RiRotate**(40.0, -1.0, 1.0, 0.0) call is another geometric transformation causing any subsequent surfaces to be **rotated** about a line in space. The first parameter specifies the amount of rotation in degrees. The last three parameters give a point in 3-space; the axis of rotation passes through this point and the coordinate origin. In this case we have specified that the whole world will rotate by 40 degrees about a line in the $z=0$ plane pointing up ($y=1.0$) and to the left ($x=-1.0$). The rotation is **left-handed**: if a person's left thumb points along the axis of rotation from the origin to the given point, the other fingers curl to point in the direction of positive rotation (see Figure

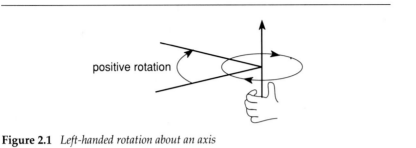

Figure 2.1 *Left-handed rotation about an axis*

2.1). As we will see in Chapter 7, the handedness of the **coordinate system** is subject to change by the application.

The *order* in which these two routines are called is very important: *the transformation specified last is performed first.* Listing 2.2 calls for a rotation followed by a translation: the axis of rotation is much nearer the object being rotated than it would be if the translation were performed first. In the latter case, the object would be rotated right out of view.

A different appearance

Listing 2.2 has a different call to **RiSurface()**, this time passing the string "matte". A matte surface varies its reflection according to the orientation of the surface. In this case, the square is still colored uniformly because its orientation is uniform, but the importance of orientation sensitivity will become clear in the next example.

Coloring the square

The call to **RiColor()** before the polygon declaration affects all objects declared after it. The color declared here is a greenish-blue. Since Listing 2.1 did not declare a color, its square came out white (*color* (1,1,1)), the default color.

The argument to **RiColor()** is an **RtColor** object, which is usually a one-dimensional array with three elements specifying the proportion of red, green and blue in the color. These values should all lie within the range 0 to 1 inclusive: the color (1,1,1) is white, and (.1,.1,.1) a dark gray.

The picture resulting from this program shows just what we have described: a square, tilted and moved away from the viewer, with a greenish-blue color.

About declarations and the graphics environment

It is important for the routines affecting objects to be called *before* the declaration of the relevant objects. If a polygon is to take on a certain color, that color must be specified before the polygon declaration.

Viewing parameters and object color are part of the **graphics environment** maintained by the interface. Whenever a transformation, a color, a light source, or any similar attribute is declared, it becomes part of the environment. Whenever an object is added to a scene, any part of the environment relevant to that object (for the square, the color defined by **RiColor**() and the surface appearance defined by **RiSurface**()) "sticks" to that object.

The environment is a set of standing attributes that apply to any relevant object. Rather than requiring the program to specify a separate color for each type of object, one routine applies a color to every object. Declaring an attribute of the environment simply replaces the previous value of that attribute. Geometric transformations, though, are somewhat more complicated. Neither the rotation nor the translation above *replaces* the previous transformation, but *modifies* it: the net effect is a rotation compounded with a translation.

All attributes of the environment have **default values** set when the interface is initialized. The simplicity of the first two example programs can largely be attributed to that fact. However, *the specification of the RenderMan Interface does not dictate the defaults for surface appearance or light source*. In the first example, we used a surface that did not require a light source, and in the second we defined both a light source and a surface that used it.

A More Complex Object

It is fairly easy to declare a square by directly describing its vertices. However, this kind of explicit description quickly becomes tedious for more complex objects. This section explores a few basic techniques for specifying objects more easily. The key idea is to use previously-defined, simpler objects to create more complex ones. Along the way, we think a bit more about geometric transformations. We also point out features of RenderMan that facilitate object description and placement.

Defining a unit cube

The main program in Listing 2.3 is similar to Listing 2.2. The translation is now by 1.5, and the call to **RiPolygon**() has been replaced by a new routine, *UnitCube*(). The previous program centered a 1-unit square on the *z* axis before moving it for viewing; this one centers a 1-unit cube on the coordinate origin.

There is not much to *UnitCube*(). It simply makes six calls to **RiPolygon**(), using the array *Cube* for data. *Cube* essentially contains six *Square*s at the various locations required to make up a cube. The problem with *UnitCube*() is that it is rather difficult to read and understand, a troubling quality for such a simple object. How can this confusion be reduced?

An alternative definition

We begin with the observation that a cube is nothing but a set of squares in different positions and orientations. If those *differences* could be described easily, then the resulting object description might be somewhat clearer.

Listing 2.4 does that by redefining *UnitCube*(). Here, we are back to the old recognizable definition of the unit square. We use the *Square* array six times to declare six polygons. The difference between them is that the last five are preceded by rotations that position the square at the six faces of the cube.

This example shows another important characteristic of the RenderMan Interface: all declarations are conceptually **call-by-value**. The data in the *Square* array can be used to call **RiPolygon**() six times because the interface can be depended upon not to change it in any way. Any transformations or other changes are performed on a *copy* of the data. Similarly, the application program may freely change any arrays passed to an

```
#include <ri.h>

static RtColor Color = { .2, .4, .6 };

main()
{
      RiBegin(RI_NULL);         /* Start the renderer */
          RiLightSource( "distantlight", RI_NULL);
          RiProjection( "perspective", RI_NULL);
          RiTranslate(0.0, 0.0, 1.5);
          RiRotate(40.0, -1.0, 1.0, 0.0);

          RiWorldBegin();
              RiSurface( "matte", RI_NULL);
              RiColor(Color);         /* Declare the color */
              UnitCube();             /* Define the cube   */
          RiWorldEnd();
      RiEnd();                        /* Clean up after the renderer */
}

#define L  -.5      /* For x: left side      */
#define R   .5      /* For x: right side     */
#define D  -.5      /* For y: down side      */
#define U   .5      /* For y: upper side     */
#define F   .5      /* For z: far side       */
#define N  -.5      /* For z: near side      */

/* UnitCube(): define a cube in the graphics environment */
UnitCube()
{
      static RtPoint Cube[6][4] = {
          { {L,D,F},   {R,D,F},   {R,D,N} },{L,D,N},      /* Bottom face   */
          { {L,D,F},   {L,U,F} },{L,U,N},   {L,D,N},      /* Left face     */
          { {R,U,N},   {L,U,N},   {L,U,F},   {R,U,F} },   /* Top face      */
          { {R,U,N},   {R,U,F},   {R,D,F},   {R,D,N} },   /* Right face    */
          { {R,D,F},   {R,U,F} },{L,U,F},   {L,D,F},      /* Far face      */
          { {L,U,N},   {R,U,N}   {R,D,N},   {L,D,N} }     /* Near face     */
      };
      int i;

      for( i = 0; i < 6; i++)      /* Declare the cube */
          RiPolygon( 4, RI_P, (RtPointer) Cube[i], RI_NULL);
}
```

Listing 2.3 *Defining a cube*

interface routine after it returns. The worlds on either side of
the interface are completely separate.

```
#include <ri.h>
/* UnitCube(): Enter a unit cube into the scene */

UnitCube()
{
    static RtPoint square[4] = {
        {.5,.5,.5}, {-.5,.5,.5}, {-.5,-.5,.5}, {.5,-.5,.5}
    };

    /* far square */
    RiPolygon(4, RI_P, (RtPointer) square, RI_NULL);

    /* right face */
    RiRotate(90.0, 0.0, 1.0, 0.0);
    RiPolygon(4, RI_P, (RtPointer) square, RI_NULL);

    /* near face */
    RiRotate(90.0, 0.0, 1.0, 0.0);
    RiPolygon(4, RI_P, (RtPointer) square, RI_NULL);

    /* left face */
    RiRotate(90.0, 0.0, 1.0, 0.0);
    RiPolygon(4, RI_P, (RtPointer) square, RI_NULL);

    /* bottom face */
    RiRotate(90.0, 1.0, 0.0, 0.0);
    RiPolygon(4, RI_P, (RtPointer) square, RI_NULL);

    /* top face */
    RiRotate(180.0, 1.0, 0.0, 0.0);
    RiPolygon(4, RI_P, (RtPointer) square, RI_NULL);
}
```

Listing 2.4 *Alternative cube definition*

The rotation commands in Listing 2.4 highlight two subtle-ties. First, their effects accumulate: the third square is rotated by 180 degrees, not 90. The second, third and fourth squares are rotated about the y axis by 90, 180 and 270 degrees, respectively. The second subtlety is that the last two transformations might not appear to work: it seems at first that the fifth square would be rotated in y by 270 degrees, then spun in x by 90, leaving it as the left face, in the same position as the fourth! But *the last transformation declared is performed first*. The rotation about x first brings the square to the bottom of the cube, and the other rotations leave it spinning, essentially unchanged. The net effect of the two x-rotations applied to the last square is to rotate it by 270 degrees before the y-rotations.

A third definition

Although this version of *UnitCube*() represents some improvement in clarity, the rotations are still a little obscure; it takes some thought to predict what happens to the last couple of squares, since the last two transformations had to account for the transformations declared previously. Even this simple example illustrates the confusion that can arise from accumulating transformations. Listing 2.5 solves the problem using two new routines. **RiTransformBegin**() makes a copy of the current transformation from the environment when it is called, and a subsequent **RiTransformEnd**() restores that copy into the environment, leaving the transformation as it was before. More precisely, **RiTransformEnd**() restores the most recently saved current transformation. As a result, these calls can be **nested**, with several saves (pushes) occurring before a restore (pop). The transformation state after each pop will be the same as before the corresponding push. In other words, geometric transformations are **stacked**.

The benefits of judiciously saving and restoring the current transformation are evident from Listing 2.5. We have enclosed the declarations of the first four faces of the cube in a begin/end transformation pair, making it possible to declare the top and bottom faces afterward in the most intuitive way: by declaring rotations in x.

This procedure makes object declaration commutative, hence less error-prone. Since the environment is the same before and after every transformation pair, the three pairs here could be rearranged arbitrarily.

Saving and restoring the transformation also eliminates side effects from the *UnitCube*() procedure. When the previous versions of the routine returned, the transformation was the one that moved the last face into place. Since the graphics environment is global within a program, returning from *UnitCube*() would *not* restore the transformation to what it had been when the routine was called. Implicit side effects of pro-

```
#include <ri.h>
/* UnitCube(): Enter a unit cube into the scene */

UnitCube()
{
    static RtPoint square[4] = {
        {.5,.5,.5}, {-.5,.5,.5}, {-.5,-.5,.5}, {.5,-.5,.5}
    };

    RiTransformBegin();

        /* far square */
        RiPolygon(4, RI_P, (RtPointer) square, RI_NULL);

        /* right face */
        RiRotate(90.0, 0.0, 1.0, 0.0);
        RiPolygon(4, RI_P, (RtPointer) square, RI_NULL);

        /* near face */
        RiRotate(90.0, 0.0, 1.0, 0.0);
        RiPolygon(4, RI_P, (RtPointer) square, RI_NULL);

        /* left face */
        RiRotate(90.0, 0.0, 1.0, 0.0);
        RiPolygon(4, RI_P, (RtPointer) square, RI_NULL);

    RiTransformEnd();

    RiTransformBegin();

        /* bottom face */
        RiRotate(90.0, 1.0, 0.0, 0.0);
        RiPolygon(4, RI_P, (RtPointer) square, RI_NULL);

    RiTransformEnd();

    RiTransformBegin();

        /* top face */
        RiRotate(-90.0, 1.0, 0.0, 0.0);
        RiPolygon(4, RI_P, (RtPointer) square, RI_NULL);

    RiTransformEnd();
}
```

Listing 2.5 *Another cube definition*

cedures are a Bad Thing. Saving and restoring the current transformation eliminated that problem in *UnitCube*(). It now does only what is expected: define a unit cube centered at the coordinate origin.

Combining Objects

Now that we have a satisfactory procedure for defining a scene with more than one object, we can experiment a bit to make a picture with a little more visual interest.

A color cube

The *ColorCube*() function in Listing 2.6 defines a color cube, in which the red, green and blue values of the cube vary with x, y and z, so that the near-lower-left corner is black and the far-upper-right corner is white. The color varies because the cube is composed of many smaller cubes stacked up in three dimensions, each given a color appropriate to its position. The number of minicubes on a side is given by the first parameter to *ColorCube*(), and each minicube can be scaled to leave empty space between them using a scale factor given by the second parameter. The color cube defined here is, as before, one unit on a side and centered about the coordinate origin.

ColorCube() begins with **RiAttributeBegin**() and ends with **RiAttributeEnd**(). These two routines are analogous to **RiTransformBegin**() and **RiTransformEnd**(): they copy and restore, not just geometric transformations, but all other attributes of the graphics environment as well. Since these include the color reset by *ColorCube*(), this procedure eliminates side effects on the rest of the environment.

The inner loop of *ColorCube*() cycles n times through x, y and z, creating unit cubes, scaling them appropriately, then translating them into position. The translation and scale commands at the beginning of the routine reduce the resulting cube to unit size and move the center of the cube to the coordinate origin.

```
#include <ri.h>
/*
 *  ColorCube(): create a unit color cube from smaller cubes
 *  Parameters:
 *    n: the number of minicubes on a side
 *    s: a scale factor for each minicube
 */
ColorCube(n, s)
int n;
float s;
{
    int x, y, z;
    RtColor color;

    if( n<=0 )
        return;

    RiAttributeBegin();
        RiTranslate(-.5, -.5, -.5 );
        RiScale( 1.0/n, 1.0/n, 1.0/n);

        for(x = 0; x < n; x++)
            for(y = 0; y < n; y++)
                for(z = 0; z < n; z++) {
                    color[0] = ((float) x+1) / ((float) n);
                    color[1] = ((float) y+1) / ((float) n);
                    color[2] = ((float) z+1) / ((float) n);
                    RiColor( color );
                    RiTransformBegin();
                        RiTranslate (x+.5, y+.5, z+.5);
                        RiScale( s, s, s);
                        UnitCube();
                    RiTransformEnd ();
                }

    RiAttributeEnd();
}
```

Listing 2.6 *Defining a larger cube from smaller minicubes*

An alternative definition

Now that we have a well-structured procedure for creating a color cube, we can improve its efficiency. The *ColorCube()* of Listing 2.6 makes n^3 calls to *UnitCube()*, each with six polygon definitions, five rotation commands, and three transformation save/restore pairs. This is *not* a complicated object; imagine the cost of defining an interesting scene!

A quick glance back at the definition of *UnitCube*() reveals the real waste of all those procedure calls. Each cube is created exactly the same way, then modified by the calling procedure. It might be useful to create an abstract definition of an object such as a cube, and then make copies, or **instances**, of it.

Listing 2.7 shows how the RenderMan Interface may be used to do just that. The new definition of *ColorCube*() begins by creating an **object description** in the first three lines. The call to *UnitCube*() in the inner loop has been replaced with the routine **RiObjectInstance**(), which creates an **instance** of the object, the cube created by *UnitCube*().

Here we see another begin/end pair: **RiObjectBegin**() and **RiObjectEnd**(). Between these calls, geometric primitives are *not* included in the scene when they are declared. Instead, each primitive is added to an internal **object description**. Once the object description is completed by calling **RiObjectEnd**(), it may be copied to add objects to the scene.

The object description is recalled using the **RtObjectHandle** returned by **RiObjectBegin**(). Every other detail of the representation is hidden; the only use for an object description is to instance it by calling **RiObjectInstance**().

An object description is like a macro triggered by **RiObjectInstance**(). It is a particularly simple macro, though, because *it includes only geometric information:* all other attributes in the environment are applied when the object is instanced, not when it is created. This fact has its uses: we were able to create a set of cubes of different colors. It has the disadvantage that varying attributes like color inside the object (by, for example, issuing **RiColor**() calls within the object definition) is impossible.

A further restriction of object declaration is not apparent in Listing 2.7. The primitives inside the declaration must all be of the same type (i.e., polygons), and geometric transformations are ignored. The version of *UnitCube*() used here must be the original one defined in Listing 2.3.

```
#include <ri.h>

/*
 *  ColorCube(): create a unit color cube from smaller cubes
 *  Parameters:
 *      n: the number of minicubes on a side
 *      s: a scale factor for each minicube
 */

ColorCube(n, s)
int n;
float s;
{
    int x, y, z;
    RtColor color;
    RtObjectHandle cube;

    if( n<=0 )
        return;

    cube = RiObjectBegin();
        UnitCube();
    RiObjectEnd();

    RiAttributeBegin();

        RiTranslate(-.5, -.5, -.5 );
        RiScale( 1.0/n, 1.0/n, 1.0/n);

        for(x = 0; x < n; x++)
            for(y = 0; y < n; y++)
                for(z = 0; z < n; z++) {
                    color[0] = ((float) x+1) / ((float) n);
                    color[1] = ((float) y+1) / ((float) n);
                    color[2] = ((float) z+1) / ((float) n);

                    RiColor( color );
                    RiTransformBegin();
                        RiTranslate (x+.5, y+.5, z+.5);
                        RiScale( s, s, s);
                        RiObjectInstance(cube);
                    RiTransformEnd ();
                }
    RiAttributeEnd();
}
```

Listing 2.7 *A more efficient color cube*

Summary of object creation

We have just seen examples of the two basic paradigms for creating objects. First was the **procedural** paradigm, in which an object was created by calling a procedure. Second was the **instance** paradigm, which also required calling a procedure but was really using data, the object description. Choosing the appropriate method in particular circumstances is a matter of judgement, which is why RenderMan provides the choice.

The important point is that both methods are hierarchical: they allow and encourage programs to build up complicated objects from more primitive ones.

A Simple Animation

Having defined a single image, we can move on to define a sequence of frames, an **animation**. Listing 2.8 uses the *Color-Cube()* routine to generate a series of pictures of a color cube. As the animation proceeds, the cube rotates, and the scale factor applied to the minicubes goes to zero, so that over the course of the animation the small cubes disappear.

Beginning the frame

Everything outside the loop is unchanged from Listing 2.3. The call to **RiDisplay()** sends the output of the different frames to different files. Within the loop, the scene description is enclosed between a pair of new calls. The program calls **RiFrameBegin()** with a frame number as argument to begin rendering a frame of the animation, and declares the frame finished by calling **RiFrameEnd()**.

The state of the geometric transformation is saved by **RiFrameBegin()** and restored by **RiFrameEnd()**. The program in Listing 2.8 invokes **RiRotate()** NFRAMES times, yet each time the rotation occurs exactly as specified instead of compounding the earlier rotations. By contrast, the three calls that set up the viewing parameters are made only once, before the first **RiFrameBegin()**, because they are restored to the same state after **RiFrameEnd()** as before **RiFrameBegin()**.

```
#include <ri.h>

#define NFRAMES 10     /* number of frames in the animation */
#define NCUBES  5      /* # of minicubes on a side of the color cube */
#define FRAMEROT 5.0   /* # of degrees to rotate cube between frames */


main()
{
    int frame;
    float scale;
    char filename[20];

    RiBegin(RI_NULL);        /* Start the renderer  */

        RiLightSource( "distantlight", RI_NULL);

        /* Viewing transformation */
        RiProjection( "perspective", RI_NULL);
        RiTranslate(0.0, 0.0, 1.5);
        RiRotate(40.0, -1.0, 1.0, 0.0);

        for (frame = 1; frame <= NFRAMES; frame++) {
            sprintf( filename, "anim%d.pic", frame );
            RiFrameBegin(frame);
                RiDisplay(filename, RI_FILE, RI_RGBA, RI_NULL);
                RiWorldBegin();
                    scale = (float)(NFRAMES-(frame-1)) / (float)NFRAMES;
                    RiRotate(FRAMEROT*frame, 0.0, 0.0, 1.0);
                    RiSurface( "matte", RI_NULL );
                    ColorCube(NCUBES, scale);        /* Define the cube */
                RiWorldEnd();
            RiFrameEnd();
        }

    RiEnd();
}
```

Listing 2.8 *A simple animation*

Summary

This chapter has provided the basic framework needed to make pictures:

*   initializing the RenderMan Interface.

- producing single frames and sequences.
- inserting objects into a scene.
- moving objects by declaring geometric transformations.
- forming compound objects from more primitive ones.
- modifying, saving and restoring the graphics environment.
- controlling the viewpoint of a scene.

Chapter 3 addresses the overall design of the interface and provides a more complete discussion of the basics.

The Structure of a RenderMan Program

The RenderMan Interface consists of a specific set of procedure calls, plus the definition of an optional shading language. The coming chapters cover individual calls, organized into groups according to domain (surface definition, viewing, shading, etc.). But first, there are some characteristics of the interface that apply across a variety of procedures: the idiosyncrasies of a procedural interface like RenderMan, the coordinate systems it uses, the syntax of procedure calls, the data types used, and the overall structure of a RenderMan program. With this material in hand, the remaining chapters may be read in almost any order.

This chapter develops a context for assembling RenderMan procedure calls into a RenderMan program, showing how they all fit together. At the end, a template program appears into which can be inserted the calls laid out in the coming chapters. A useful program for viewing typical scenes is developed in Chapter 8. The one described here is most useful for grasping the structure of a RenderMan program; the latter is more practically oriented.

RenderMan Procedures

From the programmer's point of view, RenderMan consists entirely of procedure calls whose names begin with '**Ri**' (for **R**enderMan **i**nterface). The user calls a procedure to add a surface to a scene or to modify a parameter. Depending on the system lying behind the interface, this data might be rendered immediately, archived for later rendering, sent off across a network to a remote rendering server, or piped directly to a hardware renderer.

Not all the routines in the interface are relevant all the time. Some routines, for example, address capabilities that some renderers do not provide. However, all renderers must define all RenderMan routines, even if they do nothing. This is to minimize changes required of a program using RenderMan from implementation to implementation.

Error handling

When an interface routine is passed detectably invalid data, or if the routine is inappropriate in a given context, it generates an error condition. There are very few procedures in the RenderMan Interface that return any values at all, let alone error codes. Rather, an error causes an action that is under the control of the application.

RiErrorHandler(handler)
    RtFunc handler;

RiErrorHandler() specifies how to handle errors occurring in the RenderMan Interface. *handler* is a pointer to a routine to be is called when an error occurs. There are three handlers provided by the interface: **RiErrorPrint**() prints an error message to the standard error stream. **RiErrorAbort**() prints error messages, then aborts the program if the error is severe enough. Finally, **RiErrorIgnore**() silently ignores all errors. If **RiErrorHandler**() is never called, **RiErrorPrint**() is called to handle errors.

An application may define another error-handling function. It should be declared

```
void MyHandler( code, severity, message )
RtInt code, severity;
char *message;
```

The *code* indicates the type of error, and *severity* is an index of its seriousness. Values for both are in the file *ri.h*, reproduced in Appendix C. *message* is a character string describing the error.

An interactive rendering application might define an error-handling routine that called **RiErrorPrint**(), then queried the user whether to continue the program. An application that prefers careful error handling might post the error code and severity to a global error variable and return, letting the context of the error determine the appropriate action.

Parameter lists

Since RenderMan procedures are just subroutines, parameters are passed to them in the normal way. In the case of the C language binding, the RenderMan Interface supports a mechanism allowing the set of parameters passed to a given routine to vary: a variable-length **parameter list**. Syntactically, a parameter list is a series of arguments in token-value pairs, terminated by a special token, RI_NULL.

We already saw one such parameter list in Chapter 2. The call to create a four-sided polygon,

> **RiPolygon**(4, RI_P, (**RtPointer**)Square, RI_NULL);

has a parameter list that begins with the **RtToken** RI_P paired with the data in *Square* (cast to **RtPointer**), and ends with RI_NULL. A parameter list can include many such **token-value pairs**, or none, but it must always end with RI_NULL.

Parameter lists provide syntactic flexibility. When a token expected by a procedure does not appear, a default value may be used. Applications can therefore confine their attention to relevant features, and new features can be added to a routine without threatening existing programs.

Not all parameters apply in all situations. The parameters relevant to a given procedure are included in its specification in this book. Some procedures require certain parameters. **RiPolygon**(), for example, is meaningless without an array of vertices. Any required items will also be noted in the procedure specification.

Not all RenderMan procedures take parameter lists. It depends entirely on the nature of the procedure. If a procedure does expect a parameter list, its declaration as it appears in this book will show the name *parameterlist* in italics as a pseudo-argument at the end of its argument list. *parameterlist* is meant to stand for the whole RI_NULL-terminated list of parameters.

An alternative to parameter lists

The use of variable-length parameter lists takes advantage of features of the C language that are sometimes considered dangerous or nonstandard. Some other languages (Pascal, for example) do not accept the idea at all. Therefore, RenderMan defines a vectorized version of each routine that replaces the parameter list with an integer followed by two arrays. The first array contains tokens, and the second contains the values. For example, the call

```
RiPolygon(4,  RI_P, (RtPointer)Square,
              RI_N, (RtPointer)Normals, RI_NULL);
```

could be replaced with the fragment

```
RtToken tokens[2];
RtPointer values[2];

tokens[0] = RI_P;
values[0] = (RtPointer)Square ;
tokens[1] = RI_N;
values[1] = (RtPointer)Normals ;
RiPolygonV(4, 2, tokens, values);
```

The name of the vectorized version of each *parameterlist* routine in the interface is obtained by appending 'V' to the unvectorized routine name. Its calling sequence is the same, except that the *parameterlist* is replaced with a count and two arrays, one of tokens and one of pointers. The count gives the number of elements in each array. The vectorized routines will remain implicit in the rest of this book.

Data Types

The RenderMan Interface defines a variety of data types that are always used for arguments and return values. In C, they are defined in the header file *ri.h*. Thus, any program file using RenderMan types must include that header.

The name of each data type begins with '**Rt**' (for **R**enderMan **t**ype). Depending on the implementation, it may be possible to use the underlying types instead, but it is a good idea to use the defined types anyway. Their definitions may vary between implementations, and non-rigorous use of types is flagged as an error by 'lint' and many C compilers.

Scalar types

```
typedef short      RtBoolean;
typedef long       RtInt;
typedef float      RtFloat;
typedef void       RtVoid;
typedef char       *RtString;
```

The usual scalar data types are typedef'ed to make them subject to future revision. For **RtBoolean** variables, the constants RI_TRUE and RI_FALSE are predefined. **RtString**s are used to pass names to shading language routines.

Vector types

```
typedef RtFloat    RtPoint[3];
typedef RtFloat    RtMatrix[4][4];
typedef RtFloat    RtBound[6];
typedef RtFloat    RtBasis[4][4];
```

The **RtPoint** data type is used to pass three-dimensional geometric data through the interface. **RtMatrix** is used to specify linear geometric transformations as a 4 x 4 matrix. **RtBound** is used to supply three-dimensional bounding boxes for objects. **RtBasis** is explained in Chapter 6.

Opaque data types

```
typedef RtVoid     *RtPointer;
typedef RtPointer  RtObjectHandle;
typedef RtPointer  RtLightHandle;
```

Sometimes data is passed through the interface, stored, and later passed back to the application. Other times, data returned to the application is later passed back in: light sources are turned on and off by passing an **RtLightHandle** data item, and retained models (discussed in Chapter 6) use **RtObjectHandle**. In both cases the internals of the data can and should remain invisible in the application. The data type **RtPointer** is used for these.

When arrays of data are passed through the interface, they must first be cast to **RtPointer**, as in

   RiPolygon(nsides, RI_P, (**RtPointer**)vertices, RI_NULL).

Tokens

typedef char ***RtToken**;

Whenever string identifiers are expected, **RtToken**s are used. For the strings already defined by the interface ("P", for example) RenderMan also defines, for each string, a constant that can be used in its place. These constant tokens may be used anywhere an **RtToken** can; they are named by a simple convention that capitalizes the name and prefixes it with 'RI_'. Thus, the position token "P" becomes RI_P. The calls to **RiPolygon**() we have seen thus far could be replaced with

RiPolygon(nsides, (**RtToken**) "P", (**RtPointer**) vertices, RI_NULL).

Using predefined tokens rather than strings may enable some implementations to operate more efficiently. Their use is therefore advisable. Whenever a string is described in this book, the constant will also be provided.

The line between **RtToken**s and regular character strings is sometimes indistinct. In general, an **RtToken** is used for any internal names, while a 'char *' is used for external references like file names.

Function pointers

```
typedef RtFloat     (*RtFloatFunc)();
typedef RtVoid      (*RtFunc)();
```

RenderMan may, in some contexts, be passed functions to execute later, as to **RiErrorHandler**(). These are passed either as **RtFloatFunc**, for functions returning floating-point values, or **RtFunc**, for functions with no return value.

Colors

RenderMan has adopted a particularly flexible definition of "color," extending it beyond the usual RGB representation.

typedef **RtFloat**   RtColor[3];

The idea of multi-channel color values is essential to color graphics. The number of channels in a color is so often taken to be three (red, green and blue, for example) that one can be misled into thinking that there is some fundamental principle decreeing that number. On the contrary, such color triples are just one way of describing light in the visible spectrum.

For other purposes (calculating the reflection of light from a surface, for example), more than three channels may provide a more accurate representation.

By default, a color is represented in the RenderMan Interface by a triple of values representing the relative proportions of red, green and blue in the color. However, this number can be changed.

RiColorSamples(N, nRGB, RGBn)
    RtInt   N;
    RtFloat   nRGB[N][3], RGBn[3][N];

RiColorSamples() sets the number of samples used to represent and calculate colors to N. This routine tells the rendering system to begin treating type **RtColor** as though it were defined

    typedef **RtFloat**   **RtColor**[N];

After a call to **RiColorSamples**(), all routines that take color values, even in token-value pairs, will expect **RtFloat** arrays to contain N elements.

The remaining arguments express colors in the new color space in terms of RGB. The argument *nRGB* to **RiColorSamples**() should be an $N \times 3$ matrix of floating-point values, which will multiply each N-sample color vector to obtain a 3-vector for RGB. Conversely, *RGBn* is a $3 \times N$ matrix to perform the inverse operation. *RGBn* provides the ability to transform RGB values defined in the interface into the new color space.

There is no reason that N has to be greater than 3. If a modeler prefers to operate in some linear trichromatic color space other than RGB, it can call **RiColorSamples**() with appropriate transformation matrices to change the space in which it specifies colors. A monochromatic space could also be defined.

The ability to support different color spaces can produce more accurate colors, but it is not required by the interface. If a given renderer doesn't support the capability, it simply converts all the colors it receives to RGB immediately upon input.

Graphics State

To act consistently, a procedural interface like RenderMan must maintain certain information from one interface call to the next. In fact, most of the routines in the interface do nothing but modify this **graphics environment** (also known as the **graphics state**): **RiColor**(), for example, changes the part of the state information governing surface color, known as the **current color**, **RiRotate**() modifies the **current transformation**, and so on. Almost every routine in the interface either declares a surface or modifies the graphics state. If any procedure modifies the graphics state, that fact is noted in its specification.

The graphics state consists of three types of information, each associated with one of the levels of abstraction discussed below. At the highest level are characteristics associated with individual renderers and not subject to user control. These are the **capabilities** of a renderer. At the next level down are state variables that are constant over an entire image, the **options** of the interface. Most specific are **attributes**, which are bound to individual objects and surfaces.

Every option and attribute has a default value, which is why the minimal program in Chapter 2 could be so simple: the camera has a presumed configuration, the renderer produces a standard type of output image, etc. The only unyielding requirement for a program is to provide a scene to be rendered.

Getting a handle on the difference between the types of state information and when they can be modified is essential for understanding the structure of a RenderMan application.

Capabilities

A renderer must fulfill certain requirements before it can be said to support the RenderMan Interface. It must provide each of the procedure calls in the interface, perform hidden-surface removal, and support a number of other features.

However, the RenderMan Interface also posits specific **capabilities** providing functional power, which is not strictly required for rendering, but is still nice to have if you can get it. The basic set of procedures includes routines that support each capability. Every renderer must provide the routines, even if not the capability. These capabilities are the following:

- **Solid Modeling**: performing set operations (like 'union' and 'difference') on the spaces enclosed by sets of surfaces.

- **Trim Curves**: the ability to cut away parts of free-form surfaces.

- **Level of Detail**: the ability to select one of several representations for a model depending on its apparent size in the image.

- **Motion Blur**: "streaking" an object across an image as though it moved while a shutter was open.

- **Depth of Field**: blurring objects differently according to their distance from the viewer.

- **Programmable Shading**: support for the RenderMan Shading Language.

- **Special Camera Projections**: the ability to perform nonlinear mappings from the world to the image plane.

- **Deformations**: support for nonlinear geometric transformations.

- **Displacements**: the ability to handle distortions across the surface of a single object.

Capabilities are considered to be part of the graphics state because programs using the interface should work whether a given capability is provided or not. Thus, there is a well-defined action (usually doing nothing) whenever a capability not provided by the renderer is invoked.

From the application's point of view, though, capabilities require no action at all; they are determined entirely by the choice of renderer.

Options

At the next level of flexibility, **options** are elements of the graphics state that are associated with an image as a whole. The most important options concern the viewing parameters of an image: where the camera is placed, where it's pointing, its field of view, etc. Other options pertain to the output image: its resolution and aspect ratio, the kind of data produced at each pixel, and so on.

RenderMan provides a long list of options, discussion of which fills much of this book. Each one is controlled by the application calling a specific routine. One special routine is provided to set options used by a particular implementation but not supported by the usual interface routines.

RiOption(name, *parameterlist*)
    char *name;

A call to **RiOption**() controls the *name* option via the token-value pairs in *parameterlist*. The entire parameter list is associated with *name* for use by the underlying renderer. The same mechanism that maintains the status of other options can therefore be used to communicate nonstandard ones.

Attributes

Finally, there are the components of the graphics state associated not with an image as a whole, but with individual elements of the image, the geometric primitives which appear in it. After such an **attribute** value is posted to the graphics state, each primitive passed through the interface is "stamped" with that value. The most typical attribute is color, as passed by **RiColor**(): once **RiColor**() is called, all subsequent surfaces are given that color.

As with options, there is a procedure for passing nonstandard attributes.

RiAttribute(name, *parameterlist*)
    char *name;

RiAttribute() posts the attribute denoted by *name* to the graphics state, associating it with the token-value pairs of *parameterlist*. Any particular attributes accepted are up to the implementation; any attribute posted to an implementation that doesn't expect it is simply ignored.

Chapter 3: The Structure of a RenderMan Program

Options vs. attributes

In the structure of a RenderMan program, there are only two important distinctions between options and attributes: where they can be declared and whether they can be saved and restored.

Since options apply to an image as a whole, *every option in effect for an image must have its final value before the first pixel is rendered*. Since rendering may begin after **RiWorldBegin**(), all options must have been set by then. Attributes may be modified at any time.

As noted in Chapter 2, attributes may be saved by **RiAttributeBegin**(), and restored by **RiAttributeEnd**(). This save/restore mechanism is one example of the effects RenderMan has on program structure, a topic that can now be opened in detail.

Program Structure: Blocks

Almost all modern programming languages include the notion of **blocks** of statements, sections of code that are treated as a single entity for some purpose. For example, the *then* clause of a conditional construct often consists of a series of statements grouped into a block that is syntactically considered one statement.

The RenderMan Interface also groups its procedure calls into blocks. These blocks are defined by pairs of routines, one of the form **Ri...Begin**() and another like **Ri...End**(). For example, **RiAttributeBegin**() saves the entire set of attribute values in the graphics state and **RiAttributeEnd**() restores it, so a matched pair of **RiAttributeBegin**()/**RiAttributeEnd**() calls delimits an **attribute block**. A pair of calls to **RiTransformBegin**() and **RiTransformEnd**() defines a **transformation block**: they establish a local coordinate system by saving and restoring the current transformation.

RenderMan also uses blocks to denote **modes** of the interface. From the user's point of view, RenderMan has three important ones. The first mode is in effect before **RiBegin**(). This is essentially a null mode, since the interface has not been initialized. After **RiBegin**(), options can be set, but no primitives may yet be declared. This is essentially an image definition mode. Finally, inside a block delimited by **RiWorldBegin**() and **RiWorldEnd**(), the image characteristics are frozen; options cannot be changed, and only calls that concern the scene itself are allowed: primitive declaration and attribute manipulation.

A block begun by **RiBegin**() or **RiWorldBegin**() may not contain another of the same type: you may not call **RiBegin**() twice before **RiEnd**(). This makes sense because each represents a mode switch, which can only occur once. Some RenderMan program blocks, however, do not have this restriction. An attribute block, for example, may properly contain another attribute block: they may be **nested**. This nesting is what gives a RenderMan program the ability to support hierarchical object definitions. The nesting capability of a block is noted with its specification.

Table 3.1, which ends this chapter, lists each routine of the RenderMan Interface and the types of block in which it is valid.

RiBegin(name)
    RtToken name;
RiEnd()

Every RenderMan program must begin with the call **RiBegin**() and end with **RiEnd**(). This is the **main block** of a RenderMan program.

name allows selection, by name, of a particular rendering method, if the implementation provides more than one. The default renderer is selected by passing RI_NULL.

The main block is *not* nestable: it is an error to call **RiBegin**() twice before calling **RiEnd**().

RiWorldBegin()
RiWorldEnd()

The geometric primitives of a scene are defined between calls to **RiWorldBegin**() and **RiWorldEnd**() (a **world block**). When **RiWorldBegin**() is called, the application must have finished parameterizing the image to be output. The renderer enters a state for sending the geometric data to be rendered into that image. All options are frozen, and any option-setting routines called before the matching **RiWorldEnd**() result in an error.

Depending on implementation, rendering may begin when **RiWorldBegin**() is called. But from the viewpoint of the application using the interface, rendering is complete by the time **RiWorldEnd**() returns. All the scene data declared in the world block is processed and removed by that time. This makes it possible for successive world blocks in a single program to create different images.

The world block may only appear inside the main block. Before the world block, options and attributes may be modified and light sources may be declared, but no primitives may be passed. Within the world block, options are frozen but primitives may be declared.

The world block may not be nested.

Whatever the purpose of a block, a program must maintain a strict nesting. *Every block must end before the end of any block containing it.* That is,

```
...
RiBegin();
        RiWorldBegin();
                ...
        RiWorldEnd();
RiEnd();
...
```

is correct, but

```
...
RiBegin();
        RiWorldBegin();
                ...
RiEnd();
        RiWorldEnd();
...
```

is not. This applies to nestable as well as non-nestable block types. Groups of RenderMan statements begun with **RiAttributeBegin**() and ending with **RiAttributeEnd**() are also considered to be blocks, in that nesting must be strictly maintained.

RiAttributeBegin()
RiAttributeEnd()

RiAttributeBegin() saves the current state of all attributes and **RiAttributeEnd**() restores the last set of attributes saved. Thus, the attributes outside such a pair are immune to any changes made inside it. The attributes saved include the current transformation, so that, for example,

>   **RiAttributeBegin**();
>
>>   **RiTransformBegin**();
>>   ...
>>   **RiTransformEnd**();
>
>   **RiAttributeEnd**();

is redundant.

RiAttributeBegin()/**RiAttributeEnd**() calls may be nested arbitrarily. The sequence

>   **RiAttributeBegin**();
>
>>   **RiAttributeBegin**();
>>   ...
>>   **RiAttributeEnd**();
>>
>>   **RiAttributeBegin**();
>>   ...
>>   **RiAttributeEnd**();
>
>   **RiAttributeEnd**();

is perfectly legal. Much more will be said about the usefulness of saving and restoring attributes and transformations in Chapter 7 on hierarchical object definitions.

Since options never change over the course of an image, they are not saved or restored with the rest of the graphics state. Only one routine, **RiFrameBegin**(), can save options, and only **RiFrameEnd**() can restore them.

One more block type was used in the last chapter and requires elaboration here. A **frame block** is used to generate successive, numbered frames of an animation; it occurs inside an **RiBegin**()/**RiEnd**() (main) block and it encloses an **RiWorldBe-**

gin()/**RiWorldEnd**() (world) block. It is primarily used to save the options of a program so that they may be changed from frame to frame.

RiFrameBegin(number)
    RtInt number ;
RiFrameEnd()

Within the main block, several images may be rendered. The beginning of a frame is denoted by calling **RiFrameBegin**() and ended with **RiFrameEnd**(). *number* gives a number to the frame. Frame blocks may not be nested.

Within a frame block, several world blocks may appear in sequence, perhaps to generate shadows and reflection maps before rendering the image in which they are used.

RiFrameBegin() saves all options, and **RiFrameEnd**() restores them. As a result, any options that change from frame to frame can be put inside a frame block, and those that remain constant should be put outside.

A word about data handles

The block types above have one final effect: they provide scope to data handles. Just as the graphics state defined in an attribute block ends when the block ends, data handles created within a frame or world block become invalid when the block ends. For example, a light source created before **RiFrameBegin**() will still exist after **RiFrameEnd**(), but one created after the **RiFrameBegin**() call will be deleted. Any scoping considerations will be included in the declaration of routines which create handles.

Coordinate Systems

In three-dimensional computer graphics, five different coordinate systems can be identified at different stages of the viewing process. The RenderMan Interface gives names to these five, and also supports naming of other coordinate systems.

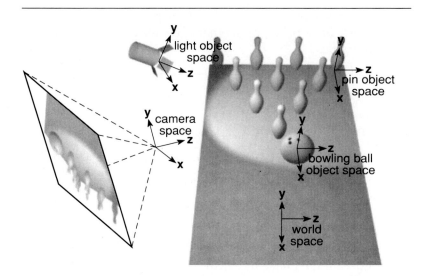

Figure 3.1 *The three-dimensional coordinate systems of RenderMan. Object space is given by the current transformation when an object is declared. World space applies at the beginning of a world block. Camera space is relative to the camera.*

RenderMan coordinate systems

Of the five coordinate systems predefined in the RenderMan Interface, three are three-dimensional spaces concerning the placement of objects and the camera. They are shown in Figure 3.1, above. The remaining two are two-dimensional, relating to coordinates in the image itself.

RenderMan's predefined coordinate systems are as follows:

- **Object space**: the coordinates in which an object is defined. When **RiPolygon()** passes a vertex list, the coordinates of the vertices are in object space by definition.

- **World space**: the "global" coordinate system of a scene independent of the camera. The interface moves objects from object space to world space by applying the current transformation as defined inside the world block.

- **Camera space**: a coordinate system with the viewpoint at the coordinate origin and the direction of view along the

Chapter 3: The Structure of a RenderMan Program

positive *z* axis. Once in world space, objects are transformed into camera space via a transformation defined before the world block is entered.

- **Screen space**: a normalized coordinate system after the scene is projected onto a viewing plane. Usually the output image occupies the range [−1,+1] in screen space, although this can be changed to provide for non-square images and skew projections. Camera space coordinates are transformed into screen space using a projection defined by **RiProjection**().

- **Raster space**: a two-dimensional space in which the top left corner of the top left pixel of the output image lies at (0,0) and pixel corners lie at non-negative integer locations.

Where defined

Object space is simply the space of the raw points used to create geometric primitives, and raster space is determined solely from the resolution of the output image, a straightforward mapping from screen space onto the pixels of the image. Camera and world coordinates are more interesting.

Throughout a RenderMan program, there is a **current transformation** affected by all geometric transformation routines. This is the transformation that is saved and restored along with the rest of the graphics state.

Within a world block, a surface is declared by passing object space coordinates to a **geometric primitive** routine like **RiPolygon**(). The current transformation is applied to those object space coordinates to move the surface into its position in the scene. The object's coordinates within the scene as a whole are then said to be in **world space**.

The current transformation is also used to define the camera transformation used to present the world for viewing. The distinction between the two uses is simple: when a world block begins, with **RiWorldBegin**(), the current transformation is accepted as the one to use for the camera and cleared for use in accumulating object-to-world transformations.

Using the current transformation for both processes allows an equally rich (in fact, identical) set of transformations to be used for both object and camera transformations.

Hider Selection

Some systems running under the RenderMan Interface may offer a variety of hidden-surface elimination techniques, called **hiders**, which can be chosen to meet various rendering demands. The specification requires, however, that every renderer offer at least three options.

RiHider(type, *parameterlist*)
   RtToken type;

RiHider() makes a selection among different methods of resolving conflicts at the image plane. There are three standard possibilities for *type*:

- "hidden" (RI_HIDDEN, the default): the renderer's standard hidden-surface elimination technique is used.

- "paint" (RI_PAINT): each surface is written to the image when it is added to the scene, without resolving hidden surfaces at all (the name derives from "painter's algorithm"). To produce a coherent image using the painter's algorithm, the farthest objects must be declared first.

- "null" (RI_NULL): hidden surfaces are not resolved at all and no output is produced.

parameterlist is the usual list of token-value pairs. It is RI_NULL for the three standard types, but may be used to pass parameters to nonstandard types.

The "null" hider type is useful mainly for checking the validity of input data.

A Boilerplate RenderMan Program

The program below more graphically summarizes the preceding discussion, illustrating what is going on at each stage in a program describing a scene to RenderMan. It may be used as a template for standard RenderMan programs, since its structure applies to most situations. However, the viewing program in Chapter 8 includes a wider variety of controls.

```
#include <ri.h>
render(nframes)          /* Basic program using the RenderMan Interface */
int nframes;
{
    int frame;

    RiBegin();              /* Options may now be set */
        /* IMAGE OPTION SECTION: See Chapter 8 */
        RiDisplay( ... );
        RiFormat( ... );

        ...

        /* CAMERA OPTION SECTION: See Chapter 8 */
        RiClipping( ... );
        RiDepthOfField( ... );
        RiProjection("perspective", RI_NULL);      /* The current  trans- */
            /* formation is cleared so the camera can be specified.     */
        RiRotate( ... );          /* These transformations address the     */
        RiTranslate( ... );      /* world-to-camera transformation        */
        ...   /* controlling placement and orientation of the camera.    */

        for(frame = 1; frame <= nframes; frame++) {
            RiFrameBegin( frame );
                /* FRAME-DEPENDENT OPTION SECTION                          */
                /* Can still set frame-dependent options, camera xforms    */
                RiWorldBegin(); /* SCENE DESCRIPTION SECTION:              */
                    /* The camera xform is now set; options are frozen     */
                    /* and rendering may begin. We are in world space.     */
                    RiAttributeBegin();   /* Begin a distinct object       */
                        RiColor( ... );            /* Attributes fit in here      */
                        RiSurface( ... );          /* See Chapter 11             */
                        RiTransformBegin();        /* See Chapter 7              */
                            RiTranslate( ... );    /* Object-positioning         */
                            RiRotate( ... );       /* commands (see Ch. 7)       */

                            ...

                            RiSphere( ... );       /* See Chapter 4              */
                            RiPolygon( ... );      /* See Chapter 5              */
                            RiPatch( ... );        /* See Chapter 6              */
                        RiTransformEnd();
                    RiAttributeEnd();        /* Restore the parent's attributes.  */
                    ...                       /* Other objects, other spaces        */
                RiWorldEnd();   /* The scene is complete. The image is ren- */
                    /* dered and all scene data is discarded. Other scenes  */
                    /* may now be declared with other world blocks.         */
            RiFrameEnd();            /* Options are restored. */
        }
    RiEnd();
}
```

Listing 3.1 *The structure of a RenderMan program*

Summary

This chapter has touched lightly on a variety of topics that span the RenderMan Interface. Most of the rest of this book simply fleshes out the basic framework given here. In particular, subsequent chapters:

- go beyond polygons to the full set of primitive object types supported by the RenderMan Interface.
- detail the full set of attributes included in the graphics environment.
- describe the extent of RenderMan's support for hierarchical models.
- provide full control over the camera used to capture scenes.
- set out procedures for adding and controlling light sources.
- give much more control over how objects can be shaded.

Valid Contexts for RenderMan Procedure Calls									
Routine Name	Outside	Beg./End	Frame	World	Attrib.	Xform	Solid	Object	Motion
General routines:									
RiErrorHandler()	•	•	•	•	•	•	•	•	•
RiDeclare()	•	•	•	•	•	•	•	•	•
Begin-end block:									
RiBegin()	•								
RiEnd()	•								
Frame block:									
RiFrameBegin()		•							
RiFrameEnd()		•							
World block:									
RiWorldBegin()		•	•						
RiWorldEnd()		•	•						
Attribute block:									
RiAttributeBegin()		•	•	•	•	•	•		
RiAttributeEnd()		•	•	•	•	•	•		
Transform block:									
RiTransformBegin()		•	•	•	•	•	•		
RiTransformEnd()		•	•	•	•	•	•		
solid block:									
RiSolidBegin()				•	•	•	•		
RiSolidEnd()				•	•	•	•		

Routine Name	Outside	Beg./End	Frame	World	Attrib.	Xform	Solid	Object	Motion
object block:									
RiObjectBegin()		•	•	•	•	•	•		
RiObjectEnd()		•	•	•	•	•	•		
motion block:									
RiMotionBegin()		•	•	•	•	•	•		
RiMotionEnd()		•	•	•	•	•	•		
options:									
RiFormat()		•	•						
RiFrameAspectRatio()		•	•						
RiScreenWindow()		•	•						
RiCropWindow()		•	•						
RiProjection()		•	•						
RiClipping()		•	•						
RiDepthOfField()		•	•						
RiShutter()		•	•						
RiPixelVariance()		•	•						
RiPixelSamples()		•	•						
RiPixelFilter()		•	•						
RiExposure()		•	•						
RiImager()		•	•						
RiQuantize()		•	•						
RiDisplay()		•	•						
RiHider()		•	•						
RiColorSamples()		•	•						
RiRelativeDetail()		•	•						
RiOption()		•	•						
lights:									
RiLightSource()		•	•	•	•	•	•		•
RiAreaLightSource()		•	•	•	•	•	•		•
attributes:									
RiAttribute()		•	•	•	•	•	•		•
RiColor()		•	•	•	•	•	•		•
RiOpacity()		•	•	•	•	•	•		•
RiSurface()		•	•	•	•	•	•		•
RiAtmosphere()		•	•	•	•	•	•		•
RiInterior()		•	•	•	•	•	•		•
RiExterior()		•	•	•	•	•	•		•
RiIlluminate()		•	•	•	•	•	•		•
RiDisplacement()		•	•	•	•	•	•		•
RiTextureCoordinates()		•	•	•	•	•	•		•
RiShadingRate()		•	•	•	•	•	•		•
RiShadingInterpolation()		•	•	•	•	•	•		•
RiMatte()		•	•	•	•	•	•		•
RiBound()		•	•	•	•	•	•		•
RiDetail()		•	•	•	•	•	•		•

Valid Contexts for RenderMan Procedure Calls (cont'd)

Valid Contexts for RenderMan Procedure Calls (cont'd)								
Routine Name	Outside	Beg./End	Frame	World	Attrib.	Xform	Solid	Object	Motion
RiDetailRange()		•	•	•	•	•	•		•
RiGeometricApproximation()		•	•	•	•	•	•		•
RiOrientation()		•	•	•	•	•	•		•
RiReverseOrientation()		•	•	•	•	•	•		•
RiSides()		•	•	•	•	•	•		•
RiBasis()		•	•	•	•	•	•		•
RiTrimCurve()		•	•	•	•	•	•		•
transformations:									
RiIdentity()		•	•	•	•	•	•		•
RiTransform()		•	•	•	•	•	•		•
RiConcatTransform()		•	•	•	•	•	•		•
RiPerspective()		•	•	•	•	•	•		•
RiTranslate()		•	•	•	•	•	•		•
RiRotate()		•	•	•	•	•	•		•
RiScale()		•	•	•	•	•	•		•
RiSkew()		•	•	•	•	•	•		•
RiDeformation()		•	•	•	•	•	•		•
RiCoordinateSystem()		•	•	•	•	•	•		
RiTransformPoints()		•	•	•	•	•	•		
polygons:									
RiPolygon()				•	•	•	•	•	•
RiGeneralPolygon()				•	•	•	•	•	•
RiPointsPolygons()				•	•	•	•	•	•
RiPointsGeneralPolygons()				•	•	•	•	•	•
patches:									
RiPatch()				•	•	•	•	•	•
RiPatchMesh()				•	•	•	•	•	•
RiNuPatch()				•	•	•	•	•	•
quadrics:									
RiSphere()				•	•	•	•	•	•
RiCone()				•	•	•	•	•	•
RiCylinder()				•	•	•	•	•	•
RiHyperboloid()				•	•	•	•	•	•
RiParaboloid()				•	•	•	•	•	•
RiDisk()				•	•	•	•	•	•
RiTorus()				•	•	•	•	•	•
general objects:									
RiObjectInstance()				•	•	•	•		
RiProcedural()				•	•	•	•	•	
RiGeometry()				•	•	•	•	•	
map-making:									
RiMakeTexture()		•	•						
RiMakeBump()		•	•						
RiMakeLatLongEnvironment()		•	•						
RiMakeCubeFaceEnvironment()		•	•						
RiMakeShadow()		•	•						

CHAPTER 4

Primitive Surfaces I: Quadric Surfaces

*"Treat nature in terms of the cylinder, the
sphere, the cone, all in perspective."*

— Paul Cezanne

The first three chapters presented RenderMan in the large by sketching out the process it represents. The remainder of the book is devoted to specifics, beginning here with the basics of **scene description**: creating surfaces. This and the following two chapters concern the **primitive surfaces** available from the interface. Everything visible in a scene is ultimately composed of these surfaces.

The words "primitive" and "prime" are related; they describe a key property of RenderMan's design: primitive surfaces are simple enough that they cannot be broken into simpler primitives without discarding important intrinsic structural information. For example, a sphere could be broken into facets, but not without losing smoothness. In general, the coherence of a surface is often lost when it is subdivided.

Three categories of primitive are available. **Quadric surfaces**, the subject of this chapter, are defined by quadratic equations in two-dimensional space. Spheres and cones are examples of quadrics. **Polygons** are surfaces whose boundaries are given by a connected series of line segments. Objects represented by polygons are often characterized by a faceted appearance and straight-edged outlines, as we will see in Chapter 5. Finally, **parametric surfaces**, described in Chapter 6, are free form polynomial curved surfaces.

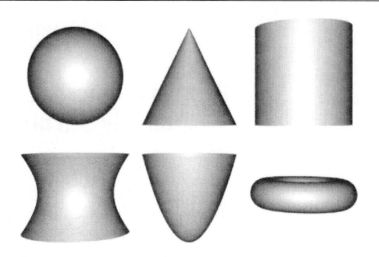

Figure 4.1 *Six different quadric types (top left to bottom right): sphere, cone, cylinder, hyperboloid, paraboloid, torus*

The quadric surfaces of RenderMan are **surfaces of revolution**, in which a finite curve in two dimensions is swept in three-dimensional space about one axis to create a surface, as in Figure 4.1. A circle centered on the origin forms a **sphere**. If the center of the circle does not lie on the origin, the circle sweeps out a **torus**. A line segment with one end lying on the axis of rotation forms a **cone**. A line segment parallel to the axis of rotation sweeps out a **cylinder**. The generalization of a line-segment sweep creates a **hyperboloid** by rotating an *arbitrary* line segment in three-dimensional space about the z axis. Finally, a parabola, defined by the equation $z = x^2$, forms a **paraboloid** when swept about the z axis.

Each type of quadric is defined in RenderMan with a single procedure call, discussed below. Listing 4.1 shows the program used to generate Figure 4.1. The axis of rotation is always the z axis, so here the quadrics are rotated about the x axis for better viewing. Each quadric routine has a **sweep angle** parameter, specifying the angular extent to which the quadric is swept about z. It is important to realize that *sweeping a quadric by less than 360.0 degrees leaves an open surface.* The hemisphere resulting from a 180.0° sweep is a cup, not a solid ball cut in half. If a solid is required, then measures must be taken to close the surface. These are discussed in Chapter 7 on composite objects.

```c
#include <ri.h>

Go()
{       ShowQuads();
}

#define OFFSET 1.2

ShowQuads()
{
        RtPoint hyperpt1, hyperpt2;

        RiRotate( -90.0, 1.0, 0.0, 0.0);

        RiTranslate( -OFFSET, 0.0, (OFFSET/2) );
        RiSphere( 0.5, -0.5, 0.5, 360.0, RI_NULL );         /* Declare a sphere     */

        RiTranslate( OFFSET, 0.0, 0.0 );
        RiTranslate( 0.0, 0.0, -0.5 );
        RiCone( 1.0, 0.5, 360.0, RI_NULL );                 /* Declare a cone       */

        RiTranslate( 0.0, 0.0, 0.5 );
        RiTranslate( OFFSET, 0.0, 0.0 );
        RiCylinder( 0.5, -0.5, 0.5, 360.0, RI_NULL );       /* Declare cylinder     */

        RiTranslate( -(OFFSET*2), 0.0, -OFFSET );
        hyperpt1[0] = 0.4;
        hyperpt1[1] = -0.4;
        hyperpt1[2] = -0.4;
        hyperpt2[0] = 0.4;
        hyperpt2[1] = 0.4;
        hyperpt2[2] = 0.4;

        /* Declare hyperboloid */
        RiHyperboloid( hyperpt1, hyperpt2, 360.0, RI_NULL);

        RiTranslate( OFFSET, 0.0, -0.5 );
        RiParaboloid( 0.5, 0.0, 0.9, 360.0, RI_NULL );      /* Declare paraboloid */

        RiTranslate( OFFSET, 0.0, 0.5 );
        RiTorus( .4, .15, 0.0, 360.0, 360.0, RI_NULL );     /* Declare torus        */

}
```

Listing 4.1 *Routine generating quadric surfaces shown in Figure 4.1*

Quadric Declaration Routines

RiSphere(radius, zmin, zmax, thetamax, *parameterlist*)
    RtFloat radius;
    RtFloat zmin, zmax;
    RtFloat thetamax;

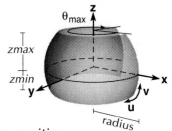

The parameters to **RiSphere**() are illustrated at right. *radius* is the radius of the sphere. *zmin* and *zmax* may be used to cut off the bottom and top of the sphere. For example, a hemisphere opening into positive z can be declared by setting *zmin* to the same value as *radius* (meaning that the bottom is not cut) and *zmax* to 0. Normally, the sphere runs from −*radius* to +*radius* in z.

thetamax is the sweep angle of the sphere. As with every quadric, the sweep begins at the x,z plane and sweeps around the z axis. If *thetamax* is 360.0, an entire sphere is swept out; if it is 180.0, a hemisphere is swept out in positive y, and so on.

RiCone(height, radius, thetamax, *parameterlist*)
    RtFloat height;
    RtFloat radius;
    RtFloat thetamax;

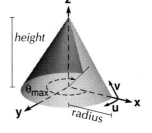

The base of a cone declared with **RiCone**() rests on the x,y plane, with the z axis passing through the center of the base and the tip of the cone, as shown at left. The *radius* parameter refers to the radius of the base, and *height* gives the distance between the base and the tip. As with all quadrics, *thetamax* may have some value other than 360.0 to sweep out some part of the cone.

RiDisk(height, radius, thetamax, *parameterlist*)
    RtFloat height;
    RtFloat radius;
    RtFloat thetamax;

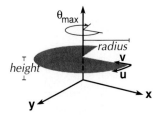

A disk is a special case of a cone with height 0. For a disk, the *height* determines the disk's displacement in z.

In other words, the call

RiDisk(height, radius, thetamax, RI_NULL);

is exactly equivalent to the sequence

RiTransformBegin();
RiTranslate(0.0, 0.0, height);
RiCone(0, radius, thetamax, RI_NULL);
RiTransformEnd();

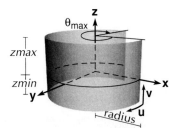

RiCylinder(radius, zmin, zmax, thetamax, *parameterlist*)
    RtFloat radius;
    RtFloat zmin, zmax;
    RtFloat thetamax;

RiCylinder() declares an open cylinder with a given *radius*, an extent in z given by *zmin* and *zmax*, and a sweep angle given by *thetamax*.

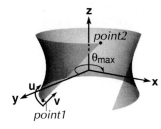

RiHyperboloid(point1, point2, thetamax, *parameterlist*
    RtPoint point1, point2;
    RtFloat thetamax;

RiHyperboloid() creates a hyperboloid from the three-dimensional points *point1* and *point2*. The surface is defined by taking the line segment between *point1* and *point2* and sweeping it *thetamax* degrees about the z axis.

Cones and cylinders are special cases of hyperboloids. A cone is simply a hyperboloid with one point on the z axis and the other on the x,z plane. The call

RiCone(1.0, 2.0, 360.0, RI_NULL);

generates a cone of radius 1, height 2; so does

RiHyperboloid(point1,point2,360.0, RI_NULL);

if *point1* = {0.0, 0.0, 2.0} and *point2* = {1.0, 0.0, 0.0}.

A cylinder is equivalent to a hyperboloid generated by a line segment parallel to the *z* axis. A cylinder with radius 1 and height 2 can be declared either with

RiCylinder(1.0, 0.0, 2.0, 360.0);

or by calling

RiHyperboloid(point1, point2, 360.0);

with point1 = {1.0, 0.0, 0.0} and point2 = {1.0, 0.0, 2.0}.

Curved hyperboloids

Cones and cylinders have straight sides, which is not surprising since hyperboloids are generated using a straight line. But the hyperboloid above has a curved profile. How can this be? From the two endpoints and midpoint of the line segment shown in the figure, there is a circle on the hyperboloid swept about the *z* axis. Every point on the line sweeps out one such circle to form the hyperboloid. The radius of each swept circle is equal to the point's distance from the *z* axis. Any line segment with an interior point nearer the *z* axis than its endpoints will sweep out an "hourglass" hyperboloid like the one shown.

One important distinction of hyperboloids concerns the meaning of *thetamax*. Unlike the other quadric types, the sweep of a hyperboloid always begins with the line segment in three-space, not with a curve on the *x,z* plane.

The image at right shows one use of hyperboloids: generating a general surface of revolution. The bowling pin was created from a profile curve defined as a set of points in the two-dimensional plane. This curve was rotated about the *z* axis to create the three-dimensional figure.

Listing 4.2 shows the routine *SurfOR()*. It takes an array of points in two-dimensional space and the length of the array. For each adjacent pair of points in two-dimensional space, it creates a pair of points in the *x,z* plane of three-dimensional space, then calls **RiHyperboloid**() to create one band of the surface as a truncated cone.

When rendered, the bottom of one hyperboloid mates perfectly with the top of the next. There is, however, a segmented appearance to the pin's profile owing to the exclusive use of hyperboloids. A smoother approximation to a curved surface can be obtained by using other quadrics as well. Faux and Pratt [FAUX80] present a method of assembling conic sections into curves with point and tangency constraints. But parametric surfaces, discussed in Chapter 6, are much more generally useful for describing curved surfaces.

```
typedef struct { RtFloat x, y; } Point2D;

SurfOR( points, npoints )
Point2D points[];
int npoints;
{
        int pt;
        RtPoint point1, point2;
        RtFloat *pp1, *pp2, *tmp;
                pp1 = point1;
                pp2 = point2;

        /*
         * For each adjacent pair of x,y points in the outline description,
         *  draw a hyperboloid by sweeping the line segment defined by
         *  those points about the z axis.
         */
        pp1[0] = points[0].y;
        pp1[1] = 0;
        pp1[2] = points[0].x;
        for( pt = 1; pt < npoints; pt++ ) {
                pp2[0] = points[pt].y;
                pp2[1] = 0;
                pp2[2] = points[pt].x;
                RiHyperboloid( pp1, pp2, 360.0, RI_NULL );
                tmp = pp1; pp1 = pp2; pp2 = tmp;          /* Swap pointers */
        }
}
```

Listing 4.2 *Using hyperboloids to create a surface of revolution*

Paraboloids

A paraboloid is a surface of revolution based on the parabola, a curve in two dimensions consisting of all points that satisfy the equation $z=ax^2$, where a is a constant.

RiParaboloid(rmax, zmin, zmax, thetamax, *parameterlist*)
    RtFloat rmax;
    RtFloat zmin, zmax;
    RtFloat thetamax;

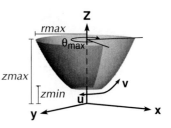

The extent of a paraboloid generated by **RiParabo-loid**() is limited by the arguments *zmin* and *zmax*. All parabolas have their tip at $(x=0, z=0)$; *zmin* and *zmax* determine where the paraboloid is cut off at the bottom and top respectively. In addition, the parameter *rmax* determines the width of the paraboloid at *zmax*. The width of the parabola is adjusted so that the parabola passes through the point $(x = rmax, z = zmax)$, so increasing *rmax* widens the paraboloid.

Due to its definition, a paraboloid must lie in positive *z*. Therefore, it is an error for *zmin* or *zmax* to be negative.

Torus

A torus is the "donut" shape that results from sweeping a circle not centered on the origin about the *z* axis.

RiTorus(majorrad, minorrad, phimin, phimax, thetamax,
      parameterlist)
    RtFloat majorrad, minorrad;
    RtFloat phimin, phimax;
    RtFloat thetamax;

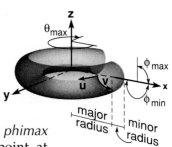

majorrad gives the distance between the center of the torus and the center of the circle being swept; *minorrad* gives the radius of the circle; *phimin* and *phimax* give sweep angles around the circle, relative to the point at the outside extreme of the torus. For example, *phimin*=180.0 and *phimax*=360.0 result in a circular trough. *thetamax* controls the wedge of the donut swept out.

Example: a toroidal "wave"

Figure 4.2 is an image generated by the program in Listing 4.3. It is a circular wavelike pattern generated by a series of tori of matched radius. The function *TorusWave()* takes a number

```
#include <ri.h>
#include <stdio.h>

Go() { TorusWave( 5, 360.0 ); }

/*
 * TorusWave( nwaves, thetamax ): create a set of concentric "waves" using
 *  a hemisphere in the middle and a set of nwaves concentric semi-tori.
 *  The sweep of the waves is given by the parameter thetamax.
 */
TorusWave( nwaves, thetamax )
int nwaves;
float thetamax;
{
        float innerrad, outerrad;
        int wave;

        if( nwaves < 1) {
                fprintf(stderr,"Need a positive number of waves\n");
                return;
        }

        /* Divide the net radius 1.0 among the waves and the hemisphere */
        innerrad = 2 / ( 8.0*nwaves + 2);
        RiRotate( 90.0, 1.0, 0.0, 0.0 );

        /* Create the cap for the center of the wave */
        RiSphere( innerrad, –innerrad, 0.0, innerrad, thetamax, RI_NULL );

        outerrad = 0;
        for( wave = 1; wave <= nwaves; wave++ ) {
                /*
                 * Each iteration creates a downward-opening half-torus
                 *  and a larger upward-opening half-torus.
                 */
                outerrad = outerrad + (innerrad * 2);
                RiTorus( outerrad, innerrad, 0.0, 180.0, thetamax, RI_NULL );
                outerrad = outerrad + (innerrad * 2);
                RiTorus( outerrad, innerrad, 180.0, 360.0, thetamax, RI_NULL );
        }
}
```

Listing 4.3 *Using **RiTorus()** to create a wavelike pattern*

Figure 4.2 *Circular "wave" pattern generated by abutting semi-tori*

of waves and a sweep angle, generating that many waves in a figure one unit in radius. A hemisphere caps the innermost wave. Figure 4.2 was created with *nwaves*=4 and *thetamax* = 250.

CHAPTER 5

Primitive Surfaces II: Polygons

P Polygons are a simple, easy-to-use class of surface. The squares in Chapter 2 were polygons, defined, like all RenderMan polygons, by a **boundary** given as an ordered series of **vertices**. Each vertex is linked to the next vertex by an **edge**, with the last vertex linked to the first. The edges are implicit; only the vertices are passed to RenderMan.

This chapter describes four routines for declaring polygons singly and in adjoining groups to form **polyhedra**. In general, the ability of polygons to describe curved objects is limited by their flatness, so this chapter also covers a technique for reducing this faceted appearance. However, we will see that it is no panacea; that fact provides the motivation for the general curved surfaces of Chapter 6.

Basic Polygon Types

Polygons are classified according to their topology. Since each vertex of a polygon may lie anywhere in three-dimensional space, the RenderMan definition of a polygon covers quite a bit of ground: a polygon could be **planar** or **non-planar**, **convex** or **concave**; there could be holes in its surface; and its vertex list could even double back in such a way that the surface intersects itself. In a **planar** polygon, all vertices lie in the same plane in three-dimensional space. The notion of convexity is conveyed by imagining a rubber band snapped around the polygon; if it follows the vertices, touching each one, the polygon is **convex**. Otherwise (if there are gaps between the band and some edges) it is **concave**. Both classes are illustrated in Figure 5.1. Only concave polygons are self-intersecting.

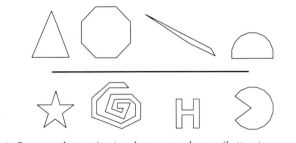

Figure 5.1 *Convex polygons (top) and concave polygons (bottom)*

In many cases, it is much easier for a renderer to handle planar, convex polygons. While the more general polygons are convenient to the user, that convenience is not without cost. Consequently, a trade-off must be made between utility and efficiency. RenderMan helps make the trade-off by providing two routines for declaring polygons. **RiPolygon**(), which we first encountered in Chapter 2, requires its input to be planar and convex. **RiGeneralPolygon**() allows planar concave polygons with holes. Even though some implementations may accept non-planar polygons, RenderMan does not guarantee the results.

The other two polygon declaration routines, **RiPointsPolygons**() and **RiPointsGeneralPolygons**(), are similar, but allow a group of polygons that share vertices (a polyhedron) to be declared at once.

Simple polygons

RiPolygon(nvertices, *parameterlist*)
    RtInt nvertices;

RiPolygon() declares a single, convex, planar polygon with no holes. The polygon has *nvertices* vertices; the vertices themselves are given in *parameterlist*, as a "P" (RI_P) token-value pair, the value of which is an array of *nvertices* points, each of type **RtPoint**.

The following examples using **RiPolygon**() show how polygons may be used to create a surface of revolution. Listing 5.1 defines the function *PolyBoid*() used to create a ring centered around the *z* axis, much like a hyperboloid. A single band is defined by two points in the *x,z* plane; when swept about the *z* axis, the line segment between the points sweeps out a band.

In Listing 5.1, *PolyBoid*() takes four parameters: *point0* and *point1*, which define the band, *ndivs* dictating the number of triangles used, and *parity*, which helps adjacent bands to mate correctly by providing a phase factor that aligns vertices with vertices.

The image at left is a bowling pin composed of polygons, paralleling the hyperboloid bowling pin in Chapter 4. *PolyBoid*() is called repeatedly for successive pairs of points along the profile of the bowling pin, as **RiHyperboloid**() was there.

Vertex Format and Information

This bowling pin has some obvious flaws: its faceted appearance is that of many adjoining flat surfaces rather than a smoothly curved surface, and its profile consists of straight edges.

Flat shading

The situation depicted in the bowling pin arises because the polygons are **flat shaded**: each polygon has the same color at all points, and the color changes abruptly in passing over the edge from one polygon to another. One way to ease that problem is to **subdivide** the object: use more, smaller polygons. The immediate result would be to reduce the magnitude of the transition from one to another. Eventually the polygons would be so small that you couldn't even *see* them individually, much less notice the difference between them.

This solution has at least two disadvantages. First, it multiplies the amount of data that must be passed through the interface. This is even worse than it seems at first, since halving the average width of the polygons requires *four times* the number of polygons (doubling horizontally *and* vertically) to cover the same area. The second disadvantage is that to avoid excessive subdivision, the extent of subdivision should be deter-

```
/*
 * PolyBoid(): approximate a hyperboloid using triangles.
 *      point0, point1: three-dimensional points as in RiHyperboloid()
 *      ndivs: number of triangles to generate
 *      parity: phase factor (0 or 1) to mate triangles from adjacent bands
 */
PolyBoid(point0,point1,ndivs,parity)
RtFloat *point0,*point1; int ndivs, parity;
{
        RtPoint     vertexpair0[2],
                    vertexpair1[2],
                    *ptrnextpair = vertexpair0,
                    *ptrlastpair = vertexpair1,
                    *temp,
                    triangle[3];
        int i;
#define SWAP(a,b,temp) temp = a; a = b; b = temp;
#define COPY_POINT(d, s)        {d[0]=s[0]; d[1]=s[1]; d[2]=s[2];}
        getnextpair(0+parity/2.0, ptrnextpair, point0, point1, ndivs);
        for (i = 1; i <= ndivs; i++) {
                SWAP(ptrlastpair, ptrnextpair, temp)
                getnextpair(i+parity/2.0, ptrnextpair, point0, point1, ndivs);
                COPY_POINT(triangle[0], ptrlastpair[0]);
                COPY_POINT(triangle[1], ptrlastpair[1]);
                COPY_POINT(triangle[2], ptrnextpair[1]);
                RiPolygon(3, RI_P, (RtPointer) triangle, RI_NULL);
                COPY_POINT(triangle[0], ptrnextpair[0]);
                COPY_POINT(triangle[1], ptrnextpair[1]);
                COPY_POINT(triangle[2], ptrlastpair[0]);
                RiPolygon(3, RI_P, (RtPointer) triangle, RI_NULL);
        }
}
#define PI 3.14159
getnextpair(offset, ptrnextpair, point0, point1, ndivs)
float offset;
RtPoint *ptrnextpair;
RtFloat *point0,*point1;
int ndivs;
{       float r;
        double sin(), cos();
        r = 2*PI*offset/ndivs;
        ptrnextpair[0][0] = point0[0]*sin(r);
        ptrnextpair[0][1] = point0[0]*cos(r);
        ptrnextpair[0][2] = point0[2];
        r = 2*PI*(offset-.5)/ndivs;
        ptrnextpair[1][0] = point1[0]*sin(r);
        ptrnextpair[1][1] = point1[0]*cos(r);
        ptrnextpair[1][2] = point1[2];
}
```

Listing 5.1 *Polygonal approximation of a hyperboloid*

mined by both the polygons' onscreen area and the magnitude of the color change from one to the next. A bowling pin half the size of the one on the previous page would require one fewer binary subdivision, and if the lighting were flatter, fewer still. For a program to dynamically make the trade-off between data volume and picture quality, information would have to be passed back across the interface, seriously compromising the interface design.

The basic problem here is that polygons are flat. As Figure 5.2 shows, the orientation of a smoothly curved surface varies smoothly across the surface. If that same surface is approximated using polygons, the orientation changes abruptly at the polygon edges.

This is a problem because the orientation of a surface directly affects its appearance: a surface that faces away from a light source appears darker than one that faces toward it. In Figure 5.2, the right polygon would appear brighter than the left one. Because the *orientation* changes abruptly at polygon edges, so does the *shade* of the object.

The orientation of a surface is represented as a vector pointing perpendicular to the surface (the surface **normal** vector), like those in Figure 5.2. It would make a polygonal object like the bowling pin appear much smoother if the surface normal used to shade the polygon varied in its interior as smoothly as it does for the underlying surface. This effect can be achieved by first associating the normal of the curved surface with the

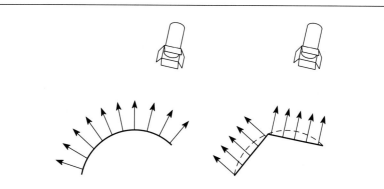

Figure 5.2 *Smooth surfaces vs. polygonal approximations*

polygon vertices, then taking the normal at interior points to be a smoothly varying combination, or **interpolation**, of those at the vertices. This is the technique of **Phong interpolation**, named for Phong Bui Tuong.

Listing 5.2 shows another version of the *PolyBoid()* function, this time providing a suitable normal at polygon vertices. The surface normal is defined at each vertex in exactly the same way as position is: the token "N" (RI_N) is followed by an array of **RtPoint**s, each giving a normal direction. The pin at right shows the result. The profile at the corresponding vertex is still segmented, but the shading is much smoother.

In the bowling pin, each vertex position is used by several adjoining polygons. This version of *PolyBoid()* makes sure the *normal* vectors assigned to a vertex are the same for all the polygons sharing that vertex. Otherwise the shading of the surface would change abruptly from one polygon to the next.

To correctly assign the surface normals to the polygon vertices, one must have some idea of the underlying surface. Frequently, a direct representation is not available. Here, for example, the bowling pin is represented by a series of profile points, with no information supplied about the profile between those points. *PolyBoid()* defines the normal at a profile point as a line perpendicular to a line segment between the surrounding two vertices (see Figure 5.3). *PolyBoid()* takes that two-dimensional normal and sweeps it about the *z* axis just as it sweeps the vertex points themselves.

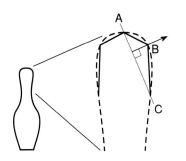

Figure 5.3 *Normal calculation from adjacent vertices. The "surface" normal at vertex B is perpendicular to the line AC.*

Chapter 5: Primitive Surfaces II: Polygons

This is by no means the best or only method for approximating the surface normals, but it emphasizes that such methods are only approximations. A common alternative is to calculate a vertex normal as the average real normal of the surrounding polygons. In any event, the important thing is that each vertex should have identical normals for each polygon sharing the vertex (unless, of course, a crease is really wanted).

Drawbacks of polygons

We have done about as well as we could with a polygonal approximation to the bowling pin. Still, problems remain which are typical of the polygonal representation. To begin with, one can do little about the straight profile edge of this object.

The second problem is a formal one: when a polygon has more than four vertices, the interior interpolation of such vertex values as color and normal is inherently ill-defined.

Even for three- and four-vertex polygons, dramatic changes in appearance over the surface can make edges visible again. Since the eye is very good at picking out differences in the visual field, even differences in the *rate* of change at edges are often visible. Some of these artifacts can be seen in the smooth-shaded version of the bowling pin.

Finally, it should be recognized that interpolation of normals is only an approximation because it interpolates vectors rather than angles (see Figure 5.4). Fortunately, the error is much smaller for relatively small changes in orientation.

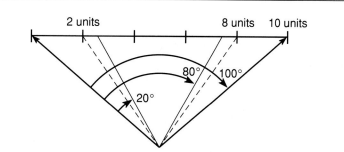

Figure 5.4 *A linear interpolation between the two vectors does not interpolate angles linearly. The error is much smaller for small angles.*

```
#include <ri.h>
#include "surfor.h"
#include "pin.hyper.h"

RtColor color = {.9,.9,.5};
Go() {
      RiColor(color);
      RiRotate( -90.0, 1.0, 0.0, 0.0 );
      PolySurfOR( points, colors, NPOINTS );
}

PolySurfOR( points, colors, npoints )
Point2D points[];
RtColor colors[];
int npoints;
{
      int pt;
      RtPoint point1, point2, normal1, normal2;
      RtFloat *pp1, *pp2,  *pm1, *pm2, *tmp;

      pp1 = point1;
      pp2 = point2;
      pm1 = normal1;
      pm2 = normal2;
      /*
       * For each adjacent pair of points in the goblet description,
       * draw a hyperboloid by sweeping the line segment defined by
       * those points about the z axis.
       */
      pp1[0] = points[0].y;
      pp1[1] = 0;
      pp1[2] = points[0].x;
      pm1[0] = points[0].x - points[1].x;
      pm1[1] = 0;
      pm1[2] = points[1].y - points[0].y;
      for( pt = 1; pt < npoints-1; pt++ ) {

            pp2[0] = points[pt].y;
            pp2[1] = 0;
            pp2[2] = points[pt].x;
            pm2[0] = points[pt-1].x - points[pt+1].x;
            pm2[1] = 0;
            pm2[2] = points[pt+1].y - points[pt-1].y;
            RiColor( colors[pt] );
            PolyBoid( pp1, pp2, pm1, pm2, 8, pt-1);
            tmp = pp1; pp1 = pp2; pp2 = tmp;
            tmp = pm1; pm1 = pm2; pm2 = tmp;
      }

      pt = npoints-1;
      pp2[0] = points[pt].y;
      pp2[1] = 0;
      pp2[2] = points[pt].x;
```

```
                    pm2[0] = points[pt-1].x - points[pt].x;
                    pm2[1] = 0;
                    pm2[2] = points[pt].y - points[pt-1].y;
                    RiColor( colors[pt] );                         `
                    PolyBoid( pp1, pp2, pm1, pm2, 8, pt-1);
}


PolyBand(point0,point1,normal0,normal1,ndivs,parity)
RtFloat *point0,*point1,*normal0,*normal1; int ndivs, parity;
{
        RtPoint vertexstrip[100][2], normalstrip[100][2];
        int i, nverts[100][2], indices[100][2][3];

        for (i = 0; i <= ndivs; i++) {
                getnextpair(i+parity/2.0,vertexstrip[i],point0,point1,ndivs);
                getnextpair(i+parity/2.0,normalstrip[i],normal0,normal1,ndivs);
        }
        for (i = 0; i < ndivs; i++) {
                nverts[i][0] = nverts[i][1] = 3;
                indices[i][0][0] = i*2;
                indices[i][0][1] = i*2+1;
                indices[i][0][2] = (i+1)*2+1;
                indices[i][1][0] = (i+1)*2+1;
                indices[i][1][1] = (i+1)*2;
                indices[i][1][2] = i*2;
        }
        RiPointsPolygons( ndivs*2, nverts, indices,
                RI_P, (RtPointer)vertexstrip,
                RI_N, (RtPointer)normalstrip,
                RI_NULL);
}


getnextpair(offset,ptrnextpair,point0,point1,ndivs)
float offset;
RtPoint *ptrnextpair;
RtFloat *point0,*point1;
int ndivs;
{
        float r; double sin(), cos();

        r = 2*3.14159*offset/ndivs;
        ptrnextpair[0][0] = point0[0]*sin(r);
        ptrnextpair[0][1] = point0[0]*cos(r);
        ptrnextpair[0][2] = point0[2];

        r = 2*3.14159*(offset-.5)/ndivs;
        ptrnextpair[1][0] = point1[0]*sin(r);
        ptrnextpair[1][1] = point1[0]*cos(r);
        ptrnextpair[1][2] = point1[2];
}
```

Listing 5.2 *Bowling pin with normals assigned to vertices*

In summary, smooth shading can help reduce the shading artifacts of the polygonal representation, especially if the polygons are relatively small, with little change of color and orientation. But it is a costly approximation: sometimes it takes thousands of polygons to approximate adequately a single smooth surface. It is much easier to define and manipulate curved surfaces directly. They are the subject of Chapter 6.

Other polygon types

RenderMan supports three other routines for defining polygons. One, **RiGeneralPolygon**(), allows a user to pass concave polygons with holes. **RiPointsPolygons**() and **RiPointsGeneralPolygons**() allow collections of abutting polygons (**polyhedra**) to be passed and stored efficiently. The four polygon routines can be arranged into a 2 x 2 matrix of capability, as below:

	One polygon	Polyhedra
Convex polygons, no holes	**RiPolygon**()	**RiPointsPolygons**()
Concave polygons with holes	**RiGeneralPolygon**()	**RiPointsGeneralPolygons**()

RiGeneralPolygon(nloops, nverts, *parameterlist*)
    RtInt nloops;
    RtInt nverts[];

A general polygon is defined as *nloops* loops, in contrast to the single loop of **RiPolygon**(). The first loop defines the outside of the polygon, and the remaining *nloops*–1 loops define holes. There should be *nloops* elements of *nverts*; the *i*th element gives the number of vertices in the *i*th loop (see Figure 5.5). In *parameterlist* there must therefore be

$$\sum_{i=0}^{nloops-1} nverts[i]$$

RtPoint vertices in the "P" (RI_P) token-value pair of *parameterlist*. As with **RiPolygon**(), there must be an identical number of vertex normals, colors or any other varying attribute, if they appear at all.

                        Chapter 5: Primitive Surfaces II: Polygons

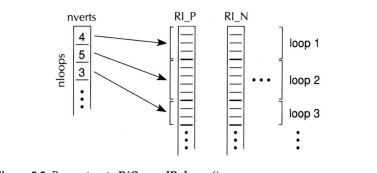

Figure 5.5 *Parameters to **RiGeneralPolygon**()*

Polyhedra

In the bowling pin example above, each vertex was used in up to six triangles, so each point was passed six times. The same was true of other attributes, like surface color and normal, associated with the polygon vertices. In rendering, each point will require six times the storage and will be transformed six times as often as it strictly needs to be.

This is a common situation when surfaces are assembled from adjoining polygons. The solution is to separate the definition of a *polygon* from the definition of its *vertices*, i.e., to define the points separately, forming the polygons by referring to the points. This is often dubbed the **points-polygons** form.

Two RenderMan routines support this strategy. As before, one accepts planar, convex polygons without holes and the other is more general.

RiPointsPolygons(npolys, nverts, verts, *parameterlist*)
    RtInt npolys, nverts[];
    RtInt verts[];

RiPointsPolygons() defines *npolys* polygons; the first polygon has *nverts*[0] vertices, the second *nverts*[1], and so on. There must be

$$\sum_{i=0}^{nloops-1} nverts[i]$$

elements in the array *verts*, each of which is not a point, but an index into the RI_P array in *parameterlist*. Since each element of *verts* is an index, it also serves to index arrays of other attributes.

RiPointsPolygons() imposes a special meaning on the RI_P token-value pair in *parameterlist*. There are only as many points as there are *distinct* vertices in the set of polygons. Each element of *verts* specifies a polygon vertex by indexing into that vertex array. For a polyhedron, where polygons share vertices, most vertices will be indexed more than once by *verts*. There is no limit to the number of polygons that can share a vertex.

For example, the effect of the call

    RiPolygon(4, RI_P, (**RtPointer**) square, RI_NULL);

can be reproduced using **RiPointsPolygons**(). If *nverts* has 1 element set to 4, and *verts* has 4 elements such that *verts[i]* = *i*, then the call

    RiPointsPolygons(1, nverts, verts, RI_P, (**RtPointer**) square, RI_NULL);

has the same effect.

For a less trivial example, consider a cube. It has six polygons with four vertices apiece, but there are only eight distinct vertex positions. Thus a cube would be described to **RiPointsPolygons**() using a vertex array of eight **RtPoint**s. *npolys* would be 6 and *nverts* would have 6 elements, each set to 4. Finally, *verts* would have 24 elements. The first four would index, in the RI_P array, the vertices of the first polygon; the second four would index the second polygon's vertices, and so on. Figure 5.6 shows the situation.

Listing 5.3 uses **RiPointsPolygons**() in one more version of the *PolyBoid*() function. Besides saving time and space, this version actually makes the resulting program cleaner. Using multidimensional arrays for indices and *nverts* inside the program makes it a little clearer, and is immaterial to the interface; they are treated as single-dimension arrays, and it all

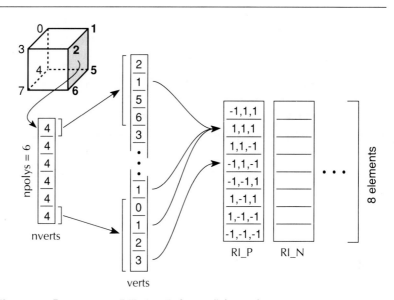

Figure 5.6 *Parameters to **RiPointsPolygons**() for a cube*

works out due to the row-major order of multidimensional arrays in C.

There must be enough elements of the vertex (or any other) array in *parameterlist* that *verts[i]* does not exceed the array bounds for any *i*. In other words, if *maxindex* is the largest element of *verts*, then there must be at least (*maxindex*+1) elements of the vertex array.

```
#define MAXVERTS 100

/*
 * PolyBoid(): declare a polygonal "hyperboloid" using RiPointsPolygons()
 */
PolyBoid(point0, point1, normal0, normal1, ndivs, parity)
RtFloat *point0, *point1, *normal0, *normal1;
int ndivs, parity;
{
    RtPoint vertexstrip[MAXVERTS][2];
    RtPoint normalstrip[MAXVERTS][2];
    int i, nverts[MAXVERTS][2], indices[MAXVERTS][2][3];
```

```
    for (i = 0; i <= ndivs; i++) {
        getnextpair(i+parity/2.0, vertexstrip[i], point0, point1, ndivs);
        getnextpair(i+parity/2.0, normalstrip[i], normal0, normal1, ndivs);
    }
    for (i = 0; i < ndivs; i++) {
        nverts[i][0] = nverts[i][1] = 3;
        indices[i][0][0] = i*2;
        indices[i][0][1] = i*2+1;
        indices[i][0][2] = (i+1)*2+1;
        indices[i][1][0] = (i+1)*2+1;
        indices[i][1][1] = (i+1)*2;
        indices[i][1][2] = i*2;
    }
    RiPointsPolygons( ndivs*2, nverts, indices,
        RI_P, (RtPointer) vertexstrip,
        RI_N, (RtPointer) normalstrip,
        RI_NULL);
}
```

Listing 5.3 *Bowling pin with normals assigned to vertices, defined using Ri-PointsPolygons()*

General polygon meshes

The final polygon routine combines the generality of **RiGeneralPolygon**() with the indirection of **RiPointsPolygons**(), using their combined syntax.

RiPointsGeneralPolygons(npolys, nloops, nverts, verts, *parameterlist*)
    RtInt npolys;
    RtInt nloops[];
    RtInt nverts[];
    RtInt verts[];

RiPointsGeneralPolygons() declares *npolys* polygons. The first has *nloops*[0] loops, the second *nloops*[1], etc. The first loop of the first polygon has *nverts*[0] vertices; its second loop has *nverts*[1] vertices, and so on. The vertices themselves are indexed in the RI_P token-value pair of *parameterlist* using *verts*.

There should be *npolys* elements of *nloops*, each giving the number of loops in one polygon. The total number of loops in the polygonal surface is

$$loopcount = \sum_{p=0}^{npolys-1} \mathrm{nloops}[p]$$

giving the number of elements of *nverts*. Lastly, there should be

$$\sum_{l=0}^{loopcount-1} \mathrm{nverts}[l]$$

elements of *verts*. As before, these index the array of **RtPoint** coordinates given in the RI_P parameter. Any other variables bound to vertices should have exactly the same number of values, and they are indexed exactly the same way. Once again, the maximum index in the *verts* array must be strictly less than the size of the vertex array in *parameterlist*.

Primitive Surfaces III: Parametric Surfaces

This chapter concerns the most general curved surface types in the RenderMan Interface. Polygonal models are useful primarily for representing objects with flat surfaces. Quadrics take a first step toward representing curved bodies, but the range of shape they can take is still very limited. By contrast, parametric surfaces enjoy a great deal of flexibility while providing intuitive control parameters to make manipulating them fairly natural.

The mathematical foundations of parametric surfaces are somewhat more sophisticated than those of polygons and quadrics. However, only a relatively small part of that background is required in order to use them effectively. This chapter discusses the facilities of RenderMan for declaring parametric surfaces, and provides several examples. Appendix B goes into the subject in more detail, providing a specification of how a wide variety of surfaces can be obtained from identical geometry. The discussion here is considerably more accessible.

The RenderMan Interface provides two classes of parametric surface. Uniform surfaces, both bilinear and bicubic, are easy to use with a minimum of mathematical background and rigor. Non-uniform rational B-splines (affectionately known as **NURB**s) are more flexible and general, but require a background beyond the scope of this book. The discussion of NURBs is confined to describing the RenderMan routine supporting them, followed by references to more complete treatments.

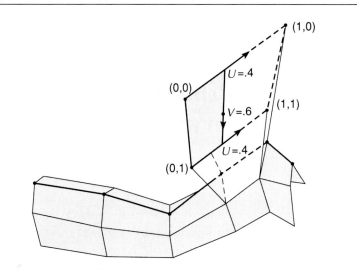

Figure 6.1 *Drawing a bilinear patch*

Uniform Bilinear and Bicubic Patches

A single **parametric surface**, or **patch**, can be visualized as an elastic square in three-dimensional space that can be stretched and twisted by a user. Even its characterization as a square is subject to change, since any edge can be shrunk to nothing by making two corners coincide.

RenderMan supports two types of uniform patch. A **bilinear patch** is a quadrilateral, not necessarily planar, formed by four vertices in three-dimensional space. Its surface is described by bilinear interpolation of the vertices' positions.

Bilinear interpolation is a generalization of linear interpolation. In linear interpolation, a line is formed between two points *p1* and *p2* and associated with a parameter *u*, which ranges from 0 at *p1* to 1 at *p2*. A point on the segment is associated with a value of *u* as the sum (*p1**(1–*u*) + *p2**u). A bilinear patch is defined by four points, as depicted in Figure 6.1: as *u* sweeps out two opposite edges of the quadrilateral, the surface is formed by lines drawn between points on the opposite segments with equal values of *u*. Equivalently, one can imagine

Chapter 6: Primitive Surfaces III: Parametric Surfaces

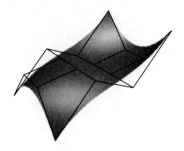

Figure 6.2 *Control hull and one possible resulting surface*

one of the edges sweeping along a path by moving its end-points along its two adjoining edges.

The second type of uniform patch in RenderMan, the **bicubic patch**, is a more interesting curved surface. It is also four-sided, but both its edges and its surface can be shaped more flexibly.

A bicubic patch is described using a set of **control points** arranged in a 4 x 4 **geometry matrix**, also known as the surface's **control hull**. Figure 6.2 shows a control hull and its associated bicubic surface. The control hull approximates, in some sense, the surface itself. Moving a point on the control hull changes the shape of the surface in a predictable way.

To render a single bilinear or bicubic uniform patch using the RenderMan Interface, an application passes a geometry matrix through **RiPatch**(). As with polygons, parameters other than position may be associated with the corners of the patch and interpolated to points on the interior of the surface.

RiPatch(type, *parameterlist*)
  RtToken type;

RiPatch() declares a single patch. *type* must be either "bilinear" (RI_BILINEAR) or "bicubic" (RI_BICUBIC). *parameterlist* must contain a token-value pair with an array of either four control points, for a bilinear patch, or sixteen, for a bicubic patch.

Three-dimensional **RtPoint** coordinates, denoted by the *type* token RI_P, are usually given for the control points. A height field, denoted by "Pz" (RI_PZ), has one z (height) value per element: x and y implicitly run from 0 to 1 in each direction, so that the first point has $x=y=0$ and the last, $x=y=1$. In all cases the array should be cast to (**RtPointer**).

Homogeneous coordinates may also be given, preceded by the "Pw" (RI_PW) *type* token, as an array of four-dimensional points. Homogeneous coordinates include a fourth variable, w, in addition to x, y and z: the ith point is expressed as a quadruple [x_i y_i z_i w_i]. The surface is evaluated in four dimensions as [$X(u,v)$, $Y(u,v)$, $Z(u,v)$, $W(u,v)$], but the surface points are given by

$$X'(u,v) = X(u,v)/W(u,v)$$

$$Y'(u,v) = Y(u,v)/W(u,v)$$

$$Z'(u,v) = Z(u,v)/W(u,v)$$

Other values, like surface normal and color, may be declared at the corners of a patch, just as they may be at the vertices of a polygon. Unlike polygons, however, there are exactly four corners of any patch, so there will be exactly four elements in each array of the token-value pairs. The values will be interpolated across the resulting surface using bilinear interpolation.

Patch example

The code fragment in Listing 6.1 produced the patch shown in Figure 6.2. It uses the 4 x 4 geometry matrix *Patch*. The control hull can be rendered by breaking the geometry matrix into individual 2 x 2 quadrilaterals and rendering them as bilinear patches.

Choice of patch type

Bilinear patches are not as flexible as bicubics, but they offer a viable alternative to polygons. First, a bilinear patch does not have the constraint of planarity. Second, a bilinear patch may be more efficient to render than a bicubic one, and so would

```c
#include <ri.h>

#define X0 -1
#define X1 -.33
#define X2 .33
#define X3 1

#define Y0 -.7
#define Y1 -.1
#define Y2 0.1
#define Y3 0.7

#define Z0 -1
#define Z1 -.33
#define Z2 .33
#define Z3 1

RtPoint Patch[4][4] = {
{ X0, Y0, Z0}, { X1, Y2, Z0}, { X2, Y1, Z0}, { X3, Y3, Z0},
{ X0, Y1, Z1}, { X1, Y2, Z1}, { X2, Y1, Z1}, { X3, Y2, Z1},
{ X0, Y1, Z2}, { X1, Y2, Z2}, { X2, Y1, Z2}, { X3, Y2, Z2},
{ X0, Y0, Z3}, { X1, Y2, Z3}, { X2, Y1, Z3}, { X3, Y3, Z3}};

PatchExample()
{
     RtPoint blpatch[2][2];
     int u, v;
#define MOVE_PT( d, s) { d[0]=s[0]; d[1]=s[1]; d[2]=s[2]; }

#ifdef PATCH
     RiPatch( RI_BICUBIC,
          RI_P, (RtPointer) Patch,
          RI_NULL);
#endif

#ifdef HULL
     for( v = 0; v < 3; v++) {
         for( u = 0; u < 3; u++) {
             MOVE_PT( blpatch[0][0], Patch[v][u])
             MOVE_PT( blpatch[0][1], Patch[v][u+1])
             MOVE_PT( blpatch[1][0], Patch[v+1][u])
             MOVE_PT( blpatch[1][1], Patch[v+1][u+1])
             RiPatch( RI_BILINEAR,
                 RI_P, (RtPointer) blpatch,
                 RI_NULL);
         }
     }
#endif
}
```

Listing 6.1 *Declaring a single bicubic patch or nine bilinear patches*

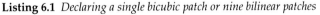

be natural for flat surfaces, or for approximating curved surfaces that are sufficiently small that interpolation can make the surface look smooth enough; as in the example above, the geometry matrix of a bicubic patch might also be rendered as a set of bilinear patches for preliminary tests of a scene. Third, they are usually more efficient to render than polygons. Fourth, interpolation is always well-defined across a bilinear patch; this is not true of polygons.

Types of Bicubic Surface

A control hull does not completely define a curved surface, in the sense that many different surfaces could reasonably result from any given control hull. For example, does the surface pass through, or **interpolate**, the vertices of the control hull, or does it merely **approximate** them? Does it interpolate all of the vertices, or just a subset? If it approximates the control hull, how close is the approximation, how closely is the surface drawn to the vertices? There are many potential types of curved surface within the bicubics.

There are four types of uniform bicubic surface supported directly by RenderMan: **Bézier**, **B-spline**, **Catmull-Rom** and **Hermite** surfaces. Just as bilinear patches are a natural extension of the mathematics of straight lines to surfaces, bicubic patches are an extension of cubic **splines**. For simplicity, we will discuss the different types of bicubic patch in terms of the corresponding splines. A spline is described using a geometry *vector* of four control points, in contrast with the geometry *matrix* of sixteen elements used to produce a surface.

Bézier splines

A Bézier spline on four control points interpolates the first and last points; the inner two points govern the curve's direction, or tangent, at the endpoints. In the diagram at right, the curve is tangent to the line segment *AB* at point *A*, and to *DC* at point *D*. Furthermore, the "inertia" of the curve at point *A* is determined by the *length* of *AB*, and likewise at *D* by *DC*. Bézier curves provide the user a great deal of control over shape.

B-splines

B-splines are fully approximating; such a curve will generally pass through its control points only if several of them are at the same location. This makes B-splines somewhat more difficult to control than interpolating splines, but they do yield a very smooth appearance.

Catmull-Rom splines

Catmull-Rom splines interpolate the middle two control points; the tangent at those points is parallel to the line between the previous control point and the next control point. Catmull-Rom splines are very convenient because they automatically fit a curve or surface to a set of points. However, they may not always interpolate in the expected way.

Hermite splines

Like a Catmull-Rom spline, a Hermite spline interpolates two of its control points, in this case the first and third. However, Hermite splines are unique among the RenderMan types in that the other two points are not positions, but *vectors* that determine the tangent of the curve at the interpolated points. The first member of the geometry vector is a position, the second gives the tangent at that position. The third is another position, the fourth another tangent.

Not only the direction but the length of the tangent vector influences the spline. Figure 6.3 illustrates the effect of varying that length on the resulting spline. As with the Bézier splines,

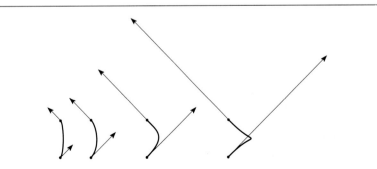

Figure 6.3 *Varying tangent vectors in Hermite curves*

the tangent's length dictates the curvature of the spline at the endpoints.

The Hermite spline example indicates an important fact: the basis type not only controls how the geometry vector influences the spline, but it also determines the *semantics* of the geometry vector: it must meet the requirements of the basis. Thus, in the Hermite case the geometry vector must contain tangents as well as positions.

Other spline types

For other types of curve (for example, the Beta splines and Cardinal splines), other parameters may influence the curve besides points and tangents. The curve's "closeness" to the control polygon (its **tension**), is a common example of such control. One way to introduce such parameters (by modifying the basis matrix used) is discussed in Appendix B. Another method, one which only involves manipulating the spline's control points, has been developed by DeRose and Barsky [DEROSE88].

Curves into surfaces

As shown above, a spline is determined by four control points. A bicubic surface is determined by sixteen, arranged in a 4 x 4 matrix. One can view that matrix as representing eight curves, four in one direction (the *u* **direction**) and four in the orthogonal (*v*) direction. The surface is a **tensor product** of the curves in the two directions: corresponding points on the four curves in the *u* direction are used to generate curves in the *v* direction or, equivalently, vice versa.

For the purpose of passing bicubic surfaces to RenderMan, this characterization of the surface as the product of orthogonal curves is important for one reason: the selection of curve type to use on a patch is independent in the two directions. For example, one can use a Bézier curve in the *u* direction and a B-spline in the *v* direction.

Selecting the bicubic patch type

Describing a bicubic patch requires not only passing a geometry matrix, but also specifying two **basis matrices**, one for the

u direction and one for the v direction of the patch. Basis matrices are predefined for each bicubic type, so using one of those types is as easy as setting the surface color. The basis matrix is an attribute of the graphics environment, passed with the routine **RiBasis()**. The Bézier basis is the default, so if, as in Listing 6.1, a Bézier surface is desired, **RiBasis()** need not be called.

```
RiBasis( ubasis, ustep, vbasis, vstep )
    RtBasis ubasis, vbasis;
    RtInt ustep, vstep;

    typedef RtFloat RtBasis[4][4];
    RtBasis  RiHermiteBasis,
             RiCatmullRomBasis,
             RiBezierBasis,
             RiBSplineBasis;
```

RiBasis() sets the current basis matrices used to create uniform bicubic surfaces from geometry matrices. Every surface declared in the current environment after a call to **RiBasis()** will use *ubasis* as its basis matrix in the u direction and *vbasis* as basis in the v direction.

ustep and *vstep* concern the "evaluation window" for a bicubic patch mesh (discussed in the next section). The following table indicates the correct step values for each of the predefined bicubic types.

Basis	Step Name	Step Value
RiHermiteBasis	RI_HERMITESTEP	2
RiCatmullRomBasis	RI_CATMULLROMSTEP	1
RiBezierBasis	RI_BEZIERSTEP	3
RiBSplineBasis	RI_BSPLINESTEP	1

As elements of the graphics environment, the current basis matrices and step values are saved and restored along with other attributes.

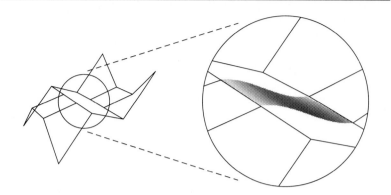

Figure 6.4 *Catmull-Rom surface generated by Listing 6.2*

Example patches

Listing 6.2 below shows a code fragment that uses the same geometry matrix as the previous example, but also specifies a Catmull-Rom basis. Figure 6.4 shows the resulting surface.

```
#include <ri.h>

DoCatmullRomPatch(patch)
RtPoint patch[4][4];
{
        RiBasis( RiCatmullRomBasis, RI_CATMULLROMSTEP,
                RiCatmullRomBasis, RI_CATMULLROMSTEP );
        RiPatch( RI_BICUBIC, RI_P, (RtPointer) patch, RI_NULL);
}
```

Listing 6.2 *Generating a Catmull-Rom bicubic surface from the previous control hull*

Bicubic Patch Meshes

Surfaces are not usually rendered singly. Normally they are declared by passing a two-dimensional array, or **mesh**, of adjoining patches to **RiPatchMesh**(). The motivation is similar to that for **RiPointsPolygon**(). It is possible, and has the same effect, to declare each patch in a mesh separately, but the conceptual elegance and storage efficiency of a mesh make it worthwhile to maintain that representation. A mesh can consist of either bilinear or bicubic patches.

A bicubic mesh can define much more complex surfaces than a single patch alone. Intuitively, a 4 x 4 control hull is limited in the amount of inflection it can describe. A patch mesh effectively allows an N x M control hull for arbitrary N and M.

If the motivation for using a mesh is to create a more complex surface, then presumably the resulting surface should be smoothly curved. In that case, the smoothness at the boundaries of the individual patches becomes an issue. The limitations and requirements for continuity at patch boundaries is an important quality of the different surface types. In general, the approximating surfaces like the B-splines are smoother in a mesh at patch boundaries.

Before presenting patch meshes directly, we return for a moment to the curve representation to discuss how a longer control hull is represented and used to generate a curve.

Longer curves

Figure 6.5 shows a series of curves generated from identical control points but different basis matrices. The first four (leftmost) points are those of the previous curve discussion.

There are 10 control points for each curve in Figure 6.5. Even on this longer geometry vector, *each point on the curve is still determined by exactly four control points*. Each of the above curves consists of a series of segments, each one determined by an **evaluation window** of four adjacent control points. The first four control points describe the first segment of the curve, then this evaluation window shifts to the next series of four points. The appropriate shift in control points between segments is an important attribute of a curve type.

Bézier evaluation window

Since a Bézier spline interpolates its first and last control points, if two segments are to join, then the last control point of one segment should coincide with the first control point of

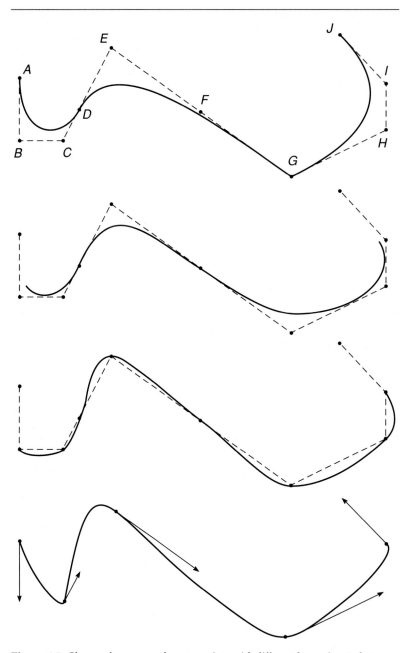

Figure 6.5 *Classes of curves on the same points with different bases: (top to bottom) Bézier, B-spline, Catmull-Rom, Hermite*

the next. That is precisely the case here: the evaluation window shifts by three control points from one segment of the curve to the next. The Bézier curve in Figure 6.5 consists of three segments, evaluated on points A through D, D through G and G through J, respectively. In general, N Bézier control points become $\lfloor (N-1)/3 \rfloor$ curve segments.

Bézier splines are a graceful, intuitive curve formulation. However, care must be taken when developing a long series of control points. The transition between the first two segments in Figure 6.5 (at vertex D) is smooth only because C, D and E are colinear. If the last pair of control points on one curve segment are not colinear with the first pair of the next segment, the curve will have a sharp break where the segments meet, as it does here at point G.

B-spline segmentation

The B-spline curve shown in Figure 6.5 is qualitatively the smoothest of the four. At the joint between segments, a B-spline segment is always smooth unless adjacent control points lie on the same point. The end of one segment coincides with the beginning of the next, the tangents are the same, *and* the rate of change in the tangent is consistent across the segment boundary.

The window of evaluation of a B-spline shifts by one from one segment to the next. In this example, there are seven B-spline segments. In general, for N control points, there will be $(N-3)$ segments.

Catmull-Rom segmentation

The Catmull-Rom curve in Figure 6.5 is smooth and unbroken from one end to the other. Since a Catmull-Rom curve segment interpolates, and is bounded by, its middle two control points, its evaluation window must shift by one control point to connect adjacent segments. For N control points, there will be $(N-3)$ curve segments.

The smoothness of the Catmull-Rom curve is intrinsic: the tangent of the curve at a given control point is parallel to a line segment between the surrounding control points, whether that control point is the end of one segment or the beginning of another.

Hermite segmentation

Since a Hermite geometry vector comes in point-tangent pairs, the evaluation window of a Hermite curve shifts by two vertices between segments. The Hermite curve in Figure 6.5 consists of $(N–2)/2$, or four, segments.

Both the position and tangent of successive segments of a Hermite curve coincide; therefore its smoothness is built in. However, it is still qualitatively less graceful than the B-spline above.

Defining surfaces with patch meshes

The discussion above indicates the economy of declaring patch meshes rather than individual patches. For example, since adjacent B-spline curve segments share three control points, a long B-spline curve can be stored in about one-fourth the space of a series of separately-defined curves. A B-spline surface mesh fits into somewhat more than one-sixteenth the space of the equivalent patches.

RiPatchMesh(type, nu, uwrap, nv, vwrap, *parameterlist*)
    RtToken type, uwrap, vwrap;
    RtInt nu, nv;

RiPatchMesh() declares a surface composed of a number of contiguous patches. *type* may be RI_BICUBIC or RI_BILINEAR, as with **RiPatch**().

nu and *nv* give the number of control points describing the surface in the *u* and *v* directions, respectively. Each must be at least 2 for bilinear and 4 for bicubic patch meshes. The array of position coordinates in *parameterlist* (RI_P, RI_PZ, or RI_PW) must have *nu*∗*nv* elements in *u*-major order: *nu* **RtPoint** points are given *nv* times.

A surface can be made to wrap in the *u* direction, the *v* direction, or both, by setting *uwrap* and/or *vwrap* to "periodic". Otherwise, they should be "nonperiodic".

Evaluation of patch meshes

A patch mesh is evaluated into patches in a manner exactly analogous to the curve case, as illustrated in Figure 6.6. The first patch is evaluated using a 4 x 4 matrix of control points starting with the first element of the RI_P array of position coordinates. The evaluation window then shifts by *nustep* points in *u* (moves to the right in the picture) for the second patch, where *nustep* and *nvstep* were passed to **RiBasis()**. If the patch is not wrapped, this process continues until the leading edge of the evaluation window runs off the end of the row of control points after (*nu*–3)/*nustep* patches. The evaluation window then moves down with a "carriage return," shifting in *v* by *nvstep*, and the process repeats. It terminates when the bottom edge of the evaluation window falls off the bottom of the mesh.

In Figure 6.6, below, the window of evaluation is illustrated on a 10 x 7 Bézier patch mesh. It first travels the *u* direction, shifting by 3 after each patch mesh, until it reaches the end of the row. Then it shifts down by 3 points and begins a new row. The process continues until it runs off the bottom.

A caveat

It is an error to have extra control points in either direction when the step size is greater than one (for example, a Bézier patch mesh might have 6 control points).

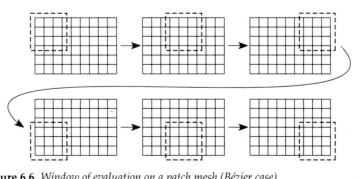

Figure 6.6 *Window of evaluation on a patch mesh (Bézier case)*

A bicubic mesh example

Listing 6.3 provides yet another way to describe a surface of revolution, with a bicubic patch mesh. It redefines *SurfOR()*, taking an array of points as a profile curve and declaring a bicubic surface from them. The major difference in this example from the previous versions (besides the fact that it employs bicubic patches) is that it expects an array of Bézier control points. These points are taken to lie in the x,z plane, and the third dimension is obtained by sweeping the curve about the z axis. The figure at right shows a bowling pin produced by this version of *SurfOR()*.

Patch wrapping

Often a bicubic patch mesh is used to represent a closed body like the bowling pin at right. In those cases, the mesh can be closed "manually" by making sure the first and last points and tangents match. An alternative, though, is to have the renderer close the patch in either *u* or *v* by setting *uwrap* and/or *vwrap* to "periodic" instead of "nonperiodic".

With wrapping in effect, the evaluation window for a surface continues to shift *after* its leading edge falls off the end of a row and/or column (see Figure 6.7). At that point, the window wraps around to the beginning of the array in the appropriate direction. Evaluation proceeds as long as the *trailing* edge of the evaluation window is within the set of control points.

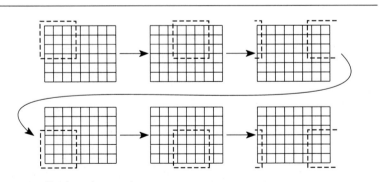

Figure 6.7 *Patch mesh wrapping*

```
#define NU 13
#define MAXNPTS 100
#define F (.4142135 * 4/3)
float coeff[NU][2] = {
      { 1, 0 }, { 1, F }, { F, 1 }, { 0, 1 }, {-F, 1 }, {-1, F },
      {-1, 0 }, {-1,-F }, {-F,-1 }, { 0,-1 }, { F,-1 }, { 1,-F }, { 1, 0} };

SurfOR(points, npoints)
Point2D points[];
int npoints;
{
      RtPoint      mesh[MAXNPTS][NU];
      int          u, v;

/*    coeff holds a matrix of coefficients for sweeping a point on the XZ
 *    plane circularly around the Z axis, with the circle approximated by
 *    4 Bezier curves
 */
      for (v = 0; v < npoints; v++) {
            /*
             * Start at the upper left of the mesh.  For each
             * control point on the circle being swept out,
             * rotate every point on the XZ curve into position
             */
            for (u = 0; u < NU; u++) {
                  /* Here comes each point on the XZ curve */
                  mesh[v][u][0] = points[v].x * coeff[u][0];
                  mesh[v][u][1] = points[v].x * coeff[u][1];
                  mesh[v][u][2] = points[v].y;
            }
      }
      RiBasis( RiBezierBasis, RI_BEZIERSTEP, RiBezierBasis, RI_BEZIERSTEP );
      RiPatchMesh( RI_BICUBIC,
            (RtInt) NU, RI_NOWRAP,
            (RtInt) npoints, RI_NOWRAP,
            RI_P, (RtPointer) mesh,
            RI_NULL);
}
```

Listing 6.3 *Version of* SurfOR() *taking profile points and producing a bicubic patch mesh by sweeping them about the z axis*

Wrapped mesh example

Listing 6.4 shows how the example from Listing 6.3 would be changed to use the wrapping feature of RenderMan. The only important difference is that the number of points in *u* is re-

```
#define MAXNPTS 100
#define BEZIERWIDTH 12

SurfOR(points, npoints)
Point2D points[];
int npoints;
{
        RtPoint mesh[MAXNPTS][BEZIERWIDTH];

        BezierSurfOR( points, npoints, mesh );
        RiBasis( RiBezierBasis, RI_BEZIERSTEP,
                RiBezierBasis, RI_BEZIERSTEP );
        RiPatchMesh( RI_BICUBIC,
                (RtInt) BEZIERWIDTH, RI_PERIODIC,
                (RtInt) npoints, RI_NONPERIODIC,
                RI_P, (RtPointer) mesh, RI_NULL);
}

#define F (.4142135 * 4/3)
float coeff[BEZIERWIDTH][2] = {
        { 1, 0 }, { 1, F }, { F, 1 }, { 0, 1 }, {-F, 1 }, {-1, F },
        {-1, 0 }, {-1,-F }, {-F,-1 }, { 0,-1 }, { F,-1 }, { 1,-F }  };

BezierSurfOR( points, npoints, mesh )
Point2D points[];
int npoints;
RtPoint mesh[][BEZIERWIDTH];
{
        int u, v;
        /*
         * coeff holds a matrix of coefficients for sweeping a point on the XZ
         * plane circularly around the Z axis, with the circle approximated by
         * 4 Bezier curves.
         */
        for (v = 0; v < npoints; v++) {
                /*
                 * Start at the upper left of the mesh.
                 * For each control point on the circle being swept out,
                 * rotate every point on the XZ curve into position.
                 */
                for (u = 0; u < BEZIERWIDTH; u++) {
                        /* Here comes each point on the XZ curve */
                        mesh[v][u][0] = points[v].x * coeff[u][0];
                        mesh[v][u][1] = points[v].x * coeff[u][1];
                        mesh[v][u][2] = points[v].y;
                }
        }
}
```

Listing 6.4 *Defining a surface of revolution using a wrapped patch mesh*

duced by one, so that there are now 12 points in the *u* direction. The thirteenth point for the fourth patch in a row is taken from the beginning of that row. We will use *BezierSurfOR()* again later on.

General wrapping

The appropriate number of points in a given direction for wrapping is also a function of the bicubic surface type. For the Bézier surface above, it is only sensible to omit the last point in *u*, which gives a position. For a wrapped Hermite patch, the number of points in the wrapping direction should be even, so that the last patch is sure to include both the position and tangent of the first point.

The appropriate wraparound point cannot be determined *a priori* any more than the shift of the evaluation window for a given type of bicubic surface. Making sure that the mesh size is appropriate for wrapping is up to the application.

Non-uniform Rational B-Spline Surfaces (NURBs)

Non-uniform rational B-splines supported by RenderMan differ in two important respects from the uniform, non-rational bicubic surfaces we have just presented. First, NURBs are based on B-splines; there is no notion of a basis matrix, and all control points are interpreted identically. Second, the bicubics are based on cubic polynomials; the degree of NURBs has no such constraint.

Another distinction of NURBs concerns the parameterization of the surface. NURBs allow, indeed require, an explicit specification of the parameters that trace out the surface, in contrast to the bicubic case, where we have avoided all concerns of parameterization. Where uniform surfaces are always evaluated in their entirety, a non-uniform surface may be partially rendered by giving a subrange of these parameter values. Finally, for renderers that support the capability, parts of a non-uniform surface may be cut away in a more general fashion by declaring a **trim curve** in the parameter space of the surface.

NURBs significantly extend the possibilities of parametric surfaces. For example, a sphere can be correctly represented using a NURB, but not with a bicubic surface. However, the theory and use of NURBs is beyond the scope of this book. For a very good presentation of this class of surfaces see the article by Tiller [TILLER83].

RiNuPatch(nu, uorder, uknot, umin, umax, nv, vorder, vknot, vmin, vmax,
   parameterlist)
 RtInt nu, nv;
 RtInt uorder, vorder;
 RtFloat uknot[], vknot[];
 RtFloat umin, umax,
   vmin, vmax;

For the u (v) directions the parameters are:

- *uorder* (*vorder*): the degree of the polynomial plus 1. A cubic is therefore of order 4.

- *nu* (*nv*): the number of control points (size of the mesh) in the u (v) direction. It must be true that $nu \geq uorder$ and $nv \geq vorder$.

- *uknot* (*vknot*): an array of knot values. The number of *knots* is *nu+uorder* (*nv+vorder*), and the knot values must appear in non-decreasing order within the arrays.

- *umin* (*vmin*) and *umax* (*vmax*): the values of u and v defining the parametric limits of the surface as evaluated. The values *umin* and *umax* must satisfy

$$uknot_{uorder-1} \leq umin < umax \leq uknot_{nu}$$

where the first knot is $uknot_0$ and the last is $uknot_{uorder+nu-1}$ (similarly for v).

The *parameterlist* must contain an array of (*nu*∗*nv*) points. If preceded with the *type* token "P" (RI_P), each element must contain three coordinates. This will yield a non-rational polynomial surface. If the *type* token is "Pw" (RI_PW), four-vectors are expected and the surface will be rational.

A B-spline as a NURB

If the basis matrices for uniform surfaces have been set to **RiB-SplineBasis** by a call to **RiBasis()**, then the call

    RiPatch(RI_BICUBIC, RI_P, (**RtPointer**)controlPts, RI_NULL);

is equivalent to the call

    RiNuPatch(4, 4, knots,0.0, 1.0,
                4, 4, knots,0.0, 1.0,
                RI_P, (**RtPointer**)controlPts, RI_NULL);

for an arbitrary 4×4 array of points *controlPts*, if *knots* contains the values $[-3, -2, -1, 0, 1, 2, 3, 4]$.

A uniform B-spline patch mesh on an *nu* x *nv* array of points could also be duplicated using **RiNuPatch()** by extending the above counts on the positive side and dividing by *nu*–3. That is, *knots* would be

$$\left[\frac{-3}{nu-3} , \frac{-2}{nu-3} , \frac{-1}{nu-3} , 0, ..., \frac{nu-3}{nu-3} , \frac{nu-2}{nu-3} , \frac{nu-1}{nu-3} , \frac{nu}{nu-3} \right]$$

General Bézier surfaces from NURBs

A bicubic Bézier surface will be produced from the same control points if *knots* contains the values $[0, 0, 0, 0, 1, 1, 1, 1]$. In fact, a Bézier patch of any degree can be expressed as a NURB. If the order is N, there should be N control points, and the knot vector should contain N 0's followed by N 1's. This is a very common way to provide Nth order Bézier patches.

Further Reading

Modeling with Bézier and B-spline bicubic surfaces is given a practical treatment in the book *Curves and Surfaces for Computer Aided Geometric Design* [FARIN88]. A more theoretical, but exhaustive, approach is taken by the book *An Introduction to Splines for use in Computer Graphics and Geometric Modeling* [BARTELS87]. The classic introduction to NURBs is the article "Rational B-Splines for Curve and Surface Representation" [TILLER83].

CHAPTER 7

Geometric Transformations and Hierarchical Modeling

The last three chapters set out the types of primitive surface accepted by the RenderMan Interface. Those primitives are the building blocks from which real objects are built. The ability to combine simple objects into more complex ones is an important capability of modeling systems. This chapter describes RenderMan's approaches to the task. We begin with a discussion of just what hierarchical modeling means, why it is so popular and what its limitations are. The following section, concerning the geometric hierarchy, includes important digressions on the coordinate systems and orientation conventions of RenderMan.

Concepts of Hierarchical Modeling

Single patches, polygons and quadric surfaces don't have much inherent visual appeal due to their limited complexity. They usually become interesting only when grouped into objects that more closely resemble things in the real world. In fact, henceforth we will use the term **object** to refer to a group of geometric primitives. A **primitive object** is just a single primitive, and an **aggregate object** consists of more than one.

An object is a set of surfaces grouped together and treated as a single entity for purposes of shading, motion, duplication or assembling other objects. It is a conceptual convenience to think, for example, of a "cube" instead of "this square and that square and that square." But that is just a human interface issue, not necessarily relevant to the design of a rendering interface. From that standpoint, the best reason for supporting aggregates is to simplify the job of assigning attributes. It makes sense to declare one color for the cube as a whole rather than having to assign colors to each face of a cube independently.

The graphics environment of RenderMan supports aggregates implicitly: all objects declared between calls that modify the environment have identical attributes. For example, a call to **RiColor**() may be followed by the declaration of any number of squares, which consequently receive the same color.

RenderMan's block structuring calls, discussed in the first chapters, strengthen this idea. In particular, **RiAttributeBegin**() and **RiAttributeEnd**() are most often used to define a single aggregate. **RiAttributeBegin**() is followed by a series of attribute-setting procedure calls, then the primitive surfaces of the aggregate, all of which will have the same attribute values. When the corresponding **RiAttributeEnd**() is reached, the attribute values return to their state before the block began. **RiTransformBegin**() and **RiTransformEnd**() have a similar purpose in the geometric domain: each object defined inside a transform block has a common coordinate system.

Hierarchical models

Any aggregate object may be made part of another aggregate just as a primitive object can. In other words, blocks may be nested within one another. Thus, RenderMan supports a **hierarchical model**. A good example of a hierarchical model is a robot. It consists of a "body," two "arms," two "legs," and so forth, with a "leg" being composed of a "thigh," a "calf," a "foot," etc. The levels of an object hierarchy are often paralleled by levels of abstraction: a door might consist of hinges, a wood panel, a doorknob and a lock. The lock could be described as a bolt, a cylinder, a keyhole, and so on.

A hierarchy allows one to think of an object, a part, a subsystem in relation to another, larger object. For example, the hands of a clock in a space capsule would turn relative to the clock face. The clock itself is fixed inside the capsule, but the capsule may be tumbling through space as it rotates about the earth, which in turn is rotating about the sun. The absolute path of the hands of this clock is complex, but the hierarchical model breaks it down into a few relatively simple motions of one object in relation to another.

Vocabulary

In a hierarchy, the **root** is the highest level of abstraction. The root has one or more **children**, which may be **leaves** (primitive objects in the current context) or **nodes** (other hierarchies) with children of their own. Two children of the same node are called **siblings**, and the node is their **parent**. There is an awkward mixing of metaphors here, but one can distinguish the genealogical terms, denoting relationships, from the botanical terms for the parts themselves.

Hierarchies and RenderMan

The RenderMan Interface supports this hierarchical model by providing a graphics environment, geometric transformation scheme, and explicit support for solids modeling. Each type of hierarchical aggregate has a particular purpose.

Graphics environment

The graphics environment stack is implicitly hierarchical. Pushing the environment with **RiAttributeBegin**() is equivalent to starting a child of the object currently being declared. Any attributes of the environment that apply to the parent also apply to the child, unless they are explicitly modified during the description of the child. **RiAttributeEnd**() restores the environment as it was originally, so that any subsequent children will share the unmodified attributes of the parent, rather than those of preceding children.

Scene description

The root of the object hierarchy is the entire scene being imaged. Every surface and object is contained within a "world object" because they are all declared in a world block bounded by **RiWorldBegin**() and **RiWorldEnd**(). There is only one world at a time; world blocks cannot be nested.

Geometric transformation environment

As introduced in Chapter 2, geometric transformations are part of the general graphics environment, but there are also routines that save and restore the current transformation: **RiTransformBegin**() and **RiTransformEnd**(). Judiciously applied geometric transformations encourage the use of **local coordinate systems**. For example, a robot arm can be made to rotate about a joint in the shoulder using a coordinate system placed in the center of the joint. The transformation environment is important enough to occupy its own section below.

Solids modeling

An extremely powerful hierarchical tool is the ability to use one object to modify the shape of another object. For example, a drilled machine part can be modeled as the undrilled part with a cylinder removed from it. This concavity would be difficult to introduce any other way. In general, this process of **Constructive Solid Geometry** (CSG) defines an object by applying set operators to the points in space inside other objects: a hole results from subtracting the cylinder from the rest of the part. An object may also be defined as the intersection of two other objects.

Object duplication

Finally, objects may be gathered into an independent description by a block bounded with **RiObjectBegin**() and **RiObjectEnd**(). A program can duplicate, or **instance**, such a description with a single routine call. We first saw this capability demonstrated in Chapter 2.

The remaining three sections of this chapter expand on the last three of these block types. They provide the most useful of RenderMan's facilities for defining hierarchical objects.

Geometric Transformation Environment

The RenderMan Interface provides a full set of capabilities for transforming object geometry within an explicit hierarchy defined by the geometric transformation environment. The most important use of a geometric hierarchy is to give each part of an object its own local coordinate system.

The current transformation

The RenderMan graphics environment includes, along with object color and other attributes, a **current transformation**.

Like any other attribute, it is applied to each object when the object is declared. Unlike those other attributes, however, routines that affect the current transformation do not *replace* it, but *modify* it. This behavior was demonstrated in Listing 2.5 of Chapter 2.

There are two ways to understand the idea of a current transformation. In one view, the current transformation acts like a stack, with the transformations comprising it applied in reverse order. The transformation declared last is applied first.

On the other hand, one can view a new transformation as applying directly to the **coordinate system** in which objects are defined (**object space**). In this model, the world begins with a set of coordinate axes, and any object is declared with geometric coordinates relative to these axes; a quadric surface is always rationally symmetric about the z axis, for example. When a new transformation is declared, it is applied to the coordinate axes. Objects will now be declared relative to these new axes. The coordinate system of the new object differs from that of its parent by the latest transformation.

It might help to think of the coordinate axes as a three-dimensional cursor, with the transformation commands serving as directives to move the cursor. "Concatenate a transformation to the current transformation" is equivalent to "Transform the cursor."

Under the latter model, **RiTransformBegin**() has the effect of retaining the coordinate system (or "cursor") in effect when it is called. **RiTransformEnd**() disposes of all coordinate systems ("cursors") defined in the meantime and restores the retained one.

RiTransformBegin( )
RiTransformEnd( )

RiTransformBegin() saves a copy of the current transformation, and **RiTransformEnd**() restores it. Transform blocks, delimited by these routines, may be nested.

RiAttributeBegin() and **RiAttributeEnd**() also save and restore the current transformation. They do the same for the rest of the graphics state, though, which is a waste of effort if only the transformation changes inside the block.

Geometric transformations in RenderMan

The routines described below all affect the current transformation. Their descriptions include an indication of whether they modify or replace it.

Translation

RiTranslate(dx, dy, dz)
    RtFloat dx, dy, dz;

RiTranslate() concatenates a translation onto the current transformation. Subsequent objects are moved by *dx* in *x*, *dy* in *y* and *dz* in *z*.

Rotation

Objects can be rotated about an arbitrary axis that passes through the coordinate origin.

RiRotate(angle, dx, dy, dz)
    RtFloat angle, dx, dy, dz;

RiRotate() concatenates a rotation onto the current transformation. The axis of rotation is the ray from the origin through the point (*dx, dy, dz*). The *angle* parameter is expressed in degrees. Under a left-handed coordinate system (the default), if the thumb of the left hand is pointed along the axis from the origin to (*dx, dy, dz*), the fingers curl to point in the direction of positive rotation. A right-handed system reverses the direction.

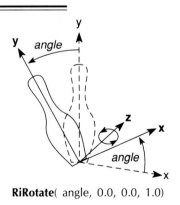

RiRotate(angle, 0.0, 0.0, 1.0)

Scaling

Objects may be scaled in *x*, *y* and *z* independently.

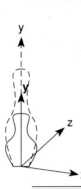

RiScale(sx, sy, sz)
    RtFloat sx, sy, sz;

RiScale() concatenates a scale transformation to the current transformation: all *x* coordinates are multiplied by *sx*, *y* coordinates are multiplied by *sy*, and *z* coordinates by *sz*. The figure to the left shows **RiScale**(1.0, 0.5, 1.0).

Skew transform

A skew transform skews points in the world by an angle between two orthogonal direction vectors.

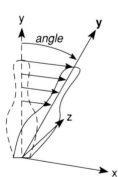

RiSkew(angle, dx1, dy1, dz1, dx2, dy2, dz2)
    RtFloat angle, dx1, dy1, dz1, dx2, dy2, dz2;

RiSkew() skews subsequent objects. (*dx1, dy1, dz1*) and (*dx2, dy2, dz2*) define two orthogonal vectors through the coordinate origin. The transformation skews the world so that the point (*dx1, dy1, dz1*) is skewed *angle* degrees toward the point (*dx2, dy2, dz2*). The figure to the left shows the effect of **RiSkew**(*angle*, 0.0, 1.0, 0.0, 1.0, 0.0, 0.0).

Figure 7.1 on the next page shows the effect of a skew transform on the bowling alley scene.

Perspective transform

Although a **perspective transformation** is usually used in a camera specification, it can also be concatenated onto the current transformation anywhere.

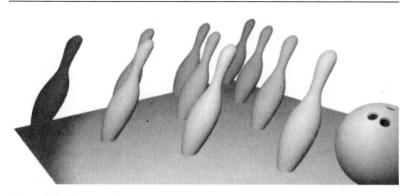

Figure 7.1 *Skew transform*

RiPerspective(fov)
    RtFloat fov;

RiPerspective() concatenates a perspective transformation onto the current transformation. The perspective transformation defines a pyramid with apex at the origin of the current
coordinate space, opening along the positive z axis, with opposite sides diverging at the angle *fov*, the field of view. *Points
within the viewing pyramid before perspective have x and y coordinates between –1 and +1 afterward.* Any points on the x,y plane
cause a zero divide.

Figure 7.2 shows the effect of a 90° perspective transform on a
cube that has been translated along the z axis. Four rays from
the origin on the left through four corners of the cube form a
pyramidal volume whose opposite sides diverge at a 90° angle. The cube is one unit across and one unit down the z axis,
so the near cube face fits perfectly inside this projection.

After the perspective divide, the rays are parallel and form a
box enclosing points that have x and y between –1 and +1. No
matter what the width of the pyramid defined by *fov*, it always
forms the same box after perspective. Any points inside the
pyramid before the perspective are inside the *box* afterwards.

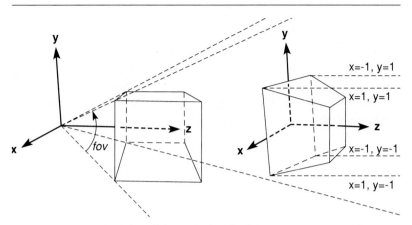

Figure 7.2 *A cube before (left) and after (right) a perspective transformation with fov=90°*

On the right, the right-hand face of the cube has shrunk relative to the left; it has become **foreshortened** with distance from the origin just as it would if viewed from there.

The right-hand cube has also moved to the coordinate origin, because the perspective transformation affects z as well as x and y. Points between the near and far clipping planes (discussed with **RiClipping**() in Chapter 8) are normalized by perspective so that a point on the near plane has a z value of 0 after perspective, and a point on the far plane lies at $z=1$. The clipping planes used by **RiPerspective**() lie at $z=1$ and $z=\infty$, so the near face of the cube goes to 0. The fact that the cube still has substantial depth after perspective indicates the perspective transformation's extreme non-linearity: a farther cube would be much flatter after perspective.

Perspective transformations cause division by 0 for points at $z=0$, and they give bizarre results for points in negative z. Therefore, they should be used with great care.

General linear transformation

In addition to the standard transformations above, more general transformations can be declared as either a **transformation matrix** or a general procedure for transforming points.

RiConcatTransform(transform)
    RtMatrix transform;

RiConcatTransform() concatenates the transformation speci-
fied by the *transform* matrix onto the current transformation.
An **RtMatrix** is a 4 x 4 homogeneous transformation matrix of
RtFloat values.

For example,

    RiScale(s1, s2, s3);

is exactly equivalent to

    RiConcatTransform(t);

if

$$t = \begin{bmatrix} s1 & 0 & 0 & 0 \\ 0 & s2 & 0 & 0 \\ 0 & 0 & s3 & 0 \\ 0 & 0 & 0 & 1 \end{bmatrix}.$$

The matrix *t* must be passed to **RiConcatTransform**() in row-
major order: [*s1* 0 0 0 0 *s2* 0 0 0 0 *s3* 0 0 0 0 1].

Clearing the current transformation

The geometric transformation environment helps to build a
"world" of objects defined with respect to a coordinate system
independent of any particular camera description. The current transformation, whatever it may be, transforms each object into this universal coordinate system, this **world space**.
When **RiWorldBegin**() is called, the object-to-world transformation represented by the current transformation is "cleared"
to the identity transformation. Therefore, in the absence of
any transformation commands, all objects are defined in
world space.

If, during the scene description, it is necessary to define an object directly in world space, the current transformation may be
reset to the identity using **RiIdentity**().

RiIdentity( )

RiIdentity() clears the current transformation. It does not affect any saved transformations; **RiIdentity()** may be enclosed in a transformation block so that the block's **RiTransformEnd()** will restore the previous transformation despite any intervening **RiIdentity()** call.

A more general transformation

RiIdentity() effectively returns the local coordinate system to world space, if used inside the world block, or camera space, if used outside. If some other specific space is desired, **RiTransform()** can establish it.

RiTransform(transform **)**
　　RtMatrix transform;

RiTransform() replaces the current transformation with the transformation specified by the *transform* matrix. **RtMatrix** is a 4 x 4 homogeneous transformation matrix of **RtFloat** values.

Calling

　　RiTransform(t **)**;

is equivalent to the sequence

　　RiIdentity( )**;
　　RiConcatTransform(t **)**;

General nonlinear transformation

If the ability to apply an arbitrary linear transformation isn't sufficient, RenderMan also allows any other transformation at all to be programmed as a procedure and applied to object geometry.

RiDeformation(name, *parameterlist* **)**
　　char *name;

An arbitrary deformation of space can be written as a **shader** using the RenderMan Shading Language. Once defined, the shader is invoked as a transformation by calling **RiDeformation**() with *name* giving the name of the shader. As usual with shaders, *parameterlist* is a series of name/value pairs supplying parameters to the shader. The shader is called for each point in space that needs to be transformed. The set of points that are actually transformed depends on the implementation. The shader will move the points according to the deformation.

The deformation expressed by the shader passed to **RiDeformation**() is conceptually the same as any other transformation. Naturally, it cannot be put on any matrix-based transformation stack, but RenderMan guarantees that it is applied just as if it were. As a result, deformations and regular transformation commands can be freely intermixed.

A deformation specified with **RiDeformation**() is applied to space as a whole. RenderMan also provides the capability to warp different parts of an object differently; this is also based on a shader, a **displacement** shader.

In- and out-facing surfaces

At this point, we pause to discuss some of the subtleties of the RenderMan geometric facilities: the interpretation of surfaces when they are assembled into objects, the conventions used to define those surfaces, and the nature of the coordinate systems used by RenderMan.

We have talked about objects as assemblies of surfaces. In general, the objects are abstractions a renderer knows little about because it has no way of knowing *a priori* whether a surface is part of a closed object. Even then it may be difficult to determine which side of a surface faces the inside of an object.

This information is important because many renderers can work more efficiently if they can discard surfaces obscured by the rest of the object they help to bound. *If a surface is part of a solid object (i.e., the object is **closed** rather than **open**), and it is on the side of the object opposite the viewer (it faces away, in other words), then the object itself obscures the surface if the object is opaque.* Any such surface can therefore usually be discarded without further ado. This will also be true of *parts* of any curved surfaces that overlap the object profile.

Most knowledge about whether a surface is part of a larger object, and whether the object is open or closed, translucent or opaque, is not explicitly passed through RenderMan. The key question is: is the surface only visible when it "faces toward" the viewer (that is, is it **one-sided**)? RenderMan depends on the user to supply that information.

RiSides(nsides)
    RtInt *nsides*;

RiSides() specifies the number of visible sides of subsequent surfaces. **RiSides**(1) declares that they are visible only on the "outside" (the forward facing side) and may be discarded otherwise. **RiSides**(2) declares both forward and backfacing surfaces important, so none are discarded. These are the only legal values of *nsides*.

Orientation

If an application is to take advantage of this feature, it must ensure that forward and backfacing surfaces can be recognized as such by the renderer. The convention used by a renderer for this decision is simple: the inside and outside of a surface are defined by its surface normal, which is assumed to point to the outside of the object. A surface is facing the viewer if and only if the surface normal points toward the camera.

For the renderer to use the normal correctly, the user must ensure that the surface normal points in the "right" direction by defining the surface properly. Quadric surfaces are defined so that normals point outward. The normals of other surfaces are defined in a straightforward way that arises from a simple, consistent coordinate system.

Left- vs. right-handed coordinates

The default coordinate system in the RenderMan Interface is the camera coordinate system, which is **left-handed**: the positive x, y and z axes point right, up and forward, respectively.

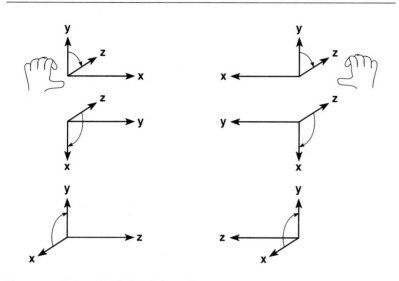

Figure 7.3 *Left- and right-handed coordinate systems*

There is a simple mnemonic for remembering the relationship between the axes of a left-handed system. If the thumb of the left hand is pointing in the positive direction along one axis, the fingers curl in the direction of "wraparound" alphabetical order: If the thumb points along x, rotation is from y to z; if along y, z to x; along z, x to y. In a right-handed system the same mnemonic holds using the right hand (see Figure 7.3 above).

The handedness of the coordinate system extends to parametric surfaces: *with the appropriate hand rotating from u to v on a surface, the thumb points along the surface's normal vector.* For example, in a left-handed system the normal to a parametric surface points toward the viewer when the surface is oriented with the u and v axes pointing right and down, respectively (see Figure 7.4). Similarly, the parameter space of a quadric is defined to obey the handedness rule in exactly the same way for both left- and right-handed systems. Finally, when the hand turns around the vertices of a polygon in the order they are declared, the thumb points along the normal. In other words, the normal of a polygon points toward the viewer

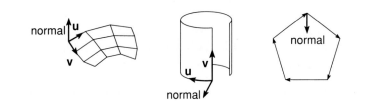

Figure 7.4 *Left-handed normals for primitive surface types*

when the vertices appear to be in clockwise order in a left-handed system and counterclockwise in a right-handed one.

The user may explicitly set the handedness of the RenderMan coordinate system by calling **RiOrientation**().

RiOrientation(orientation)
   RtToken orientation;

orientation should be either "lh" (RI_LH), to set the orientation of subsequent surfaces to be computed using a left-handed rule, or "rh" (RI_RH), for a right-handed rule. *orientation* is an attribute of the graphics state and so is saved and restored by **RiAttributeBegin**() and **RiAttributeEnd**().

A change in orientation turns subsequent surfaces "inside out," so that they must be defined with the opposite handedness. **RiOrientation**() should generally be called only if the user knows that subsequent surfaces will obey the opposite convention.

A geometric transformation (such as a scale) can change the handedness of a coordinate system implicitly by reversing the sense of its axes. In Figure 7.3, corresponding left- and right-handed examples differ only in that one axis is reversed. For example, the transformation command **RiScale**(-1.0, 1.0, 1.0) would turn the top left coordinate system into the top right one.

When a linear transformation which changes the handedness is specified, RenderMan detects it and automatically compensates so that the left-handed system is retained from the user's point of view. If the user wishes to force a change of handedness (perhaps to turn a primitive inside-out), it should be done with **RiReverseOrientation**() to avoid interfering with the tracking mechanism.

RiReverseOrientation( )

The sense of subsequent surfaces is toggled between left- and right-handed and so flips normals from their previous sense.

RiReverseOrientation() should be used with care, because a subsequent **RiTransformEnd**() can remove any number of transformations which changed the sense of the coordinate system. The system will correctly track these, but the **RiTransformEnd**() will *not* compensate for the sense-reversal of **RiReverseOrientation**(), since it is an attribute.

This is a good place to use **RiAttributeBegin**() and **RiAttributeEnd**() instead, since the orientation is an attribute and **RiAttributeEnd**() restores the transformation as well. If the orientation was correct before an attribute block, it will be again afterward.

Named coordinate systems

We have already touched on the equivalence between geometric transformations and coordinate spaces. Each transformation effectively defines a new set of coordinate axes that differ from the previous set by that transformation.

While each transformation "moves the cursor," not all of the coordinate spaces defined by the cursor are very interesting. However, there are five such spaces important enough to be given names. They span the rendering process from object definition to pixels.

- "raster" is the coordinate system of the image being rendered, where (0, 0) is the top left corner of the top left pixel, and each pixel has a non-negative integer location.

- "screen" is a device-independent coordinate system based on the image plane after perspective projection. Depending on its aspect ratio, the image being rendered usually covers approximately the square [-1,+1] in x and y of screen space.

- "camera" space is a left-handed three-dimensional space with its origin at the camera viewpoint and positive z axis pointed along the direction of view. Its coordinate axes differ from those of the world space by the current transformation as it exists when **RiWorldBegin**() is called.

- "world" space is defined as the coordinate system in effect immediately after **RiWorldBegin**(). It is the "root" coordinate system of the geometric transformation hierarchy.

- "object" space for any particular object is the coordinate space prevailing when the object is declared.

Only the last space differs for each object in a scene. Since "object" space differs for each object, RenderMan has a facility for giving a coordinate space a name for later reference.

RiCoordinateSystem(space)
    RtToken space;

RiCoordinateSystem() marks the current coordinate system with a name, given by the token *space*, that can be referred to later. It is an error to mark two coordinate systems with the same name.

When an object is declared, its geometric coordinates are interpreted relative to the current ("object") coordinate space, as given by the current transformation from object space to world space. That is, the current transformation is always applied to an object. Therefore, if object geometry is supposed to exist in some other space, the geometry must be transformed into the current space before using it.

RtPoint *RiTransformPoints**(fromspace, tospace, npoints, points)
    RtToken fromspace, tospace;
    RtInt npoints;
    RtPoint points[];

RiTransformPoints() converts a set of points defined in the space named *fromspace* into the space named *tospace*. Either space may be one of the standard named coordinate systems ("object", "world", "camera", "screen", or "raster"), or it may have been previously marked using **RiCoordinateSystem**(). *points* is an array of points to be transformed and *npoints* is its size.

RiTransformPoints() cannot be expected to work correctly if the transformation represented by *tospace* is not invertible, i.e., if it includes deformations, or if non-invertible matrices are supplied to **RiTransform**() or **RiConcatTransform**().

RiTransformPoints() is useful for providing a common coordinate system to the individual primitives of an object. Since the current transformation is used both for assembling objects and arranging the scene, there is no intrinsic information about the "object" coordinate system of a composite as a whole. By marking the appropriate coordinate system, and then transforming object points from a lower level of the hierarchy into that system, the application can provide a common reference to each primitive. This is most useful for providing consistent parameters to shaders.

Bounding box

The last topic under the geometric environment concerns the size of objects. Many image synthesis programs use the spatial extent of objects or collections of objects to more efficiently determine their visibility or fix the order in which they are processed. This spatial extent is usually given in the form of a **bounding box**, a rectilinear box in 3-dimensional space defined by its maxima and minima in x, y and z. The bounding box includes every point in space between *xmin* and *xmax* in x, etc. (see Figure 7.5).

The bounding box of almost all geometric primitives supported by the RenderMan interface can be easily calculated, so most renderers can and will calculate it as objects are passed across the interface. Bounding boxes may be supplied by the application in order to save calculations, or to give renderers help in situations where the bounding box is difficult to calculate, as in procedural models or CSG volumes.

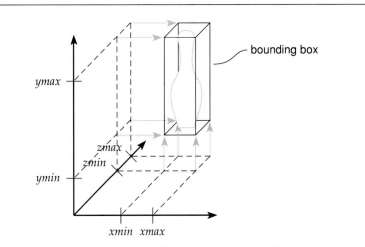

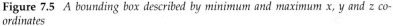

Figure 7.5 *A bounding box described by minimum and maximum x, y and z coordinates*

RiBound(bound)
   RtBound bound;

The routine **RiBound**() promises that all subsequent primitives will lie within the bounding box *bound*. *bound* is an array of six **RtFloat** values [x_{min} x_{max} y_{min} y_{max} z_{min} z_{max}].

The bounding box is expressed in object coordinates in the current coordinate system.

Since it is an attribute, the bounding box remains in effect for the duration of the current environment (i.e., until it is replaced with **RiAttributeEnd**()).

Note that the **RtBound** data is not two points, but a series of three pairs, each giving a bound on one axis.

Constructive Solid Geometry

The technique of **Constructive Solid Geometry (CSG)** allows an object to be defined as a Boolean combination of other objects. For example, machined parts commonly have significant concavities after tools remove material. A drilling operation on an object may be modeled as the subtraction of a cylinder from that object. Depicting the resulting surface any other way could well be prohibitively difficult.

A **solid** is defined as a set of points in three-dimensional space, with a surface separating points in the set from those not in the set. Given a number of solid objects (sets of points) in space, one can either combine them into composite objects (using the set operation **union**), use only those points they have in common (set **intersection**) or use one solid to "carve out" another by subtraction (set **difference**).

Since the results of these set operations can be used in further set operations, CSG is also a hierarchical definition tool.

Terms

A **solid** is defined under RenderMan as a **boundary representation**, a set of surfaces that enclose a space. The surfaces must join together to completely enclose the space, providing a well-defined inside and outside such that *every point in space is either inside or outside the solid*. The points of the solid are not necessarily contiguous (two spheres may be considered a single solid even without overlapping), but dire consequences and bizarre results can occur if there is any way to get inside a "solid" without passing through some surface. RenderMan assumes that any object declared as a solid is sealed.

The inside of the solid is defined as the set of all regions with finite volume, and the outside is the sole region with infinite volume. Note that this definition is independent of the orientation of the surfaces making up the object.

A **primitive solid** is created as an assemblage of the primitive surface types discussed in Chapters 4, 5 and 6. **Composite solids** are formed from primitive solids and other composite solids in the usual hierarchical fashion.

RiSolidBegin(type)
    RtToken type;
RiSolidEnd( )

All CSG solids, whether primitive or composite, are declared by enclosing a series of RenderMan routines between calls to **RiSolidBegin**() and **RiSolidEnd**(). *type* is a token for the operation to be performed on the objects declared between the two calls. If *type* is RI_PRIMITIVE, the intervening RenderMan surface primitives are taken to define a CSG solid. If *type* is RI_UNION, RI_DIFFERENCE or RI_INTERSECTION, **RiSolidBegin**()/**RiSolidEnd**() blocks are the only object declarations allowed.

RiSolidBegin(RI_PRIMITIVE)

type "primitive" (RI_PRIMITIVE) forms a solid CSG object from a set of surface primitives. Between calls to **RiSolidBegin**(RI_PRIMITIVE) and **RiSolidEnd**(), any set of geometric primitives may be declared. The primitives must join to *completely* enclose a volume of space.

Listing 7.1 shows how a solid is defined. In preceding chapters we have defined several versions of *SurfOR*() for generating surfaces of revolution. In *SolidSurfOR*(), one of these objects is made into a primitive solid by using disks to make sure the two ends are closed.

```
/* SolidSurfOR(): create a solid surface of revolution from a set of points */
SolidSurfOR(points, npoints)
Point2D points[];
int npoints;
{
    RiSolidBegin( RI_PRIMITIVE );
        SurfOR( points, npoints );          /* ... from Chapter 4 */
        if(points[0].y != 0.0)              /* Seal the object at the ends */
            RiDisk( points[0].x, points[0].y, 360.0, RI_NULL );

        if(points[npoints-1].y != 0.0)
            RiDisk( points[npoints-1].x,
                    points[npoints-1].y, 360.0, RI_NULL );

    RiSolidEnd();
}
```

Listing 7.1 *Using hyperboloids to create a solid surface of revolution*

CSG composites

Composite solids are also declared by a block of routines delimited by **RiSolidBegin**() and **RiSolidEnd**(). An object going into a composite may be either a primitive solid or another CSG composite solid.

   RiSolidBegin(RI_INTERSECTION)

The intersection of a set of solids is defined as the set of points that lie inside all of them.

One use for solid intersection is in closing partial quadrics. For example, a sphere formed with *thetamax* not equal to 360 or 180 would have a wedge shape when solidified. It is impossible in general to close this surface exactly using the straight edges of a polygon. The intersection operation, however, does so elegantly. Listing 7.2 shows how; Figure 7.6 shows the result.

```
/* SolidWedge(radius, zmin, zmax, thetamax): make a solid from a (partial)
 *      sphere as the intersection or union of two hemispheres.
 */
SolidWedge( radius, zmin, zmax, thetamax )
float radius, zmin, zmax, thetamax;
{
     if (thetamax == 180.0) {
          SolidHemisphere( radius, zmin, zmax );
     } else if (thetamax == 360.0) {
          SolidSphere( radius, zmin, zmax );
     } else if (thetamax < 180.0) {
          RiSolidBegin( RI_INTERSECTION );
               SolidHemisphere( radius, zmin, zmax );
               RiRotate( thetamax-180.0, 0.0, 0.0, 1.0 );
               SolidHemisphere( radius, zmin, zmax );
          RiSolidEnd();
     } else if (thetamax < 360.0) {
          RiSolidBegin( RI_UNION );
               SolidHemisphere( radius, zmin, zmax );
               RiRotate( thetamax, 0.0, 0.0, 1.0 );
               SolidHemisphere( radius, zmin, zmax );
          RiSolidEnd();
     }
}

/* SolidHemisphere: create a solid hemisphere from a sphere and a cylinder*/
SolidHemisphere( radius, zmin, zmax )
float radius, zmin, zmax;
```

```
{
    RiSolidBegin( RI_INTERSECTION );
        SolidSphere( radius, zmin, zmax );
        /*
         *  A cylinder is defined with the same radius as the sphere and
         *  rotated so that its bottom bisects the sphere in the x/z plane.
         */
        RiRotate( 90.0, 1.0, 0.0, 0.0 );
        /* Rotate the cylinder 90 degrees in x */
        SolidCylinder( radius, 0.0, radius );
    RiSolidEnd( );                          /* intersection */
}


/* SolidSphere: create a closed sphere */
SolidSphere( radius, zmin, zmax )
RtFloat radius, zmin, zmax;
{
    RiSolidBegin( RI_PRIMITIVE );

        RiSphere( radius, zmin, zmax, 360.0, RI_NULL );

        if(fabs(zmax) < radius)                 /* The top is chopped off      */
            RiDisk(zmax, sqrt(radius*radius - zmax*zmax), 360.0, RI_NULL);

        if(fabs(zmin) < radius)                 /* The bottom is chopped off   */
            RiDisk(zmin, sqrt(radius*radius - zmin*zmin), 360.0, RI_NULL);

    RiSolidEnd();
}


    /*
     *  SolidCylinder() makes a solid cylinder of the given radius, extending
     *  from zmin to zmax along the z axis.
     */
SolidCylinder( radius, zmin, zmax )
float radius, zmin, zmax;
{
    RiSolidBegin( RI_PRIMITIVE );

        RiCylinder( radius, zmin, zmax, 360.0, RI_NULL );

        RiDisk( zmax , radius, 360.0, RI_NULL );      /* Close the top     */
        RiDisk( zmin, radius, 360.0, RI_NULL );       /* Close the bottom  */

    RiSolidEnd( );
}
```

Listing 7.2 *Generating solid partial spheres and cylinders*

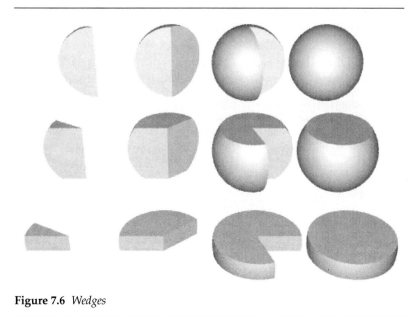

Figure 7.6 *Wedges*

The *SolidWedge*() function above uses a second CSG combination operator, RI_UNION, which joins two other CSG solids.

>**RiSolidBegin**(RI_UNION)

The CSG "union" (RI_UNION) operator forms a solid from a number of other solids. The solid resulting from an **RiSolidBegin**(RI_UNION) block includes all the CSG solids therein.

At the scene level the RI_UNION operation might seem redundant since it is equivalent to simply declaring a series of objects individually. Within a CSG hierarchy, however, it is sometimes necessary to explicitly gather a set of objects together to treat them as a single object. To subtract one solid from several other solids, for example, is easier if the latter are gathered into a single composite under the RI_UNION operator. The next example, in Listing 7.3, will demonstrate.

>**RiSolidBegin**(RI_DIFFERENCE)

The "difference" (RI_DIFFERENCE) operation subtracts CSG solids from one another. After **RiSolidBegin**(RI_DIFFERENCE), there should be a series of solid blocks. The first solid is a "basis" solid, and any subsequent solids within the RI_DIF-

FERENCE block are carved out of the initial solid. Listing 7.3 shows the creation of such a difference solid, a bowling ball made by subtracting the union of three plugs from a solid sphere. On the left of Figure 7.7, the plugs are rendered outside the ball, and the right shows the result of Listing 7.3.

```
BowlingBall()
{
    static RtColor plugcolor = { 0.1, 0.1, 0.1 };

    RiSolidBegin( RI_DIFFERENCE );

        RiSolidBegin( RI_PRIMITIVE );
            RiSphere( 0.3, -0.3, 0.3, 360.0, RI_NULL );
        RiSolidEnd();

        RiSolidBegin( RI_UNION );
            RiColor( plugcolor );
            RiRotate( 170.0, 1.0, 0.0, 0.0 );
            BowlingBallPlug();
            RiRotate( 30.0, 0.0, 1.0, 0.0 );
            BowlingBallPlug();
            RiRotate( 30.0, 1.0, 0.0, 0.0 );
            BowlingBallPlug();
        RiSolidEnd();

    RiSolidEnd();
}

BowlingBallPlug()
{
    RiSolidBegin( RI_UNION );
        SolidCylinder( 0.03, -0.3, -0.15 );
        RiTranslate( 0.0, 0.0, -0.315 );
        SolidCone( 0.075, 0.045 );
    RiSolidEnd();
}

SolidCone( height, radius )
RtFloat height, radius;
{
    RiSolidBegin( RI_PRIMITIVE );
        RiCone( height, radius, 360.0, RI_NULL );
        RiDisk( 0.0, radius, 360.0, RI_NULL );
    RiSolidEnd();
}
```

Listing 7.3 *Routine for generating a bowling ball*

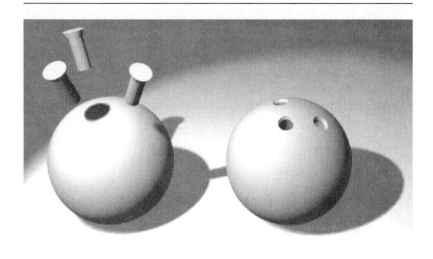

Figure 7.7 *The bowling ball: (left) exploded, (right) as in BowlingBall()*

Subtraction

The right of Figure 7.7 shows what happens to parts of the plugs that are not inside the sphere: they are invisible. It is perfectly legal for parts of a subtractor solid to lie outside the basis. Surfaces of the subtractor appear only if they are inside the basis solid. If the two solids don't intersect at all, the subtractor has no effect on the picture whatsoever.

Shading

In Listing 7.3, the plugs are assigned a color different from that of the sphere. It may seem peculiar to assign a color to a negative solid, but Figure 7.7 shows the result: the boundary surface between the two solids is colored by the subtractor solid. This may seem counterintuitive, but it actually adds some extra control over appearance: the subtractor solid can always be given the same surface characteristics as the basis if desired.

The surface appearance of a composite solid is always well defined, because every point on the surface of a composite is on the surface of one of the primitives making it up. The appearance of the composite is the appearance of the underlying primitive.

Object Instancing

The last hierarchical tool of the RenderMan Interface was introduced in Chapter 2 and needs little elaboration here: the ability to predefine models and subsequently create **instances** of them.

Retained models

Since RenderMan completely discards its scene data each time an image is rendered, it is easy to spend a lot of effort in animation redeclaring complex objects or parts of objects that change little, if at all, from one frame to the next. The same is true of a single image that depicts a number of identical instances of one part or object.

Defining a retained model

RenderMan allows such repetitive data to be gathered into a single aggregate and copied with one procedure call.

RtObjectHandle RiObjectBegin( )
RiObjectEnd( )

A block of RenderMan surface declaration calls bounded by calls to **RiObjectBegin**() and **RiObjectEnd**() define a **retained model**. The model is thereafter referred to by the **object handle** returned by **RiObjectBegin**(). The object is destroyed and its data handle invalidated at the end of the nearest enclosing frame or world block. An object created before **RiFrameBegin**() will be valid for all frames, while one created within a frame block will only be valid for that frame, and similarly for **RiWorldBegin**()/**RiWorldEnd**().

Between these two calls, only procedures that declare object geometry can be called. No transformation procedures are allowed; all surfaces are described in the same object coordinate system. Furthermore, *only surfaces of the same type may be included in one retained model.*

The current transformation is *not* applied to the surfaces of the model when it is created. Rather, the model is defined in exactly the coordinates supplied to the primitive routines. Those coordinates are transformed by the current transformation in effect when the object is instanced. In fact, it is often a good idea to define a retained model outside the **RiWorldBegin()**/**RiWorldEnd()** block, so that it can be used in a series of frames.

RiObjectInstance(handle)
    RtObjectHandle handle;

An instance of the model is created in the current space by calling **RiObjectInstance()**, passing it the model's *handle*. This includes in the scene any primitives in the model exactly as they were defined previously. The current transformation is applied to the surface geometry when the object is instanced, not when it is defined. The same is true of the rest of the graphics environment: *all attributes are assigned during instancing, not during definition.*

Listing 7.4 shows a routine, *PlacePins()*, which uses object instancing to set up the bowling pins of a bowling alley. This one defines a retained bowling pin using an apocryphal routine *BowlingPin()*, then instances it ten times with suitable translations.

After the model is opened by calling **RiObjectBegin()**, the handle it returns is tested. If the model couldn't be created, that handle is NULL and we must abort. In that case, there is no need to match the failed call to **RiObjectBegin()** with one to **RiObjectEnd()**.

The pins are set by rows; each row is diagonally offset from the previous one. The *N*th row (beginning with 0) gets *N*+1 pins. The separation between rows and between pins in a row is given by the procedure parameters *xseparation* and *yseparation*.

There is some redundancy here. The pins in a row could be moved incrementally by *yseparation* each time, without saving and restoring the transformation state each time through the inner loop. Also, the translation in each loop is 0 the first time through the loop. However, these "features" are left in because they make each loop independent and make the intention of the translations somewhat clearer.

```
/*
 * PlacePins: set up ten bowling pins using object instancing. We assume
 *     that the pin is centered on the z axis, and separate the rows by
 *     xseparation.
 */
PlacePins( xseparation, yseparation )
RtFloat xseparation, yseparation;
{
     int row, pin;
     RtObjectHandle phandle;
     phandle = RiObjectBegin();
         if(!phandle)                            /* If can't create a retained model */
             return;
         BowlingPin();
     RiObjectEnd();

     for( row = 0; row < 4; row++ ) {                        /* For four rows */
         RiTransformBegin();        /* Independent movement for each row */
             RiTranslate( row*xseparation, row*yseparation/2, 0.0 );
             for( pin = 0; pin <= row; pin++ ) {        /* #pins == row#-1 */
                 RiTransformBegin();
                     RiTranslate( 0.0, -pin * yseparation, 0.0 );
                     RiObjectInstance( phandle );
                 RiTransformEnd();
             }
         RiTransformEnd();
     }
}
```

Listing 7.4 *Setting up bowling pins in the x,y plane using object instancing*

The *PlacePins()* routine blithely calls *BowlingPin()*, but there is a critical assumption disguised here: *BowlingPin()* must declare only one kind of primitive, and any other RenderMan commands are ignored, especially transformation commands. There could be at least three possible versions of *BowlingPin()*, employing either polygons, hyperboloids or parametric surfaces. All could be constructed without transformations, and so obey this stricture. But the point is worth emphasizing: *retained models can include only one kind of surface.*

Semantics of instancing

The most important fact this example shows is that the model given by an object handle consists only of geometry. That is, the instance of the model is made by copying the *geometric* data appearing between **RiObjectBegin**() and **RiObjectEnd**(), ignoring the graphics environment.

This has two important consequences: first, any characteristics of the object that are taken from the environment (for instance, its color or the set of light sources that apply to it) are set when the object is instanced, not when it is declared. This makes it possible to color different instances differently. On the other hand, it also means that *every part of the model receives exactly the same characteristics*, those prevailing when **RiObject-Instance**() is called.

Uses of retained models

The main reason for using a retained model rather than repeated object declarations is efficiency. A renderer can potentially represent a retained model much more compactly, and perform a certain amount of processing only once rather than many times. Actual savings naturally depend on the implementation.

Perhaps an equally important aspect of retained models is their use as a conceptual tool. The ability to invoke an entire model with a simple handle, rather than requiring a long series of modeling commands, makes it easier to manipulate and use that model.

The usefulness of retained models is limited, however, by a lack of control over the internal environment of the object. Each instance is created as though by a series of primitive declarations. All environment modifications, including specifications of color and shading, are surrendered to the environment as it exists when the object is instanced.

CHAPTER 8

Viewing I:
The Digital Camera

The discussion in this book so far has centered on geometry: how to create surfaces and assemble them into a coherent scene. We now address how to **render** that scene into a digital image. As always, there are RenderMan routines which set various options controlling the rendering process. Since there are many such options, the rendering specification can become quite involved. However, all options have sensible defaults, so in most cases a simple specification suffices.

There are three major concerns in going from a three-dimensional scene to a two-dimensional digital image. First, the *content* of the image is determined by a **virtual camera** which projects the scene into two dimensions. The two-dimensional area which goes into the rendered image is the **screen window**, analogous to the standard photographic film frame.

After determining the content of the image via the camera definition, an array of pixels must be defined to *represent* the scene in a file or on a display. The rectangle of pixels which represents the content of the screen window is termed the **frame**. Finally, the image is produced by deriving a digital (usually color) value at each pixel, which represents the part of the scene that projects to the neighborhood of that pixel.

Following an example program for orientation, this chapter covers the specification of a screen window and frame in two sections. Chapter 9 provides a detailed model of the rendering process, covers the RenderMan controls over pixel production, and concludes by presenting two special effects in rendering. Statements emphasized *with italics* are key rules in understanding the image definition process.

An Example Viewing Program

The generic RenderMan program in Listing 8.1 shows the basic routines for setting up the viewing parameters of an image. We'll begin this chapter with a quick pass through this example, then discuss its routines in more detail. The next chapter covers some other routines that affect viewing.

The reader with access to a RenderMan renderer is encouraged to experiment with this program. Any of the scene description routines of previous chapters may be called between **RiWorldBegin**() and **RiWorldEnd**() to set up a scene for viewing. Toying with the parameters of the routines shown here is at least as educational as a textual discussion of their meaning.

```
main()
{
    RtFloat fov;
    RiBegin(RI_NULL);

            /* Output image characteristics */
            /* Output to file "ri.pic" */
            RiDisplay( "ri.pic", RI_FILE, RI_RGBA, RI_NULL );
            RiFormat( 640, 480, 1.0 );                /* Image resolution       */
            RiCropWindow( 0.0, 1.0, 0.0, 1.0 );   /* Rendered subregion     */

            /* Camera characteristics */
            RiScreenWindow(-1.33, 1.33, -1.0, 1.0);
                                            /* Window on image plane  */

            /* Nature of the projection to the image plane */
            fov = 90;
            RiProjection( "perspective",          /* Perspective view        */
                RI_FOV, (RtPointer)&fov, RI_NULL );

            /* Camera position and orientation */
            RiRotate( 0.0, 0.0, 0.0, 1.0 );        /* Camera roll             */
            RiRotate( 0.0, 0.0, 1.0, 0.0 );        /* Camera yaw              */
            RiRotate( 0.0, 1.0, 0.0, 0.0 );        /* Camera pitch            */
            RiTranslate( 0.0, 0.0, 0.0 );          /* Camera position         */

            /* Now describe the world */
            RiWorldBegin();
                    /* <Scene is described here> */
            RiWorldEnd();
    RiEnd();
}
```

Listing 8.1   *A boilerplate viewing program*

Overall organization

The routines in Listing 8.1 appear in five groups. The first four control aspects of viewing; only the world block deals with scene data. This grouping and ordering of procedure calls makes sense for most RenderMan programs.

Often, some of these groups will have more routine calls than those shown here (the others are presented in the next chapter), and often fewer or none. In fact, every call shown here between **RiBegin**() and **RiWorldBegin**() could be omitted because the values they assert are exactly the default. The set of defaults for the viewing parameters is designed to be widely useful to minimize the number of routines that any given program needs to call.

Image characteristics

The first group of statements controls the physical characteristics of the output image:

- the type and name of the device (normally either a display or file) to which the image will be output, and whether each output pixel contains color, depth and/or coverage information (**RiDisplay**());

- the horizontal and vertical resolution of the image, and the aspect ratio (width/height) of the individual pixels (**RiFormat**());

- what portion of the image as defined will actually be rendered (**RiCropWindow**()).

Camera characteristics

Next, the example specifies where the film frame lies on the image plane (**RiScreenWindow**()).

Projection

The call to **RiProjection**() controls how the three-dimensional geometry of the scene is cast onto the two-dimensional **image plane** from which the image will be taken. This call to **RiProjection**() specifies that the scene will be rendered using a perspective projection with a 90° field of view.

Camera placement

The last set of viewing parameters concerns the placement of the camera. Any geometric transformations occurring after **RiProjection**() and before **RiWorldBegin**() concern the camera. The most important routines for camera control are **RiTranslate**(), to control where it lies, and **RiRotate**(), to control its orientation. The fact that the routines as called here do nothing reflects the fact that the default camera placement is at the world-coordinate origin, facing along the positive z axis. In other words, world and camera coordinates are identical by default.

Options vs. transforms

One might wonder how important it is for the routines in Listing 8.1 to appear in this order. Each one either sets options (e.g., **RiFormat**(), **RiDisplay**()) or affects the viewing transformation (**RiRotate**() and **RiTranslate**()). Basically, routines of the first kind are independent of the order in which they appear (as long as they all appear after **RiBegin**() and before **RiWorldBegin**()), while the order of the transformation commands is critical. The reasons for this relate to the nature of geometric transformations and how options are assumed to be processed.

When **RiWorldBegin**() is invoked, all options are frozen and cannot be changed until **RiWorldEnd**(). This is primarily due to the RenderMan assumption that rendering may begin any time after scene description begins. Therefore, any image-wide parameters (options) must be fixed by then. However, there is a second issue: a number of option defaults are not specific values, but are derived from other options. For example, the default screen window, if **RiScreenWindow**() is not called, is derived from the image aspect ratio given to **RiFormat**() or **RiFrameAspectRatio**(). These defaults are calculated during **RiWorldBegin**(). In that sense, options are not really "accepted" until then, so all non-geometric option declarations are order-independent.

Order of transforms

The same is not true of geometric commands for positioning the camera. As with the other options, **RiWorldBegin**() *marks*, or accepts, the current transformation as the viewing transformation. But the order of transformations making up the current transformation is just as important for viewing as it is for modeling.

A Virtual Camera

This section describes the geometric considerations for setting up the synthetic camera. No matter how automatic a camera is, someone still has to decide where to put it (that is, provide a **viewing location**) and point it (impose a **viewing direction**). In the real world, photographers also affect the resulting image by choice of camera type, lens and film. Among other things, these decisions influence how much of the world the camera sees in the direction it points (its **field of view**) and the camera's output (the film frame in conventional photography) as a rectangular region (the **screen window**) of the **image plane** on which the lens focuses. This information together er defines the **virtual camera** for viewing a scene.

The parameters above are not always orthogonal. For example, an object may be made larger in the image by either moving the camera closer or narrowing the lens' field of view. Similarly, the effect of narrowing the field of view can be duplicated by making the screen window smaller. In the first case the image looks somewhat different for the two approaches, but in the second case the results are identical.

Partly because the physical camera model is ambiguous (in the sense that its parameters are not completely orthogonal), RenderMan does not provide a specific camera model, but a set of routines that can be used to construct a variety of reasonable camera models. This section presents one such virtual camera, controlled by two routines that RenderMan calls to describe it. These camera routines should provide some insight into the RenderMan calls that they use.

The viewing transformation

In the RenderMan model, a scene is rendered from a viewpoint at the coordinate origin *of camera space*, looking out along the positive *z* axis. If the camera needs to be some place other than the world origin, or pointing in some other direction, then a **viewing transformation** must be provided to transform points from world space into camera coordinates.

RenderMan allows the user to apply *any* geometric transformation to the world in order to position it before the camera. The only difference between a geometric transformation used to assemble a scene and one used to build up a viewing transformation is context: *any transformation routines called before **RiWorldBegin**() are assumed to be part of the viewing transformation.* Any such calls made afterward are considered part of the modeling transformation.

A simple camera procedure

Listing 8.2 shows a useful setup procedure for a viewing transformation based on the position, direction and orientation of a camera.

```
#include <ri.h>

/*
 * PlaceCamera(): establish a viewpoint, viewing direction and orientation
 *      for a scene. This routine must be called before RiWorldBegin().
 *      position: a point giving the camera position
 *      direction: a point giving the camera direction relative to position
 *      roll: an optional rotation of the camera about its direction axis
 */

PlaceCamera ( position, direction, roll )
RtPoint position, direction;
float roll;
{
        RiIdentity();                /* Initialize the camera transformation */
        RiRotate( -roll, 0.0, 0.0, 1.0 );
        AimZ( direction );
        RiTranslate( -position[0], -position[1], -position[2] );
}

/*
 * AimZ(): rotate the world so the direction vector points in
 *      positive z by rotating about the y axis, then x. The cosine
 *      of each rotation is given by components of the normalized
 *      direction vector. Before the y rotation the direction vector
 *      might be in negative z, but not afterward.
 */
```

```
#define PI 3.14159265359
#include <math.h>
AimZ( direction )
RtPoint direction;
{
        double xzlen, yzlen, yrot, xrot;

        if(direction[0]==0 && direction[1]==0 && direction[2]==0)
              return;
        /*
         * The initial rotation about the y axis is given by the projection of
         * the direction vector onto the x,z plane: the x and z components
         * of the direction.
         */
        xzlen = sqrt(direction[0]*direction[0]+direction[2]*direction[2]);
        if(xzlen == 0)
              yrot = (direction[1] < 0) ? 180 : 0;
        else
              yrot = 180*acos(direction[2]/xzlen)/PI;


        /*
         * The second rotation, about the x axis, is given by the projection on
         * the y,z plane of the y-rotated direction vector: the original y
         * component, and the rotated x,z vector from above.
         */
        yzlen = sqrt(direction[1]*direction[1]+xzlen*xzlen);
        xrot = 180*acos(xzlen/yzlen)/PI;       /* yzlen should never be 0 */

        if( direction[1] > 0 )
              RiRotate( xrot, 1.0, 0.0, 0.0 );
        else
              RiRotate(-xrot, 1.0, 0.0, 0.0 );
        /* The last rotation declared gets performed first */
        if( direction[0] > 0 )
              RiRotate(-yrot, 0.0, 1.0, 0.0 );
        else
              RiRotate( yrot, 0.0, 1.0, 0.0 );
}
```

Listing 8.2 *A simple camera specification*

Camera translation

The initial call to **RiIdentity**() clears the viewing transformation. Since the camera will be rotated about the viewpoint,
the translation to make the viewpoint coincide with the coor-

dinate origin must be applied first. Therefore it is declared last. The negative camera position coordinates in **RiTranslate()** are important: the world is being translated away so as to move the "camera location" to the coordinate origin.

Camera direction

The function *AimZ()* points the *z* axis in an arbitrary direction. Similarly to the translation, we are really rotating the world so that the desired direction vector points along the *z* axis: any point that formerly lay along the direction vector from the viewpoint now lies on the *z* axis.

Camera roll

When taking pictures in the world, "up" on the film is usually aligned with "up" in the world. *AimZ()* assumes that "up" parallels the positive *y* axis. The rotation performed by **RiRotate()** in *PlaceCamera()* provides for "head tilting" via a rotation about *z* controlled with the *roll* parameter.

General camera transformation

The above camera specification underscores the fact that positioning, pointing and orienting (in short, transforming) a camera from the coordinate origin in world space is equivalent to applying the inverse transformation to the rest of the world. One can also view the camera transformation as moving the world coordinate axes away from the camera system. Its inverse, then, expresses the camera relative to the world.

Formally, if one treats the camera as an object defined at the coordinate origin of world space pointed along the *z* axis, it might be positioned by *N* *geometric* transforms *xform*$_1$() through *xform*$_N$():

$$xform_N(xform_{N-1}(... xform_1(cam) ...))$$

where *xform*$_1$() is performed first. The RenderMan camera specification uses the fact that this series of transforms on the *camera* is equivalent to the following transformation applied to the *world*:

$$xform_1^{-1} (... xform_{N-1}^{-1} (xform_N^{-1} (world))...)$$

where *world* stands for every object in the world defined with geometric coordinates.

Looking at the camera transform this way yields a very useful fact: if the specification of a camera in world space can be reduced, as it often is in modeling systems, to a 4 x 4 transformation matrix (call it *CameraMatrix*), and that matrix can be inverted as *CameraMatrixInverse*, then

RiTransform(CameraMatrixInverse)

is a complete specification of camera geometry.

Describing the camera

The procedures in Listing 8.2 concern the *placement* of a camera. The second part of a reasonable camera specification concerns characteristics of the camera itself. A synthetic camera is defined by how it derives a bounded image on some image plane from the three-dimensional world before it. The objects of the scene are first clipped to discard elements behind the camera.

Clipping planes

Only objects which are in front of the camera should appear in an image. In most renderers, this is expressed as a **clipping plane** perpendicular to the z axis in camera space and usually close to the camera. It is declared as a single depth (z) value. Any object nearer in depth is invisible. RenderMan also supports a far clipping plane, beyond which any object is invisible.

RiClipping(near, far)
　　RtFloat near, far;

near and *far* are distances from the camera, z values in camera space (after the camera transformation). The special value RI_EPSILON is slightly greater than 0, and is the minimum value allowed for *near*. RI_INFINITY is the largest representable value and may be used in *far* to include all objects. If **RiClipping**() is not called, *near* and *far* are RI_EPSILON and RI_INFINITY, respectively, so that almost all data in front of the camera is rendered.

The main reason for moving the clipping planes from their default is to declare bounds for a scene. Rendering is often more efficient if the clipping bounds are close to the actual bounds of the scene.

Model of projection (a digression)

The essential purpose of the camera is to derive a two-dimensional image from a three-dimensional scene. Whether one is rendering a three-dimensional digital model or snapping pictures with a camera, the basic purpose is to **project** a three-dimensional array of illuminated objects onto a plane, and take a rectangular area of that plane as a two-dimensional image. The perspective projection typically used in computer graphics mimics a physical camera, in which light rays pass through a lens, converge at a **focal point** and focus on an **image plane**. The focal point of a RenderMan camera is the same as the viewpoint located at the coordinate origin. The image plane is one unit away in positive z (in front of the viewpoint), which means that the projection passes through the image plane on the way to the focal point. In an orthographic projection, a point in the scene is projected directly onto the image plane along a line parallel to the z axis.

A rectangular region of the image plane is captured in the image itself. That region is called the film frame in photography and the **screen window** in RenderMan. The distance between the focal point and the image plane is the **focal length** of the camera.

An important fact is that *the size of the output image in pixels is independent of the size of the screen window.* The screen window concerns the *content* of the image, while the size of the output image is a function of how that content is represented. Once again, photography provides the model: the size of an enlargement made from a negative is independent of the negative itself.

For a given screen window and focal length, there is a pyramidal volume of space containing the parts of the scene that project within the screen window and thus appear in the image. The same is true of a physical camera: what actually appears in the film frame is a clearly defined part of the world.

Chapter 8: Viewing I: The Digital Camera

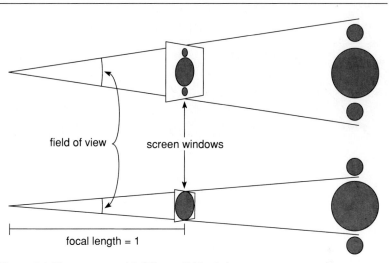

Figure 8.1 *Two cameras with different fields of view*

The pyramid is characterized by the angle between opposite sides, termed the camera's **field of view**.

If the size of the screen window is fixed, then moving the focal point closer to the image plane widens the field of view, and moving it farther away narrows it. Conversely, if the focal point is fixed (as it is with the RenderMan "camera"), then the field of view can be manipulated by defining a larger or smaller screen window.

Figure 8.1 shows two abstract cameras with fixed focal length but different fields of view, as determined by varying the screen window. The wider screen window includes more of the world in the frame and generally makes objects appear smaller. A narrower field corresponds to a telephoto lens, which excludes more of the scene and enlarges farther objects.

The fact that the focal length of the RenderMan camera is fixed at 1 might seem a limitation. However, the important thing is how the world is projected onto the image plane within the screen window. Figure 8.2 shows that the field of view is completely determined by the *ratio* of the focal length to the

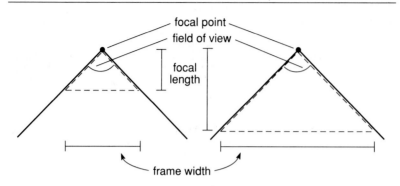

Figure 8.2 *Constant ratios of focal length and frame width give constant field of view. Doubling the focal length and frame width at the same time leaves the field of view unchanged.*

frame width, since doubling both leaves the field of view unaffected. A little trigonometry indicates that

$$field\ of\ view = 2*atan\left(\frac{frame\ width/2}{focal\ length}\right)$$

Notice that if the screen window is not square, the field of view will be different in the horizontal and vertical directions. Specifically, it will be wider in the longer dimension. In RenderMan, the field of view is measured in the narrower of the two directions.

In a physical camera, the screen window is fixed by the film format, and the focal length is varied by selecting a lens or by setting a zoom lens. Under the RenderMan Interface, the focal length is always 1, but both the screen window and the field of view can be set directly to bring more or less of the world within the screen window. There is interplay between the two parameters, since widening the screen window has the same effect as widening the field of view.

Listing 8.3 shows a simple routine, *FrameCamera()*, which takes a camera description in terms of the focal length of a lens and the width and height of the film. *FrameCamera()* manipulates the screen window to simulate that camera, leaving the field of view fixed.

```
/* FrameCamera(): give physical parameters for a camera.
   Parameters:
        focallength: the "camera's" focal length.
        framewidth: the width of the film frame
        frameheight: the height of the film frame
*/
FrameCamera( focallength, framewidth, frameheight )
float focallength, framewidth, frameheight;
{
        RtFloat normwidth, normheight;

        /* Focal length of 0 is taken to be an orthographic projection */
        if( focallength != 0.0 ) {
                RiProjection( "perspective", RI_NULL );
                normwidth = (framewidth*.5)/focallength;
                normheight = (frameheight*.5)/focallength;
        } else {
                RiProjection( "orthographic", RI_NULL );
                normwidth = framewidth*.5;
                normheight = frameheight*.5;
        }
        RiScreenWindow( -normwidth, normwidth, -normheight, normheight );
}
```

Listing 8.3 *Camera specification in terms of a physical camera*

Perspective projection

FrameCamera() takes three parameters: the width of the film image (*framewidth*), its height (*frameheight*), and the focal length of the lens used (*focallength*) in a hypothetical camera. The units used are unimportant. It might be inches or millimeters if one wants to model a film camera; it might be square pixels for a digital representation. But the units must be the same for all three parameters.

Projection

The first RenderMan call in Listing 8.3 is **RiProjection**().

```
RiProjection( name, parameterlist )
    char *name;
```

RiProjection() takes the *name* of a projection method for going from three-dimensional points onto the image plane. Two

standard projection methods, "perspective" and "orthographic",
are predefined in RenderMan. The former provides a perspective transformation that includes all objects within a 90° field
of view. Other fields of view may be supplied using the
RI_FOV parameter, as in the following:

RtFloat fov;
RiProjection("perspective", RI_FOV, (**RtPointer**) &fov, RI_NULL);

The RI_FOV parameter must be less than 180°. This parameter
causes the perspective projection to also scale the world so
that the requested field of view angle exactly fills the −1 to 1
square on the image plane.

An orthographic projection projects each point onto the image plane along a path parallel to the z axis, simply discarding
the z coordinate of any point.

The *parameterlist* of **RiProjection**() may also be used to pass parameters to nonstandard projections.

Figure 8.3 illustrates the effect of varying the RI_FOV parameter from a small value at top (corresponding to a telephoto
lens) to a large value (a fisheye lens) at bottom. The middle
image is the default.

Screen window

FrameCamera() defines the screen window according to the ratio between the frame width and the focal length (see Figure
8.4), normalizing the "camera" to a focal length of 1. *Frame-
Camera*() takes a special focal length of 0 to indicate an infinitely long lens, necessitating an orthographic projection onto
the image plane. Normally a perspective projection is used.

RiScreenWindow() specifies the screen window as a bounding
box in x and y on the image plane.

RiScreenWindow(left, right, bottom, top)
    RtFloat left, right, bottom, top;

RiScreenWindow() declares a screen window, the boundaries
of an image on the image plane. *The image will consist of exactly
the part of the scene that projects onto the image plane within the*

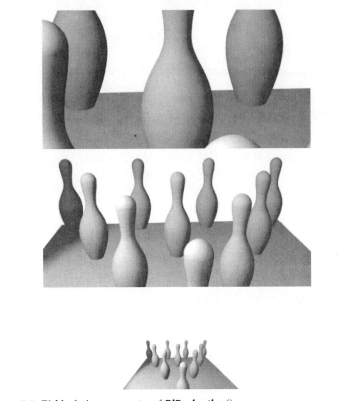

Figure 8.3 *Field-of-view parameter of **RiProjection**()*

screen window. left and *right* are the bounds of the window in the negative and positive x direction, respectively, and *bottom* and *top* are its bounds in the negative and positive y directions. If *left > right* or *bottom > top*, the image will be reflected about the appropriate axis.

The parameters of **RiScreenWindow**() are defined in screen space, in which x is positive to the right and y is positive upward. Thus, a typical screen window is the unit square

$$left = -1$$
$$right = +1$$
$$bottom = -1$$
$$top = +1$$

The default screen window is the same shape as the output frame, and contains the unit square on the image plane. The frame shape is affected by **RiFormat**(), **RiDisplay**() and **RiFrameAspectRatio**().

Uncentered windows

FrameCamera() centers the screen window about ($x=0,y=0$) on the image plane, where the viewing direction is perpendicular to the image plane. This corresponds closely to the design of almost all modern cameras. However, it is quite reasonable to define uncentered windows.

At large offsets, an image becomes significantly tilted with respect to the viewing direction. This property recalls view cameras, which can tilt the film plane to compensate for perspective distortion. A picture taken from street level can make tall buildings appear less sharply raked if the film plane can be made parallel to the buildings even though the camera is looking up. An uncentered window could be passed to **RiScreenWindow**() to achieve the same effect.

An alternative camera

The usual screen window is –1 to +1 in both x and y. Since the RenderMan focal length is fixed at 1, the perspective projection into this window corresponds to a field of view of 90 degrees (see Figure 8.4). This is roughly the equivalent of a 35mm lens on a 35mm camera, slightly wider than a "normal" lens. The version of *FrameCamera*() above simulated a change in the field width of the lens by changing the size of the screen window. It might not be considered convenient or intuitive to control the size of the field by sizing the screen window; it would be like changing film formats instead of using a zoom lens. It is actually unworkable if one wants the screen window to be set automatically based on the output frame. One must avoid calling **RiScreenWindow**() in that case. The field of view can be controlled directly by leaving the screen window alone and providing an RI_FOV parameter to **RiProjection**(), which will then control what falls inside the default screen window, rather than resizing the screen window

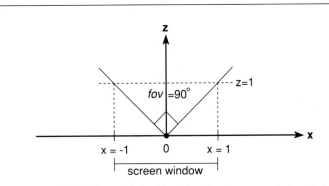

Figure 8.4 *90° field of view with focal length of 1 puts screen window at 1*

itself. Specifically, *fov* is the angle between sides of the viewing frustum enclosing objects which are projected within the unit square on the image plane. In other words, if it's inside the viewing frustum, its image space coordinates will be between –1 and +1 on the image plane.

The RI_FOV parameter to **RiProjection**() frees us from the geometry of the focal point, screen window and field of view, to give us what we really want: direct control over the field of view seen by a given screen window on the image plane. It determines exactly what will appear in any given screen window.

That makes two nearly equivalent ways to select part of the world along the direction of view for rendering: **RiScreenWindow**() and **RiProjection**(). Just to make this relationship clear, Listing 8.4 shows an alternative version of *FrameCamera*() that uses the latter method.

This version of *FrameCamera*() replaces **RiScreenWindow**() with a new routine, **RiFrameAspectRatio**(). It sets the default screen window indirectly: rather than giving specific bounds, it says only that the output frame, and by implication the screen window, should have a specific shape, specified as the ratio of width to height. The resulting screen window just encloses the unit square on the image plane. In Listing 8.4, the field of view is again derived from the focal length, frame width and the frame height. Here, though, the minimum of

```
/* FrameCamera(): give physical parameters for a camera.
 * Parameters:
 *     focallength: controls the width of the camera's field of view.
 *     framewidth: the width of the film image
 *     frameheight: the height of the film image*/
#include <ri.h>
#include <math.h>
FrameCamera( focallength, framewidth, frameheight )
float focallength, framewidth, frameheight;
{
        RtFloat fov;
        /* A nonzero focal length is taken to be a "normal" lens */
        if( focallength != 0.0 ) {
                fov = 2 * atan( (min(framewidth,frameheight)*.5)/focallength );
                RiProjection( "perspective",
                        RI_FOV, (RtPointer)&fov, RI_NULL );
        } else
                RiProjection( "orthographic", RI_NULL );
        RiFrameAspectRatio( (RtFloat)(framewidth/frameheight) );
}
```

Listing 8.4 *Alternative camera description using **RiPerspective**() to control the field of view*

the width and height is used to calculate the field of view because the minimum dimension maps to the unit square.

This completes the discussion of RenderMan's controls for determining what part of the three-dimensional world will appear in the output image. We can now turn to the question of how that information is represented in the image.

The Digital Image

The camera procedures *PlaceCamera*() and *FrameCamera*() are as valid in an analog world as in a digital one because they concern a continuous image within the screen window on the image plane. The next part of the viewing process concerns how the visual information within that window is represented as a digital image with specific vertical and horizontal pixel resolution.

Display description

First, the destination of the image must be specified, whether it is to be displayed on a frame buffer or stored in an image file. At the same time, the nature of the information recorded at each pixel is detailed.

RiDisplay(name, type, mode, *parameterlist*)
    char *name;
    RtToken type, mode;

RiDisplay() declares the destination of the image being rendered. *type* determines the device type, e.g., "file" (RI_FILE) or "framebuffer" (RI_FRAMEBUFFER). *name* gives a specific display device name or the name of the output file. *mode* is a string specifying the information to be stored at each pixel. It contains combinations of "rgb", "a" and "z", for full color, coverage, and depth information, respectively.

By default, the upper left pixel of the image — (0,0) in screen space — is placed at the upper left pixel of the file or display. The "origin" (RI_ORIGIN) parameter of *parameterlist* may be used to change this. Its value is an array of two **RtInt** values giving a horizontal and vertical offset for the image relative to the display or file. If the image goes to a file, the origin is stored in the file for possible later use in displaying it. If the image is being rendered to a display, a positive origin displaces the upper left pixel of the image to the right and down from the top left pixel of the display. The origin does *not* affect the content of the image as rendered; it will contain exactly the same portion of the scene no matter what the origin. The origin affects only the physical destination of the pixels.

The *parameterlist* of **RiDisplay**() may also be used to pass any device- or implementation-dependent display parameters.

Display type *and* name

type, which concerns the physical destination, is usually either RI_FRAMEBUFFER or RI_FILE. If the image is to be stored in a file, then *name* gives the file's name. The meaning of *name* for frame buffers depends on the nature of the frame buffer and its interface to the renderer. This is an especially implementation-dependent parameter in the RenderMan Interface; it is meant to signify a device name, whether on a display or on external storage.

Display mode

mode indicates the type of information that should be stored at each pixel. For simple display, the pixel's color is usually sufficient. The *mode* string "rgb" (RI_RGB) indicates that color values should be stored. Some renderers can be used to extract other information from scenes. For example, it is often useful to retain coverage information indicating the extent to which a pixel was formed from objects in the scene as opposed to the background. Historically known as **alpha**, this information can be stored with the pixels of an image by including "a" in the *mode* string. The distance of the surface nearest the viewing plane at a pixel may be recorded by including "z" in the *mode* string.

mode may include combinations of the above strings. By convention, they should appear in the order "rgb", "a" and "z". For example, if *mode* is "rgba" then both color and coverage information are stored in the pixels. A *mode* of "az" stores coverage and depth. "rgbaz" stores all the above information, and could be used to composite a number of images that depict different objects in the same scene [DUFF85].

Image resolution

RiDisplay() determines the physical destination of the image data. The other key attributes of the output are its resolution (numbers of rows and columns of pixels) and the aspect ratio of individual pixels. The **pixel aspect ratio** is simply

$$ar_p = \frac{pixelwidth}{pixelheight}$$

where the *pixelwidth* and *pixelheight* are the horizontal and vertical size of each pixel on the display.

RiFormat(xresolution, yresolution, pixelaspectratio)
    RtInt xresolution, yresolution;
    RtFloat pixelaspectratio;

RiFormat() sets the horizontal and vertical resolution of an image, and declares the aspect ratio (width/height) of its pixels. *pixelaspectratio* may be negative to indicate that the default of the display as specified by **RiDisplay**() should be used.

When an image is rendered to a file, *xresolution* and *yresolution* specify the horizontal and vertical resolution of that file. When the image is being rendered to a display device with **RiDisplay**(), presumably the device has a physical pixel aspect ratio. **RiFormat**() can defer to that value by giving a negative *pixelaspectratio*. *xresolution* and *yresolution*, together with any "origin" parameter provided to **RiDisplay**(), define a rectangular region of pixels to be rendered onto the display. If this image does not fit on the display (either because it is too big or because the origin given to **RiDisplay**() causes the raster to overlap the display bounds), any pixels that cannot be displayed are cropped. That is, *a given pixel within an image will be assigned exactly the same portion of the scene independent of the capabilities of the display.* This is in contrast to shrinking the image to fit it into the display, which would inevitably change the relationship between pixels and the scene.

Figure 8.5 shows the relationship between the origin given to **RiDisplay**(), the resolution of the image and that of a display. The pixels at the top and left of the display are left untouched, while those outside the display bounds at the right and bottom are cropped.

Relationship between screen window and image

We can now predict what portions of the scene appear in the image (namely the screen window) and the size of the output image. The single remaining issue is the relationship between the two.

The pixel aspect ratio supplies an important piece of information: together with the horizontal and vertical resolutions, it determines the **image aspect ratio**, its physical shape when displayed.

The aspect ratio of an image is given by the ratio of its physical width and height. If res_h and res_v are the horizontal and vertical resolution of the display, then the aspect ratio of the image is

$$ar_i = \frac{ar_p * res_h}{res_v}$$

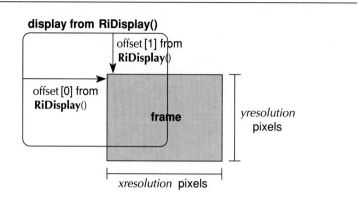

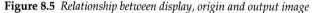

Figure 8.5 *Relationship between display, origin and output image*

If pixels are square, then the image aspect ratio is simply the ratio between the horizontal and vertical resolution as measured in pixels.

The image aspect ratio is important for one reason: *the projected contents of the screen window map directly to the pixels of the image. If the image aspect ratio does not match that of the screen window, the image will appear distorted.* RenderMan normally avoids distortion by using a screen window which matches the image aspect ratio. If no screen window is specified (**RiScreenWindow**() is never called), then RenderMan defines a screen window with the same shape as the image and the output is undistorted.

If a screen window *is* defined by the application, and it fails to match the shape of the image, distortion normally results. However, sometimes a particular output aspect ratio is desired, regardless of the display used. *FrameCamera*() was an example of that: we wanted an output in the shape of a physical film frame. In the second version of *FrameCamera*(), **RiFrameAspectRatio**() did exactly that.

How is this desired frame reconciled with the shape of the image defined by **RiDisplay**() and **RiFormat**()? Simple: *if the shape of the frame given by **RiFrameAspectRatio**() does not match that of the output image, then pixels are left untouched at either the right or the bottom of the image.*

RiFrameAspectRatio(frameratio)
    RtFloat frameratio;

RiFrameAspectRatio() decrees that the picture contained in the output image will have width/height = *frameratio* regardless of the display or file being generated. If this **frame aspect ratio** differs from that of the output image as a whole, then pixels will be untouched at either the right or the bottom.

If **RiScreenWindow**() is never called, **RiFrameAspectRatio**() also determines the screen window. The default screen window always just fits the square from –1 to +1 in x and y into the display. Therefore, if *frameratio* > 1 (the frame is "horizontal"), the default screen window is *–frameratio* to *+frameratio* in x and –1 to +1 in y. If *frameratio* < 1, it will be –1 to +1 in x and $-1/frameratio$ to $+1/frameratio$ in y. If both **RiFrameAspectRatio**() and **RiScreenWindow**() are called, and the screen window does not match *frameratio*, then the output image will be distorted.

Image vs. frame

Since the pixels in the output image may not all be rendered, we now have the motivation for a bit of new nomenclature. We will use the word **image** to refer to the array of pixels defined by **RiDisplay**() and **RiFormat**(), all of which are rendered in the absence of a call to **RiFrameAspectRatio**(). The **frame** is the subset of the image stipulated by **RiFrameAspectRatio**(). It has two important roles.

First, the frame limits the set of pixels in the image that are actually rendered. The image and the frame may differ only in their aspect ratios; pixels may be untouched at either the right or the bottom of the image, but not both. If **RiFrameAspectRatio**() is never called, the frame and the image are the same.

Second, the pixels within the frame form a digital rendition of the contents of the screen window. *The screen window is always mapped to the frame, not the image.* Therefore, the important issue in avoiding distortion is to match the aspect ratios of the screen window and the frame.

This relationship between the frame and the screen window completely specifies the relationship between data in the scene and pixels in the image. It does *not* imply that all the pixels of the frame are actually rendered. If part of the frame lies outside a display, that part is simply not rendered; the remaining pixels will receive exactly the same information that they would if the image were complete.

The following few paragraphs give examples of how to meet some common formatting needs.

Filling the display

If the user wants only to fill the display with the scene, then only one line is required. Assuming that the name of the display is "mydisplay", that line is as follows:

```
RiDisplay("mydisplay", RI_FRAMEBUFFER, RI_RGB, RI_NULL);
```

The screen window will be defined to match the shape of the display (just enclosing the –1 to +1 range on the image plane), and the frame will be defined to encompass every pixel in the display.

Creating an image file

Since a RenderMan renderer produces a file by default, if the user wants to create an image file 700 pixels wide and 500 pixels high, then only the call

```
RiFormat( 700, 500, 1.0 );
```

is needed. If the file should be called "myfile" instead of "ri.pic"(the default), then the sequence

```
RiDisplay("myfile", RI_FILE, RI_RGB, RI_NULL);
RiFormat( 700, 500, 1.0 );
```

would be used instead. Finally, if the file will be used on a display with pixel aspect ratio 0.9, the only way for RenderMan to know that would be with the call

```
RiFormat( 700, 500, 0.9 );
```

Windowing onto a display

To render into a window on a display device, one need only specify the size and origin of the window, the former to **RiFormat**(), the latter to **RiDisplay**(). If one wanted to render a

512 x 384 window on "mydisplay", offset by 128 pixels in x and 200 pixels in y, then the following fragment would apply:

```
RtInt origin[2];

origin[0] = 128;
origin[1] = 200;
RiDisplay("mydisplay", RI_FRAMEBUFFER, RI_RGB,
        "origin", (RtPointer) origin, RI_NULL);
RiFormat( 512, 384, -1.0 );
```

This specification is designed to be independent of the particular display device used. Since the pixel aspect ratio passed to **RiFormat**() is –1.0, that of the display is used. If the display doesn't have enough resolution to display the window, then only the part of it that does fit will be seen.

Enforced frame aspect ratio

The handiest use of an enforced aspect ratio is in specifying the shape of the output independent of the display. The resolution and aspect ratio of a display are implicit in the **RiDisplay**() command that sets it up. If an image should be rendered onto display "mydisplay" with aspect ratio 4:3, the sequence

```
RiDisplay("mydisplay", RI_FRAMEBUFFER, RI_RGB, RI_NULL);
RiFrameAspectRatio( 4.0/3.0 );
```

takes care of everything: the screen window will be –4.0/3.0 to +4.0/3.0 in x and –1 to +1 in y, and the image will be as large as can fit on the display without distortion.

If output is to a file, there is little point in defining the file to be of a different shape than the frame. For example, the call

```
RiFormat( 1024, 768, 1.0 );
```

would provide a 1024 x 768 image with square pixels, which would have exactly the same shape. So would a file with

```
RiFormat( 1024, 1024, 4.0/3.0 );
```

Use of image distortion

You may want a distorted image. **Anamorphic** wide-screen movie formats (Panavision, for example) laterally compress a wide field into a conventional 35mm frame and reverse the process optically during projection.

Declaring a screen window with a different aspect ratio than the image is an easy way to achieve this effect. Suppose a screen window with an aspect ratio of 2:1 is to fit within a frame of aspect ratio 4:3. Then the sequence

```
RiFrameAspectRatio( 4.0/3.0 );
RiScreenWindow( -2, 2, -1, 1 );
```

will do the job no matter what the characteristics of the display or output file. So will the sequence

```
RiFormat( 512, 384, 1.0 );
RiScreenWindow( -2, 2, -1, 1 );
```

RenderMan will fill the entire 512 x 384 image. The physical output will therefore have aspect ratio 4:3.

Rendering a subwindow

Sometimes a user wishes to render only a part of the frame, or to render it in tiles and assemble them later.

RiCropWindow(left, right, top, bottom)
    RtFloat left, right, top, bottom;

left, *right*, *top* and *bottom* are floating-point values between 0 and 1 such that *left* < *right* and *top* < *bottom* (they are swapped to suit if they are not passed that way). They define a rectangular subregion, the **crop window**, of the output frame (not the image); the call

```
RiCropWindow( 0.0, 1.0, 0.0, 1.0 )
```

renders the entire frame, which is the default.

The values passed to **RiCropWindow**() are expressed in screen space, in which x increases positively to the right and y increases positively downward: the screen window [.75 1 0 .25] describes the upper right sixteenth of a frame.

RenderMan does not render fractional pixels. The window defined by *left*, *right*, *top* and *bottom* is taken to integer pixel locations. Specifically, if pixels in the frame run from 0 to (*xres*–1) horizontally and 0 to (*yres*–1) vertically, then the window actually rendered is

$$rxmin = \lceil \text{left} * xres \rceil$$
$$rxmax = \lceil (\text{right} * xres) - 1 \rceil$$
$$rymin = \lceil \text{top} * yres \rceil$$
$$rymax = \lceil (\text{bottom} * yres) - 1 \rceil$$

Under this definition, if *left=right* or *bottom=top* no pixels are rendered. That can even be true when *left* is slightly less than *right*. However, this definition of the rendered pixels *does* have the property of perfect tiling. One can divide the [0,1] square into a set of panels and render them separately. As long the panels do not overlap in the floating-point parameters to **RiCropWindow**(), no pixel will be rendered twice, and as long as the square is covered completely, every pixel will be rendered in one of the panels.

A final example

Figure 8.6 illustrates the pixels rendered by the following specification:

```
RiFormat( 1280, 1024, 1.0 );
RiFrameAspectRatio( 1.0 );
RiCropWindow( .125, .75, .125, .5 );
RiDisplay( "mydisplay", RI_FRAMEBUFFER, RI_RGB, RI_NULL );
```

A large horizontal image with square pixels is defined by **RiFormat**(1280, 1024, 1.0). The square image demanded by **RiFrameAspectRatio**(1.0) crops the raster to 1024 x 1024 and specifies the square screen window shown. The declared crop window runs from .125 to .75 horizontally and .125 to .5 vertically, excluding an eighth of the target raster at the left and top, a quarter at the right and half at the bottom. Assuming that "mydisplay" is 640 x 480 pixels, the rendered image is reduced even further.

It might seem strange to format an image so much larger than the display. However, it makes sense if one is developing a very large image and testing small parts of it by rendering them to a display.

Summary of output specification

To summarize, the rectangular region of pixels actually rendered represents the *intersection* of:

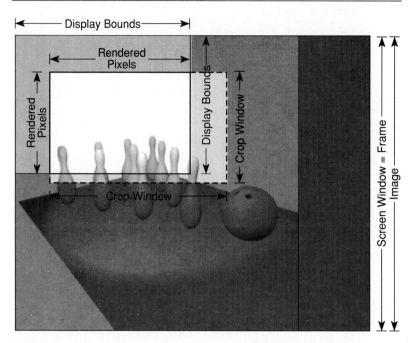

Figure 8.6 *Pixels actually rendered for one set of imaging calls*

- the frame,
- the crop window, and
- the display, if any.

If output is to a file, the crop window is usually rendered in its entirety, although some file formats may have limited resolution. No pixels at all will be rendered if the crop window occupies a part of the frame outside the display.

Figure 8.7 summarizes how the frame and screen window are determined. Each box shows a factor in this process, and each factor has a priority list for determining its value. The lowest level has the lowest priority. This should enable the user to predict the effect of any given set of commands. The order of the various formatting commands within a program is irrelevant; since the output image is not determined until scene description begins with **RiWorldBegin**(), only the priority of the routines matters.

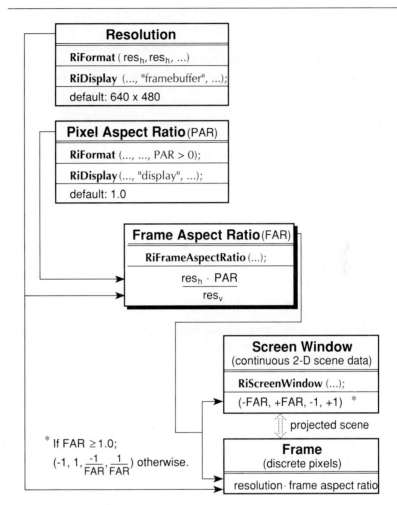

Figure 8.7 *Arriving at rendered pixels*

The single most important factor in Figure 8.7 is the frame aspect ratio. It determines the default screen window and absolutely determines the shape of the frame irrespective of the shape of the image or display.

Pixel aspect ratio

RenderMan assumes that pixels are square by default (in other words, the default pixel aspect ratio is 1.0). However, if **Ri-**

Display() is called to send output to a display device, then the pixel ratio of the display prevails. The pixel aspect ratio given to **RiFormat**() has higher priority in case of conflict, but only if it is specified to be positive. (It might be negative or zero if one wishes to dictate the resolution with **RiFormat**() but leave the pixel aspect ratio alone.)

Image resolution

The default output image resolution is 640 pixels horizontally and 480 vertically, giving a frame aspect ratio of 4:3 (assuming square pixels). The default dimensions of the output image can be overridden by either **RiDisplay**() or **RiFormat**(). If both are called, the size given by **RiFormat**() has priority. **RiDisplay**() affects the size of the output image the output image only if it directs output to a physical display device (i.e., its *type* parameter is RI_FRAMEBUFFER).

Frame aspect ratio

If there is no call to **RiFrameAspectRatio**(), the frame aspect ratio is calculated from the resolution and pixel aspect ratio of the output image as

$$ar_f = \frac{ar_p * res_h}{res_v}$$

where ar_p is the pixel aspect ratio, and res_h and res_v are the horizontal and vertical resolution of the image.

The frame aspect ratio determines both the *default* screen window and the *actual* frame. The default screen window contains the unit square on the image plane, widened or lengthened to match the frame aspect ratio. It can be set directly using **RiScreenWindow**(). The frame is the largest area of pixels in the output image which has the stipulated frame aspect ratio.

Once the screen window and target raster are defined, the relationship between pixels and the screen window is fixed, and the renderer will attempt to calculate those pixels using that screen window. A subset of those pixels will be rendered if either **RiCropWindow**() is called or the target raster does not fit into the display used.

Chapter 8: Viewing I: The Digital Camera

Synthetic camera model

Figure 8.8 is a graphic representation of the discussion of this chapter. It indicates a significant difference from the physical camera model. In a physical camera, light converges on a focal point or viewing location, then projects onto an image (film) plane behind the focal point. The synthetic image plane is best visualized *in front* of the viewpoint. Specifically, RenderMan posits an image plane located at $z=1$, which leads to a more intuitive coordinate space: using an image plane in positive z means that the image is right-side-up after projection (unlike a conventional camera), and that the y axis is still positive upward.

A Better Viewing Program

Listing 8.5 shows a revised version of Listing 8.1. It uses *FrameCamera*() and *PlaceCamera*() as well as a set of predefined constants to set parameters. These have the default values for the corresponding options. This program may be used by modifying these parameter values and defining a scene between **RiWorldBegin**() and **RiWorldEnd**().

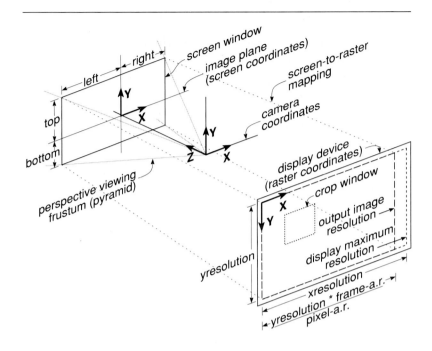

Figure 8.8 *Projection into screen space (camera-to-raster projection geometry)*

```
#include <ri.h>

/* viewbasics.c: file compiling view options into a rendering shell. */

#define FILENAME "ri.pic" /* output file name; delete to render to display*/
#define DATATYPE RI_RGBA          /* Pixels have RGB and coverage    */
#define PICXRES ( ( RtInt ) 640 )  /* Horizontal output resolution    */
#define PICYRES ( ( RtInt ) 480 )  /* Vertical output resolution      */

#define CROPMINX ( ( RtFloat ) 0.0 )   /* RiCropWindow() parameters    */
#define CROPMAXX ( ( RtFloat ) 1.0 )
#define CROPMINY ( ( RtFloat ) 0.0 )
#define CROPMAXY ( ( RtFloat ) 1.0 )
#define CAMXFROM 0.0                /* Camera position  */
#define CAMYFROM 0.0
#define CAMZFROM 0.0

#define CAMXTO 0.0                  /* Camera direction */
#define CAMYTO 0.0
#define CAMZTO 1.0
```

```
#define CAMROLL 0.0                    /* Camera roll      */

#define CAMZOOM 1.0                    /* Camera zoom rate*/

RtPoint CameraFrom    = { CAMXFROM, CAMYFROM, CAMZFROM },
        CameraTo      = { CAMXTO, CAMYTO, CAMZTO };

main()
{
     RiBegin( RI_NULL );               /* As always */

            /* Output image characteristics */
#ifdef FILENAME                        /* output to file */
            RiDisplay(FILENAME, RI_FILE, RI_RGBA, RI_NULL);
#else                      /*...to frame buffer */
            RiDisplay( "", RI_FRAMEBUFFER, RI_RGBA, RI_NULL);
#endif

            RiFormat( PICXRES, PICYRES, 1.0 );          /* Image resolution */
            /* Region of image rendered */
            RiCropWindow(  CROPMINX, CROPMAXX,
                             CROPMINY, CROPMAXY );
            /* Camera characteristics */
            FrameCamera(    (float)PICXRES*CAMZOOM, (float)PICXRES,
                             (float)PICYRES );
            /* Camera position and orientation */
            CameraTo[0] -= CameraFrom[0];
            CameraTo[1] -= CameraFrom[1];
            CameraTo[2] -= CameraFrom[2];
            PlaceCamera( CameraFrom, CameraTo, CAMROLL );
            RiClipping( RI_EPSILON, RI_INFINITY );          /* Clipping planes*/

            /* Now describe the world */
            RiWorldBegin();
                   ...     /* ...Your scene here... */
            RiWorldEnd();

     RiEnd();
}
```

Listing 8.5 *An improved boilerplate viewing program*

CHAPTER 9

Viewing II: A Model of the Rendering Process

This chapter rounds out the discussion of camera specification. Chapter 8 presented the viewing process in terms of a physical camera, a model that is sufficient for many cases. However, there are enough differences between the physical model and the way digital rendering works that the physical model breaks down eventually. This chapter concerns general issues of quality arising from the digital image synthesis process. The first section addresses the exactness of curved surface representation. The second covers the process of producing the pixels of an image. The last two sections introduce two of the most novel features of the RenderMan Interface: motion blur and depth-of-field calculations.

Surface Approximation

The first quality issue concerns the approximation of curved surfaces. Under many rendering schemes, for example, polygons are much easier to render than curved surfaces, so quadric or parametric surfaces may be **approximated** by the renderer using small polygons. As the number of polygons goes up, so does the quality of the approximation, but so does the cost of creating, storing and rendering the polygons. Ideally, the approximation should be adaptive: a more tightly curved surface needs more small polygons than a smoother one for the same quality of approximation. Different measures of "quality" may also apply in different situations.

RenderMan provides a routine for determining whether a set of polygons or other surfaces constitutes an adequate approximation to the underlying surface.

RiGeometricApproximation(type, value)
    RtToken type;
    RtFloat value;

RiGeometricApproximation() sets the criterion for approximating the surface primitives of a scene with other, more easily rendered, primitives. *type* is the type of criterion and *value* gives a value in a metric meaningful for that criterion. There is one predefined *type*, "flatness" (RI_FLATNESS), the default, under which a polygon is a good enough approximation if it never deviates more than *value* pixels from the true curved surface in raster space.

The default *value* is .5, so that no polygon deviates by more than half a pixel from the surface it is approximating.

Raster Output

Now that we know how the geometry of a scene is projected onto a raster image, the only remaining question is how the parts of the scene landing near a pixel affect the color and intensity of the pixel as output. We need to discuss how that output is determined, again beginning with a conceptual model to help understand just what is going on.

Model of pixel rendering

An image formed using RenderMan is a **raster**, a rectangular grid of **pixels**, which represents the scene data projecting inside the screen window on the image plane. To physically display an image, each pixel supplies color information for lighting the phosphors of a cathode-ray tube or for controlling a color halftone. It is essential to realize, however, that the single color value at a pixel represents a finite *area* of the image plane, which may contain a variety of surfaces. Its color may actually vary a great deal across its extent. Generating an output pixel value, then, requires analyzing the scene information at the pixel, settling on an external representation for the result, and possibly supplementing the color with other kinds of information.

Sampling

Rendering a pixel begins with the very small portion of a scene that projects onto the target raster near the center of the pixel. It must produce a single color value for that pixel; that is, it must **sample** the scene.

In the simplest methods, the scene data is simply point sampled: the color of the entire pixel is taken from the surface at the center of the pixel. Point sampling invariably diminishes image quality with aliasing artifacts. RenderMan supports a variety of methods for filtering the scene geometry, in order to improve the quality of the resulting image by allowing more surface information to influence the output pixel.

Quantization

Once the color at a pixel is determined, it is usually **quantized**, or reduced to a small set of discrete colors. These are typically represented using a range of integers, usually [0,255], in which integer steps represent equal differences in the original color. In other words, quantization is a linear mapping by default.

This linear quantization has shortcomings of its own, since it leads to high contrast between adjacent quantized values at low levels.* RenderMan directly supports logarithmic exposure mapping, and provides the ability to specify any other function for converting pixel colors for output. These could be used to convert to other color systems before quantization.

Associated image information

Finally, RenderMan allows information other than color to be output. The depth in space of the surface projecting onto a pixel (its z value) can be made available using **RiDisplay()**, for use in combining images with hidden-surface resolution. It may also be important to record the fraction of a pixel that

---

*A good measure of the contrast between values C_1 and C_2 is

$$\frac{C_1 - C_2}{C_1 + C_2}$$

Values near 0 have much higher contrast than higher values.

surfaces from the scene (its **alpha** value), in order to composite images accurately.

The imaging pipeline

Figure 9.1 expands on the above model to show the pixel production process schematically. It begins once the projection and hidden-surface processes have determined the scene information projected in the vicinity of the pixel. Two paths proceed in parallel, one for color values and one for depth values. We'll discuss each stage in the pipeline together with the routines that govern it.

Filtering and sampling

The process of choosing an output value to represent the part of an image under a pixel is known as **sampling**. The most common method of sampling is simply to determine the color of the light arriving from the scene in the center of the pixel. This creates problems in realistic rendering, since fine detail (a tiny picket fence is the usual example) that is too small to be resolved can nonetheless create huge, inappropriate fluctuations in adjacent pixel values (**aliasing**), depending on which part of the detail falls on the pixel center. The staircases, or **jaggies**, that are seen along edges that are close to being horizontal or vertical are a familiar artifact of primitive sampling.

The ideal is to completely integrate all that lies under a pixel into the sample, carefully affording each surface its due in the output pixel value. Unfortunately, this process is extremely laborious, impractical and sometimes impossible to perform correctly. In practice, computer graphics falls back on a number of compromises that offer improvements over point sampling at reasonable cost.

One strategy is to **supersample** the pixel: compute the arriving colors at several regularly spaced locations inside the pixel and **filter**, or weight the resulting values to obtain the pixel value. This strategy, too, has disadvantages, beginning with the fact that it multiplies the cost of computing the image without increasing its resolution. Supersampling can only reduce aliasing, not eliminate it. Nevertheless, it does qualita-

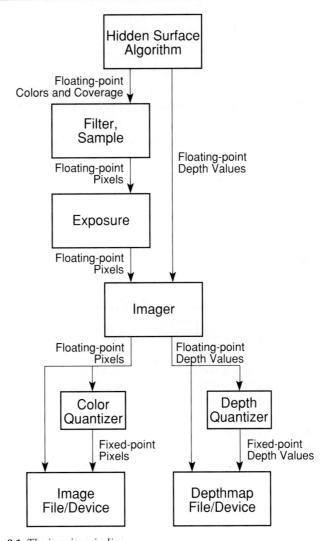

Figure 9.1 *The imaging pipeline*

tively improve the picture. Furthermore, aliasing artifacts can be converted to much less noticeable noise by **jittering** the supersamples (randomly displacing them individually from their uniform placement) [COOK86].

RiPixelSamples(xsamples, ysamples)
  RtFloat xsamples, ysamples;

The parameters of **RiPixelSamples**() give the ratio of the number of samples taken to the number of pixels in each direction. The default is 2 samples in each direction, meaning that each pixel contains 4 samples.

Filtering the supersamples

The final output value of a pixel is a weighted average of the supersamples. Generally, the farther a sample from the center, the less its weight. Specifically, a **filter function** gives sample weight as a function of x- and y-displacement.

All practical filter functions decrease to zero at some distance from the pixel center. Otherwise, all of space would have to be sampled to compute one pixel. The width of this **support** of the function may be greater than the size of a pixel. In other words, the samples that go into a pixel can come from the "grid cells" of nearby pixels. This can increase the quality of filtering at little additional expense, since a single sample can be used on a number of pixels.

RiPixelFilter(function, xwidth, ywidth)
  RtFloatFunc function;
  RtFloat xwidth, ywidth;

Pixel filter functions are specified by passing a pointer to a function returning an **RtFloat** value (see below). *xwidth* and *ywidth* specify the support of the filter in pixels. The weight of a filter is 0 outside its support. A width of 1 means that only samples within the grid cell of a given pixel will influence that pixel.

The five filter functions **RiGaussianFilter**() (the default), **RiBoxFilter**(), **RiTriangleFilter**(), **RiSincFilter**() and **RiCatmullRomFilter**() are defined with RenderMan. Each function weights samples according to their distance from the pixel center.

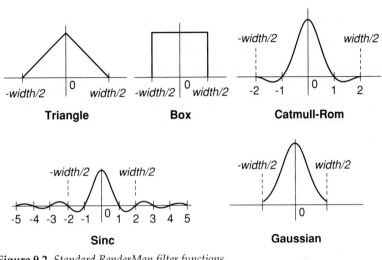

Figure 9.2 *Standard RenderMan filter functions*

Samples affect a pixel from a two-dimensional area whose extent is *xwidth* in *x* and *ywidth* in *y*. Assume that $F(x,y)$ is a two-dimensional filter function. A sample at position (x,y) *relative to the pixel center* is weighted (scaled) by $F(x,y)$ if

$$-(xwidth/2) \leq x \leq (xwidth/2)$$

and

$$-(ywidth/2) \leq y \leq (ywidth/2),$$

and 0 otherwise. For the sinc and Catmull-Rom filters, some samples have negative weight.

Figure 9.2 shows the standard filter functions in one dimension. In two dimensions, the triangle and box filters are bilaterally symmetric, i.e., the triangle becomes a pyramid and the box a cube. The other filters are circularly symmetric. Formally, if $f(x)$ is a one-dimensional filter function, then

$$F(x,y) = \min(f(x),f(y))$$

for triangle and box filters, and

$$F(x,y) = f(sqrt(x^2+y^2))$$

for Catmull-Rom, sinc and Gaussian filters.

The *xwidth* and *ywidth* parameters to **RiPixelFilter**() affect different filter functions differently. The triangle, box and Gaussian filters are widened or narrowed so that they are nonzero within the specified bounds and zero outside. The sinc filter, on the other hand, is clipped: the filter always has the same shape, and its width only determines the bounds over which it is evaluated. A width of 2 means that each sample is given a non-negative weight, for example. The Catmull-Rom filter is also clipped.

Other filters can be programmed by the user and passed to the interface. They are declared as follows:

```
RtFloat filterfunc( x, y, xwidth, ywidth )
RtFloat x, y;
RtFloat xwidth, ywidth;
```

x and *y* give a displacement from the pixel center, where pixel centers are a distance of 1.0 apart. *xwidth* and *ywidth* give the filter support passed to **RiPixelFilter**(). *filterfunc* should return the weight of the filter (usually a value between −1 and +1) at that point.

Typically, *filterfunc* is called only enough times to build up a table of filter weights. It is never called with $abs(x) > xwidth/2$ or $abs(y) > ywidth/2$.

Pixel fidelity

RiPixelSamples() directly determines how frequently the scene is sampled. Usually, the higher the sampling rate the better the image quality. However, the sampling rate can be made adaptive. Portions of an image whose shade varies relatively slowly can be sampled less frequently, hence more efficiently. Conversely, image areas of greater detail can be sampled more frequently, hence more accurately. Adaptive sampling is a way to put rendering effort where it will do the most good.

RiPixelVariance() is a more general and flexible way to specify sampling rate than **RiPixelSamples**(). For a given set of samples, the accuracy of the resulting pixel value can be statistically estimated; increasing the number of samples decreases this **variance** of the sample from the true value. The sole parameter of **RiPixelVariance**() dictates an acceptable level of variance. More samples are taken at a pixel until the variance is below the requisite threshold.

RiPixelVariance(variance)
    RtFloat variance;

RiPixelVariance() limits the acceptable variance in the output value of pixels. The *variance* parameter is expressed before quantization. For example, if pixel values are normally between 0 and 1, a variation of $1/255$ in the context of 8-bit quantization will mean that the pixel as output should not vary by more than one quantization level.

Since it is based on statistical methods of predicting the likely deviation of a pixel value, the sampling criterion of **RiPixelVariance**() is probabilistic. However, it is predictable in the sense that lowering the variance will improve the overall quality of a picture.

Exposure

After a single (color) value is derived at a pixel, it enters the second step of the pixel production pipeline, **exposure**, in which pixel values are passed through an arbitrary function that models the rendering system's "response" to incoming light.

Every sensor of light responds according to the amount of impacting light. This relationship is not always, or even usually, linear. Photographic film, for example, increases in density as a logarithmic function of the total light striking it. RenderMan supports such nonlinear encodings of color data in order to serve better the needs of both display technology and the human visual system.

Considering for a moment the display of an image, cathode-ray tube monitors are driven by applying a voltage to each of its red, green and blue electron guns. The intensity of the resulting colors is nonlinearly related to the applied voltage. In fact, the output intensity I approximates a power curve in input voltage V: $I=V^\gamma$, for some γ different for each type of monitor. Often a display has a lookup table accompanying its image memory that can be used to compensate for this characteristic. It is also possible to perform this compensation in the rendering stage, although that makes the resulting image more specific to the target display.

Perhaps the most compelling reason for nonlinear encoding concerns the discrimination capabilities of the human eye. In a linear encoding, the difference of brightness from one quantization level to the next is constant. But by the time the visual information on the surface of a monitor passes through the human visual system, the perceived difference between two levels of brightness is related less to their absolute difference than to their proportion. As a result, the perceived difference between intensity levels of 3 and 4 is far greater than that between 200 and 201. A nonlinear encoding of brightness data offers the opportunity to make the best use of the bits of output.

RiExposure(gain, gamma)
    RtFloat gain, gamma;

After a call to **RiExposure**(), every color component of every pixel is transformed as follows:

$$color_{output} = (color_{input}*gain)^{1/gamma}$$

gain and *gamma* must be positive. Each is 1.0 by default, meaning in essence that exposure mapping is turned off in the normal case.

Figure 9.3 shows input vs. output for *gamma* > 1. If the output is quantized into sixteen levels, as shown, then the quantization levels will be distributed as shown on the ordinate, clustered at the lower intensity levels. Nonlinear exposure is a relatively cheap way to improve the apparent color resolution of a display system.

Figure 9.4 demonstrates the effect of changing *gain* and *gamma*. Each column was rendered with identical *gain*, and each row with identical *gamma*. From left to right, the columns have *gain* of 0.5, 1.0 and 2.0. *gamma* goes from 0.5 on the top row to 1.0 in the middle and 2.0 on the bottom.

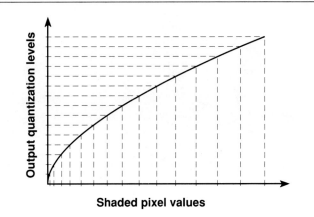

Figure 9.3 *Effect of quantizing pixel values after gamma-mapping*

Imaging

After exposure, the color components of a pixel are passed through an **imaging** process. This allows users to modify output pixel values in any way they choose.

RiImager(name, *parameterlist*)
    char *name;

The *name* passed to **RiImager**() refers to a shader written in the RenderMan Shading Language. *parameterlist* is a series of token-value pairs used to pass parameters to the shader.

The imager shader is an option, and so cannot be set after **Ri-WorldBegin**().

By writing an imaging shader and invoking it with **RiImager**(), a user has a chance to transform the colors of output before quantization. For example, if output is intended for color separations, an imaging shader might convert RGB coordinates into CMYK output, placing the cyan, magenta and yellow coordinates into the RGB components, and black into alpha. The user could also use an imager to implement a more sophisticated exposure mechanism than that provided by **RiExposure**().

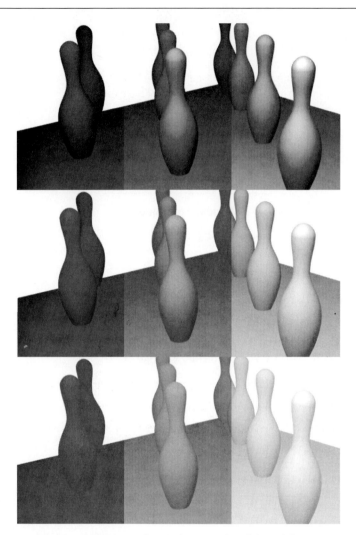

Figure 9.4 *Results of **RiExposure**(): gain* increases from left to right, gamma *from top to bottom*

Quantization

For realistic imagery, pixel values may be calculated at high resolution, often up to 32 or 64 bits per channel. Only rarely do they need to be stored with such precision, especially since few displays can present data with more than 10 bits of color resolution per channel. The format of the data also matters, since even fewer displays handle anything but integer values.

As a result, almost all images are stored using low-resolution fixed-point numbers to represent the color values at each pixel. There are two basic aspects of mapping from floating-point values to integer format: what range of floating-point values maps to what range of integer values, and how the errors associated with this mapping can be reduced.

RiQuantize(type, one, min, max, ditheramplitude)
    RtToken type;
    RtInt one, min, max;
    RtFloat ditheramplitude;

RiQuantize() is used to specify quantization and dithering. It may be called independently for color values and depth values. *type* should be the token "rgba" (RI_RGBA) for the former and "z" (RI_Z) for the latter.

When quantization is turned on, the floating-point values at each pixel are assumed to lie in the range [0,1]. Each channel value is multiplied by *one*, and the resulting integers are **clamped** to the range [*min,max*]. In other words, if *fvalue* is the computed value of a channel, then the corresponding quantized value is

$$ivalue = fvalue*one$$

This maps the range [0,1] into the range [0,*one*]. If *ivalue<min*, then clamping raises *ivalue* to *min*; if *ivalue>max*, then it is lowered to *max*.

ditheramplitude can be used to introduce a little randomness into the pixel value before quantization. If *random()* is a function generating a random number between −1 and 1, then

$$ivalue = fvalue*one + ditheramplitude*random()$$

ivalue is then clamped as before.

ditheramplitude is 0.5 by default, which randomly perturbs the output by one quantization level up or down.

For example, the call

> **RiQuantize**(RI_RGB, 255.0, 0, 255, 0.0);

quantizes the red, green and blue channels of an image without dithering. It maps the range [0,1] into the integer range [0, 255], suitable for storage at eight bits per channel. If, instead, the channels were calculated in the range [0,255], then

> **RiQuantize**(RI_RGB, 1.0, 0, 255, 0.5);

would provide the proper quantization, and also dither the pixel values before quantization.

Dithering and false contours

The contrast (ratio of intensities) between adjacent fixed-point values is very high for values near zero. Very dark, slowly-varying surfaces may have large adjacent regions with high contrast between them, which may be seen as **false contours** in the image (see Figure 9.5). This is a problem largely because the human visual system emphasizes contrast, and it is especially troublesome for quantization to a fixed-point range with low resolution. The nonlinear encoding provided by **Ri-Exposure**() can help, but it is no panacea.

One solution to the contouring problem is to **dither** pixel values by adding a random amount of noise before quantization. A proper dither will thus perturb the resulting fixed-point value by a step up or down at random. While this doesn't mean much at the level of a single pixel, adjacent *groups* of pixels will vary in their *average* intensity according to their mean floating-point value. This group average has considerably more resolution than the color of a single pixel.

This style of dithering can be invoked by setting the *ditheramplitude* parameter of **RiQuantize**() to a nonzero value (0 turns dithering off). Typically the noise range should randomly round the pixel value up or down to the next level. This is accomplished by using a *ditheramplitude* value of 0.5, as in the example above.

We have now covered all RenderMan routines that address the pixel production process. Now we can step back and present two large-scale quality issues: the fact that physical cameras have a limited ability to resolve detail in space, and

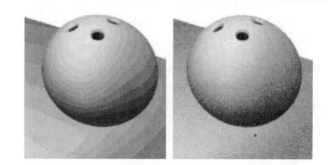

Figure 9.5 *False contours (left); contouring reduced by dithering (right)*

in time. These artifacts are introduced into synthetic images via depth-of-field calculations and motion-blur effects.

Depth of Field

Cameras that focus light through a finite-sized aperture render objects sharply over only a limited range of distances. The sharpness of an object in a photograph depends on its distance relative to that range. The extent of the range of acceptable focus is related to the diameter of the lens opening, or aperture: the smaller the opening, the wider this **depth of field**. The uniformly perfect focus of most computer images may be enviable to photographers, but it does eliminate an esthetic tool and a cue for depth perception.

A photographer sets the optical system of a camera to a **focal distance** at which objects appear sharpest. The depth of field is then determined by 1) the ratio of the **focal length** to the size of the aperture admitting light into the camera (the **f-stop**), and 2) the focal distance.

RiDepthOfField(fstop, focallength, focaldistance)
  RtFloat fstop, focallength, focaldistance;

The parameter *focaldistance* to **RiDepthOfField**() gives the distance at which surfaces appear in focus. *focallength* declares the focal length of the lens being used. *fstop* declares the f-stop to which the lens is set. An *fstop* of RI_INFINITY, the default, signifies a pinhole camera rendering objects equally well-focused everywhere in the world, turning depth of field off.

In photography, the focal length of a lens is commonly expressed in millimeters, but the units used in *focallength* are unimportant; they need only be the same as the units used for *focaldistance*.

Figure 9.6 shows the effect of varying the f-stop of an image. The three panels were generated with identical data; the only variation was the f-stop, which was *f*1.4, *f*8, and *f*22 at the top, middle, and bottom, respectively.

Motion Blur

A camera that could record a scene with perfect sharpness, no matter how quickly objects or the camera moved might seem like an enviable technical achievement. However, a *series* of perfectly sharp images, when presented in rapid sequence as an animation, creates a strobing effect, destroying the sense of smooth motion. Objects needn't be blindingly fast to suffer from this **temporal aliasing**: the eye *expects* to see a loss of detail in moving objects. Even in a single image, a little ''streaking'' of a moving object can give a sense of dynamics.

Plate 24 shows a frame from the animated film *Luxo Jr. in "Light Entertainment."* Part of the satisfying sense of physical realism in that film arises from the motion blur used for even the smallest movements.

Specifying motion blur

A photograph may appear blurry because objects, lights or the camera move while the shutter is open. For a synthetic scene, this movement is set out explicitly by 1) defining the scene's geometry at a series of moments in time, and 2) specifying the time period the shutter is open. Each of the geometry definitions represents a **temporal sample** of the changing scene configuration at one moment. For times in between, the parameters of the objects in the scene are interpolated between adjacent sample moments. The nature of the interpolation (linear, cubic, etc.) is left up to the implementation.

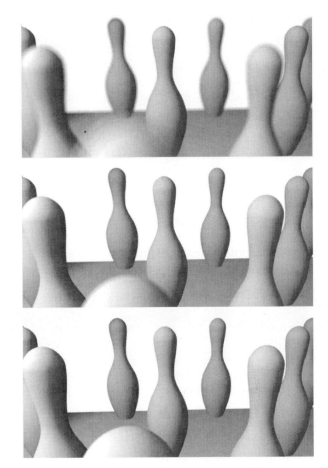

Figure 9.6 *Effect of f-stop on depth of field. Focal length and distance were fixed, but f-stop was varied from 1.4 at top to 8 in the middle to 22 at bottom.*

Moving the scene

There are two basic approaches to describing changes in a scene over time. The first would involve a complete description of the entire scene at each sample moment; i.e., "here's the scene at time t_1; here it is at t_2; here's..." Presumably all the values of the scene (positions, light colors, etc.) that differed from one time to another would be interpolated.

RenderMan takes a different approach. Rather than move an entire *scene* between times, the scene is described once, but the moving objects and/or transformations are described several times, with their *parameters* changing from one time to the next. For example, a geometric translation can be declared at time t_1 and time t_2. In between those two times, any object affected by that translation will move smoothly between the two positions resulting from the translations at the extremes.

Using this parameter interpolation technique, the geometry of objects themselves may also vary over time. For example, if a polygon command is declared at two different times, the two versions are matched vertex for vertex, so that the polygon's shape, as well as its motion, may change. A sphere can have one radius, top, bottom and sweep angle at one time and another set of parameter values at another time. In between times, it will interpolate smoothly between the extremes. The latter change would be difficult or impossible to describe correctly using interpolation for an entire scene because potentially complex motion information would be lost.

The time-varying parameter approach has three advantages. First, it is only necessary to describe those parts of the scene that actually change. Second, each part can be sampled differently. For example, an object moving along a tight curve may need many samples to correctly approximate its motion. Another object in the same scene might be moving along a straight line, requiring only two samples. Third, motion can be interpolated in the semantically appropriate way: the interpolated rotation of a point can be very different from the endpoints of the rotation, interpolated.

Declaring motion

The basic method for moving objects or commands is simple: they are declared exactly as usual, with the same RenderMan procedure calls. Each routine to be moved is replaced by a *series* of calls to the same routine, with any time-varying parameters changing from one call to the next. This series of procedure calls is identified as a series of time samples, rather than independent static calls, by bracketing this **motion block** with calls to **RiMotionBegin**() and **RiMotionEnd**(). The former routine also spells out the time associated with each procedure call in the block.

RiMotionBegin(N, time1, ..., timeN)
    RtInt N;
    RtFloat time1, ..., timeN;
RiMotionEnd( )

A RenderMan Interface procedure is sampled over a sequence of N times by calling **RiMotionBegin**(), calling the procedure exactly N times, and finishing with **RiMotionEnd**(). **RiMotionBegin**() declares N, the number of samples, and the time of each sample. The first is assumed to take place at *time1*, the second at *time2*, etc. The time values *time1...timeN* must increase from one to the next. If an implementation does not support motion blur, then the sample at *time1* is used.

Within the motion block there should be exactly N calls of exactly one RenderMan procedure. Moving three routines, even over the same interval, requires three motion blocks.

Examples

If a transformation is given different values at different times, all objects affected by that transformation will move over time. For example:

```
RiTransformBegin();

    RiMotionBegin( 2, 0.0, 1.0 );
        RiRotate( 10.0, 1.0, 0.0, 0.0 );
        RiRotate( 20.0, 1.0, 0.0, 0.0 );
    RiMotionEnd( );

    RiSphere( 1.0, -.7, .7, 270.0, RI_NULL );

RiTransformEnd();
```

The clipped sphere will be rotated by ten degrees about the x axis at *time1*, and rotated twenty degrees at *time2*. In between times, the amount of rotation will vary smoothly between ten and twenty degrees.

The motion block above is similar to a single rotate command. Any RenderMan commands could appear between **RiMotionEnd**() and **RiTransformEnd**(), including object descriptions, light sources, environment modifications and transformations. Any object affected by the current transformation would be moved in time.

Moving objects

Object declarations are moved in a similar way:

```
RiTransformBegin();

    RiRotate( 10.0, 1.0, 0.0, 0.0 );

    RiMotionBegin( 2, 0.0, 1.0 );
        RiSphere( 1.0, -.7, .7, 270.0, RI_NULL );
        RiSphere( 1.0, 1.0, 1.0, 360.0, RI_NULL );
    RiMotionEnd( );

RiTransformEnd();
```

This time it is the definition of the sphere that moves. Between time 0.0 and time 1.0, the sphere is closed at the top and bottom, and its sweep is completed.

Opening and closing the shutter

RiMotionBegin() and **RiMotionEnd**() define the time-varying behavior of a scene. The procedure calls in a motion block define the *exact* configuration of the scene at *any* time within the intervals. Only one other piece of information is required: the interval of time over which the shutter is open.

RiShutter(opentime, closetime)
    RtFloat opentime, closetime;

RiShutter() declares when the virtual shutter opens and when it closes. *opentime* and *closetime* can be any times at all, as long as *opentime* ≤ *closetime*. If *opentime* = *closetime*, the scene is defined for the fixed configuration at $t = opentime$, and no motion blur is done at all.

The open shutter interval is applied to an image as a whole. Therefore it must be specified before **RiWorldBegin**().

The shutter times should resemble the times declared for the moving primitives. If *opentime* < $time_1$ or *closetime* > $time_N$ for some primitive's $time_1$ and $time_N$, no guarantee is made as to the primitive's position.

What can move

Not all procedures can appear within a motion block. For example, since options are fixed for an entire image, it makes no sense to blur them. The set of commands allowed inside a motion block are listed in Table 9.1 below. In general, any floating-point parameter values of geometry or attributes may change.

Transformations	Geometry	Shading
RiTransform()	RiBound()	RiColor()
RiConcatTransform()	RiDetail()	RiOpacity()
RiPerspective()		
RiDisplacement()	RiSphere()	RiLightSource()
RiDeformation()	RiCone()	RiAreaLightSource()
	RiCylinder()	RiSurface()
RiTranslate()	RiHyperboloid()	RiInterior()
RiRotate()	RiParaboloid()	RiExterior()
RiScale()	RiDisk()	RiAtmosphere()
RiSkew()	RiTorus()	
	RiPolygon()	
	RiGeneralPolygon()	
	RiPointsPolygons()	
	RiPointsGeneralPolygons()	
	RiPatch()	
	RiPatchMesh()	
	RiNuPatch()	

Table 9.1 *Time-variable RenderMan Procedures*

Further Research

The sampling process and filtering theory involve some of the most elegant mathematics around. Frank Crow [CROW77] first pointed out the aliasing problem in synthetic imagery. Two recent articles that treat the problem in the context of computer graphics are [DIPPE85] and [COOK85]. An excellent text encompassing concepts of analog and digital signal processing is [OPPEN75]. Finally, a full treatment is [PRATT78].

On the lighter side, the credibility added by good motion blur, and the degradation resulting from nonexistent motion blur, can be seen in the stop-motion animation of popular films.

CHAPTER 10

Procedural Models and Level of Detail

The surface types set out in chapters 4, 5 and 6 can be used to represent a wide variety of objects. However, a given object may lend itself to many valid representations varying from the crudest to the most detailed. For example, a curved surface can be approximated using a number of polygons. The *number* of polygons used for a given surface affects both the amount of data the renderer must deal with and the quality of the resulting image. If the polygons approximating a curved surface are only about a pixel in size, then the approximation may be indistinguishable from the real thing. At the other extreme, a bicubic patch can be approximated very crudely by the nine bilinear quadrilaterals defined by its control hull.

This trade-off between quality and complexity is not static, but depends in part on the viewing parameters of an image. Even approximating a parametric surface with its control hull may be appropriate if the surface occupies only a few pixels. Conversely, it can be wasteful to use detail that gets lost between the pixels. We already saw in Chapter 9 that renderers often make this trade-off in splitting curved surfaces into polygons for rendering, subject to some quality criterion.

There is an analogous problem with models as a whole. For example, does one depict a tree trunk with a cylinder, or with an elaborate curved surface? If the tree is so small in the output image that the two are indistinguishable, the answer is obvious.

With viewing functionality residing on the other side of the interface, how can an application determine the best way to approximate its models with RenderMan primitives? A more intimate relationship must be established between the software defining a scene and the renderer producing the image.

A model's definition should vary according to its size as measured in pixels. The RenderMan Interface supports two different means to this end. The first, discussed in the next section, allows the application to specify several alternative representations for a model and let the renderer choose between them. The model chosen in a particular rendering depends on the on-screen size of the object (its **level of detail**), with a smooth transition between alternatives.

The second method is more general, hence more flexible, but also more involved for the application. It defines an object, not as a data structure containing geometric coordinates, but as a *procedure* invoked by the renderer. This procedure then declares the geometric data according to image information the renderer passes to it. This gives the application an opportunity to define its objects in the context of rendering. These **procedural models** are covered in the second section of this chapter.

Level of Detail Calculations and Models

There is an important trade-off in image synthesis between the complexity that can provide visual interest, and the cost of rendering complex objects. Many applications work well with a simple representation for a model if it is far away, but require a more complex version when it looms larger. Rather than always forcing the application to pay for rendering the most complex available representation, RenderMan allows a set of alternatives to be specified, then chooses the appropriate one based on its apparent size in the image. Varying the complexity of a model according to its apparent size is a key strategy for providing the right level of visual interest at reasonable cost.

Support for level of detail calculations is an optional capability in the RenderMan Interface. Renderers that do not support it will simply ignore the information discussed below and always draw the most complicated model.

Level of detail defined

The apparent size of an object depends on several variables: the actual size of the object, its distance from the camera, the camera's field of view, and the resolution of the output image. Fortunately their net effect can be expressed as a single factor, the number of pixels covered by the object in the image. We call this area in raster space the object's **level of detail**.

Calculating level of detail

All the imaging parameters that go into determining the level of detail of an object are fixed by the time it is defined, but the object's size must be declared to the interface.

Every object occupies a definite range [*xmin...xmax*] along the *x* axis, another range in *y*, and a third in *z*. The six orthogonal planes *x=xmin*, *x=xmax*, *y=ymin*, *y=ymax*, *z=zmin*, *z=zmax* intersect to define a three-dimensional rectangular box barely enclosing the object. For simplicity, the level of detail calculation for an object uses this **bounding box**: the box is projected onto the image plane, where the level of detail is calculated as the on-screen area of its bounding box.

The level of detail of the bounding box is at least as large as, and usually larger than that of the object itself, especially for very diagonal, elongated objects. But the bounding box has the virtue of simplicity.

Bounding box declaration

The bounding box for an object is declared explicitly.

RiDetail(bound)
   RtBound bound;

RiDetail() declares a bounding box by giving the minimum and maximum *x*, *y* and *z* coordinates in *bound* in the order [*xmin*, *xmax*, *ymin*, *ymax*, *zmin*, *zmax*]. All points in *bound* should be in object coordinates. The interface calculates the level of detail of that bounding box and uses it to set the **current level of detail**. The larger the bounding box, the higher the level of detail. That value is an attribute in the graphics state, so it applies to all subsequent objects declared within the same block.

Level of detail metric

A high level of detail demands a more detailed object than a lower level, but this is still just a relative measure. Some renderings of the same scene may require more detail than others. The interface allows the application to boost or diminish the *relative* importance of pixel area by declaring that all level-of-detail values should be scaled by a certain amount. This means that the rendered quality of an entire image can be controlled by a single parameter.

RiRelativeDetail(relativedetail)
    RtFloat relativedetail;

RiRelativeDetail() causes all level-of-detail values to be multiplied by the factor *relativedetail*. A value greater than 1 causes models employing level-of-detail calculations to be rendered in greater detail; if it is less than 1, they are generally rendered more crudely.

The relative level of detail is an option, so it must be declared before **RiWorldBegin**(), and it applies to an image as a whole. It cannot be adjusted for individual objects.

Using level of detail

An application controls the complexity of a model by presenting a number of **alternative representations** for it, associating each with a range of level-of-detail values. The renderer chooses among the alternatives based on the current level of detail, as determined from the model's bounding box above.

Presumably the simpler alternatives will be assigned to the lower ranges of detail, when the model occupies a small area of the image. The more complex alternatives will be used at higher levels, when the model appears larger and more detail is required. Depending on the implementation, the system may either select one alternative to the exclusion of all others, or smoothly blend two alternatives.

Level of detail declaration

Each alternative is described as a series of surfaces and objects. Before presenting an alternative, its relevant range of detail is declared with **RiDetailRange()**.

RiDetailRange(offlow, onlow, onhigh, offhigh)
    RtFloat offlow, onlow, onhigh, offhigh;

RiLevelOfDetail() prefaces one alternative representation for a model, and declares four level-of-detail values that specify the importance of the alternative at four different levels of detail. The special value RI_INFINITY may be used for *onhigh* and/or *offhigh* to declare the most detailed alternative.

The model has importance 0 for levels of detail below *offlow* and above *offhigh*. It has importance 1 for levels between *onlow* and *onhigh*. In the range of level of detail from *offlow* to *onlow*, the importance increases from 0 to 1. From *onhigh* to *offhigh*, it decreases from 1 to 0.

Meaning of level of detail

Figure 10.1 should help to illustrate the meaning of these ranges. Essentially, **RiDetailRange()** says that the coming alternative should be used at levels of detail between *onlow* and *onhigh*. The alternative is less relevant in the "fuzzy ranges" between *offlow* and *onlow* and between *onhigh* and *offhigh*, and it is considered too fine for levels of detail below *offlow*, and too crude for levels higher than *offhigh*.

If the level of detail falls into the fuzzy range of two alternatives at once, as at level L between $model_{i-1}$ and $model_i$ in Figure 10.1, then the renderer has two alternatives:

- It can choose one of the two models, ignoring the other.

- It can "mix" the two models according to their importance. At level L, if $model_i$ has importance .3 and $model_{i-1}$

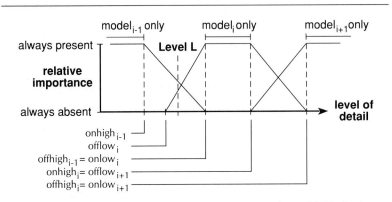

Figure 10.1 *Levels of detail for alternative representations of a model. The horizontal axis shows level of detail, and the vertical axis shows the relative importance of the alternative models at each level of detail.*

has importance .4, a renderer could present them in that proportion.

RenderMan does not dictate any one of these choices, or define "mix" in the last choice. Its purpose is only to specify how different models are associated with different levels of detail.

An example

Listing 10.1 shows a routine using level of detail. It uses a hypothetical routine, *Dome()*, which declares a geodesic dome, a polygonal approximation of a sphere of a given granularity. The higher the value of the parameter to *Dome()*, the more polygons go into the approximation. The routine *Domes()* declares several alternative domes, each with its own level-of-detail range.

Domes() first declares the bounding box of the dome, which we know from the hypothetical definition of *Dome()* to be a unit cube. The level of detail of the dome is a function of the unit cube in image space as it is projected onto the image.

```
/*
 * Domes(): render a geodesic dome divided according to level of detail.
 */
```

```
Domes()
{
    RtBound bound;
    bound[0] = bound[2] = bound[4] = -1.0;
    bound[1] = bound[3] = bound[5] =  1.0;

    RiAttributeBegin();        /* Push attributes to save level of detail */
        RiDetail( bound );
        RiDetailRange( 0.0, 0.0, 10.0, 20.0 );
            Dome(4);
        RiDetailRange( 10.0, 20.0, 40.0, 80.0 );
            Dome(8);
        RiDetailRange( 40.0, 80.0, 160.0, 320.0 );
            Dome(16);
        RiDetailRange( 160.0, 320.0, RI_INFINITY, RI_INFINITY );
            Dome(32);
    RiAttributeEnd();
}
```

Listing 10.1 *Routine specifying geodesic domes with different granularities*

Smooth transition between alternatives

The fuzzy ranges of alternatives can be used to provide a smooth transition from one alternative to another as a scene changes during an animation. If the model looms larger as a sequence proceeds, then it makes sense to switch gradually from one representation to another one with a higher level of detail. Declaring the various alternatives with overlapping fuzzy ranges can ensure that result if the renderer supports this kind of continuous segue.

Such a transition works best in the situation of $model_i$ and $model_{i+1}$ in Figure 10.1. As level of detail increases, $model_i$ begins to decline in importance just as $model_{i+1}$ becomes relevant, and the former switches off just as the latter is switching full on. In general, for the ith and $(i+1)$th alternatives, it is a good idea to have

$$offlow_{i+1} = onhigh_i,$$

and

$$onlow_{i+1} = offhigh_i.$$

RenderMan guarantees the level of detail facility to work consistently only when the level of importance of all alternatives sums to 1 at every level of detail. The condition above meets this criterion if, for N alternatives,

$$onlow_1 = 0$$

and

$$onhigh_N = RI\_INFINITY.$$

This property, which is obeyed in *Domes()*, provides a well-defined choice under all selection schemes. If a model's level of detail is such that the total importance is not 1, then the result is undefined.

A simple special effect

A good set of alternative representations, together with the relative level-of-detail facility, can produce an intriguing special effect even at a fixed absolute level of detail. Listing 10.2 shows a program fragment for fading from one representation to another. The geodesic dome from Listing 10.1 is viewed at the same size in every frame, but the relative level of detail increases from frame to frame. In the first frame, it is very small and the dome is crude, but in the last frame the relative level of detail is 1, and the dome is seen in its full complexity.

```
/*
 * The following program fragment generates a series of frames
 * dissolving from a crude geodesic dome to a more detailed one
 * of the same size.
 */
        ... /* Statements here set up the viewing transform for the dome */
        for( i = 1; i <= NFRAMES; i++ ) {
                ... /* Statements here initialize a new image */
            RiFrameBegin(i);
                RiRelativeDetail( ((float)i)/NFRAMES );
                RiWorldBegin();
                    Domes();
                RiWorldEnd();
            RiFrameEnd();
        }
```

Listing 10.2 *Program to dissolve a crude model into a refined one*

Procedural Models

A **procedural model** declares a model not as a series of surfaces like polygons and quadrics, but as a *procedure* that is called to define the model during rendering. The procedure is usually called when the portion of the image then being rendered includes the on-screen projection of the model's bounding box. Using a procedural model can save on the cost of storing the model, as well as give the procedure an opportunity to generate the model with a complexity appropriate to the situation. Procedural models generally have a much smaller external representation than the data that is ultimately rendered. This **data amplification** of procedural models can save a great deal of storage space, and also makes them much easier for a user to manipulate.

Declaring a procedural model

A procedural model is passed to the interface as four elements: the data the procedure will use, a bounding box for the model, a pointer to a procedure for the interface to call to refine the model (the **refinement procedure**), and a second procedure pointer for disposing of the data. The refinement procedure uses the data in further describing the model. The renderer may use the bounding box to calculate the primitive's level of detail and to determine when to call the refinement procedure.

RiProcedural(data, bound, refineproc, freeproc)
    RtPointer data;
    RtBound bound;
    RtFunc refineproc, freeproc;

RiProcedural() declares a single procedural model. *data* is a pointer to a block of data. *bound* is the bounding box of the model in object space. *refineproc*() is the refinement procedure called to express the model using RenderMan function calls; it may even define the model as a series of other procedural models. *freeproc*() is a function called when the data is no longer needed.

The data to which *data* points remains owned by the application. The renderer is forbidden to do anything with it except use it as a parameter to *refineproc*() or *freeproc*(). However, some renderers may recreate a procedural model several times by passing *refineproc*() that same pointer. Consequently, neither *refineproc*() nor the application should modify it in a way that changes the resulting model. It is passed once, at most, to *freeproc*(). which is the application's only opportunity to dispose of the associated data. *Only freeproc*() *is allowed to free up the data.*

bound must completely enclose the model because it represents a promise to the renderer that the model is confined to that region of object space. If the model touches a pixel then so must the *bound.*

The refinement procedure

The *refineproc*() procedure is called by the renderer when the model is needed for the rendering process. When *refineproc*() is called, the graphics state is the same as during the original call to **RiProcedural**(). Thus, any attributes extant when **RiProcedural**() was called will apply to any object created by *refineproc*().

Depending on the implementation, *refineproc*() may be called before **RiProcedural**() returns. The application should make sure that this does not affect the resulting model.

refineproc() is called as if it were declared thus:

```
refineproc( data, levelofdetail )
RtPointer data;
RtFloat levelofdetail;
```

data is the value passed to **RiProcedural**(), and *levelofdetail* is the level of detail of the model as determined from the bounding box originally passed to **RiProcedural**(). The graphics environment is restored to its state as of the original **RiProcedural**() call, except that the current level of detail is set to *levelofdetail*. If *levelofdetail* is RI_INFINITY, the model should be subdivided to the maximum possible extent. This is an important case to handle correctly, because if a renderer does not

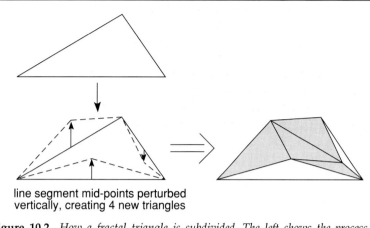

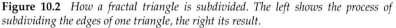

line segment mid-points perturbed
vertically, creating 4 new triangles

Figure 10.2 *How a fractal triangle is subdivided. The left shows the process of subdividing the edges of one triangle, the right its result.*

support procedural models it may simply call *refineproc()* once with *levelofdetail* set to RI_INFINITY.

A caveat

Unlike other pointers passed to the RenderMan Interface, no effort is made to copy or otherwise protect the data supplied by the *data* pointer. The pointer is simply passed back across the interface as a parameter to the model's *refineproc()*. The interface does nothing to affect the data except call *freeproc()*. However, the data is not protected from corruption by the application.

Example: a simple fractal generator

Listing 10.3 shows an example of a procedural model, a simple fractal generator. A triangle can be rendered as a fractal by recursive subdivision: each edge is bisected and the midpoint perturbed vertically by a random amount. The original triangle vertices and the three new vertices form four triangles. The process, shown in Figure 10.2, ends when the resulting triangles are sufficiently small, as judged by their level of detail.

```
/* Fractal(): procedural model for a fractal triangle.  If the triangle's level of
 *      detail is below a threshold, or the triangle has been subdivided more
 *      than a certain number of levels, it is presented directly as a
 *      triangle; otherwise it is divided into four smaller triangles
 */
#include <ri.h>
/* A fractal point is a location plus a random-number seed */
typedef struct fractalpoint {
        RtPoint location;
        int seed;
} FractalPoint;

/* A fractal triangle is three vertices and a level number used
 *      to limit subdivision */
typedef struct fractaltriangle {
        FractalPoint vertices[3];
        int level;
} FractalTriangle;

#define MOVEPT(src,dst) {dst[0]=src[0]; dst[1]=src[1]; dst[2]=src[2]; }

/* FractalDiv(): RenderMan refinement procedure for subdividing a fractal
 *      triangle. */
FractalDiv( data, levelofdetail )
RtPointer data;
RtFloat levelofdetail;
{
    FractalTriangle *pTriangle = (FractalTriangle *)data, *pChild;
    RtPoint vertices[3];
    if (levelofdetail<1.0 || pTriangle->level>MAXLEVELS ) {
            /* Small enough to be rendered */
            MOVEPT(pTriangle->vertices[0].location, vertices[0]);
            MOVEPT(pTriangle->vertices[1].location, vertices[1]);
            MOVEPT(pTriangle->vertices[2].location, vertices[2]);
            RiPolygon( 3, RI_P, (RtPointer) vertices, RI_NULL );
    } else      /* Too large; subdivide */
            TriangleSplit( pTriangle );
}

/* TriangleSplit(): subdivide a FractalTriangle, giving it an array of
 *      four dynamically-allocated children. */
TriangleSplit( pFT )
FractalTriangle *pFT;
{
    int childnum;
    RtBound bound;
    FractalTriangle *pChildren;

    pChildren = (FractalTriangle *)malloc( 4*sizeof(FractalTriangle) );
    /* Give each child a level number  */
    for(childnum = 0; childnum < 4; childnum++)
        pChildren[childnum].level = pFT->level+1;
```

```
        /* Give the first three children one vertex from the parent and one
         *     edge midpoint as vertices */
        for( childnum = 0; childnum < 3; childnum++ ) {
            pChildren[childnum].vertices[0] = pFT->vertices[childnum];
            EdgeSplit( &(pFT->vertices[childnum]),
                    &(pFT->vertices[(childnum+1)%3]),
                    &(pChildren[childnum].vertices[1]));
        }
        /* Give the fourth (inside) child vertices from the split edges, and give
         *     the other three children their third vertex. */
        for( childnum = 0; childnum < 3; childnum++ ) {
            pChildren[3].vertices[childnum] =
                pChildren[(childnum+1)%3].vertices[2] =
                    pChildren[childnum].vertices[1];
        }
        for( childnum = 0; childnum < 3; childnum++ ) {
            /* TriangleBound() computes the bounding box for a triangle */
            TriangleBound( pChildren, bound );
            RiProcedural( pChildren++, bound, FractalDiv, free );
        }
}

#define SEEDTODISPLACEMENT(seed) (seed/((double)(1<<31)))
double EdgeLen( );

/* EdgeSplit(): split an edge between two vertices to derive a third vertex */
EdgeSplit( pFP1, pFP2, pFPOut )
FractalPoint *pFP1, *pFP2, *pFPOut;
{
    double displacement =
        SEEDTODISPLACEMENT( (pFP1->seed + pFP2->seed)/2);
    srandom( (pFP1->seed + pFP2->seed)/2);
    pFPOut->seed = random();
    EdgeMidpt( pFP1->location, pFP2->location, pFPOut->location );
    pFPOut->location[2] += 0.25 * displacement *
                    EdgeLen( pFP1->location, pFP2->location );
}

/* EdgeMidpt(): return the midpoint of an edge */
EdgeMidpt( pt1, pt2, midPt )
RtPoint pt1, pt2, midPt;
{
    midPt[0] = (pt1[0]+pt2[0])/2;
    midPt[1] = (pt1[1]+pt2[1])/2;
    midPt[2] = (pt1[2]+pt2[2])/2;
}

/* EdgeLen(): return the Euclidean length of an edge */
double EdgeLen( pt1, pt2 )
RtPoint pt1, pt2;
{
    double xdel = pt2[0]-pt1[0],
           ydel = pt2[1]-pt1[1],
           zdel = pt2[2]-pt1[2];
```

```
        double len = sqrt( xdel*xdel + ydel*ydel + zdel*zdel );
        return( len );
}

/* TriangleBound(): calculate the fractal bounding box of a triangle as
 *       the union of the bounding boxes of its edges  */
TriangleBound( pFT, bound )
FractalTriangle *pFT;
RtBound bound;
{
    RtBound tmpBound;
    EdgeBound( pFT->vertices[0].location, pFT->vertices[1].location, bound );
    EdgeBound(  pFT->vertices[1].location,
                        pFT->vertices[2].location, tmpBound );
    BBoxUnion( bound, tmpBound, bound );
    EdgeBound( pFT->vertices[2].location,
                        pFT->vertices[0].location, tmpBound );
    BBoxUnion( bound, tmpBound, bound );
}

#define min(a,b) ((a)<(b)?(a):(b))
#define max(a,b) ((a)>(b)?(a):(b))
#define SPHEREBUMP 1.4

/* EdgeBound: calculate the fractal bounding box of an edge, with its y
 *       range expanded to allow for midpoint perturbation. */
EdgeBound( pt1, pt2, bound )
RtPoint pt1, pt2;
RtBound bound;
{
    double radius;
    RtPoint midpt;

    bound[0] = min(pt1[0], pt2[0]); bound[1] = max(pt1[0], pt2[0]);
    bound[2] = min(pt1[1], pt2[1]); bound[3] = max(pt1[1], pt2[1]);
    EdgeMidpt( pt1, pt2, midpt );
    radius = (EdgeLen(pt1, pt2)/2)*SPHEREBUMP;
    bound[4] = midpt[2] - radius; bound[5] = midpt[2] + radius;
}

/* BBoxUnion: set a bound to be the union of two other bounds */
BBoxUnion( bound1, bound2, ubound )
RtBound bound1, bound2, ubound;
{
    ubound[0] = min( bound1[0], bound2[0] );
    ubound[1] = max( bound1[1], bound2[1] );
    ubound[2] = min( bound1[2], bound2[2] );
    ubound[3] = max( bound1[3], bound2[3] );
    ubound[4] = min( bound1[4], bound2[4] );
    ubound[5] = max( bound1[5], bound2[5] );
}
```

Listing 10.3 *A procedural fractal generator*

Modus operandi of FractalDiv()

The data passed to *FractalDiv*() is a pointer to a triangle, an array of three points. If the level of detail of the triangle is below a threshold, the triangle is simply declared outright as a polygon. Otherwise, the triangle is divided into smaller triangles as follows: each edge of the triangle is bisected, and the y coordinate of the midpoint is perturbed by a random amount. The resulting perturbed midpoints and the existing vertices are used to form four smaller triangles, one formed from the three midpoints and the others from two original vertices and one midpoint each.

Data structures

FractalDiv() uses two data structures. A *FractalPoint* represents a triangle vertex. It consists of an **RtPoint** for the vertex location, plus a seed for random-number generation in subdivision. The tricky thing about fractals is ensuring that coinciding edges from two triangles that abut, are divided in exactly the same way. The only way to do that is to make sure they are both divided using the same random-number seed, so each vertex carries the seed for one of the edges it adjoins.

A *FractalTriangle* consists of three *FractalPoints* (its vertices) and a number indicating the level of subdivision this triangle represents. Level 0 is given to the original triangle declared to **RiProcedural**(), and it is increased by 1 in its children. The level number is used to limit the maximum extent of subdivision.

Bounding-box calculation

The only other interesting thing about this program is the method used to calculate the bounding box of an edge. Since the midpoint of the edge may potentially be perturbed above the upper vertex or below the lower one, the bounding box needs to be expanded in y. This is done here by calculating the edge's bounding circle in y, expanding it by the factor SPHERE-BUMP, then using that in the bounding box.

Figure 10.3 depicts the results of a maximal subdivision on a triangle. Properly colored, it effects a remarkable rendition of a tortilla chip.

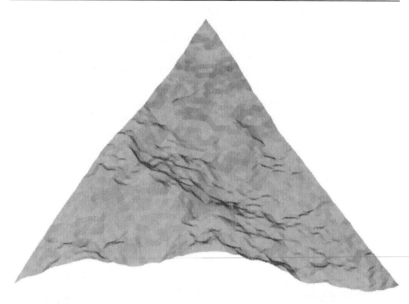

Figure 10.3 *A fully subdivided fractal triangle*

This fractal procedure is illustrative of procedural models, but it could be improved in a number of ways. First, the fraction of edge length that limits the perturbation could be made a parameter of the triangle. Second, to model more closely a real fractal, this fraction should be diminished at each subdivision by a factor that could also be made a parameter. Third, the bounding box calculation could be made tighter by an analysis of the maximum possible perturbation. Finally, the possibility exists here that, of two adjoining triangles with appropriate levels of detail, one could subdivide and the other not, yielding a crack. Fixing that problem would require the subdivision criterion to apply to edges independent of triangles.

Chapter 10: Procedural Models and Level of Detail

Lighting and Shading

This chapter discusses RenderMan's facilities for manipulating the *appearance* of objects: how to create and position light sources, and how to color surfaces with something other than a flat color. Thus begins a change in emphasis from geometric **shape** to that of **shading**: calculating the color of each surface as seen in the output image, as well as its shape and position. We will consider how shading works for a single point, a sample of the surface, under the assumption that an entire surface can be shaded as a number of sample points.

Before any point on a surface can be shaded, it must be placed in a scene and given surface properties like color and transparency. Light sources for illuminating the object must be specified in terms of their color, intensity and propagation. The position of the camera is also important, since many surfaces reflect light differently in different directions. Given all this information, the color of any surface point can be calculated.

RenderMan summarizes all those influences as a model of a specific physical process. This **shading pipeline** is illustrated in Figure 11.1. For each visible point on a surface, shading it involves the following:

- Illumination: determining the intensity and color of light, from various light sources and even other surfaces, that arrives at this point.

- Reflection/Transmission: simulating the interaction of the arriving light with the material making up the surface. The simulation calculates the intensity and color of

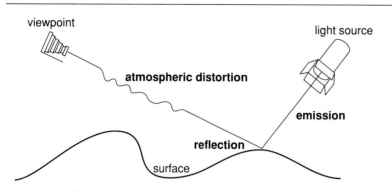

Figure 11.1 *Three basic parts of the shading process: emission at the light source, interaction of the light with the surface, and atmospheric effects between the surface and the viewpoint*

the light reflected from the surface toward the viewer or in a particular direction of interest.

- Atmospheric effects: modification of the light's color as it travels from the object to the viewer, perhaps by particles in the atmosphere.

Rendering systems generally implement these processes as one monolithic shading process that proffers a large array of parameters. The RenderMan Interface, on the other hand, defines each of the tasks above as a **shader**: there are **light source shaders**, **surface shaders**, **volume shaders**, and others. Each shader is a programmed procedure, written in the RenderMan Shading Language, which embodies one of those processes *individually*.

While the physical model is fixed, the shading calculation is controlled in part by the selection of a shader for each task. A variety of standard shaders is a part of the definition of the RenderMan Interface: there are point light sources, distant light sources and spotlights, for example. An application would invoke a point light source or a distant light source by an appropriate selection of shader. Even a single shader (for example, a distant light source) can be made to exhibit different characteristics by manipulating its parameters for things like color, intensity and direction.

Chapter 11: Lighting and Shading

The main purpose of this chapter is to introduce shader selection and control, and present the standard shaders. But the possibilities of the shading process are not limited to the standard choices shown here. Special-purpose light sources are easy to imagine, for example. There are also important trade-offs to be made between shading accuracy and computational expense. Much of the justification for a rendering structure that incorporates shaders is to allow users to define their own. This is an exciting area that is discussed in depth in the final four chapters of this book.

Using Shaders

A **shader** is a procedure called to compute a value or set of values needed during rendering. For example, a light source shader is called when the direction and color of light sent by the light source to a particular point on a surface is needed. The shader for a light source uses as input the direction toward the surface point, the light's color, direction, and so on.

Shaders as procedures

Shaders are procedures written in the RenderMan Shading Language, and they usually exist as autonomous modules invoked by a renderer at runtime. The routine that adds a light source to a scene is just a directive to access a named shader.

Shader instances

One important distinction between shaders and normal procedures is that there are commonly several "flavors," or **instances**, of a given shader in use at once. Instances of a single shader vary not in functionality but in their parameters. In this respect, shaders resemble classes in an object-oriented programming paradigm, with instances corresponding to objects. For example, there may be several point light sources in a scene (several instances of the "pointlight" shader), each with a different color, intensity and position. Similarly, while a given surface is always shaded by the same surface shader, different surfaces may use distinct instances of the same shader just as easily as they could use different shaders altogether.

The shader used for a given shading task may be an attribute (part of the graphics environment just like surface color) or an option, depending on its type. There is a **current instance** of a surface shader that is attached to each object as it is declared, a current atmosphere volume shader, and so on. For each type of shader (light source, surface, atmosphere, etc.) there is a RenderMan routine to declare its current instance.

The information distinguishing one instance from another takes the form of procedure parameters known as **instance variables**. Values are bound to the instance variables of a shader when the shader is entered into the graphics environment. They are passed to the interface routine declaring the shader in a *parameterlist* of token-value pairs: **RiLightSource**(), for example, adds a light source shader, taking the color, intensity and position of the light source in its *parameterlist*. These assign values to the instance variables of the shader. Assignment to instance variables is optional; default values for each unassigned instance variable are provided by the shader.

It may be useful to think of a shader instance as an object bundling the functionality of the shading procedure with values for the instance variables used by the procedure.

Uniform vs. varying instance variables

Instance variables are usually **uniform**: every time the shader is invoked by the renderer, they have the value that was given them when the shader was instanced. However, there is an alternative: the value of a **varying** instance variable can change systematically. Varying instance variables are most commonly used for interpolated surface parameters. If the *parameterlist* of a geometric primitive declaration includes a vertex variable with the same name as an instance variable of the current surface shader, then that is used for the instance variable. The value is interpolated to each point on the surface, and the shader will have the interpolated value when it is called. For example, a visualization process might bind a temperature value, *temp*, to the vertices of a polygon; if its surface shader uses a *temp* instance variable, it will receive the interpolated temperature at interior points.

This ability to interpolate arbitrary parameters is a powerful feature of RenderMan. It allows the information influencing the appearance of an object to be completely unconstrained.

Chapter 11: Lighting and Shading

Environment variables used by shaders

In addition to their instance variables, shaders may use certain elements of the graphics environment. In Chapter 2, we first encountered the RenderMan procedure for setting the reflectiveness of the surface as a color.

RiColor(Cs)
    RtColor Cs;

RiColor() replaces the current surface color in the graphics environment with the new color *Cs*. The current color is an attribute of the graphics environment, saved and restored like any other.

If a surface color "Cs" (RI_CS) is declared in the *parameterlist* of a geometric primitive, it overrides that declared with **RiColor**(), but only for that particular primitive.

When a surface is declared, it is assigned the current color in the graphics environment. Shaders generally use the surface color to compute the color of light reflecting from the surface toward the eye. They may also use the current opacity.

RiOpacity(Os)
    RtColor Os ;

RiOpacity() changes the current surface opacity in the graphics environment. *Os* is a color giving the proportion of each color channel that the surface absorbs in passing light through it. A completely transparent surface has opacity 0 in all channels, a completely opaque surface opacity 1. A colored filter would have different values in each channel.

Both color and opacity may be made uniform (constant over a surface), by using the above routines, or varying (bound to vertices and interpolated), by use of vertex variables. This is a special case, provided because surface color is a particularly important attribute. In general, the instance variables of a shader are declared to be *either* uniform *or* varying.

Shading attributes

We mentioned earlier that a surface is shaded by calculating its appearance at a number of points and using those values for other points. If this frequency of shading (the **shading rate**) is large compared to the number of pixels touched by the surface (and uniformly distributed across the surface), the resulting image will be able to depict rapid changes in appearance across the surface. On the other hand, a surface with a smooth, slowly changing shade may be perfectly well rendered with far less frequent shading. In either case, an application might use relatively infrequent shading in the early stages of developing an image ("draft mode") and more frequent shading for final rendering. In neither case can the renderer determine *a priori* how rapid a shading rate is "good enough."

The shading rate sounds very reminiscent of the sampling rate discussed in the last chapter, but RenderMan assumes that the frequency with which the *shade* of a surface is calculated is independent of sampling rate. The latter might be more frequent because the configuration of surfaces in a scene can easily change much more rapidly than the color of any one surface, or vice versa. The shading rate concerns how frequently a given surface is shaded. The sampling rate addresses the sampling of the scene as a whole. The two are not necessarily related.

RenderMan allows control over shading rate in two ways. First, it may be declared as an area (measured in pixels) per sample. Second, the application may determine whether the shade between samples is interpolated or not.

RiShadingRate(size)
    RtFloat size;

RiShadingRate() controls the frequency of shading a surface. *size* is specified as an area in pixels: if *size* is 1, a surface is shaded about once per pixel. Large values of *size* cause cruder but faster shading.

The shading rate is an attribute of the graphics environment. It can vary for each surface, and is saved and restored with the rest of the graphics environment.

The ability to vary the shading rate, intelligently used, can be a powerful tool for optimizing the trade-off between appearance and rendering speed.

Shading interpolation

The shading rate determines how frequently the appearance of a surface is fully calculated. The next routine determines how to depict other points on the surface in terms of nearby samples.

RiShadingInterpolation(type)
    RtToken type;

type should be either "constant" (RI_CONSTANT) or "smooth" (RI_SMOOTH). If the former, points on the surface between samples take the shade of the nearest calculated sample. If the latter, other points are interpolated from neighboring samples so that the appearance varies smoothly.

Constant shading is most useful when the shading rate is on the order of a pixel (and the in-between points are not resolved), when a surface changes relatively little from point to point, or when relatively coarse shading is "good enough." Smooth shading is more appropriate when a large shading rate causes abrupt transitions between samples that can be seen in the output image.

So-called Gouraud shading is a special case of sampling and interpolation: the surface shade is calculated at polygon vertices and interpolated for points in the interior.

When the shading rate is set to a value larger than any polygon and the type of shading interpolation is "smooth", Gouraud shading results. The shade is calculated for polygons at their vertices and smoothly interpolated across their interiors.

A special kind of shading

A very special-purpose option for shading suppresses the entire shading process. In motion-picture work, it is often useful to use objects to describe holes in an output image so the image can later be merged with other information. An object used this way is said to function as a **matte object** (a three-dimensional equivalent of what is commonly called a **hold-out matte**). RenderMan allows an object to be used as a matte object by calling **RiMatte()**.

RiMatte( )

RiMatte() causes each subsequent object to act as a matte object, i.e., to be rendered without shading but with objects behind them hidden. The areas where a matte object appear in an image are rendered black and transparent, regardless of what lies behind it. **RiMatte()** controls an attribute in the graphics state, so its effect is cancelled the next time the state is restored.

Light Source Shaders

The first class of shaders are the light source shaders, which calculate the intensity and color of light sent by the light source to a point on a surface. Figure 11.2 shows the basic idea.

RtLightHandle RiLightSource(name, *parameterlist* **)**
    char *name;

RiLightSource() adds a new light to a scene by creating an instance of the shader identified by *name*. The standard light source shaders defined under the RenderMan Interface are described below. *parameterlist* is a series of token-value pairs giving the instance variables of the shader. The relevant token-value pairs for each standard shader are listed with it. Any instance variables declared in *parameterlist* but not used by the shader are ignored. The value returned by **RiLightSource()** is a handle that may be used later to turn the light on and off. Lights are on when they are created.

There is no defined limit on the number of light sources, but individual implementations may have their own limitations.

Light source shaders are the only shaders that may have multiple instances available at the same time. That is, when a light source is instanced by **RiLightSource()**, it does not replace

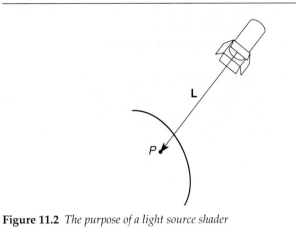

Figure 11.2 *The purpose of a light source shader*

any existing light source, but is added to the light list. Once a light source is created, it remains defined until the end of the enclosing frame or world block. That is, if a light source is created before **RiWorldBegin**(), it still exists after the corresponding **RiWorldEnd**(), and similarly for **RiFrameBegin**() and **RiFrameEnd**(). This mechanism allows exactly the right set of light sources to persist from frame to frame of an animation, for example.

Switching a light on

Since light sources remain once they are created, RenderMan provides the ability to turn them on and off individually. Surfaces are illuminated by each light source that is on when they are created.

RiIlluminate(light, onoff)
    RtLightHandle light;
    RtBoolean onoff;

RiIlluminate() turns a light on or off. *light* is a light source handle as returned by **RiLightSource**(). If *onoff* is RI_TRUE, the light source is turned on; if RI_FALSE, the light is switched off. Light sources are on by default.

The state of each light source is part of the graphics environment. Therefore, restoring the graphics state can turn lights on or off without a call to **RiIlluminate**().

The *list* of light sources is maintained outside of the graphics state. The *state* of each light, on the other hand, is part of the graphics state. Conceptually, a light is off before it is created. As a result, restoring an environment that was saved before a light source was created will not destroy the light source, but only turn it off. Therefore, *exactly the same set of lights is on after an attribute block as before it*. Other sources created inside the block may be turned on.

Predefined light sources

The set of light source shaders predefined by the RenderMan Interface is explained below. They are available regardless of whether the implementation supports the RenderMan Shading Language. Figure 11.3 demonstrates them in action; Listing 11.1 gives the program used to produce those four images.

Default light source

Since light sources can only be added to the scene, not deleted, *there is no default light source.* The examples of earlier chapters either declared a light source explicitly, or used a constant surface shader, which requires no light source.

Ambient

```
RiLightSource( "ambientlight",
                "intensity", intensity,
                "lightcolor", color,
                RI_NULL)
    RtFloat *intensity;
    RtColor color;
```

An **ambient light source** distributes light uniformly throughout space in all directions. Therefore it throws the same light on every surface regardless of the surface's position or orientation. Most scenes include a small ambient light source to prevent any surface from being completely unilluminated.

Chapter 11: Lighting and Shading

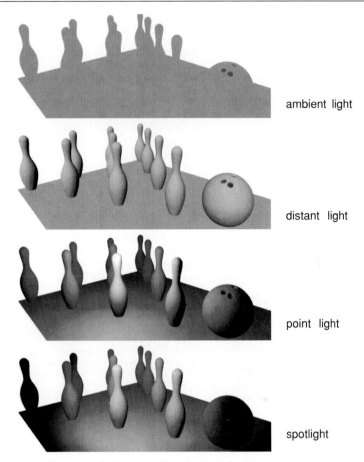

ambient light

distant light

point light

spotlight

Figure 11.3 *Four basic light sources illuminating a basic scene*

The declaration of an ambient light source may optionally include the *intensity* and *color* of the source. If not supplied, the *intensity* is set to 1 and the *color* to maximum white (1 in all components).

Distant light

RiLightSource("distantlight",
        "intensity", intensity,
        "lightcolor", color,
        "from", from,
        "to", to, RI_NULL)

```
RtPoint from, to;
RtFloat intensity, conedeltaangle, coneangle;
from[0] = ...;        from[1] = ...;        from[2] = ...;
to[0] = ...;          to[1] = ...;          to[2] = ...;
intensity = ...;
RiFrameBegin(1);
    RiLightSource("ambientlight",
            (RtToken)"intensity",            (RtPointer)&intensity,
            RI_NULL);
    RiWorldBegin();
        ...
    RiWorldEnd();
RiFrameEnd();

...
RiFrameBegin(2);
    RiLightSource("distantlight",
            (RtToken)"intensity",            (RtPointer)&intensity,
            (RtToken)"from",                 (RtPointer)from,
            (RtToken)"to",                   (RtPointer)to,
            RI_NULL);
    RiWorldBegin();
        ...
    RiWorldEnd();
RiFrameEnd();

...
RiFrameBegin(3);
    RiLightSource("pointlight",
            (RtToken)"intensity",            (RtPointer)&intensity,
            (RtToken)"from",                 (RtPointer)from,
            RI_NULL);
    RiWorldBegin();
        ...
    RiWorldEnd();
RiFrameEnd();

...
RiFrameBegin(4);
    RiLightSource("spotlight",
            (RtToken)"intensity",            (RtPointer)&intensity,
            (RtToken)"conedeltaangle",       (RtPointer)&conedeltaangle,
            (RtToken)"coneangle",            (RtPointer)&coneangle,
            (RtToken)"from",                 (RtPointer)from,
            (RtToken)"to",                   (RtPointer)to,
            RI_NULL);
    RiWorldBegin();
        ...
    RiWorldEnd();
RiFrameEnd();
...
```

Listing 11.1 *Program invoking four basic light sources*

RtFloat *intensity;
RtColor color;
RtPoint from, to;

The light of a **distant light source** flows uniformly in space in one direction. As a result, surfaces of like orientation receive the same amount of light independent of location. However, surfaces of *different* orientation are illuminated differently. Those facing directly toward the light source appear brightest and those facing away are completely unilluminated.

The best-known example of a distant light source is the sun. As viewed from the earth its rays are essentially parallel and position makes no practical difference in its intensity.

The two **RtPoint** parameters *to* and *from* give the direction of the source. It faces along the vector (*from–to*). The default *from* is (0, 0, 0) and *to* is (0, 0, 1). If the distant light is declared in camera space, this yields a direction straight along the positive *z* axis, illuminating all surfaces visible from the viewpoint. The defaults for *intensity* and *color* are 1.0 and white, as with ambient sources.

Point sources

RiLightSource("pointlight",
            "intensity", intensity,
            "lightcolor", color,
            "from", from, RI_NULL)
    RtFloat *intensity;
    RtColor color;
    RtPoint from;

A **point light source** distributes light through space from a single point. It shines evenly in all directions, but the intensity of the light falls off with the square of the distance from the light to the surface.

The location of a point light source is given by the **RtPoint** *from* parameter, which is (0, 0, 0) by default. Any explicit *from* positions are in the object space of the light source declaration. As before, *intensity* gives the intensity of the source, which is 1.0 by default.

Spotlight

RiLightSource("spotlight",
                    "intensity", intensity,
                    "lightcolor", color,
                    "from", from,
                    "to", to,
                    "coneangle", coneangle,
                    "conedeltaangle", conedeltaangle,
                    "beamdistribution",beamdistribution, RI_NULL)
        RtFloat *intensity;
        RtColor color;
        RtPoint from, to;
        RtFloat *coneangle, *conedeltaangle, *beamdistribution ;

A **spotlight** is a light source with both position and direction. It simulates a cone of light emitted from one point *from* toward another point *to*. The intensity of the emitted light falls off exponentially with angle from the center of the cone.

The first four instance variables of a spotlight have the same meaning as those of point and distant sources. A spotlight has a **falloff with angle** $F_{coneangle}$ from the spotlight direction to the direction of the surface point. $F_{coneangle}$ is controlled by the last three instance variables. It decays from 1 in the spotlight direction (*from–to*) to 0 *coneangle* radians away, and so is nonzero only inside a cone 2*coneangle* radians wide. The exponent of decay is given by *beamdistribution*: larger values give a narrower light source, smaller values a wider one.

Formally, $F_{coneangle}$ is the product of two decay functions F_1 and F_2. If **L** is the direction from the surface point to the spotlight, and **A** is the direction in which the light source points, then F_1 is

$$F_1 = (\mathbf{L} \cdot \mathbf{A})^{beamdistribution}$$

which is 1 for points in the direction of the spotlight, decaying geometrically with the cosine of the angle between **L** and **A**. It is 0 for points 90 degrees off-center. More precisely, it is the cosine of the angle of the point with respect to the spotlight direction, raised to the power *beamdistribution*.

The second angular falloff, F_2, is given by a smooth, continuous function that is 1 from the spotlight direction to (*coneangle–conedeltaangle*) radians away and 0 for points more than *coneangle* degrees from the spotlight direction,

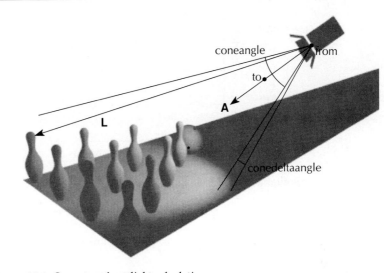

Figure 11.4 *Geometry of spotlight calculation*

with a smooth falloff in between. This function provides a penumbra-like decay, which helps prevent aliasing at the edges of the spot.

Figure 11.4 illustrates $\mathbf{L}$ and $\mathbf{A}$. Figure 11.5 plots F_1, F_2 and F_{dist} as a function of the angle between $\mathbf{L}$ and $\mathbf{A}$ for the values of *coneangle*, *conedeltaangle*, and *beamdistribution* used in Listing 11.1.

Positioning light sources

The positional and directional coordinates of light sources are treated like those of any geometric object. The position and direction are transformed by the current transformation as defined when the light source is declared. This allows a great deal of flexibility in placing light sources. If a positional source is declared after **RiProjection**() but before the camera transformation, it is in camera space and fixed relative to the viewpoint. If it is declared after **RiWorldBegin**() but before any transformations, its points are in world space. Inside the world block, a light can be attached to an object by simply declaring it next to the object. All of these can be very handy in animating scenes with moving light sources.

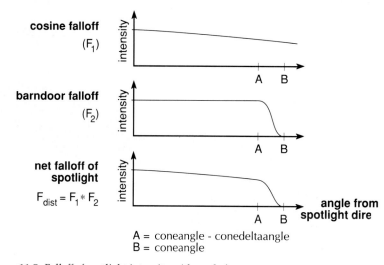

cosine falloff (F_1)

barndoor falloff (F_2)

net falloff of spotlight $F_{dist} = F_1 * F_2$

angle from spotlight dire

A = coneangle - conedeltaangle
B = coneangle

Figure 11.5 *Falloff of spotlight intensity with angle from center*

In a sense, the *from* and *to* parameters of the spot, point and distant sources are redundant because all are defined to lie at the coordinate origin, pointing along the positive *z* axis in object space. A light can be positioned or pointed just as well by using a modeling transformation to position and point the light's object coordinate system. In fact, this is a good practice because light source shaders that do not use *from* instance variables are more widely applicable, since they may be used in the area light sources described next. The standard shaders above use those variables because they make it easier to set up lights using an explicit position and direction.

Area light sources

One of the traditional limitations on the realism of synthetic imagery is the non-physical character of many types of light source: a point light is infinitesimal in size, so it casts a harsh light. Almost any real source emits light over some area in space. Two examples are frosted glass light bulbs and fluorescent tubes.

The RenderMan Interface provides the capability to describe such **area light sources**, although renderers are not required to support them. The basic procedure is to instance the light source shader, then declare a series of geometric surface primitives. All primitives declared before the next call to **RiAttributeEnd**() will be added to the area light.

RtLightHandle RiAreaLightSource(name, *parameterlist*)
   char *name;

As before, *name* is the name of the shader to be applied to the area light. In general, any light source shader that does not have a "from" positional instance variable may be applied to an area light.

From **RiAreaLightSource**() up to the next restoration of the graphics environment, usually by **RiAttributeEnd**(), any surface primitive that is declared will be added to the area light.

Area light sources are added to the set of current light sources and subsequently treated exactly as any other light source.

Surface shaders

A surface shader is called to determine the color of light reflecting from a point on a surface in a particular direction. Usually this happens when the point is found to be visible. Most surface shaders use the light arriving at the surface (as obtained from a light source shader) and the nature of the surface itself to calculate the color and intensity of the reflected light, but shaders may be written to use any other information deemed appropriate.

A surface shader also has the opportunity to set the opacity of the surface at the point. With the cooperation of the renderer, the shader can thus let a surface reveal, either partially or completely, the surfaces behind it.

The character of the surface is embodied partly in the definition of the shader and partly in the shader's instance variables. For example, there is a shader defined by the interface for a specular (shiny) surface. However, the shininess of a particular surface is given by an instance variable of the specular shader.

Elements of surface shading

To characterize the light emerging from a surface, surface shaders may use any or all of the following information:

- the direction, color and intensity of the arriving light.

- the color of the surface, as given by **RiColor**() or assigned to the vertices of the surface when it was defined.

- the opacity of the surface, the extent to which the surface absorbs light coming from behind. Opacity is expressed as a color to **RiOpacity**() or assigned to vertices and interpolated.

- the orientation of the surface, as given by the **surface normal** vector. The actual **geometric normal** may differ from the **shading normal**, which is a fiction used solely for shading.

- the direction in which the surface is viewed, the **incident vector I**. Mirrorlike surface reflections (**highlights**) are seen in specular surfaces when the camera lies in the mirror direction from the light. For other surfaces, the *color* reflected may depend in part on the incident vector. Though light striking a surface may be scattered arbitrarily in many different directions, the surface shader is concerned *only* with the light leaving the surface along the incident vector.

The last two factors above, so-called geometric factors, are calculated by the rendering system and provided for the shader with no action by the application.

The geometric factors **I**, **L** and **N** are illustrated in Figure 11.6 along with the "halfway vector" **H**, which points halfway between the light vector **L** and the incident vector **I**. If **H** and **N** coincide, then a mirror reflection of the light from the surface reaches the camera.

Color of reflections

Light arriving at a surface is described as a color. Computer graphics systems typically express the color of light as a triple giving the proportions of red, green, and blue in the light, although **RiColorSamples**() can be used to change this characteristic. When red, green, and blue, for instance, are mixed in the specified proportion, the result will be the specified color.

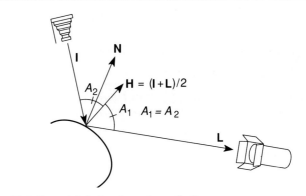

Figure 11.6 *Geometric factors in surface reflection*

The *surface color* is expressed as a similar triple, but one giving the *reflectivity* of the surface by three values between 0 and 1, each giving the proportion of red, green, or blue that the surface *reflects*:

$$red_{reflected} = red_{incident} * red_{reflectivity}$$

$$green_{reflected} = green_{incident} * green_{reflectivity}$$

$$blue_{reflected} = blue_{incident} * blue_{reflectivity}$$

Thus, white light (with *red=green=blue=1*) striking a surface reflects in the surface color.

If the reflectivity of a surface is less then 0, negative amounts of light will be reflected from the surface. If it exceeds 1, more light reflects from the surface than strikes it. Both these cases are clearly non-physical. Light sources, on the other hand, frequently have much larger values than 1 because intensity can have any finite value. Generally, the intensity of light arriving at the eye—the product of light intensity and reflectivity in each color—should fall between 0 and the value *one* passed to **RiQuantize()**. This ensures that the output of the renderer will not fall outside the range of representable values.

Types of reflection

The predefined surface shaders treat reflected color as a weighted sum of three components: ambient, diffuse, and specular reflections. The principal difference between the

```
RtFloat ka, kd, ks;
RiFrameBegin(1);
    RiWorldBegin();
        kd = 1; ka = ks = 0;
        RiSurface( "plastic",  (RtToken)"Ka",   (RtPointer)&ka,
                               (RtToken)"Kd",   (RtPointer)&kd,
                               (RtToken)"Ks",   (RtPointer)&ks,
                               RI_NULL);
                               ...

    RiWorldEnd();
RiFrameEnd();
RiFrameBegin(2);
    RiWorldBegin();
        ks = 0.5; ka = kd = 0;
        RiSurface( "plastic",  (RtToken)"Ka",   (RtPointer)&ka,
                               (RtToken)"Kd",   (RtPointer)&kd,
                               (RtToken)"Ks",   (RtPointer)&ks,
                               RI_NULL);
                               ...

    RiWorldEnd();
RiFrameEnd();
RiFrameBegin(3);
    RiWorldBegin();
        ka = 0.3; ks = kd = 0;
        RiSurface( "plastic",  (RtToken)"Ka",   (RtPointer)&ka,
                               (RtToken)"Kd",   (RtPointer)&kd,
                               (RtToken)"Ks",   (RtPointer)&ks,
                               RI_NULL);
                               ...

    RiWorldEnd();
RiFrameEnd();
RiFrameBegin(4);
    RiWorldBegin();
        ka = 0.5;
        ks = 2;
        kd = 0.5;
        RiSurface( "plastic",  (RtToken)"Ka",   (RtPointer)&ka,
                               (RtToken)"Kd",   (RtPointer)&kd,
                               (RtToken)"Ks",   (RtPointer)&ks,
                               RI_NULL);
                               ...

    RiWorldEnd();
RiFrameEnd();
```

Listing 11.2 *Ambient, diffuse and specular reflections, and a summation of all three*

shaders is in how they handle those three components, the weight they give to each.

Figure 11.7 illustrates the different effects of these three components. It was generated by the program like the one in Listing 11.2.

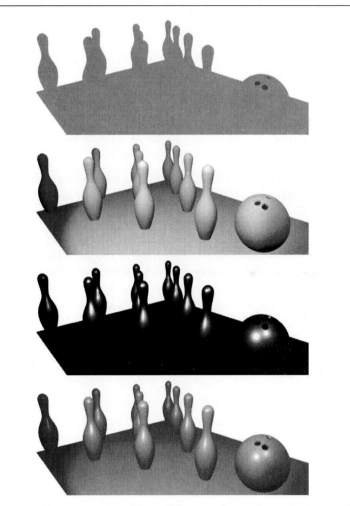

Figure 11.7 *Appearance of ambient, diffuse, and specular reflections, and a scene summing all of them. The top uses an ambient light source, the middle two a distant source and a spotlight, and the bottom all three.*

Ambient reflection

Ambient reflection is the name given to surface reflection of ambient light sources. The intensity of the reflection is independent of both surface location and orientation, but its color is affected by both the color of the light source and the reflectivity of the surface. The top of Figure 11.7 shows that ambient reflection is completely flat.

Diffuse reflection

If a surface scatters light uniformly, the surface appears equally bright from all points of view. The intensity of light *striking* the surface, on the other hand, is proportional to the area the surface presents to the light source. Thus **diffuse reflection** is brightest for a light source directly above the surface; a light near the surface's "horizon" lights it obliquely, hence dimly; below the horizon, no light at all reaches the surface.

The second image in Figure 11.7 shows how the diffuse component of reflection affects the appearance of a surface under a distant light source: the apparent brightness of the surface varies only with the orientation of the surface.

Formally, the color of the diffuse reflection is that of the incident light scaled by the cosine of the angle between the surface normal and the incident direction. If C_L is the color of the incident light, $\mathbf{N}$ the surface normal vector, and $\mathbf{L}$ the direction to the light source, then the reflected intensity is

$$C_I = C_L * \max(0, \mathbf{N} \bullet \mathbf{L})$$

Specular reflection

Specular reflection is the mirrorlike reflection of a surface at or near the **mirror direction**, the light source direction reflected about the surface normal. If the camera lies in the mirror direction, a specular reflection appears very bright. For a perfect mirror, *only* viewpoints in the mirror direction receive any specular reflection at all.

Few surfaces are perfect mirrors, but many surfaces exhibit some degree of "shininess," greater brightness when the viewpoint is near the mirror direction. The specular brightness is strongly determined by how close the incident vector is to the mirror direction. The brightness generally decays rapidly as the vector deviates from that direction.

The reflectivity of a specularly-reflecting surface falls off sharply with angle away from the mirror direction. The following simple shading rule approximates this behavior. The incident light is scaled by

$$S_{spec} = (\mathbf{N} \bullet \mathbf{H})^{1/roughness}$$

where the vectors $\mathbf{N}$ and $\mathbf{H}$ are as shown in Figure 11.6. The larger the value of roughness, the rougher (less specular) the surface.

A specular reflection is somewhat like a blurred image of the light source reflected in the surface. The question that naturally arises is: does a highly specular surface reflect the rest of its environment as well? Environment reflections may be provided automatically, usually by a ray-tracing renderer that treats the reflections from other surfaces as it does other sources of light. The RenderMan Interface also supports the use of an **environment map** to represent the rest of the scene as viewed from the surface. Use of an environment map is optional with the shader and will be covered in Chapters 15 and 16.

Specular reflections are important to the perceived realism of objects. Few surfaces are so diffuse that they scatter light uniformly, and rendering all objects with just diffuse reflection lends an image an artificial "computer" look. Conversely, the focus and brightness of a specular highlight provide a lot of visual information about the shape and texture of a surface.

Choosing a surface shader

RiSurface(name, *parameterlist*)
    char *name;

RiSurface() sets the current surface shader by *name*, thus controlling the appearance of the surface. The standard surface shaders are described below, together with their instance variables for *parameterlist*. The default surface shader depends on the implementation.

In contrast to light sources, there is only one surface shader in the graphics state at a time, and when a surface is declared the current surface shader is permanently associated with the surface and always used to shade it.

Constant surface

RiSurface("constant", RI_NULL)

The constant shader ignores all light sources, and simply returns the color of the surface and its opacity.

Matte surface

RiSurface("matte",
        "Ka", ambient,
        "Kd", diffuse, RI_NULL)
   RtFloat *ambient, *diffuse;

A matte surface combines ambient and diffuse reflections weighted by the instance variables "Ka" (RI_KA) and "Kd" (RI_KD). They are coefficients (usually between 0 and 1, to respect conservation of energy) that scale the respective components before summing them.

The ambient component of a matte surface's shade is just the summed contribution of all ambient light sources that are turned on for the surface, scaled by Ka.

The diffuse reflection is calculated from non-ambient light sources as described above. It is scaled by Kd.

Both Ka and Kd are 1 by default.

Metal surface

RiSurface("metal",
        "Ka", ambient,
        "Ks", specular,
        "roughness",roughness, RI_NULL)
   RtFloat *ambient, *specular, *roughness;

A metal surface reflects light with only an *ambient* and a *specular* component. Similar to the matte case, the metal surface shader uses the "Ka" (RI_KA) and "Ks" (RI_KS) instance variables to scale the ambient and specular components of the surface reflection. Both variables default to 1.

The sharpness of the specular reflection is controlled by the *roughness* parameter. The reflection falls off away from the mirror direction as rapidly as 1/*roughness*: a value of *roughness* near 0 sharpens the highlight to a point. As *roughness* increases toward infinity, the specular falloff goes to 0.

Plastic surface

RiSurface("plastic", "Ka", ambient,
   "Kd", diffuse,
   "Ks", specular,
   "roughness", roughness,
   "specularcolor", specularcolor, RI_NULL)
  RtFloat *ambient, *diffuse, *specular, *roughness;
  RtColor specularcolor;

A plastic surface has ambient, diffuse, and specular reflections. As before, they are scaled by the instance variables named "Ka", "Kd", and "Ks", respectively, declared with the shader and defaulting to 1. As with metal surfaces, the smoothness, or polish, of the specular component is controlled with the *roughness* parameter. The nearer *roughness* is to 0, the tighter the highlight.

Unlike metal, the plastic shader colors the specular reflection differently than the ambient and diffuse components. Given by the instance variable *specularcolor* above, the specular color is used to govern the color of the specular reflection in the same way that the surface color governs the ambient and diffuse reflections. The components of the specular reflectivity scale the color components of the incident light. *specularcolor* defaults to white.

Volume Shaders

The idea of atmosphere affecting light passing through space between a surface and the eye is generalized in the concept of volume shaders. A **volume** is a region of space filled with any material that affects light passing through it. A volume can be as simple as a fog bank or a jello mold, or as complex as a human body captured by a CAT scan. Each has different effects on the "light" passing through them.

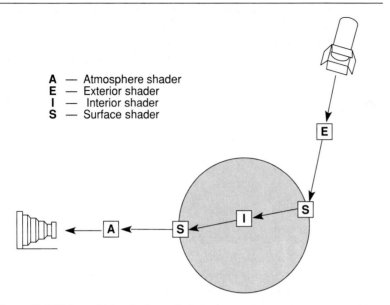

Figure 11.8 *Volume shaders in the rendering process*

The effect of a volume cannot be captured by a surface description. Jello, for example, affects light all along the path through the volume. The effect of a volume is fundamentally different from that of a surface.

RenderMan specifies that volume calculations are performed by **volume shaders**. They are invoked by the renderer and given the intensity, color and direction of light entering a volume. They calculate the intensity and color of the light leaving that volume.

Figure 11.8 shows how volume shaders fit into the rendering process. After a light source determines the light arriving at a surface, the exterior volume shader associated with the surface is called to modify the light, then the surface shader does its work. If the surface is not opaque, light passes through the volume interior to the surface, and the interior shader is called to calculate the effect on that light in traversing that path. On the path from surface to camera, the atmosphere shader is called.

The job of specifying volume shaders is complicated somewhat by the fact that there is no notion of a volume as, say, a geometric primitive in RenderMan. Instead, volume shaders are associated with the surfaces that bound them. The shader that represents the volume on the inside of an object is declared with **RiInterior()**, and the volume on the outside is declared with **RiExterior()**. The volume through which light moves in going from a surface to the camera is declared with **RiAtmosphere()**.

RiInterior(name, *parameterlist*)
    char *name;

RiExterior(name, *parameterlist*)
    char *name;

RiAtmosphere(name, *parameterlist*)
    char *name;

RiInterior() sets the current interior volume shader associated with subsequent surfaces, and **RiExterior**() sets the current exterior shader. **RiAtmosphere**() sets the current atmosphere shader.

Whenever light approaches a surface (as from a light source), the surface's exterior shader is called to modify the light before it strikes the surface. Whenever light passes through an object, the interior shader associated with one end of the path is called to modify the light. It is an error to associate different interior shaders with different parts of an object. When light reflects from a surface on an unobstructed path toward the eye, the current atmosphere shader is called.

The current shader of each type is an attribute of the graphics state, saved and restored like any other. There are no default volume shaders of any kind.

The use of interior and exterior volume shaders is beyond the scope of this book. In fact, volume rendering is just coming into its own as a technique for visualizing multidimensional data. The orientation of this book is toward realistic computer graphics, but volume rendering creates the possibility of a variety of other "realities" for computer graphics.

On the other hand, atmospheric effects, which modify light after it leaves a surface but before it reaches the eye, are more tractable. They can provide powerful visual cues about an environment. The apparent distance of mountains in a range and a strong sense of their scale can be conveyed by intervening haze.

A volume shader can be used to introduce any atmospheric effects into the light reflecting from a surface toward the eye. As with surface shaders, there is only one of these shaders in the environment at a time, and it is associated with each object independently so that different objects may have different atmosphere shaders. Unlike surface shaders, there need be no atmosphere shader, and that is the default. If no atmosphere shader has been specified, light passes free of any atmospheric effects between a surface and the viewer.

Depth cues

RiAtmosphere("depthcue",
                "mindistance", mindepth,
                "maxdistance", maxdepth,
                "background", backgroundcolor, RI_NULL)
    RtFloat *mindepth, *maxdepth;
    RtColor backgroundcolor;

The depth-cue shader mixes the color *backgroundcolor* into the reflected light according to the distance between the surface and the viewpoint. If the surface is more than *maxdepth* away, the arriving color is entirely *backgroundcolor*. Nearer than *mindepth*, the reflected color arrives at the camera unchanged. From *mindepth* to *maxdepth*, *backgroundcolor* is mixed linearly into the reflected color.

Fog

RiAtmosphere("fog",
                "background", fogcolor,
                "distance", distance, RI_NULL)
    RtColor fogcolor;
    RtFloat *distance;

The fog shader, like the depth-cue shader, mixes a color into the light according to the distance between the surface and the viewpoint. The difference is that fog-shaded light always re-

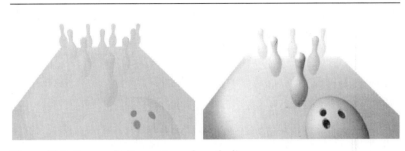

Figure 11.9 *Fog vs. depth-cue atmosphere shading*

tains some of the original reflected color. The fog is mixed in with weight $(1-e^{-depth/distance})$, which is 0 at *depth* 0 and increases with increasing *depth* but never reaches 1.

Figure 11.9 illustrates the difference. The scene is shown at right with depth-cueing and at left with fog.

Other Shaders

This chapter has discussed and presented the standard light source, surface and atmosphere shaders, and touched lightly on volume shaders. A variety of other types of shader are specified by the RenderMan Interface, but none have standard shaders associated with them, which makes discussion difficult. However, using any other shader should be straightforward after mastering the basic protocol presented here. Chapters 13 through 16 provide more information.

Further Reading

The topic of lighting and shading is a rich one in the computer graphics literature, because there is both so much to do and so much room for clever tricks. The model of specular reflection used in RenderMan is due to Jim Blinn [BLINN77], and the model of metallic reflection to Rob Cook [COOK81]. A good recent survey of the field is the book *Illumination and Color in Computer Generated Imagery* [HALL89].

CHAPTER 12

Surface Mapping

The lighting and shading discussion of the last chapter covered the broad aspects of coloring objects in a scene, in the following sense: both shaders and light sources apply to objects in their entirety. However, singly-colored objects, no matter how well lit, provide only simple visual information. It is the small variations of shape and shading within a single object that provide much of the visual interest and credibility of natural scenes: the wood grain of a piece of furniture, the tiny marks of paint on a wall chipped and cracked with age, the play of light on a fine fabric, the veins on a leaf, the subtle blushes and textures of human skin, even the text on the cover of a book or a picture in a frame demonstrate a richness in the visual world well beyond the complexity of the objects themselves.

It might be possible to provide these kinds of texture by using smaller and more numerous surfaces, but it multiplies the cost of transmitting and storing data and of resolving their hidden surfaces. Conceptually, detail is not associated with the shape and configuration of the objects, but with their *appearance*. From a modeling standpoint, it seems sensible to deal with the two domains separately; to design, for example, the shape of a book first, then its cover. Finally, it is not clear that using a multiplicity of tiny objects will even work in all cases. There must be a better way to depict a photograph in a scene than to model every little change over its surface with a polygon. The better way is to distinguish **shape**, the geometry of a scene providing the basic conformation of objects, from **shading**, governing the appearance of those objects.

This is actually quite a natural idea. An interesting way to express it is to visualize objects in the real world shaded by old-style computer graphics techniques. Imagine, for example, a wooden chair in a uniform, untextured, flat plastic color. What is left is shape; what is left out, the difference between the visualization and the reality, is shading.

We have already mentioned the interpolation process by which surface parameters such as shading normal or color can be bound to the extrema of a surface and interpolated to interior points. If separation of shape from shading is to have much meaning, there must be some finer level of control over object appearance than simple interpolation. Shading characteristics must vary *within* an object, as well as *among* the separate objects in a scene. The discussion of this methodology still needs to be completed by specifying exactly the form and extent of these capabilities under the RenderMan Interface, including specifying exactly *how* shading is mapped onto surfaces. That is the subject of the first part of this chapter.

A second part of the discussion is entirely new in this chapter. It is a venerable subject in computer graphics: the domain loosely described as **texture mapping**, in which a planar image is mapped onto a surface in the manner of a decal. The discussion of texture maps has been deferred until now because their use is an optional capability under RenderMan, and none of the standard shaders use them. However, texture maps can be an extremely powerful tool for introducing detail and making a scene visually interesting. The third part of this chapter deals with generalizations of texture mapping to include shadows, changes in the surface normal and reflections from the environment.

These two topics of interpolation and mapping are linked by the process used to lay textures onto surfaces. Textures are accessed using the two-dimensional **texture coordinates** associated with each point on a surface. These coordinates are interpolated across a surface in exactly the same way as the vertex-bound normals we used in Chapter 5.

A sample texture

Figure 12.1 shows a texture and a partial sphere to which the texture has been applied. The texture is applied as a reflectivi-

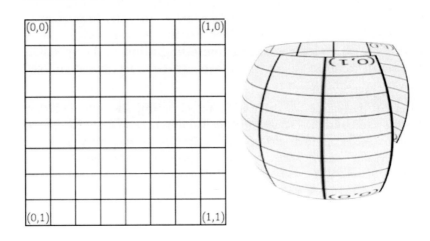

Figure 12.1 *Mapping a texture onto a surface*

ty used exactly as a color specified with **RiColor**() would be used to calculate the surface shading. Since the "constant" surface shader is used in this example, it reveals no changes in lighting.

Simple Surface Mapping

Earlier chapters have set out the *parameterlist* mechanism for binding an extensible set of parameters to surfaces and shaders when they are passed to the interface. We've mentioned several times the examples of color and surface normal bound to the vertices of polygons, but much is still unexplained: what kinds of values can be interpolated? How are values interpolated for surfaces which, like quadrics, have no vertices? How can these interpolated values be used for the kinds of surface variations we seek?

Varying vs. uniform variables

Our purpose in this chapter is to allow the appearance of a surface to vary across its extent in as many ways as possible.

Therefore, it seems a natural extension of the interpolation scheme to allow, not just surface color and shading normal, but *any* instance variable used by a shader to vary across a surface. For example, it might be interesting to make the specularity coefficient Rl_KS of a surface shader vary in some way based on vertex values.

RenderMan supports that idea by equating the *parameterlists* of shaders and surfaces: *If a name-value pair can be provided as an instance variable to a surface shader, then that same variable can be used in the parameterlist of a surface primitive.* The value will be interpolated for every point on the interior of the surface as usual. When the corresponding surface shader is called to shade that point, its like-named instance variable will have the interpolated value.

Sometimes we want a value to be constant across a surface. We declare the variables carrying these values to be **uniform**. When we want a variable to be interpolated across the surface, the variable is declared to be **varying**. For example, if an application wishes to force the geometric normal of a polygon to some value, it can include an Rl_NP name-value pair in the *parameterlist* of **RiPolygon**().

For an arbitrary value to be used in the *parameterlist* of a primitive surface, the system must know the type and number of values to expect in each token-value pair. There is a set of variables predefined in RenderMan, listed in Table 12.1. All but "s", "t" and "st" have already been discussed in previous chapters; they will be covered in the next section.

Extending the set of variables

Other variables may be added to the list of Table 12.1 by using the function **RiDeclare**():

RtToken RiDeclare(name, declaration)
    char *name;
    char *declaration;

RiDeclare() makes a new variable known to the interface for use in the *parameterlist* of geometric primitive routines and shader declaration functions. *name* will be used in the token-value pair to identify instances of the new variable. *declaration* is a string giving the variable's storage modifier (either "varying" or "uniform") followed by its type, either "float", "point", "color" or "string". The call

RiDeclare("temp", "varying float");

declares that variable "temp" has a single floating-point value at each vertex.

Only the predefined "st" and "Pw" variables have more than one element at each vertex. No such variables may be declared with **RiDeclare**().

The RI_P variable in Table 12.1 would be declared as

RiDeclare("P", "varying point");

RiDeclare() returns a value of type **RtToken**, which can be used as a token in a token-value pair for the variable involved, as in

RI_TEMP = **RiDeclare**("temp", "varying float");
RiPolygon(4, RI_P, (**RtPointer**) vxvals,
        RI_TEMP, (**RtPointer**) tempvals, RI_NULL);

Using an **RtToken** this way may be more efficient than passing strings.

Information	Name	Class	Type	Number of Values
Position	"P"	varying	**RtPoint**	1
	"Pz"	varying	**RtFloat**	1
	"Pw"	varying	**RtFloat**	4
Normal	"N"	varying	**RtPoint**	1
	"Np"	uniform	**RtPoint**	1
Color	"Cs"	varying	**RtColor**	1
Opacity	"Os"	varying	**RtColor**	1
Texture Coordinates	"s"	varying	**RtFloat**	1
	"t"	varying	**RtFloat**	1
	"st"	varying	**RtFloat**	2

Table 12.1 *Predefined Variables*

In passing these variables to a *parameterlist*, the values must correspond to the declaration. A "uniform" variable is passed as a pointer to a single value of the appropriate type (or, equivalently in C, an array with one element); a "varying" variable must be passed as an array of values of the appropriate type, one per vertex. For a "float" variable the array must consist of **RtFloat** values. For a "point", each element must be an **RtPoint**, 3 floating-point values. A "color" is also 3 floating-point values, unless the application has called **RiColorSamples()** to change that number.

The interface provides for special handling of **RtPoint** variables: they are transformed using the current transformation so that they "track" the geometric coordinates used to describe the primitives. In this respect, the RI_PZ, RI_PW, RI_N and RI_NP variables have special semantics beyond a simple declaration. The former two are transformed even though they are not declared as **RtPoint** variables, and the latter two are transformed as vectors so that their directions remain consistent.

Basis of interpolation

We now know how to declare and interpolate arbitrary variables, but it is not yet clear what that interpolation means in every case. Polygons obviously get one value for each vertex, but what about quadrics and parametric surfaces? What is the basis for interpolation there? How many values should be passed in for such surfaces, and how is a value determined for an interior point?

Except for polygons, every type of surface supported by the RenderMan Interface can be treated as a topological rectangle. A patch, for example, is passed through the interface as a rectangular grid of control points. Regardless of the shape of a surface, a two-dimensional rectangular coordinate system can be imposed on it, with a unique mapping from points in that coordinate system to points on the surface: each point between the four corners of the coordinate system has a corresponding point on the surface. The reverse mapping is not always well determined. At the poles of a sphere, for example, two corners of the rectangle coincide.

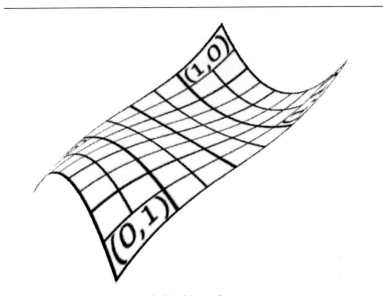

Figure 12.2 *Parameter space of a bicubic patch*

The underlying rectangular coordinate system imposed on a surface is known as the surface's **parameter space**. The names used by RenderMan for the coordinates of its parameter space are the conventional u and v.

Patch and mesh interpolation

The parameter space of a bicubic or bilinear patch occupies exactly the range 0 to 1 in both directions: points along the edges of the surface have either a u value of 0 (which we will refer to as the "left" edge of the surface), a u of 1 (the "right" edge), a v of 0 (the "top" edge) or a v of 1 (the "bottom"). The parameter coordinates of all interior points lie within those bounds. Figure 12.2 illustrates.

This parametric coordinate system can therefore be used to find an interpolated value at any interior point on the surface, given values at the four corners. Specifically, if $val_{0,0}$ is the value at the top left corner, and so on as shown in Figure 12.2, then the value at any interior point (u,v) is given by bilinear interpolation:

$$val_{u,v} = (val_{0,0}*(1-u)+val_{1,0}*u)*(1-v)+(val_{0,1}*(1-u)+val_{1,1}*u)*v$$

The meaning of this for applications is very simple: the *parameterlist* of any parametric surface or quadric can be used to interpolate any value just as it can for polygons. The application need only provide a token-value pair, where the value is an array with exactly *four* elements: the values at $(u,v) = (0,0)$, $(1,0)$, $(0,1)$, and $(1,1)$, in that order. *This is different from the order of polygon vertices*, which are circular around the surface. The interpolant has one of the array values at each of its four corners, and each interior point is a bilinear interpolation between the two.

The case of bilinear and bicubic patch *meshes* is slightly more complicated. Recall that a patch mesh is a more compact way of representing a rectangular array of patches that fit together continuously at their boundaries. A patch mesh declared with *nu* vertices in the u direction and an evaluation step of *nustep* will have $N = \lceil (nu-3)/nustep \rceil$ patches in u, and similarly for v. For a patch mesh with N patches in the u direction and M patches in the v direction, the array of vertex values will contain exactly $(N+1)*(M+1)$ values in u,v order if the patch doesn't wrap around, and $N*M$ if it does. This declaration of patch vertex values has *no* effect on the coordinate system: the entire mesh is still covered by the range [0,1] in u and v.

The parameter space of a patch has another important use. A patch or patch mesh may be specified as a **height field** by passing each point on the control mesh as a single floating point value, the height of that point. The x and y coordinates of the mesh are set equal to the u and v parametric surface values. Therefore, a patch derived from a height field will have an x and y extent across the square covering the range [0,1]. This scheme provides a compact representation for terrain data, and is also a convenient form for rendering functions in two dimensions.

Quadric parameter space

How does interpolation work for a quadric surface? What are the corners of a sphere, for example? Quadrics are also rectangles for purposes of binding values. A cylinder may be imagined as a rectangle twisted around to make two opposite edges

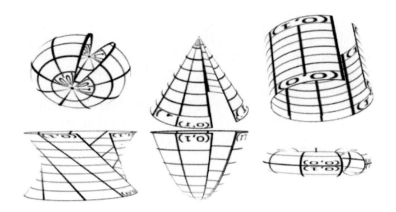

Figure 12.3 *Parameter space on quadric surfaces*

coincide; similarly for a cone, if one edge has no length. A hyperboloid is formed from a line segment in 3-space swept about a coordinate axis; the starting and ending positions of that line segment define two opposite edges of the rectangle, and the circles swept out by its endpoints the adjacent edges. For a sphere, the coordinate space is that of latitude and longitude. Figure 12.3 should help in visualizing this. The quadric declaration diagrams in Chapter 4 included this u,v information.

The parameter space of a quadric arises naturally from the fact that quadrics are surfaces of revolution equivalent to sweeping a curve in 3-space around some coordinate axis. In a quadric surface, v runs from 0 to 1 along that basis curve, and u runs from 0 to 1 about the circumference of the revolution. In other words, u is longitude and v is latitude.

This is true regardless of the radius of curvature, and especially regardless of the sweep angle of the quadric, or *zmin* and *zmax* values in the case of a sphere. *The surface of a quadric always exactly occupies the parameter range [0,1].* A hemisphere covers the same "parameter area" that a sphere does.

Polygon parameter space

Now, what about polygons? Quadrics and parametric surfaces have a simple mapping to rectangles. Polygons are more complicated because they can have any number of vertices and even holes. There are many possible definitions of the polygon parameter space, none of them entirely satisfactory. The parametric coordinates of a point on a polygon are defined by RenderMan to be the x and y coordinates of that point *in object space*. This choice means that polygons have a uniform, well-defined parameter space. It also means that a polygon can be used like a "cookie cutter" for a texture on the x,y plane.

There are two things to beware of, however. First, if a polygon is perpendicular to the x,y plane, then its parameterization becomes strange. Second, if polygons may be nonplanar, two points on the surface may have the same x and y location, so the mapping from parameter space to points on the polygon is no longer unique.

Uses of parameter space

The ability to map between points in parameter space and points on the surface of a geometric primitive is key to controlling the appearance of surfaces. We have already seen how surface parameterization defines interpolation of values across the surface. But there are at least three other important uses of parameter space: shading, trim curves and texture mapping.

Shaders and surface maps

Surface shaders operate with a very restricted view of the world: they are called once for each point on the surface independently and only have information about such *local* properties of the surface as normal, texture coordinates and parametric derivatives. If a shader is to vary its effect coherently across the surface, it must know where on the surface a particular point lies. The surface parameterization provides that information, thanks to the correspondence between points in the parameter space and points on the surface.

Trim curves

Using an optional capability defined under the RenderMan Interface, an application can cut out arbitrary regions of a non-uniform rational B-spline (NURB) surface. Standard patch descriptions result in a surface which is basically a warped rectangle. The ability to describe **trim curves** on a NURB surface can provide more flexible shapes.

Declaring trim curves

A trim curve is a set of **loops** defined in the parameter space of a NURB. Each loop divides the surface into points inside the loop and points outside it. If the loop is defined counterclockwise (as viewed on a rectangle with u positive to the right and v positive downward), the interior points are discarded from the surface (the loop cuts a hole). If the loop is clockwise, the exterior points are excluded (the loop is a cookie-cutter). The final surface consists of points left after every loop cuts points away. Using trim curves, a surface can be broken into an arbitrary number of disjoint pieces.

Each loop of a trim curve is a closed series of non-uniform, rational B-splines in two dimensions, the parameter space of the surface being cut.

RiTrimCurve(nloops, ncurves, order, knot, min, max, n, u, v, w)
    RtInt nloops, ncurves[], order[], n[];
    RtFloat knot[], min[], max[], u[], v[], w[];

RiTrimCurve() declares a list of *closed* **loops**. Each loop consists of a sequence of NURB curves in *(u,v)* parameter space with homogeneous coordinate *w*. The curves of a loop must join to form a closed path.

The number of loops is *nloops*. The number of curves in the Nth loop is given by *ncurves[N]* for $0 \leq N < nloops$.

The total number of curves in the trim set is

$$C = \sum_{N=0}^{nloops\text{-}1} ncurves[N]$$

If $0 \leq m \leq C-1$, then *order*[m] gives the order of the *m*th NURB and *n*[m] the number of control points on that spline. For the *m*th spline, there should be *n*[m] elements of *u*[], *v*[], and *w*[], giving control points for the spline in the parameter space of the NURB. There should also be (*order*[m]+*n*[m]) values in *knot*[] giving the knot values of the spline. The spline will be evaluated between *min*[m] and *max*[m].

Parameter space in texture mapping

The final important use of surface parameterization is in texturing: modulating the appearance of a surface based on the contents of an independent image. In fact, surface parameterization is the link between variable interpolation and the next section, which describes RenderMan's texturing facilities.

Using Texture Maps

The rectangular parameter space of quadrics and parametric surfaces is good for more than just interpolating vertex values. It also makes it straightforward to map textures onto those surfaces.

A texture map is a rectangular digital image, so it too has a rectangular coordinate system: each point in the image has a unique pair of coordinates, designated *s* and *t*. A texture map in the RenderMan Interface exactly covers the unit square [0,1] in *s* and *t*, regardless of the resolution of the map. The top left corner of the image is at (0,0) and the bottom right is at (1,1). It is no coincidence that this range exactly matches the parameter space of the most common primitive surfaces: *a texture map applied to a quadric or parametric surface will exactly cover that primitive under the default parameterization.*

Parameter- to texture-space mapping

There is a reason, though, for making a distinction between the parameter space of a surface and the texture space of a texture map. Surfaces are commonly joined together to form larger composite objects. In these cases, the need arises to apply a texture over the object as a whole. There must be some way of going from the "local" parametric coordinate system of a primitive to the "global" coordinate system of the object. This projection is specified using the routine **RiTextureCoordinates**().

The mapping between parameter space and texture space is controlled by giving the four coordinates of a quadrilateral in texture space. The unit square [(0,0),(1,0),(0,1),(1,1)] in parameter space (which just covers most surfaces) of a single surface is projected onto the given rectangle in texture space. This projection is akin to pinning that part of the texture map down onto the entire surface primitive. A set of adjoining surfaces can be textured by **RiTextureCoordinates**() calls that assign independent but adjoining portions of the texture space to each surface.

RiTextureCoordinates(s1, t1, s2, t2, s3, t3, s4, t4)
    RtFloat s1, t1;
    RtFloat s2, t2;
    RtFloat s3, t3;
    RtFloat s4, t4;

RiTextureCoordinates() declares a projection from the unit square [(0,0),(1,0),(0,1),(1,1)] in parameter space to quadrilateral [(*s1,t1*),(*s2,t2*),(*s3,t3*),(*s4,t4*)] in texture space. It therefore projects a *part* of a map onto an entire quadric or parametric surface (if the quadrilateral is within the unit square), or distributes multiple copies of the map across the surface (if the quadrilateral is much larger than the unit square).

The mapping projection defined by **RiTextureCoordinates**() is an attribute contained in the graphics environment. It is saved and restored with other attributes, and it is assigned to a surface when the surface is declared, unless the surface is a polygon.

The texture coordinates of polygons are the same as their parameter-space coordinates, unless the former are bound to vertices and interpolated; that is, **RiTextureCoordinates**() has no effect on polygons: texture coordinates must be explicitly bound to polygon vertices if the default is not sufficient.

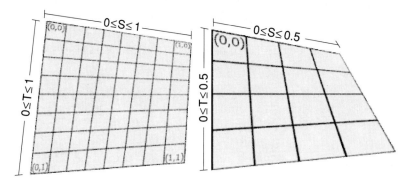

Figure 12.4 *Surfaces generated by the program in Listing 12.1. On the left, a bilinear patch with default texture coordinates; on the right, the texture space is [0,.5], [0,.5].*

Texturing and parameterlist

The texture coordinates for a primitive can be specified in the *parameterlist* of the procedure creating the surface. The tokens "s" (RI_S) and "t" (RI_T) label an array of single-value texture coordinates, and "st" (RI_ST) labels an array of texture coordinate pairs that are applied to vertices and interpolated the same way as any other parameter. The coordinates themselves are **RtFloat** values.

Two examples

Listing 12.1 shows a program fragment exercising the texture-mapping facilities of RenderMan. The result is shown in Figure 12.4. Both of these examples assume that the shader "mytexture" used to render the surface uses a texture map. None of the standard RenderMan shaders do, but as we will see in later chapters, such shaders are easy to construct in the RenderMan Shading Language.

There is only one noteworthy feature of this example: the means of passing the name of the texture map to the "mytexture" surface shader. The string pointer to the name "grid.txt" is passed *by address*, in contrast to the usual (in C) method of passing it by value.

```
static RtColor color = { 0.9, 0.9, 0.9};
static RtPoint corners[] = {    { -1,  .3,  1 },
                                {  1, -.1,  1 },
                                { -1, -.1, -1 },
                                {  1,  .3, -1 }
};
static struct { RtFloat x, y } textcoords[] = {
    { 0, 0 }, { 0.5, 0 }, { 0.5, 0.5 }, { 0, 0.5 }
};
char *tmap = "grid.txt";

RiDeclare( "tmap", "uniform string" );
RiSurface( "mytexture", ( RtToken )"tmap", ( RtPointer )&tmap, RI_NULL);
RiColor( color );

RiTransformBegin();
    RiTranslate( -1.3, 0.5, 1.0 );
    RiRotate( -50.0, 1.0, 0.0, 0.0 );
    RiPatch( "bilinear", RI_P, ( RtPointer ) corners, RI_NULL );
RiTransformEnd();

RiTransformBegin();
    RiTranslate( 1.0, 0.5, 1.0 );
    RiRotate( -40.0, 1.0, 0.0, 0.0 );
    RiPatch( "bilinear",  RI_P, ( RtPointer ) corners,
                        RI_ST, ( RtPointer ) textcoords, RI_NULL );
RiTransformEnd();
```

Listing 12.1 *Program fragment for generating Figure 12.4*

Textured quadric

Figure 12.5 shows the bowling pin from Chapter 4, this time textured with the "grid.txt" texture used in Figure 12.2. The routine in Listing 12.2, used to generate Figure 12.5, defines a textured surface of revolution formed from a number of hyperboloids. The most useful function of the routine is to divide the texture map among the segments of the surface. Normally, each hyperboloid in the surface would be just covered by the entire texture map; here, however, they were textured smoothly by dividing texture space among the hyperboloids. On the left, each of the N surfaces gets $1/N$th of the texture space. On the right, the distribution of texture is equalized among the rings based on the surface's vertical extent.

```
#include <ri.h>

typedef struct { RtFloat x, y; } Point2D;

/*
 * MapSurfOR(): produce a surface of revolution from a profile curve.
 *      The first surface has a texture distributed evenly among its
 *      individual rings. In the second surface, the texture distribution
 *      is equalized according to the size of the ring.
 */

MapSurfOR( points, npoints )
Point2D points;
int npoints;
{
        double totlen, xlen, ylen;
        RtFloat tcoords[NPOINTS];
        int pt;

        /* Distribute the texture interval [0,1] linearly among the surfaces */
        for(pt = 0; pt < npoints; pt++)
                tcoords[pt] = ((float)pt)/(npoints-1);
        RiTransformBegin();
                RiTranslate( -0.6, 0.0, 0.0 );
                TextSurfOR( points, tcoords, npoints, 360.0 );
        RiTransformEnd();

        /* Equalize the texture coordinates */
        tcoords[0] = totlen = 0;
        for(pt = 0; pt < npoints-1; pt++) {
                xlen = points[pt+1].x-points[pt].x;
                ylen = points[pt+1].y-points[pt].y;
                /* Set tcoords[i] to the accumulated length of all segments <= i */
                tcoords[pt+1] = (totlen += sqrt(xlen*xlen+ylen*ylen));
        }

        /* Normalize the accumulated lengths to the interval [0,1] */
        for(pt = 1; pt < npoints; pt++)
                tcoords[pt] /= totlen;

        /* Declare the surface again */
        RiTransformBegin();
                RiTranslate( 0.6, 0.0, 0.0 );
                TextSurfOR( points, tcoords, NPOINTS, 360.0 );
        RiTransformEnd();
}
```

```
/*
 * TextSurfOR(): create a surface of revolution with a texture, distributing
 *      texture space among the segments
 */

TextSurfOR( points, tcoords, npoints, thetamax )
Point2D points[];
int npoints;
RtFloat tcoords[], thetamax;
{
        int pt;
        RtPoint point1, point2;
        RtFloat *pp1, *pp2, *tmp;
        RtFloat thisT, nextT;
        char *tmap = "grid.txt";

RiAttributeBegin();
        pp1 = point1;
        pp2 = point2;

        /*
         * For each adjacent pair of points in the description,
         * draw a hyperboloid by sweeping the line segment defined by
         * those points about the z axis.
         */
        pp1[0] = points[0].y;
        pp1[1] = 0;
        pp1[2] = points[0].x;
        nextT = tcoords[0];
        RiSurface("mytexture",
                    (RtToken) "tmap", (RtPointer) &tmap, RI_NULL);
        RiRotate(90.0, 0.0, 0.0, 1.0);
        for( pt = 1; pt < npoints; pt++ ) {
            pp2[0] = points[pt].y;
            pp2[1] = 0;
            pp2[2] = points[pt].x;
            thisT = nextT;
            nextT = tcoords[pt];
            RiTextureCoordinates(0.0,thisT, 1.0,thisT, 0.0,nextT, 1.0,nextT);
            RiHyperboloid( pp1, pp2, 360.0, RI_NULL );
            tmp = pp1; pp1 = pp2; pp2 = tmp;          /* Swap pointers */
        }
RiAttributeEnd();
}
```

Listing 12.2 *Routine used to draw Figure 12.5*

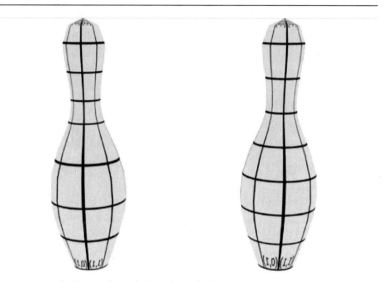

Figure 12.5 *Surfaces of revolution formed by abutting hyperboloids joined in texture space*

Making a texture map

A texture map is created from an image file using **RiMakeTexture**():

RiMakeTexture(imagefile, texturefile, swrap, twrap, filterfunc,
        swidth, twidth, *parameterlist*)
    char *imagefile, *texturefile;
    RtToken swrap, twrap;
    RtFloatFunc filterfunc;
    RtFloat swidth, twidth;

RiMakeTexture() creates the texture file named *texturefile* from an image file named *imagefile*. The resolution of the texture file is similar to that of the image file, but the texture *space* of the map is still over the range [0,1] in both *s* and *t*, regardless of resolution. By definition, channels of the image are converted to channels of the texture map. Neither file format is dictated by RenderMan, but should be specified in any implementation.

filterfunc is a pointer to the function used to filter the pixels of the image. As with pixel filtering in image rendering (see Chapter 9), the functions **RiGaussianFilter()**, **RiCatmullRomFilter()**, **RiSincFilter()**, **RiTriangleFilter()** and **RiBoxFilter()** are pre-defined under RenderMan, and the application can define others as **RtFloatFunc** *func()*. *swidth* and *twidth* give the support of the filter, the number of pixels in *s* and *t* used in filtering each element of the texture map. *swidth* and *twidth* are typically 1 or 2.

swrap and *twrap* refer to the behavior of the texture map when it is accessed outside the range [0,1]. If "periodic" (RI_PERIODIC), the texture wraps with a period of 1. If "clamp" (RI_CLAMP), the value at the nearest edge will be returned for out-of-bounds access. "black" (RI_BLACK) means to return 0 outside [0,1]. The *parameterlist* of **RiMakeTexture()** may be used to pass implementation-dependent information to the texture creation routine, but no standard parameters are defined.

As noted above, the resolution of the input image file affects *only* the quality of the texture, which always exactly occupies the range [0,1].

Texture Mapping Generalized

Given the ability to modulate the reflectivity of a surface across its extent by using a texture map, one might wonder whether it would be useful to modulate other surface properties in the same way. The RenderMan Interface provides direct support for three generalizations of simple texture access. A **bump map** controls the surface orientation under shading, providing for subtle "bumpiness" effects on an otherwise flat surface. An **environment map** can provide glossy and mirror-like reflections of other objects from a surface via a rendition of what a scene looks like from the point of view of the surface. And a **shadow map** provides information for determining whether a surface point falls in a shadow cast by a particular light source.

Bump mapping

All of the primitive object types in the RenderMan Interface have very well-defined surface normals: a polygon has a single surface normal over its entire area, the normal of a quadric surface changes smoothly from place to place, and the normal of a parametric surface is given by the cross-product of the tangents to the surface in the u and v directions. While consistent, these variations in surface orientation are normally about as interesting as the single color that is used for shading in the absence of texture maps.

Texture due to surface modulation

The classic example in computer graphics of texture due to surface orientation is an orange. At a superficial level, an orange appears to have a fairly simple, nearly spherical shape, one single color everywhere on its surface and a constant specularity. One subtlety that makes an orange far less mundane is the tiny pits and undulations of its surface.

Modeling surface modulations

Obviously, these small modulations of the surface could be represented by a parametric surface in which someone took the trouble to introduce all the little variations of shape individually. On a practical level, that procedure is not only painfully cumbersome, but it would only be good for one orange at a time. On a conceptual level, it seems to be using an *object* description to set out what should be a property of the *surface*. It fails to distinguish shape from shading.

Once we recognize that we are dealing with a property of the surface, the key observation is that the position of each point on the surface of the orange is relatively unimportant. The amount of light arriving in the middle of a pit is not significantly different from that arriving at the surface. Only the variation in the orientation of points on the surface makes much difference to the ultimate appearance of the orange.

Whereas a texture map describes variations in the *reflectivity* of a surface, a **bump map** describes the variations in a surface's *orientation*. Otherwise, bump mapping is identical to texture mapping: a bump map file covers the texture-space range [0,1], with coordinates out of that range handled according to the wrap mode declared with the bump map.

Making a bump map

Just as with texture maps, a bump map can be made from an image file.

RiMakeBump(imagefile, bumpfile, swrap, twrap, filterfunc,
        swidth, twidth, *parameterlist*)
    char *imagefile, *bumpfile;
    RtFloatFunc filterfunc;
    RtToken swrap, twrap;
    RtFloat swidth, twidth;

RiMakeBump() creates a bump map file named *bumpfile* from an image file named *imagefile*; its parameters have the same meaning as those of **RiMakeTexture**(). The image file should have a single channel which gives a displacement, or height, along which the surface should be perturbed. The perturbation is converted into changes in the normal by examining adjacent perturbations. Thus, a uniform displacement will cause no bumps at all. The formats of the two files are implementation-dependent.

An alternative for bump mapping

Bump maps have an honorable history in computer graphics, and can dramatically enhance the appearance of a surface. They do have one shortcoming, though. A bump map affects only the shading normal of a surface, not its true shape. This means that profile edges will never change, and there is no possibility of self-shadowing in the pits. This is not a big problem if the modulations of the surface are much smaller than the surface itself, as they are in the case of the orange.

RenderMan supplements bump maps with an optional facility that can modify the actual geometry of a surface. A user can write and apply a **displacement shader**. Called once during rendering for each point on a surface, the displacement shader has the opportunity to modify both the position and normal of the surface at that point.

RiDisplacement(name, *parameterlist*)
    char *name;

RiDisplacement() posts a displacement shader to the graphics state. Any surface declared under that state will be shaded only after the displacement shader is called to perturb the surface. *name* is a string giving the name of the shader. If *name* is RI_NULL, then no displacement shader is defined and surface points are not perturbed. *parameterlist* is an optional series of token-value pairs providing the instance variables of the shader.

The current displacement shader is an attribute in the graphics state, and as such it is saved and restored with the rest of the state.

Since displacement shading is an optional capability, no standard displacement shaders are specified under the RenderMan Interface, but displacement shaders will be demonstrated among the example shaders of Chapter 16.

Environment mapping

Environment maps address the problem of interobject reflections. In the real world, an observer sees parts of the world reflected in glass, metal, water and other shiny surfaces as from a mirror. The most popular rendering method to include interobject reflections in an image is **ray tracing**. A ray tracer renders a pixel by casting an imaginary ray back into the world from the viewpoint, through that pixel. If the ray strikes a surface, it is shaded by casting rays from the point of intersection toward each light source in the scene. If the surface is sufficiently shiny, another ray is cast along the mirror direction from the surface. Any object that this latter ray strikes is seen as a reflection of the second object in the first. Figure 12.6 shows this process.

Ray tracing can be an expensive method due to its cost in computing time and the fact that it must store a scene in its entire-

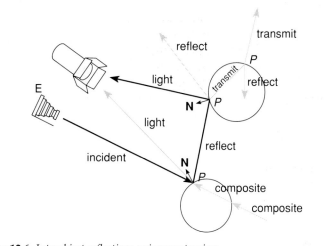

Figure 12.6 *Interobject reflections using ray tracing*

ty throughout the rendering process. Ray tracing also often suffers from aliasing problems due to the nature of cast rays as infinitely narrow. There is an alternative which also provides interobject reflections and which can often be more efficient, although it is less flexible. It is based on a simple fact of projective geometry. A flat mirror reflects light toward a given viewpoint as though the surface were transparent, with the viewpoint behind it (see Figure 12.7). For purposes of rendering from the original viewpoint, a **reflection map** can be precomputed from a viewpoint behind the surface. It can then be used to depict the reflections by an appropriate mapping.

Environment maps defined

Many shiny surfaces can be approximated in a similar way by assuming a single viewpoint somewhere in the middle of the object and precomputing an image from that viewpoint. An **environment map** gives an image of the environment in all directions from a location inside an object. Unlike texture and bump maps, an environment map is not accessed by surface location, as expressed in texture-space coordinates. Rather, an environment map contains the appearance of the scene from a fixed point varying by *direction*. When rendering a surface us-

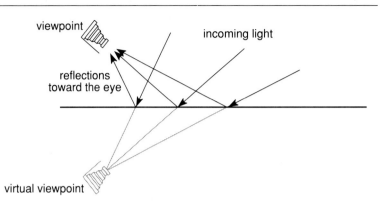

Figure 12.7 *Reflections from a flat surface appear as if they had been viewed from behind the surface.*

ing an environment map, the map tells the color of the light arriving from the environment in a specific direction.

Environment mapping is a relatively inexpensive way to render a few highly specular objects. It works best when the surfaces are fairly small compared to the distance to the objects in the environment map (e.g., mountains on the horizon). The technique is less well suited to rendering highly convoluted surfaces that reflect themselves, and to rendering object interreflections. However, since few objects in a typical real scene are mirrorlike, environment maps are often a good choice.

Another strong argument for environment maps is that they bring the same filtering technology as other kinds of maps to the problem of depicting accurate reflections. Since the "spread" between adjacent traced rays can vary wildly in direction, having a global representation like an environment map makes it much more tractable to filter reflections.

Making an environment map

There are two routines for creating an environment map. The first uses an image indexed by the latitudinal and longitudinal coordinates of a sphere. The second uses a set of six images whose size, shape and viewing directions collectively form a cube.

RiMakeLatLongEnvironment(imagefile, reflfile, filterfunc, swidth, twidth,
      parameterlist)
   char *imagefile, *reflfile;
   RtFloatFunc filterfunc;
   RtFloat swidth, twidth;

This makes the environment map *reflfile* from the image called *imagefile*. Except for the omission of the wrap parameters (which make no sense in this context), the parameters are identical to those of **RiMakeTexture**() and **RiMakeBump**().

The image file must be indexed according to a spherical projection: if the map will be used under a left-handed coordinate system, longitude varies from 0 at the left to 360 at the right; under a right-handed coordinate system longitude is 360 at the left and 0 at the right. In both cases, latitude is −90 at the bottom and 90 at the top. A direction in space (*dx, dy, dz*) is a function of *latitude* and *longitude*:

$dx = \cos(longitude) * \cos(latitude)$
$dy = \sin(longitude) * \cos(latitude)$
$dz = \sin(latitude)$

Any flat representation of a sphere (a map of the earth, for example) contains some distortion. The latitude-longitude environment map makes objects seen at the top and bottom appear much larger than the same objects seen near the equator.

A latitude-longitude environment map is often created using a paint system. An environment map can also be made by rendering a scene six times, once for each face of a cube centered on the object that will bear the reflection. Once rendered, the environment map is made by the following:

RiMakeCubeFaceEnvironment(px,nx, py,ny, pz,nz, reflfile,
      fov, filterfunc, swidth, twidth, *parameterlist*)
   char *px, *nx, *py, *ny, *pz, *nz;
   char *reflfile;
   RtFloat fov;
   RtFunc filterfunc;
   RtFloat swidth, twidth;

This routine makes an environment map named *reflfile* using six images corresponding to the six sides of a cube. Each image has its viewing location at the center of the cube with viewing direction along the positive and negative *x*, *y* and *z* axes, respectively. *filterfunc, swidth* and *twidth* are the same as before. *fov* is the horizontal and vertical field of view of the images. An *fov* value of 90 would fit the cube faces exactly, but two or three degrees extra can provide a little overlap to improve the quality of the resulting map.

The six face views must have an orientation that depends on the axis they sight along, as detailed in the table below.

Face View	Axis toward top	Axis toward right
px	$+y$	$-z$
nx	$+y$	$+z$
py	$-z$	$+x$
ny	$+z$	$+x$
pz	$+y$	$+x$
nz	$+y$	$-x$

The orientation of these views is natural in a left-handed coordinate system. For a right-handed coordinate system they represent left-to-right mirror images.

The orientations required of the images of the environment cube are (in a left-handed coordinate system) those of a viewer facing the positive *z* direction who then swivels his head to face the various directions. They are illustrated in Figure 12.8 and Plate 14.

If the environment is rendered under a right-hand coordinate system, the orientation of each view is exactly the same, and the same camera transformation may be used to render the images. However, they will *appear* to be flipped right-to-left.

An environment map should be precomputed from the scene being rendered, but without the reflecting object so that the reflections are accurate. Since the faces of the cube parallel the coordinate axes of camera space, the viewing transformation should do the following:

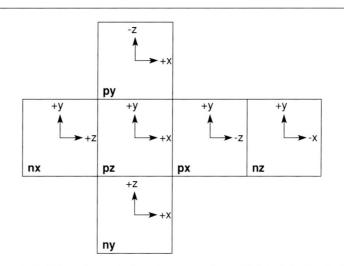

Figure 12.8 *Orientations of the views passed to* **RiMakeCubeFaceEnvironment**()

- use a perspective projection with field of view of 90 degrees or slightly more (see above),

- translate from the origin of world space to the center of the object in question.

Listing 12.3 gives a version of the rendering process to create six reflection images via six renderings, then create an environment map.

Listing 12.4 provides a routine to use the resulting reflection map in a scene. It declares the object which will reflect the environment (a sphere) after declaring a translation to the location of the environment map rendered earlier, then goes on to show the rest of the world. As before, this example posits the existence of a surface shader, "myreflector", which uses a reflection map.

Plate 15 shows the result of using the environment map created from Plate 14. While the reflection on the teapot is quite convincing, closer inspection reveals that neither the spout nor the handle are reflected in the body. However, the service to realism is substantial nonetheless.

```
/* MakeRefl.c: create and use an environment map at a given viewpoint. */

#include <ri.h>
#define BUFSIZE 256
RtPoint CameraFrom;

main()
{
        RtInt resolution;
        char filename[BUFSIZE], tfilenames[6][BUFSIZE+4];

        GetCubeParms( CameraFrom, filename, &resolution );
        RiBegin(RI_NULL);               /* As always */
                RiDeclare( "reflmap", "uniform string");
                /* Render the faces of the cube */
                Snap( "x+", tfilenames[0], resolution );
                Snap( "x-", tfilenames[1], resolution );
                Snap( "y+", tfilenames[2], resolution );
                Snap( "y-", tfilenames[3], resolution );
                Snap( "z+", tfilenames[4], resolution );
                Snap( "z-", tfilenames[5], resolution );
                RiMakeCubeFaceEnvironment(
                        tfilenames[0], tfilenames[1],
                        tfilenames[2], tfilenames[3],
                        tfilenames[4], tfilenames[5],
                        filename, 90.0, RiGaussianFilter, 2.0, 2.0, RI_NULL );
                RiFrameBegin(7);
                        RiWorldBegin();
                                Go(filename);
                        RiWorldEnd();
                RiFrameEnd();
        RiEnd();
}

Snap( direction, tfilename, resolution )
char *direction, tfilename;
int resolution;
{
        int axis;
        static int framenum = 1;
        RtPoint CameraTo;

        sprintf(tfilename, "%s.%s", filename, direction);

        RiFrameBegin(framenum++);

                RiDisplay(tfilename, RI_FILE, RI_RGB, RI_NULL);
                RiFormat( resolution, resolution, 1.0 );        /* image resolution */
                /* Nature of the projection to the image plane */
                RiProjection( "perspective", RI_NULL );    /* perspective view */
```

```
                    /* Camera characteristics */
                    FrameCamera( resolution/2.0, (float)resolution, (float)resolution );

                    /* Camera position and orientation */
                    CameraTo[0] = CameraTo[1] = CameraTo[2] = 0;
                    switch(direction[0]) {
                    case 'x': axis = 0; break;
                    case 'y': axis = 1; break;
                    case 'z': axis = 2; break;
                    }
                    CameraTo[axis] = (direction[1]=='-') ? -1 : 1;
                    PlaceCamera ( CameraFrom, CameraTo, (RtFloat) 0.0 );

                    /* Now describe the world */
                    RiWorldBegin();
                            Go(NULL);
                    RiWorldEnd();
            RiFrameEnd();
}
```

Listing 12.3 *Function for creating environment maps for an object in a scene*

```
/*
 * Object description function for creating and using a reflection
 *      map on a sphere. If mapname is non-NULL, the function
 *      assumes it to be the name of a reflection map. Otherwise,
 *      the function ignores the object and simply declares the rest
 *      of the world.
 */
extern RtPoint CameraFrom;
Go(mapname)
char *mapname;
{
        if(mapname != NULL) {
                RiAttributeBegin();
                    RiSurface("myreflector",
                            (RtToken) "reflmap", (RtPointer) &mapname,
                            RI_NULL);
                        RiTranslate(CameraFrom[0],CameraFrom[2],CameraFrom[2]);
                        RiSphere( 1.0, -1.0, 1.0, 360.0, RI_NULL );
                RiAttributeEnd();
        }
        ShowRestOfWorld();
}
```

Listing 12.4 *Function for using an environment map in a scene*

Figure 12.9 *Depth-rendered shadow map (data recorded by shadow maps)*

Shadow maps

The fourth type of map provided by RenderMan covers another special capability of ray tracing: rendering shadows resulting from objects blocking light sources. A **shadow map** begins as a depth image, rendered from the viewpoint of a light source. If the image contains, at each pixel, not the color of the nearest surface, but its distance, the result can be used to determine whether any point in the scene is in shadow. Figure 12.9 shows the depth image used in creating Figure 7.7; darker points are nearer the light. Any point visible in the depth rendering is illuminated by the light, and any points "behind" an illuminated surface are in shadow.

A depth image is created by giving **RiDisplay**() the token RI_Z as its *mode*, indicating that depth values rather than colors are being rendered. Once the depth image is created, it is transformed into a shadow map by the following:

RiMakeShadow(picfile, shadowfile, *parameterlist*)
    char *picfile;
    char *shadowfile;

As usual, **RiMakeShadow**() takes a depth-rendered picture file *picfile*, producing a shadow map file *shadowfile* suitable for use by a shader that attends to these matters. *picfile* contains depth ("z") information.

Listing 12.5 shows a simplified example for creating and using a shadow map. It assumes that *Setup*() calls the RenderMan routines used to position the light source, *SetupInv*() declares the inverse transformation, and *DoScene*() declares all the objects in the scene.

In the first frame block, *SetupInv*() is used to position the world with respect to the camera; in the second, Setup() positions the spot light. As explained in Chapter 8, a camera transformation must be described as the *inverse* of a transformation used to position an object (in this case, a light) in the same location with the same orientation as the camera.

The **RiDisplay**() call at the beginning of the first frame passes RI_Z in the mode parameter to cause a depth image "shdw.z" to be output. Since that call occurs *inside* the frame block, that specification is removed at the end, and the second frame uses the default display parameters. In the second world block the light source is positioned and declared at the beginning because the setup transformation is expressed relative to world space.

A spot light has a default location at the coordinate origin of its object space and points along the positive z axis, just as a camera does. For that reason, both the camera and light point in the same direction after the transformation. As a result, the shadow is cast back into the world from whence it was taken. This only works because the "from" and "to" parameters of the spot light are left with their default values. If they were not, it would ruin the coincidence of light and shadow.

This example assumes the existence of a spot light shader named "shadowspot" which takes the name of a shadow map

```
/* Create and use a shadow map for a spot light. */
char *shadowfile = "shadowfile";
RiBegin(RI_NULL);
      RiDeclare( "shadowfile", "uniform string");
      RiFrameBegin(1);
             RiDisplay( "shdw.z", RI_FILE, RI_Z, RI_NULL);
             SetupInv();
             RiWorldBegin();
                   DoScene();
             RiWorldEnd();
      RiFrameEnd();
      RiMakeShadow( "shdw.z", shadowfile, RI_NULL );
      RiFrameBegin(2);
             RiWorldBegin();
                   RiTransformBegin();
                         Setup();
                         RiLightsource( "shadowspot",
                                (RtToken)"shadowfile",(RtPointer)&shadowfile,
                                RI_NULL );
                   RiTransformEnd();
                   DoScene();
             RiWorldEnd();
      RiFrameEnd();
RiEnd();
```

Listing 12.5 *Function for creating and using a shadow map for a light source*

in its "shadowfile" instance variable. None of the standard
RenderMan shaders use shadow maps but any implementation may support them and, of course, if the implementation
supports the RenderMan Shading Language they may be written directly. "shadowspot" is defined in Chapter 16.

Conclusion

There are four different kinds of maps defined by RenderMan
because their indexing and data are of different kinds. Otherwise, the basic idea of mapping, that of varying surface properties across an object, applies equally to all.

Although the data in each type of map has an implied meaning (color for texture maps, normal perturbation for bump
maps, etc.), there is no reason that these interpretations must
apply. For example, the information in a texture could be

used for any purpose. It might provide perturbation information to a displacement shader. It could represent airflow speed and pressure to a shader visualizing dynamic stresses. In fact, any variable relevant to shading can be stored in a map and accessed by a shader that knows about it.

Standard surface shading parameters apply to surfaces as a whole. In the first part of this chapter, we described how these parameters can be varied linearly across a surface by binding values to corners or vertices and letting the renderer interpolate them and pass them to the instance variables of a shader. The different types of maps are nothing but the ultimate generalization of this idea, allowing *any* numerical input to the shading process to vary arbitrarily.

Further Reading

The original work on texture mapping was done by Ed Catmull [CATMULL74], but perhaps a better source is Paul Heckbert's survey [HECKB84]. Bump maps were first discussed by Jim Blinn [BLINN78]. The use of environment maps to simulate reflections is set out by Blinn and Newell [BLINN76] and detailed by Greene [GREENE86]. Feibush, Levoy and Cook [FEIBUSH80] give insight into the filtering of texture maps. Finally, the RenderMan shadow mapping technique is based on work by Reeves, Salesin and Cook [REEVES87].

CHAPTER 13

The RenderMan Shading Language I: Introduction

Writing computer programs to synthesize digital images has always been a challenging undertaking. It begins with a marathon of programming: designing and implementing a hidden-surface algorithm, managing an array of complex data structures, performing a battery of geometric tasks and simulating the physics of light emission, transmission and reflection. When the first picture finally emerges, it is a cause for celebration.

An important part of any renderer is the **shader**, the section that calculates the appearance of visible surfaces in the scene. The rest of a renderer deals with a fairly bounded, well-defined problem centering around data management and projective geometry. Since the visual world is so rich, since appearance can vary so widely, the shader is the center of flexibility and power in a renderer.

Once an image synthesis program exists, the shader also becomes the focus of users' expectations. As visually oriented animals, people are very sensitive to subtleties of shading, and that sensitivity expresses itself as a nearly limitless demand for subtle, flexible control over shading. At the same time, the more successful a program is, the wider the range of physical reality it is expected to duplicate. Both of these facts place extraordinary demands on the shading portion of any renderer.

Usually, the shader is a large, complex body of routines embedded within a renderer. Viewed from outside, it appears as a nest of interacting options, parameters, maps and light sources, a massive, mysterious system that can be massaged into doing more or less what the user wants by a circumspect approach and a delicate manipulation of parameters. Its behavior can only be modified, not extended. If, in the end, the shader is simply not able to provide a particular feature, someone must revise the renderer itself. This is the domain of the programmer, and even for a skilled programmer it is likely to be a protracted, touchy process.

This all raises the cost of creating truly compelling synthetic imagery and impedes the free flow of experiment and result that should exist between the creator and his or her work. It is no accident that the most striking images in computer graphics are produced by programmers or artists working closely with programmers. The complex nature of physical reality and the breadth of the visual imagination ensure that this process will never end. There will always be unanticipated demands on a monolithic shader.

There is an alternative, based on giving the user more access to the shading system itself, rather than its external interface. The critical thing is to give users access to the useful parts of the system without burdening them with irrelevant details. Just as one shouldn't have to know about the chemistry of pigmentation to use a paint brush, there should be a way to control the appearance of objects in a synthetic scene without an in-depth knowledge of the entire rendering program. Fortunately, the shading process can be tamed and brought under control that way.

One key idea is to tease apart rendering issues dealing with substance from those of appearance. Image synthesis can be divided into two basic concerns: the **shape** realm of geometric objects, coordinates, transformations and hidden-surface methods; and the **shading** realm of light, surface, material and texture. The former is very specific: I want a telephone here, a 3-D logo there, a building over there. Geometry must be controlled more or less explicitly by the user. This is most often accomplished with the aid of modeling software.

Most of the visual interest of a typical scene, the place where credibility resides, is at a level more subtle than the overall geometry: the veins on a leaf, the aged sheen of the paint on a car, the textures of various materials, the subtle differences between real wood grain and those plastic simulations. A quick glance around any room is enough to convince anyone of the astonishing variety of materials in the real world.

The confusion between shape and shading is wasteful if it leads users to seek complexity in geometry when it could be provided more easily during shading. As an example, consider fabric. Theoretically, a piece of cloth could be described geometrically as a net of polygons or parametric surfaces for each individual thread. But a more reasonable approach might be to describe the overall fabric geometrically, taking the *appearance* of the cloth as a shading problem.

The RenderMan Interface is largely motivated by the idea that a lot of geometric complexity can be supplanted, with an equal level of visual interest and realism, by more flexible shading methods.

It is difficult to provide this sort of flexibility in a monolithic shader. The presentation of shading as a predefined process under the control of a fixed set of parameters has fundamental limitations. What could possibly take its place? The most adaptable creature in computing is the procedure, or subroutine. The key idea in the RenderMan Shading Language is to control shading, not only by adjusting parameters and options, but by *telling the shader what you want it to do directly* in the form of a procedure.

The programming procedure can become an uncommonly powerful lever for control over shading, both because its job can be very tightly defined in terms of the elements of the shading process (e.g., describing the light emerging from a light or reflecting from a surface), and because the author of the procedure doesn't have to worry about such issues as eliminating hidden surfaces or determining the geometric context of the procedure call.

By writing an appropriate shader in the shading language, a programmer can extend old shading models or implement entirely new ones, light sources can be defined with any radiant distribution, and new and novel surface properties can be introduced easily. Any parameter to these processes can be set up with a constant value, a value that varies smoothly over a surface, or one modulated arbitrarily by a surface map.

The performance of shaders is not even limited to optical processes. The color at each point on the surface of an airplane wing, for example, could be calculated from stresses at that point or the velocity of airflow over it. Realism may be a convenient benchmark for quality in rendering, but really exciting images may also be produced by non-physical shaders.

This chapter introduces the RenderMan Shading Language, giving essential background as well as an overall discussion. The next two chapters get into the specifics of language syntax and the tools available for writing shaders. The book closes with Chapter 16, "A Gallery of Shaders," which suggests the possibilities of the shading language approach and provide some examples of useful tricks and techniques.

Shaders from the Outside Looking In

Figure 13.1 shows the shading process as a dataflow model, with the calculation of a surface color proceeding from emission at the light source, through reflection at the surface and on through the atmosphere. The process begins when a renderer recognizes the need to determine the color of light reflecting from a surface toward the camera. The renderer enters the shading realm when it asks the question: what color is *that* surface at *that point?*

Shading as data flow

In Figure 13.1, information flows from light to camera. A light source has a single purpose, to calculate the light *arriving* at a surface point, taking into account such factors as the distance between source and surface.

A surface shader uses color of the light arriving from the light source, together with the color of the surface and other factors, to calculate the light *leaving* the surface at that point. That information in turn is passed to an atmosphere shader, which may further modify it in calculating the light arriving at the image plane. Similarly, a volume shader affects light passing through some material.

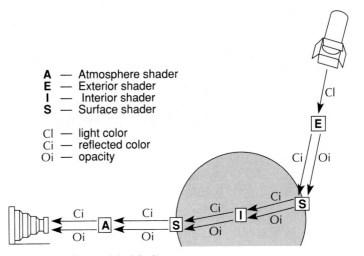

A — Atmosphere shader
E — Exterior shader
I — Interior shader
S — Surface shader

Cl — light color
Ci — reflected color
Oi — opacity

Figure 13.1 *Dataflow model of shading*

Dataflow modules

One of the important aspects of the shading language is that the shaders are functionally independent. The interaction between one module and another is limited to the data items (light color, primarily) that pass between them. From the standpoint of the model as a whole, the internal operation of a shader is completely unconstrained. It doesn't matter how the surface shader determines its reflected color; it is only important that it provide one.

The normal view of programming procedures is that of fixed "black boxes" that have well-defined input and output and unknown internals so that they can be assembled into large systems based only on that external view. Shaders, by contrast, are embedded in a predefined system (the renderer), and the user's freedom lies in implementing or selecting the module itself.

Shader types

The RenderMan Interface specifies six types of shader, distinguished by the inputs they use and the kinds of output they produce. Several types of shader may each be used in different parts of the shading process.

Light source shaders

A **light source shader** is given the position of a light source, and the direction of a surface point from the light. It returns the color of the light originating in the light source and striking that surface point.

Unlike most other shaders, there may be several light sources in a scene at once, each declared with **RiLightSource**() or with **RiAreaLightSource**(). Any subset of them may be turned on or off for any surface in a scene.

Volume shaders

Volume shaders are associated with volumes of space both inside and outside the objects of a scene. They describe the effects on light of passing through a volume from an origin to a destination. If the path is inside some object, an **interior volume shader** is called. An **exterior volume shader** is used to affect light which passes through "empty space" outside any object. A volume shader is called for light approaching the camera.

A volume shader is associated with the volume interior to a surface by calling **RiInterior**(), with its exterior by **RiExterior**(), and with the atmosphere by **RiAtmosphere**(). All the surfaces facing the interior of an object should have the same interior volume shader, or an error results. If there are several different exterior volume shaders defined in a scene, the choice of which one to use for a given path is implementation-dependent, but it will be the exterior shader bound to one of the surfaces at either end of the path.

Transformation shaders

Transformation shaders are really part of the geometric process rather than shading. The geometric transformation capabilities specified by RenderMan include both matrix operations and the ability to apply arbitrary nonlinear transformations (called **deformations**) to geometric coordinates. These are specified with a **transformation shader**, which takes a point in space and outputs another point. A transformation shader is concatenated onto the current transformation by calling **RiDeformation**(). A nonstandard geometric projection from camera space onto the image plane is specified by calling **RiProjection**(), naming a transformation shader instead of "perspective" or "orthographic".

Displacement shaders

Transformation shaders and displacement shaders are similar in their mission of moving points in space. They differ, however, in their respective place in the rendering process and their relationship to object geometry. A transformation shader is the nonlinear equivalent of a transformation matrix in a concatenated series, transforming points without regard to any associated surface. Consequently, a deformation may be embedded within a series of linear and nonlinear transformations and used to deform any geometric aspect of a scene. The purpose of a transformation shader, then, is to modify a *coordinate system*.

The purpose of a **displacement shader**, on the other hand, is to perturb the surface of an object point by point, providing detail in the form of small variations that would be much more difficult to specify geometrically. It operates entirely on the surfaces of objects. Unlike a transformation shader, a displacement shader may use the surface normal, parametric derivatives or any other property of the surface in calculating the displacement. Finally, a deformation is made part of the current transformation, while a displacement is associated with individual surfaces like any other attribute. Displacement shaders are instanced with **RiDisplacement**().

In Chapter 16, the *threads*() shader in Listing 16.24 is a displacement shader based on a phased sinusoid in parameter space. Those few lines of code are all that are required to create the threads on a light bulb from a simple cylinder.

Surface shaders

When light strikes a surface, it frequently bounces around in the material of the surface and emerges in some direction with some color usually different from when it arrived. A **surface shader** has the job of computing reflected light in a particular direction (often, but not always, toward the camera) using the location of a point on the surface, the orientation of the surface, a set of light sources and other information. As discussed earlier, surface shaders are invoked by **RiSurface**().

Imager shaders

An **imager** shader may be invoked by calling **RiImager**(). It will transform floating-point pixel color values as supplied by the renderer after rendering the pixel to the output values of a pixel once it is completely rendered. An imager shader takes a color on input and places another set of values, of arbitrary meaning, on output. It might be used, for example, to convert RGB output into a device-dependent format like YIQ or a four-color separation. The place of an imager shader in the pixel-production pipeline was discussed in Chapter 9.

Shaders from the Inside Looking Out

Since shaders are part of the rendering pipeline, there is no question of "calling" them in the usual sense from an application using RenderMan. Instead, each shader is plugged into the system using a call like **RiLightSource**(), referring to the appropriate shader by name. Chapter 11 covered the process of using existing shaders, considering them from the outside in, as it were. From the standpoint of *writing* shaders, life looks a little different.

Services supporting shading

A key difference between shaders and standard programming "hooks" is that RenderMan goes to great lengths to simplify the task of writing shaders, both by an appropriate design and specification, and by setting out an extensive array of support services. Thanks to the rich environment shaders operate in, they are often just a few lines of code, and rarely exceed a page of text in length.

Orthogonal definition

One aid for shader writers is RenderMan's definition of a canonical rendering process. Each shader has a well-defined role, and the shaders as a group are functionally independent. A surface shader may be chosen without regard to what light sources or volume shaders are in use, and its behavior is independent of them.

Rendering environment

Taken individually, each shader operates in an environment in which the bulk of what normally constitutes shading work is already done. When a shader is called, geometric data is fully transformed, and a variety of relevant information (the position of a surface or light, the direction to the eye, etc.) is immediately available in a set of global variables, which are preset every time the shader is called. The problem of resolving hidden surfaces is completely managed by the renderer.

Special data types

The shading language provides two special data types, **point** and **color**, for manipulating geometric and color information. The language includes special operators for the **point** type, and the standard programming language operators are able to operate on both types.

Varying variables maintained

As discussed in Chapter 12, any variables that go into shading a surface can be interpolated across the surface, but that fact is invisible to the shader itself. The interpolation takes place behind the scenes; the only difference is that the shader's instance variables differ from one invocation to another.

Integration constructs

In addition to the usual programming language control constructs like **for** and **if-then-else**, the RenderMan Shading Language includes special constructs for spatial integration of light emerging from light sources and impinging on a surface.

Filtered map access

Texture maps and other forms of mapped data are accessed from shaders as simple function calls, with prefiltered return values. Any multichannel value can be stored in a map, accessed by a shader and used to control any aspect of shading.

Function library

The shading language includes a large library of mathematical, color, optical, geometric and noise functions. The common shading functions for calculating ambient, diffuse, specular, and Phong reflections are also predefined.

An Example Shader

We conclude this chapter by dissecting the example shader below, which reveals some of the features of the shading language.

```
1    /* clouds(): a surface shader for a cloudy surface */
2    surface
3    clouds(
4          float  Kd=.8,
5                 Ka=.2 )
6    {
7       float sum ;
8       float i, freq;
9       color refl;
10
11      sum = 0;
12      freq = 4.0;
13      for (i = 0; i < 6; i = i + 1) {
14          sum = sum + 1/freq * abs(.5 - noise( freq * P)) ;
15          freq = 2 * freq;
16      }
17      refl = Cs * sum;
18      Ci = refl*( Ka*ambient() + Kd*diffuse(faceforward(normalize(N),I)) );
19      Oi = 1.0;        /* Always make the surface opaque */
20   }
```

Listing 13.1 *An example shader*

Overview

clouds() is a surface shader that gives a wispy, cloudlike appearance to the shading of a surface, as shown in the bowling pin at left. It is called whenever a renderer needs the color of the light reflecting from a surface at a given point. This shader can be roughly divided into two sections. The first section, through line 17, computes the reflectivity of the surface as a summed noise function that scales the input surface reflectivity *Cs*. Line 18 calls the **ambient**() and **diffuse**() functions, weighting the color values they return by the instance variables *Ka* and *Kd*, respectively.

ambient() returns the summed contributions of all ambient light sources. **diffuse**() is passed the normal vector to the surface, also provided by the renderer and reversed, if necessary by the function **faceforward**() to point toward the viewer. **diffuse**() polls all relevant light sources, scaling the light from each according to the surface's orientation and summing the resulting eyeward reflections into its returned color.

Resemblance to C

The most obvious characteristic of this shader is a superficial resemblance to a function in the C programming language. The shading language is syntactically similar to a subset of C, but is tailored to its task. This makes the shading language easier to learn, but one must beware of assuming the shading language *is* C.

Declaration

The first distinction between the shading language and C is that *clouds*() is not a function or a procedure, but a **shader**: that fact is denoted by the keyword **surface** preceding the declaration and indicating that this shader is devoted to computing surface reflections.

Instance variables initialized

The declared parameters (here, *Kd* and *Ka*) of a shader are its instance variables. For example, the *clouds*() shader might be instanced by the fragment

```
RtFloat Kd = 0.3;
RiSurface( "clouds",
        RI_KD, (RtPointer)&Kd,
        RI_NULL );
```

That would give the instance variable *Kd* the value .3, which it would have every time this instance of the shader is called. Unlike a C function, a shader must specify default values for its parameters (instance variables) because providing values when instancing a shader is always optional. In this example instance, *Ka* would have the default value .2.

Local variables

clouds() has the local variables *i, freq, sum* and *refl*, which are analogous to C. The shading language supports type **float**, but it also defines two vector types: **color**, giving a light or reflectance color, and **point**, giving a point in three-dimensional space.

Global variables

Four variables appear in *clouds*() that are neither local to the shader nor instance variables. These **global variables** are shown underlined: *I, P, N, Cs* and *Ci*. The first three are the implicit parameters of the shader, giving the viewing direction *I*, the surface point being shaded (*P*), the surface normal at that point (*N*), and the color of the surface expressed as a reflectivity (*Cs*). All such variables are set before the shader is called. The output of the shader, the light emerging from the surface, is passed back to the renderer in the global variable *Ci*.

Special operators and functions

The RenderMan Shading Language has predefined extensions both in operators and functions. The functions **noise**() and **abs**() on line 14, and **faceforward**(), **normalize**(), **ambient**() and **diffuse**() on line 18, are standard in the language.

Expressions with vector types

In the RenderMan Shading Language, arithmetic operations work on **point**s and **color**s as well as **float**s. On line 14, the surface position **point** P is multiplied by a scalar before passing it into **noise**(). On line 18, the **color** returned by **diffuse**() is multiplied by the scalar Kd and added to Ka to obtain a **color**, which is then multiplied by the **color** *refl*. Since the shading language handles vector operations itself, any operation on color is independent of the number of color samples specified by **RiColorSamples**().

Statements and control constructs

Standard control constructs for looping (**while**, **do**, **for**) and conditional execution (**if-then-else**) are included in the shading language, as can be seen on line 13.

No return value

The final feature of a shader is that it has no explicit return value. It communicates its results by setting one or more global variables. The surface shader is calculating the light leaving a surface, and it leaves its result in the global **color** variable Ci. Chapter 16 discusses the results expected of the different types of shader.

Further Reading

The RenderMan Shading Language is based on the shade trees of Rob Cook [COOK84]. His paper provides much historical background and motivation.

CHAPTER 14

The RenderMan Shading Language II: Description

ŗ This chapter details the form of the RenderMan Shading Language. After a quick introduction, the second section describes the data types supported: the set of global variables that allow shaders to do their work, and the form of instance variables. The third section concerns syntax, the form of expressions and statements. The fourth and fifth sections present three special constructs for gathering light at surfaces.

Defining Shaders and Functions

Using the data types and syntax described in this chapter, a programmer can define both shaders for including in the rendering process, and user-defined functions for inserting into shaders. Shaders may only be invoked by the renderer, functions only by shaders and other functions. Except as noted, all features and constructs of the shading language may be used within either.

A shader is defined by preceding its declaration with one of the shading language keywords **light**, **displacement**, **surface**, **volume**, **transformation**, or **imager**.

A function is declared just as in C, by preceding its definition with an optional type, either **float**, **color**, **point**, or **string**. If not declared explicitly, the return value of a function is **float**.

An important difference between C and the shading language is that parameters to functions are passed by *reference*. In practical terms, this means that if a function changes the value of a parameter, that change persists after the function returns. This allows functions to calculate several values and return them in its parameters.

Finally, the shading language forbids recursion, either directly or indirectly: no function may call itself, no function it calls may call it, etc.

Functions and shaders are otherwise syntactically identical, except that shaders do not support return values, so the **return** statement cannot be used. Access to shaders is restricted: they can be invoked only from within a RenderMan program, not by other shaders or by functions. Functions can be called by shaders and other functions, but cannot be called from outside the shading language.

Data

The set of data types in the shading language is small, but includes two special types. Except for those two, no aggregate data types are supported. In the following discussion and the remaining chapters, the names of global variables are emphasized by underlining them.

Data types

The shading language provides for one scalar and two vector data types, and also includes the capability to define and use, but not modify, character strings as names.

float
: The only scalar data type supported by the shading language is **float**. All integer calculations must be performed using floating-point variables.

string
: Character strings are used only for naming such external entities as texture maps. They may be either constants or instance variables.

point
: A **point** is a vector of three floating-point values; such items are usually used to represent positions and directions in three-dimensional space. In *clouds*(), the example in the previous chapter,

many of the global variables are **point**s. The **point** _P_, for example, gives the position of a surface point being shaded.

The individual components of a point are accessed using the special functions **xcomp()**, **ycomp()**, **zcomp()**, **setxcomp()**, **setycomp()** and **setzcomp()**, discussed in the next chapter.

color

color is another type unique to the shading language, representing either the color and intensity of a light, or the reflectivity and opacity of a surface used to scale a light during reflection and transmission. In _clouds()_, the **color** _refl_ is used to store the reflectance of the surface for modifying the light arriving from the light source(s).

In computer graphics a color is usually represented as a triple of values, typically red, green and blue, used to drive the three guns of a color monitor. However, other color spaces do exist. In the RenderMan Shading Language, **color** is an abstract data type of undefined structure. The programmer should make no assumptions about the meaning of the values in a color.

Not only the type but also the size of a color may vary. Renderers supporting the Spectral Color capability allow the user to redefine the number of elements in a **color**, as well as their meaning. The language is defined so that the programmer needn't know the details of the color representation if he or she sticks to the standard color operations on **color** data.

Coordinate systems

Both **color** and **point** values can be expressed in a variety of coordinate systems. Colors may be expressed in the standard RGB system, but also in a variety of other coordinate systems (HSV—hue, saturation and value—and CIE XYZ, for two examples), each of which has a name associated with it. Geometric coordinates stored in **point** values can occur in object space, camera space and any other standard or user-definable coordinate spaces. Coordinate spaces are named as well.

Within a shader, however, all operations occur in uniform coordinate spaces, one for geometry and one for colors. A shader might operate in the geometric object space existing when the shader was declared, or world space. Colors might be expressed in any of a variety of color spaces. But within a given shader, all **point**s will be in the same geometric coordinate space, and all **color**s will be in the same color space, so that the programmer need never worry about consistency. Points expressed in another space will be automatically converted.

Constants

Constants can be assigned to **float** variables just as in any programming language. So can **point** and **color** values. Syntactically, a **color** expression is of the form

> **color** [spacename] (v1, v2, v3)

where **color** is a keyword in the shading language; *v1*, *v2* and *v3* are any floating-point expressions containing only scalar values, and *spacename* is an optional string constant giving the color space in which (*v1*, *v2*, *v3*) is expressed. For example,

> **color** c = **color** "hsv" (.8, .2, .1);

declares a **color** variable *c* and initializes it to an HSV value. That value will be converted to the common color space before storing it into *c*.

There are five predefined color coordinate systems, listed in Table 14.1 together with the meaning of each component of color constants in that system. "rgb" is the default; if *spacename* is omitted in the expression, "rgb" is assumed.

Coordinate System	Meaning
"rgb"	red, green, blue as defined by NTSC
"hsv"	hue, saturation, value
"xyz"	CIE xyz coordinates
"xyY"	CIE xyY coordinates
"YIQ"	NTSC coordinates

Table 14.1 *Color Spaces in the RenderMan Shading Language*

point *coordinate systems*

Expressions of type **point** can be specified using a similar syntax. The relevant coordinate systems for a **point** are those of the rendering process ("object", "world", etc.), plus any named coordinate systems the user may already have defined in the RenderMan program using **RiCoordinateSystem**() (see Chapter 7 for more information). The shading language also defines two other coordinate systems. "current", the default, is the space in which calculations are being performed (normally "camera" or "world", depending on the implementation). "shader" is the object space in which the **RiSurface**() call (as opposed to the object being shaded) was made. This allows several surfaces, each with its own object space, to share a common coordinate system for purposes of shading.

A point *pt* can be declared in the shading language and initialized to the value (*x, y, z*) in the "spacename" coordinate system as follows:

> **point** pt = **point** "spacename" (x, y, z);

(*x, y, z*) is expressed in the space named by "spacename" and transformed into the "current" space. Again, *x, y,* and *z* may be any scalar expression. If "spacename" is omitted, a point constant is in "shader" space if it appears in the shader parameter list, and in the "current" space elsewhere. "shader" space is similar to object space: points defined therein are transformed by the current transformation as it is defined when the shader is instanced.

Global Variables

Global variables have a special meaning in the shading language, supplying shaders with information they may use in performing their calculations. The renderer makes sure those values are valid when a shader is called. Since a surface shader, for example, is concerned with computing the color of light reflecting from a surface in a particular direction, it generally needs to know the position of that point in 3-dimensional space and the direction from which it is to calculate a reflection. The global **point** variables $\underline{P}$ and $\underline{I}$, respectively, supply that information.

Table 14.2 lists each predefined global variable available to surface shaders, together with its data type, storage class and a summary of its meaning. Different sets of global variables are available to other shader types. They appear in Table 14.3.

Type	Name	Storage Class	Purpose
color	*Cs*	varying/uniform	Surface color (input)
color	*Os*	varying/uniform	Surface opacity (input)
point	*P*	varying	Surface position
point	*dPdu*	varying	Change in position with u
point	*dPdv*	varying	Change in position with v
point	*N*	varying	Surface shading normal
point	*Ng*	varying/uniform	Surface geometric normal
float	*u,v*	varying	Surface parameters
float	*du,dv*	varying/uniform	Change in u,v across element
float	*s,t*	varying	Surface texture coordinates
color	*L*	varying/uniform	Direction from surface to light source
color	*Cl*	varying/uniform	Light color
point	*I*	varying	Direction of ray impinging on surface point (often from camera)
color	*Ci*	varying	Color of light from surface (output)
color	*Oi*	varying	Opacity of surface (output)
point	*E*	uniform	Position of the camera

Table 14.2 *Global Variables Available to Surface Shaders*

Surface color and transparency

Cs and *Os* represent the current surface color and opacity, respectively, as declared in **RiColor**() and **RiOpacity**() and bound to the surface being shaded when it was created.

Cs and *Os* are used as filter values. The color of reflected light from a surface with surface color *Cs* under incident light with color *Cl* is often taken to be *Cl* ∗ *Cs*. In other words, each component of *Cs* scales the corresponding component of the incoming light according to the absorption of the surface. *Os* has the same effect on light passing *through* the surface. Normally, every component of *Cs* and *Os* lies in the range [0,1].

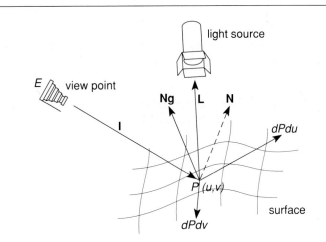

Figure 14.1 *Surface position, normal, and parametric derivatives*

Surface position and change

The **point** value P represents the position of the point being shaded in world space, and Ng is the **geometric normal vector**, perpendicular to the surface, at that point. The **shading normal vector** N is by default equal to Ng, but may be different for shading purposes. If a displacement shader changes the surface normal, it usually works on N and leaves Ng alone.

Parameter space

The floating-point values u and v give the position of the current point on the current surface in parameter space. The **point**s $dPdu$ and $dPdv$ are parametric derivatives, giving the derivative of surface position P with respect to u and v, respectively. The surface normal Ng is defined to be the cross-product of these two vectors. u and v always range between exactly 0 and 1 on all surfaces except polygons.

Figure 14.1 illustrates P, Ng, $dPdu$ and $dPdv$. The normal vector Ng is the cross product of $dPdu$ and $dPdv$ by definition.

Texture space

The floating-point values s and t give the texture-space coordinates of the current point on the surface. They may be used to index into textures or bump maps (see the section on built-in functions, below), etc. for modulating surface properties coherently. They may also be used as input to any function in two dimensions for varying the appearance of the surface.

s and t are equal to u and v, unless vertex variables or **RiTextureCoordinates**() changed the texture space of the primitive being shaded. By default, though, all quadrics, patches and patch meshes exactly cover the texture range [0,1].

Reflection variables

A surface shader reports its reflected light back by setting the global **color** variable Ci, and reports in **color** Oi the extent to which it blocks light from behind the surface. The default values of both Ci and Oi are undefined. Consequently, all shaders must take care to set them explicitly. *clouds*() in Chapter 13 always set Oi to 1.0, producing an opaque surface with variations only in reflected color Ci.

Light variables

The color Cl gives the color of light arriving at the surface at a given point, and the point L gives the direction in which it is arriving. If the light source has a position, then L's length is the distance between the light point and the surface point.

While the variables above are always defined when a shader is called, L and Cl are redefined for each light source. Since a surface shader is called only once at each surface point, but there may be light from many sources impinging on that surface, the shading language provides the **illuminance** construct, described in the fourth section of this chapter. In concept, it "loops" over all light sources, setting L and Cl once for each light source. (This may not be strictly true for all renderers.)

Camera and surface position

When a shader is called, the point E is set to the position of the camera in world space. Frequently the reflection being calculated is toward the camera, so that the incident direction $I = P - E$. However, in the context of a ray tracer, rays may be calculated in any direction, so that one should not assume that this equality always holds. Consequently, E should be used rarely if ever by a surface shader.

Surface derivatives

Two other global variables are provided in support of **surface elements**. Some renderers operate by dividing surfaces into pieces small enough to be rendered with a single color. Surface elements are typically smaller than a pixel as seen in the image, in which case flatness of either color or geometry is usually not discernible.

Small size notwithstanding, some shaders may find it handy to know how large a surface element is being shaded. For these purposes, the global floating-point values du and dv give the change in parametric surface parameters u and v across the element. Of course this assumes that the boundaries of an element are rectangular in parameter space.

The names du and dv hint at a third characteristic of surface elements: they are usually small enough that the absolute change in u and v across the element mimic the surface's derivatives at the current point. In fact, the following relationship holds: if the surface location $P(u, v)$ is P at parameter location (u, v), then

$$P(u+du, v) = P(u, v) + dPdu*du$$

and

$$P(u, v+dv) = P(u, v) + dPdv*dv$$

Global variables in other shaders

Table 14.3 lists the complete set of global variables that are part of the RenderMan Shading Language. Not all of them are available within all shaders, however, so the table also indicates what variables are available inside which types of shader. In a cell of the table, 'R' indicates that a shader of the given type may read the variable, and 'W' indicates that it may write values to that variable.

When a shader of a given type is called, the renderer guarantees the validity of all of the 'R' global variables listed under

Type	Name	Surface	Light	Displ.	Transform	Volume	Imager
color	*Cs*	R					
color	*Os*	R					
point	*P*	R	R	RW	RW	R	R
point	*dPdu*	R	R†	R			
point	*dPdv*	R	R†	R			
point	*N*	R	R†	RW	RW		
point	*Ng*	R	R†	R			
point	*Ps*		R				
float	*u,v*	R	R†	R			
float	*du,dv*	R	R†	R			
float	*s,t*	R	R†	R			
point	*L*	R*	R*				
color	*Cl*	R*	RW*				
point	*I*	R				R	
color	*Ci*	RW				RW	RW
color	*Oi*	RW				RW	RW
point	*E*	R	R			R	
float	*A*	R					R

* *inside* **solar**(), **illuminate**(), *or* **illuminance**()
† *only sensible in area light sources*

Table 14.3 *Global Variables in the RenderMan Shading Language*

that type in Table 14.2. A shader of a particular type returns a value by setting one or more of the 'W' variables, and cannot modify any others.

Instance variables

If global variables are effectively the parameters of a single *call* of a shader, instance variables are the parameters of an *instance* of a shader. A single light source shader, for example, can be instanced a number of times as distinct light sources differing in position, color, etc.

Instance variables are declared for a shader as if they were parameters to the shader routine. In *clouds*(), the instance variables are *Ka* and *Kd*, representing the weight accorded to ambient and diffuse reflections from the surface. When the shader is instanced, the application gives them values by passing token-value pairs to **RiSurface**(). Those values are passed to the shader every time the instance is invoked. They cannot be changed after the instance is created.

Default values

Instance variables differ from procedure parameters in one important respect. They must be assigned default values when they are declared. In *clouds*(), *Ka* has the default value .8 and *Kd* is .2. This constraint makes all instance variables optional when instancing the shader; any variable whose value is not specified receives the default.

Local variables

Shaders may have local variables as well as instance variables and global variables. They may be declared only at the beginning of a shader and may be **float**, **point**, or **color**, but not **string**.

Storage classes

The **float**, **point**, and **color** data types may be declared under two different storage classes, **uniform** and **varying**. A **uniform** instance variable is assumed to be constant over a surface, so it has the same value every time an instance of a shader is called. A **varying** instance variable can differ for each point on the surface. It may or may not actually be different each time an instance of a shader is called. Declaring a variable to be **uniform** may allow the shader to be executed more efficiently: any expressions involving only **uniform** variables need only be evaluated once, when the shader is instanced. By default, instance variables are **uniform** and local variables are **varying**.

Syntax

The syntax of the RenderMan Shading language is like C in many respects, but is tailored to the job of expressing shading calculations.

Expressions

The shading language supports both arithmetic and logical expressions on **float**, **point**, and **color** values, adding two special operators for **points** and **colors**. Table 14.4 gives the set of operators, their precedence and purpose.

Operation	Associativity	Function
( )	left	expression grouping
– !	right	unary arithmetic & logical negation
.	left	dot product
* /	left	multiplication, division
^	left	cross product
+ –	left	addition, subtraction
< <= => >	left	arithmetic comparison
== !=	left	equal, not equal
&&	left	logical AND
||	left	logical OR
? :	right	conditional expression
=	right	assignment

Table 14.4 *Operators in the Shading Language*

Operators

Both arithmetic and relational operators have the same meaning for floating-point values in the RenderMan Shading Language as they do in C.

Arithmetic on special types

When the arithmetic operators '+', '–', '*' and '/' are used on two **point** values or two **color** values, they are applied to each component of the two individually, forming a like-typed result. To be consistent with the definition of **color** as an abstract type, they are illegal between a **point** and a **color** even though the two types often have the same number of components.

When an arithmetic operation is performed between a **float** and a **point** or a **float** and a **color**, the scalar is promoted by duplicating its value in each component of the vector. This is equivalent to performing the operation between the **float** and each component in turn.

Comparison of special types

The result of a comparison is always a single Boolean value, even if the operands include a **point** or a **color**. In fact, the only relational operators allowed between two **point**s or two **color**s are '==' and '!='. If a **float** is compared to a **point** or a **color**, it is promoted just as for arithmetic operations.

Dot product

In C, the '.' operator is used to access an element of a structure, but there are no structured data types in the shading language. Here, the '.' operator is a dot product, taking two **point** operands and forming a **float** by multiplying corresponding elements of the two **point**s, then summing the products.

Meaning of dot product

The dot product is a simple way of measuring the angle between two vectors. If |**A**| is defined as the Euclidean length of vector **A**, then for vectors **A** and **B**,

$$\mathbf{A}.\mathbf{B} = |\mathbf{A}||\mathbf{B}|\cos\theta$$

where θ is the angle between **A** and **B**. If **A** and **B** have been normalized such that |**A**| = |**B**| = 1, then $\mathbf{A}.\mathbf{B} = \cos\theta$.

Dot product operands

The dot product takes either two **point**s or two **color**s as operands, never one **point** and one **color**. If one of the operands, but not both, is a **float**, it is promoted to the appropriate type by duplicating its value in all elements of the type. The dot product of two **color** values is allowed.

Cross product

The cross-product operator '^' applies to **point** values and forms a **point** result, unlike the dot product. If **A** and **B** are vectors represented by a **point**, then **A**^**B** is a vector perpendicular to both **A** and **B**. The length of **A**^**B** is

$$|\mathbf{A}^{\wedge}\mathbf{B}| = |\mathbf{A}||\mathbf{B}|\sin\theta$$

where θ is the angle between **A** and **B**.

Meaning of cross product

The cross product is commonly used to find the normal to a surface at a point, given two nonparallel vectors tangent to the surface at that point. The geometric surface normal vector expressed in the global variable *Ng* is defined as the cross product of the parametric derivative vectors *dPdu* and *dPdv*. In other words,

$$Ng \equiv dPdu \wedge dPdv.$$

Cross product operands

As with the dot product, the cross product of a **point** and a **float** is performed by promoting the latter to a **point** by setting all components of the **point** to that value. Doing so doesn't usually make sense, however.

Statements

In addition to the assignment statements expected of any algebraic programming language, the shading language supports statement grouping using the delimiters '{' and '}', together with the control constructs for which they are most useful.

Both conditional execution and looping are controlled by boolean expressions. These typically result from a binary comparison between two values. In C, any arithmetic value can be used to form a boolean expression; if the value is nonzero, the boolean is true. In the shading language, however, it is illegal to use a **float**, **point** or **color** value where a boolean expression is expected.

if-then-else One of two alternative statements can be chosen for execution with the usual **if-then-else** construct:

> **if**(boolean expression) statement [**else** statement]

where statement is either a single statement or a series of statements between the delimiters '{' and '}'. The **else** clause is optional.

while A statement can be executed repeatedly with the **while** construct:

> **while** (boolean expression) statement

The *expression* is tested before *statement* is first executed, and *statement* is executed repeatedly as long as the *expression* is true.

for

The shading language includes the C **for** statement:

> **for** (expr; boolean_expression; expr) statement

clouds() shows that the **for** construct in the shading language parallels the C version: the first *expr* is executed only once, before *statement* is first executed; *boolean_expression* is evaluated before every execution of *statement*; and the second *expr* is executed after *statement*. Since an assignment statement is accepted as an *expr*, the two *exprs* can be, and most commonly are, used to initialize and increment loop variables.

break

A **for** or **while** loop can be terminated regardless of the state of its controlling boolean by using

> **break** [n]

with a constant value *n* to specify that *n* levels of nested loops should be terminated, beginning with the innermost. *n* is optional, defaulting to 1, terminating the innermost enclosing loop.

continue

A loop can also be restarted with the **continue** construct,

> **continue** [n]

which redirects execution to the bottom of the *n*th nested loop. If the loop is a **for** construct, this is effectively a branch to the increment *expr*. Again, *n* must be a constant and its default is 1, the innermost loop.

return

A function (not a shader) can be terminated at any time using

> **return** expr

where *expr* will be the value returned from the function, and is cast to the expected return type if possible. *expr* may be omitted.

illuminance

One of the novel constructs of the RenderMan Shading Language is **illuminance**. The basic idea is to give surface shaders a way of collecting samples of all the light arriving at a surface at the point being shaded.

Figure 14.2 shows the expected configuration. Light reflected in the direction I may be influenced by light striking the surface from anywhere in the **incident cone** W (which in this case is a hemisphere). For a very diffuse surface, light striking from anywhere above the surface can be reflected toward the camera, so W opens at a 180° angle in this case. The first job of the **illuminance** construct is to limit the attention of the surface shader to the appropriate direction.

illuminance The syntax of **illuminance** is

> **illuminance**(position[, axis, angle]) statement

position is the only required argument, a **point** giving the position of the apex of the incident cone. It is usually P for a surface shader (see Figure 14.2 for clarification). *axis* is a **point**, a vector giving the center of the cone as a direction from *position*. *angle* is a **float** giving the angle between a side of the cone and the axis, in radians, so the cone is 2*angle* radians wide. No samples will be taken outside this cone.

If *axis* and *angle* are omitted, light contributions are summed over the entire sphere centered at *position*. The usefulness of this default is limited because surfaces are normally not illuminated by lights behind them, but the hemisphere of illuminance needed to do that is impossible to define in the absence of an *axis*. If that behavior is desired, *axis* would be the surface normal and *angle* would be PI/2. If *angle* is 0, the cone is infinitesimally thin, a single ray in fact, and only light coming in from *exactly* that direction is used for shading the surface. A mirror would be the surface most likely to use such an *angle*. A specular surface might use a narrow *angle*, and an *axis* obtained by reflecting I about the surface normal.

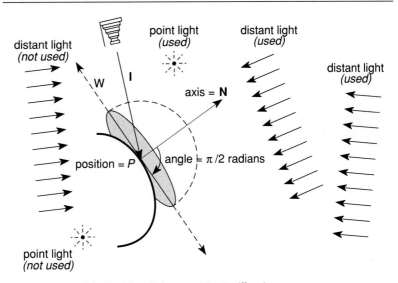

Figure 14.2 *Model of incident light served by the **illuminance** construct*

For each source of illumination within the incident cone, *statement* is executed once, with Cl set to the arriving light and L the direction toward the source. In most cases the shader will use both Cl and L to calculate the color reflected toward the eye from that direction.

illuminance statements cannot be nested. In other words, *statement* cannot include another **illuminance** statement.

How illuminance works

The **illuminance** construct is designed to support different rendering approaches. For simpler shading models, the only important elements in illuminating a surface are light sources. Renderers operating under such models will usually sample only the light sources, executing the **illuminance** statement once for each light source within the cone. With two exceptions, this reduces the **illuminance** construct to a simple loop over all relevant light sources. One exception is ambient light sources, which have no direction. Their contribution must be handled separately by having the shader call the built-in function **ambient**(). The other exception is an area light source, which may be treated as if it were many individual point light sources.

Sampling reflections

More sophisticated rendering approaches (for example, ray-tracing and radiosity methods) may illuminate a surface with light reflected from other surfaces as well as a light from light sources. Rays are cast from $\underline{P}$ to determine the light $\underline{Cl}$ arriving from different directions $\underline{L}$, regardless of whether that light was emitted by a light source or reflected from a surface. All this is transparent to the shader that uses an **illuminance** statement.

Ray tracing and illuminance

Fans of rendering by ray tracing may have recognized by now the resemblance between sampling under **illuminance** and ray tracing. In ray tracing, rays would be cast from $\underline{P}$ within the **illuminance** cone [WHITTED80]. The reflection at the first surface struck by each ray is calculated recursively, then used in the reflection at the original surface. Rays would normally be cast toward light sources within the cone.

The shading language supports ray tracing implicitly by ignoring the difference between light coming in from light sources and light from surfaces. (This is why a surface shader should always use $\underline{I}$ as the view direction rather than ($\underline{P}$–$\underline{E}$) even though they are equivalent when viewing a surface from the camera.) Shaders pass the problem of deriving the incoming light back to the renderer by using the **illuminance** construct. Not all renderers support this generality, however.

illuminance *and radiosity*

Another popular shading technique calculates diffuse reflection using a complete analysis of the distribution of light energy (**radiosity**) in a scene [GORAL84]. A radiosity-based renderer may return the results of the radiosity calculation in the **dif-**

fuse() function, but the **illuminance** *statement* could easily serve the same purpose. The renderer might present the arriving radiosity in a variety of directions as iterations of the **illuminance** *statement.*

illuminance *and integration*

The **illuminance** construct is really meant to model the integration of incoming light over a specified cone. There *are* ways to accurately compute the integral, and that's what **illuminance** does, at least in principle. However, a given implementation may take short cuts. Even within a given implementation there may exist controls over the accuracy of the approximation. No approximations in the renderer, though, should affect the way an **illuminance** statement is used by the shader.

illuminate and solar

The **illuminance** construct allows surface shaders to integrate the light impinging on a surface over a finite cone. Two similar constructs exist for light sources to denote the distribution of light emerging from the source. Both of them are specified over a cone, and the statements within may be executed for any direction inside the cone.

Model of light emission

Many light sources are **directional**, casting all their light in one direction and none in others. The classic example of this behavior is the sun as seen from the earth, where rays are essentially parallel. At the opposite extreme are so-called point lights, which emit light uniformly in all directions from a single point.

Since the **illuminance** construct of surface shaders is executed once for each directional sample, it would help the underlying system to know what light sources are relevant in a particular direction: there's no sense evaluating a light source shader if it's pointed in the wrong direction. The **solar** and **illuminate** constructs for light source shaders provide that information, declaring a solid cone of emission such that surface points outside the cone of emission of a light source are considered to be in the dark.

The illumination constructs are declared in a manner similar to the **illuminance** construct. They are driven by a solid cone specified in the header. The body specifies the cast light as a function of direction within the cone, as though the body were called repeatedly to spread light throughout the cone. In fact, the body is only executed when a surface requires light from within the cone.

Though the illumination constructs have the superficial appearance of looping constructs, they are more in the nature of coroutines operating in conjunction with the **illuminance** construct: the renderer calculates the intersection of the cones provided by the two. Each body is executed only if the apex of each cone is within the other cone.

The difference between the two illumination constructs is that one includes a position for the light source and the other doesn't (infinitely distant light sources have no position). Since in both cases the solid cone is optional, between them they cover both directional and non-directional light sources, with and without position.

illuminate   The **illuminate** construct has the syntax

> **illuminate**(position [, axis, angle]) statement

statement is a statement in the RenderMan Shading Language. *position* and *axis* are any valid **point** expressions, while *angle* must be a **float** expression. The value of *position* gives the location of the apex of the cone, and *axis* specifies the direction of the center of the cone. *angle* is the angle between the center of the cone and its outside in radians, so that an *angle* of PI/2 covers a hemisphere. If *axis* and *angle* are omitted, the light emits over the entire sphere centered at *position*.

Within *statement*, $\underline{L}$ is set to the vector from *position* to a surface point in three-dimensional space. The length of $\underline{L}$ is the distance between the light source position and the surface point. The light source shader should set $\underline{Cl}$ to the color and intensity of the light emerging from the source and ar-

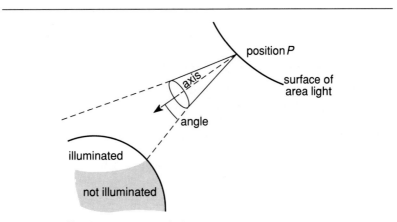

Figure 14.3 illuminate *on an area light source*

riving at the surface. Many shaders will diminish the intensity of the light with distance from the surface.

A point light source

A point light source is given in terms of the **illuminate** construct by

> **illuminate**($\underline{P}$)
> $\underline{Cl}$ = (intensity * lightcolor) / ($\underline{L}$.$\underline{L}$);

$\underline{P}$ is the position of the light source, *intensity* the relative intensity of the source and *lightcolor* its color. (Presumably the latter two are instance variables). Since $\underline{L}$ is preset to the vector from $\underline{P}$ to the point being illuminated, the dot product $\underline{L}$.$\underline{L}$ gives the square of that distance and dividing by the result implements an inverse-square law falloff.

An area light source

The **illuminate** construct makes it easy to define an area light source. Inside an area light source, the global value $\underline{P}$ is set by the renderer to a point on the surface of the geometric primitive that describes the area light, and most standard surface variables are defined. Figure 14.3 shows the situation.

The following statement implements a simple area light source:

illuminate(P, N, PI/2)
    Cl = (intensity * lightcolor) / (L.L);

The axis $\underline{N}$ and angle *PI/2* allow the source to cast light over the hemisphere centered at $\underline{P}$. The assignment to $\underline{Cl}$ distributes the emitted light uniformly over the hemisphere without regard to angle.

solar   The **solar** construct restricts illumination to a range of directions without specifying a position for the source. At two extremes of behavior, it encompasses distant light sources, which cast light in only one direction, and starlight in space, which comes from all around and doesn't vary with different positions.

The **solar** construct appears as:

    solar([axis, angle]) statement

axis, angle and *statement* have the same meaning as in the **illuminate** construct: *statement* is executed (light is cast) only for directions within *angle* radians from the direction vector given by *axis*. If the arguments are omitted, *statement* is always executed (light may be emitted in any direction). Within *statement*, $\underline{Ps}$ is set to the position of the surface point being shaded. This contrasts with $\underline{L}$ in **illuminate**, since a solar source has no position and $\underline{L}$ runs between the surface and light source positions.

A light source representing a distant light source such as the sun is easy to specify:

    solar(D, 0)
        Cl = intensity * lightcolor;

$\underline{Cl}$ is nonzero only in directions matching the direction *D* of the light source.

A skylight shader

A skylight source is almost as easy, and serves as an example of the **solar** construct. In the earth's atmosphere, light from the sun illuminates objects both directly (directionally, as in the distant source above) and indirectly by means of refraction and scattering in the atmosphere. To a first approximation, this indirect light can be treated as a uniformly-illuminated hemisphere, and the light arriving at a surface can be treated as a summation of all the light from the hemisphere toward the surface.

The **solar** statement below implements a simple version of skylight:

```
point D = point "world" (0, -1, 0);
solar( D, PI/2 )
     Cl = intensity * lightcolor;
```

It assumes that the surface of the world is in the x,z plane in world space, so that y is up. It takes light from the "sky," the hemisphere centered on the y axis and opening to negative y. For a surface shader that uses **illuminance** to sum incoming light over a broad incident cone, the intensity of sky light will be greatest for surfaces facing the zenith, and fall off to 0 in the opposite direction.

In reality, for any angle within the sky light hemisphere, both the color and the brightness of the light depend in a complex way on the angle's nearness to the sun and the horizon. But that is left as an exercise for the reader.

CHAPTER **15**

The RenderMan Shading Language III: Tools

The RenderMan Shading Language specifies numerous functions that shaders and other functions can call—tools of the shading trade, you might say. That functionality is described in this chapter.

Mathematical Functions

The mathematical functions supported by the shading language are summarized in Table 15.1. Most of them are generic scalar mathematical functions, for which no further explanation is necessary. All arguments are floating-point expressions and all functions return **float** values. Angles are expressed in radians.

There are other mathematical functions, described below, that aren't limited to **float** values but can also take, as well as return, **point** or **color** values. Unlike the case in many programming languages, the same function name is used for all three cases, so that, for example, any type of expression can be interpolated by the **spline**() function. Needless to say, all arguments must be the same type in a given call. The functions below are also more exotic than those in Table 15.1 in terms of their capabilities.

---

spline(value, f1, f2...fn, fn1)

The **spline**() function returns a point on a curve fitted to a number of values using a Catmull-Rom interpolatory spline.

Name	Returns
sin(a)	sine of angle a, a **float** expressed in radians
asin(a)	arcsine of angle a
cos(a)	cosine of angle a, expressed in radians
acos(a)	arccosine of angle a
tan(a)	tangent of angle a, expressed in radians
atan(a)	arctangent of a
atan(y,x)	arctangent of (y/x)
float PI	predefined float value of *PI*
radians(a)	degree-to-radian conversion
degrees(a)	radian-to-degree conversion
sqrt(x)	square root of x
pow(x,y)	x^y of x and y
exp(x)	e^x for x
log(x)	natural logarithm of x
mod(a, b)	a modulo b
abs(x)	absolute value of x
sign(x)	+1 or −1, depending on sign of x
min(a,b)	minimum of a and b
max(a,b)	maximum of a and b
clamp(a,min,max)	a clamped to the range [*min*,*max*]
ceil(x)	smallest integer greater than or equal to x
floor(x)	largest integer less than or equal to x
round(x)	closest integer to x
step(min, val)	0 if *val* < *min*; 1 if *val* ≥ *max*
smoothstep(min, max, val)	0 if *val* < *min*; 1 if *val* ≥ *max*; otherwise, a smooth Hermite interpolation between 0 and 1

Table 15.1 *Shading Language Scalar Math Functions (all arguments and return values are type* **float***)*

value should lie between 0 and 1. If it is 0, *f2* is returned; if it is 1, *fn* is returned. Otherwise, a point on the fitted curve is returned. The curve passes through all the points *f2...fn. f1* and *fn1* are used to determine the direction of the curve at its endpoints: at *f2*, the curve's tangent is (*f3-f1*), and at *fn*, (*fn1–f(n-1)*).

The arguments to **spline()** may be **float, point** or **color** expressions, but all arguments must be of the same type. The return type matches that type.

Derivative functions

Surface shaders frequently can make use of various derivatives on the surface, typically expressed in the parameter space of the surface.

Du(expr)

Dv(expr)

Within a surface, displacement or deformation shader, or a light source shader operating on an area light source, **Du()** and **Dv()** compute the parametric derivative of the expression *expr* with respect to the *u* and *v* parameters of the underlying surface.

It only makes sense to take the derivative of expressions that depend on **varying** variables: the derivatives of **uniform** expressions are always 0.

The derivative of a variable with respect to variables other than *u* and *v* may be taken using **Deriv()**.

Deriv(num, denom)

Deriv() computes the derivative of expression *num* with respect to *denom*. The arguments may be of arbitrary but identical types. The result (of the same type) is calculated using the rule:

$$\mathbf{Deriv}(num, denom) = \frac{\mathbf{Du}(num)}{\mathbf{Du}(denom)} + \frac{\mathbf{Dv}(num)}{\mathbf{Dv}(denom)}$$

As with **Du()** and **Dv()**, **Deriv()** is only useful when *num* and *denom* are **varying** expressions.

Noise

noise(val)
    float val;

noise(u, v)
    float u, v;

noise(pt)
    point pt;

The **noise()** function computes either a 1-, 2- or 3-dimensional noise function, depending on the number and type of its arguments. It returns a **float** value between 0 and 1 by default, but **point** and **color** values can be obtained, as in

        p = **point noise**(...);

and

        c = **color noise**(...);

noise() is based on random-number generation, but it is guaranteed to be consistent from one frame to another. Any appearance parameters based on **noise()** will be stable in an animation as long as the parameters to **noise()** are stable.

A word about magic

Some of the functions above might seem problematic to implement. Just how, for example, do **Du()** and **Dv()** know the derivative of, not just **varying** *variables*, but *expressions* as well? How does **spline()** know what type of data to return?

The existence of these functions is a benefit of special-purpose programming language design. The compiler for the shading language knows how **varying** variables change over a surface, and can approximate the derivative of a variable using its change over a surface element. The compiler knows *a priori* about the predefined data types, and can determine the appropriate version of **spline()** from the context.

These kinds of functions work well enough that it is not worth discussing their internals. However, there are small but significant inherent dangers associated with some of the functions to follow. These pitfalls will be highlighted as they arise.

Shading, Coloring and Lighting Functions

The functions described next aid the process of writing surface shaders by implementing some common shading algorithms. Each one calculates a basic type of reflection over all light sources, summing them into a net reflection. They allow a surface shader to break down the process of shading a point into two parts. The first part modifies the contribution of each light source according to the orientation of the surface with respect to the light; the second part factors in the color of the surface *after* summing the lights.

None of the functions below concern themselves with the color of the surface. In other words, the color is returned as if the surface were completely white. The calling shader must decide what to do with that value: whether to multiply it by the surface color Cs to color the reflection, or to look up the reflectance in a texture map, or whatever. The shading functions concern themselves only with geometry and light source characteristics. Any other property of the surface must be attended to separately.

These functions are intended to aid in developing a variety of shaders, and are not meant to be universal. Specifically, they are inappropriate if the reflectivity of a surface varies with incident angle, since the returned value represents a simple summation of light from all incident directions.

Ambient illumination

---

color ambient()

The **ambient**() function sums the contributions of all ambient light sources in a scene and returns it as a **color**. An ambient light source is one with no **illuminance** or **solar** statement. (See Chapter 14 for a discussion of these constructs.)

Most surface shaders will multiply the return value of **ambient**() by the **color** of the surface (for example, Cs or a texture value) to get the ambient contribution to reflected color.

Diffuse illumination

---

color diffuse(norm)
    point norm;

diffuse() calculates diffuse reflection for a given surface normal, given by *norm*. **diffuse**() sums the diffuse reflection for all light sources as follows:

```
color C = 0;
point unitnorm = normalize(norm);
illuminance( P, unitnorm , PI/2)
        C += Cl* normalize(L).unitnorm ;
return C ;
```

Since **diffuse**() uses the **illuminance**() construct, the incoming light *Cl* may arise from object reflections as well as light-source emissions, depending on the renderer. Radiosity-based renderers will do much of their work in the guise of the **diffuse**() function.

Phong illumination

---

color phong(norm, eye, size)
    point norm, eye;
    float size;

Like **diffuse**(), **phong**() sums the contribution of all light sources over a surface. The Phong shading model assumes that reflections are greatest in the "mirror" direction **R**, opposite the eye vector with respect to the surface normal, falling off rapidly from **R***. The exponent is given by the *size* parameter: the greater the value of *size*, the sharper a highlight appears. *eye* is the direction of the viewpoint from the surface (normally *I*), and *norm* is the "normal" about which the *eye* is reflected

---

* Note on typeface conventions: In this discussion, **R**, **L**, **N**, **I**, and **H** are vectors, and are shown in **boldface**. Of these, **L**, **N** and **I** are available in the RenderMan Shading Language in the global variables *L*, *N*, and *I*. This is represented by underlining the boldface type as in **L**, **N** and **I**.

to obtain **R**. *norm* is usually $\underline{\mathbf{N}}$. For each light source, **phong**() scales the incoming light by

$$c = \left(\frac{\mathbf{R}.\mathbf{L}}{|\underline{\mathbf{L}}|} \right)^{size}$$

raising the cosine of the angle between **R** and $\underline{\mathbf{L}}$ to the power *size*.

Specular reflection

The specular shading model is similar to the Phong model in basing its falloff on the angle between two vectors. Whereas the Phong model uses the angle between light-source direction $\underline{\mathbf{L}}$ and the mirror direction **R**, the specular shading model uses the angle between the normal vector $\underline{\mathbf{N}}$ and the "halfway" vector **H**, which points exactly between $\underline{\mathbf{L}}$ and the incident direction $\underline{\mathbf{I}}$.

color specular(norm, eye, roughness)
    point norm, eye;
    float roughness;

specular() accumulates specular reflections in the direction *eye* off a surface with normal *norm*. For a given light source, the reflection falls off as follows: the direction vector **H** halfway between $\underline{\mathbf{L}}$ and *eye* is compared to *norm*. The cosine of the angle between **H** and *norm* is raised to the power $1/roughness$. The light source color *Cl* is scaled by the result. The surface color must be factored in elsewhere. **specular**() scales the contribution of each incoming light source by

$$c = \left(\frac{norm.\mathbf{H}}{|norm| \, |\mathbf{H}|} \right)^{(1/roughness)}$$

Figure 15.1 shows the difference between Phong and specular reflection for a distant light source in front of and below the scene, and one behind and above it. At the top are four spheres using **specular**() with *roughness* values of (from left to right) 0.4, 0.2, 0.1 and 0.05; the bottom four use **phong**() with

Figure 15.1 *Specular(top) vs. Phong(bottom) reflection*

size set to 5, 10, 20 and 40. In addition to providing a subjectively more credible highlight, the specular model avoids the sudden discontinuity in brightness visible in the bottom left sphere. That transition occurs because the Phong model gives a bright reflection even for points near the "horizon" of the sphere with respect to the light source. As a result, the cutoff occurring where the surface turns away from the light seems abrupt.

Ray tracing

As discussed in the last chapter, the **illuminance** construct collects samples of light falling at surface position P in a variety of directions. This is equivalent to invoking a ray tracer in each direction. This same capability can be accessed directly using the built-in function **trace**():

color trace(location, direction)
    point location, direction;

trace() determines the color of light incident on surface point *location,* from the direction *direction.* Implementations may vary, but **trace**() is equivalent to the **illuminance** statement

> Ci = 0;
> **illuminance** (location, direction, 0)
>   Ci += Cl;

Map Access Functions

Chapter 12 discussed how to apply maps to surfaces. This section describes the support within the shading language for using those maps during the shading process.

There are four basic types of map: texture, environment, shadow and bump maps. Their names indicate their nominal purposes. However, no rule dictates how the data from a map is used. A map may be viewed as a multi-valued function in (usually) two dimensions, where the two dimensions cover the surface. This makes mapping the natural extension of vertex-value interpolation for modulating arbitrary properties of a surface across its extent. With a little thought, mapping can become a powerful tool for creative shading.

Maps and channels

As discussed in Chapter 12, a map is a digital representation of a function in either two or three dimensions. Most maps are defined with a number of **channels**; a color texture map, for example, may have separate channels for red, green, blue and sometimes opacity (alpha). Accessing a point on the map returns a subset of the channel values at the specified location.

Map types

The RenderMan Interface describes maps of four kinds. **Texture maps** are generally used to modulate the reflectivity of surfaces. **Bump maps** are used to specify small variations in the shading normal of a surface, giving it the appearance of roughness with no change in geometry. Both texture and bump maps are indexed by relative surface location. **Environment maps** depict the world as viewed from an object, and are used for mirror reflections. They are indexed by direction of reflection from a surface. A **shadow map** contains information about how a light source is obscured by objects in a scene. A shadow map is indexed by the location of a point in three-dimensional space.

Mapping functions

Each of these four types has its own map access function. The arguments to the map access functions are divided into three groups. The texture-map index function illustrates.

texture(name [channel] , *textcoords, parameterlist*)

name is a string, the name of a texture map file as created by **RiMakeTexture**(), discussed in Chapter 12. *channel* selects a set of the map's channel(s) to be accessed. The channel specification is optional, but if present it must include the square brackets. It is a small non-negative integer constant giving the number of the first channel accessed. If an RGB texture map is to be accessed in all three channels, *channel* may be given as 0, but that is the default if *channel* is omitted. The alpha channel of an RGBA texture map has a *channel* of 3.

textcoords is not an expression but an optional set of texture coordinates. If there are two coordinates, they specify a location on the map to access. The call

    texture("amap" [1], sloc, tloc, ...);

samples the texture map "amap" at location (*sloc,tloc*) beginning with channel 1. If there are eight coordinates, as in

    texture("map2", s1,t1, s2,t2, s3,t3, s4,t4, ...);

the map is accessed from channel 0 over the quadrilateral specified by the four points in texture space. Texture values over that area will be filtered to produce the value returned. If the texture coordinates are omitted, the texture map is accessed at location ($\underline{s}$, $\underline{t}$), the current global texture coordinates.

The *parameterlist* at the end of a map access is a series of to-ken-value pairs. The main idea is to use them to control the quality of filtering done in the access, and there are four standard parameters that exert this control. However, future versions of the interface specification and other implementations may extend this list.

The following discussion assumes this texture access:

```
float lowval, nsamples, swid, twid;
texture("anothermap",  "variance", lowval,
                       "samples", nsamples,
                       "swidth", swidth,
                       "twidth", twidth );
```

This call accesses "anothermap" at the current global (s,t) beginning with channel 0, the "red" channel. (Note that no RI_NULL token is required at the end of *parameterlist*.)

The remaining parameters concern the sampling of the texture map. Just as an image pixel represents scene data projected onto a finite area of the image plane, an access of the texture map represents data spread over a finite area of the map. The extent of this area, and the rate at which it is sampled to determine the output value, are parameters of the access function.

The "variance" token-value pair controls how close the sampled value is to the underlying value in the texture map. The meaning of variance in this context is the same as that in the discussion of **RiPixelVariance**() in Chapter 9.

"samples" specifies an effective sampling rate. For values greater than 1 (it makes no sense for it to be less), the texture map is accessed *nsamples* times for each call of **texture**().

The "swidth" and "twidth" token-value pairs control the area of the texture map over which an access is sampled. In the example above, *swidth* will multiply the width of the sampled area in *s*, and *twidth* will do the same in *t*. Thus, if both *swidth* and *twidth* are 2, the area sampled is four times larger. It is appropriate to take samples over a larger area of the texture map when the map is being sampled infrequently, as might happen when a surface is being shaded at infrequent intervals. Normally, though, the area of the texture map sampled is matched to the spatial frequency with which it is sampled.

Texture access

---

color texture(name[channel], *textcoords, parameterlist*)
float texture(name[channel], *textcoords, parameterlist*)
    string name;
    float channel;

A location in the named texture map is read using the built-in shading function **texture**(). It may return a **float** or a **color**; if the latter, the access is from three (or more, if the number of color samples has been increased) successive channels beginning with *channel*. *textcoords* and *parameterlist* are discussed above.

Bump map access

The function for accessing a bump map differs from that for texture maps in both its parameters and its return type. **bump**() returns a **point** value that is generally used to perturb the surface normal by vector addition.

The general idea in normal perturbation is that it affects a surface in the same way regardless of the surface's position or orientation. Therefore, the relative perturbation must depend not only on the surface's normal vector, but also on its orientation about the normal. See Figure 15.2.

---

point
bump(name[channel], norm, dPds, dPdt, *textcoords, parameterlist*)
    string name;
    float channel;
    point norm, dPds, dPdt;

The *name, channel, textcoords* and *parameterlist* arguments to **bump**() have the same meaning and defaults as they do in **texture**(). The remaining three arguments, all **point**s, are used to define a "local" set of coordinate axes for the normal perturbation. They should be mutually orthogonal. The **point** returned from **bump**() is normally used to perturb the surface normal *norm* by simply adding the two together.

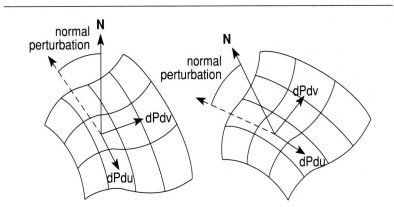

Figure 15.2 *Dependence of normal perturbation on surface location and orientation.*

Since *N*, *dPdu*, and *dPdv* are mutually orthogonal by definition, they make good values of *norm*, *dPds*, and *dPdt*.

bump() may be used even in an implementation that does not support bump mapping. There, the returned point is always (0, 0, 0), safely indicating no perturbation.

Environment maps

color
environment(name[channel], direction, *parameterlist*)
    string name;
    float channel;
    point direction;

The function **environment**() accesses a reflection map. It is indexed, not by texture coordinates (s, t), but by a **point** value giving a direction vector. The *direction* will generally be the "mirror" direction given by the incident vector as reflected about the surface normal. It should be specified in the coordinate system in which the environment map was originally specified. The **color** returned is the color of the environment in that *direction* from the viewpoint at which the environment map was rendered. The direction may also be specified as a comma-separated set of four **point**s, in which case colors from the environment are filtered over the interior of the region delimited by the four directions.

Shadow maps

A shadow map allows light sources to cast shadows on objects without ray tracing. Typically, a shadow map stores the depth of the surface nearest a particular light source in a given direction. Figure 12.9 shows the shadow data used in Figure 7.7. Surfaces nearer the light are darker; only they are illuminated.

Shadow maps, like reflection maps, represent the world as viewed from an object, in this case a light source. They are also accessed similarly.

float
shadow(name[channel], position, *parameterlist*)
    string name;
    float channel;
    point position;

The arguments to **shadow**() are similar to those of **environment**(). *position* is the location of a point in "current" space, and *name* is the external name of a shadow map file created from the point of view of the light source accessing the map. The *shadowspot*() example in the next chapter will show exactly how to use **shadow**().

The return value of **shadow**() is a single floating-point value. It gives the extent to which the surface point is in shadow, 1 indicating complete shadowing and 0 complete exposure. A typical light source shader using a shadow is shown below; it uses the shadow value and provides a square-law falloff.

```
light shadowlight( color lightcolor=color (1,1,1); float intensity=1)
{
    illuminate( P )
        Cl = lightcolor * intensity * (1-shadow("map", Ps))/(L.L);
}
```

Geometric Functions

The shading language defines a variety of functions for geometric calculations. These are summarized in Table 15.2 and discussed below.

Return Type	Declaration	Meaning
float	**xcomp**(P)	return x component of **point** P
float	**ycomp**(P)	return y component of **point** P
float	**zcomp**(P)	return z component of **point** P
—	**setxcomp**(P, v)	set x component of **point** P to **float** v
—	**setycomp**(P, v)	set y component of **point** P to **float** v
—	**setzcomp**(P, v)	set z component of **point** P to **float** v
float	**length(V)**	return the Euclidean length of **point V**
float	**distance**(P1,P2)	return the Euclidean length of ($P1$–$P2$)
float	**area**(P)	return the surface element area at P, in pixels
point	**normalize(V)**	return **V**/**length(V)** for **point V**
point	**faceforward(V,I)**	return **V** flipped to point opposite **I**
point	**reflect(I, N)**	return reflection of incident ray **I** about normalized vector **N**
point	**refract(I,N**,eta)	return incident ray **I** refracted through surface with normal **N** and index of refraction **float** *eta*
	fresnel(I, N, eta, Kr, Kt [, **R, T**])	return reflectance coefficient **float** *Kr*, transmittance coefficient **float** *Kt*, reflected ray **R**, and refracted ray **T**, given incident ray **I**, surface normal **N** and relative index of refraction **float** *eta*
point	**transform**([fromspace,] tospace, P)	transform the **point** P from the coordinate system named by string *fromspace* to the coordinate space named by *tospace*
float	**depth**(P)	return depth of **point** P in camera space, normalized between 0 at the near clipping plane and 1 at the far one
point	**calculatenormal**(P)	return the normal to a surface at **point** P

Table 15.2 *Geometric Shading Functions*

A number of these functions depend on the concept of a **surface element**. Under RenderMan, a surface element is a quadrilateral piece of a larger surface, which spans the distance between adjacent shading samples.

For purposes of shading, a surface element is also assumed to be geometrically infinitesimal, in the sense of the theory of limits in calculus. Specifically, the tangents of a surface element are equated with the change in position across its edges, and its normal can be calculated directly from those. In fact, the derivative of any *varying* value at an element is assumed to be the same as the values's change across the element. The "real" meaning of the global variables _du_ and _dv_, which give the derivatives of the surface parameters at a point, is their change across the surface element. _du_ is nothing but the change in _u_ across one surface element, and similarly for _dv_.

Point components

Since the shading language does not support structured data types, the components of a point are accessed by predefined functions.

---

float xcomp(P)
float ycomp(P)
float zcomp(P)
    point P;

These functions fetch the x, y and z components from a **point** data object. These components are set with

setxcomp(P, val)
setycomp(P, val)
setzcomp(P, val)
    point P;
    float val;

Vector length

---

float length(V)
    point V;

length() returns the Euclidean length of the vector *V*:

$$\begin{aligned}
\textbf{length(V)} &= \textbf{sqrt(} \ \textbf{xcomp(V)*xcomp(V)} + \\
&\quad\ \ \textbf{ycomp(V)*ycomp(V)} + \\
&\quad\ \ \textbf{zcomp(V)*zcomp(V))} \\
&= \textbf{sqrt(} \ \textbf{V.V} \ \textbf{)}
\end{aligned}$$

Distance between points

float distance(p1, p2)
    point p1, p2;

distance() returns the Euclidean distance between points *p1* and *p2*:

        distance(p1, p2) = **length**(p1-p2);

Differential surface area

float area(P)
    point P;

area() returns the raster space area of the surface element at **point** *P*, its area in pixels.

Vector normalization

point normalize(V)
point V;

normalize() returns a vector of length 1 that points in the same direction as **point** vector *V*. If the length of *V* is 0, then

        normalize(V) = point(0,0,0 **)**

Otherwise,

        normalize(V) = V / length(V)

Normal flipping

Function **faceforward**() ensures that two vectors have a particular relative orientation (i.e., they point in opposite directions). It is most frequently used in shading to ensure that a surface normal points toward a light source or the viewpoint.

---

point faceforward(V, R)
    point V, R;

If **V** and **R** form an acute angle when placed head to tail, then **faceforward**() returns **V**. If not, it returns −**V**.

Refraction

Transparent surfaces like glass typically alter the path of light passing through them from other materials like air. The amount of refraction (the angle of deflection) depends on the angle between the entering ray and the surface normal, as well as a **relative index of refraction**, the ratio of the speed of light in the two materials involved.

---

point refract(I, N, eta)
    point I, N;
    float eta;

refract() takes an entering ray direction **I**, a surface normal **N** and a relative index of refraction *eta*. It returns the direction of the refracted ray.

If the angle between **I** and **N** is too great for a given *eta*, the ray is reflected from the surface and none of it enters the material. In that case, **refract**() returns **point** (0, 0, 0).

Proportional reflection and refraction

In most cases, a ray striking a refractive material is partly reflected and partly refracted. The function **fresnel**() calculates the respective fractions. It may also return the reflected and refracted direction vectors, so that it subsumes **refract**().

fresnel(**I**, **N**, eta, Kr, Kt[, **R**, **T**])
    point I, N;
    float eta, Kr, Kt;
    point R, T;

As in **refract**(), *I, N* and *eta* are the incident direction vector, the surface normal vector, and the relative index of refraction between two materials, respectively. When **fresnel**() returns, *Kr* is set to the fraction of light reflected and *Kt* is the fraction of light refracted/transmitted. In general, *Kr* and *Kt* do not sum to 1. They are fractions of intensity, and refraction changes intensity due to focusing and defocusing effects. Both must be variables, of course.

If *R* and *T* are supplied, they are set to the direction vector of the refracted ray and the transmitted ray, respectively.

Coordinate system conversion

When a shader is called, all points are defined in the same ("current") coordinate system. As mentioned in the last chapter, a **point** constant can be expressed in any named coordinate system and implicitly converted to the "current" system. To convert **point** variables, or to convert constants to systems other than "current", requires an explicit function:

point transform([fromspace,]tospace, P)
    string fromspace, tospace;
    point P;

transform() converts the **point** *P* from the coordinate system named by *fromspace* to the coordinate system named by *tospace*. If *fromspace* is omitted, "current" is used.

Relative depth

float depth(P)
    point P;

depth() takes a **point** coordinate in three-dimensional space and returns its distance in *z* from the camera. The depth returned is normalized so that points on the near clipping plane are at depth 0, and on the far clipping plane, 1.

Normal calculation

When a displacement or deformation shader transforms the global surface **point** *P*, it also has the responsibility for resetting the surface normal *N*. This can usually be accomplished easily by calling:

point calculatenormal(P)
    point P;

calculatenormal() determines the surface normal of a surface element based on the change in *P* across the element, as in Figure 15.3:

$$\mathbf{N} = \underline{dPdu} \char94 \underline{dPdv}$$

Color functions

Four functions are provided to perform basic operations on colors.

Accessing color components

Treating color as an abstract data type works out in almost all cases, but when it is really necessary to access the individual components of a color, **comp**() and **setcomp**() are available.

float comp(c, index)
    color c;
    float index;

setcomp(c, index, value)
    color c;
    float index, value;

float ncomps;

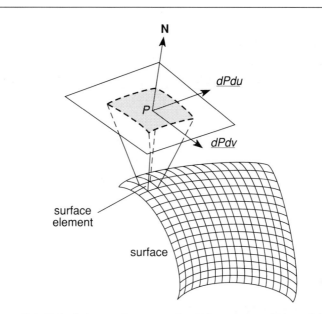

Figure 15.3 Calculating surface normal at _P_ from points _dPdv_ and _dPdu_

comp() returns the value of the *index*th component of **color** _c_. **setcomp**() sets it. For purposes of driving loops over the components of a color, the actual number of components being used is stored in the global variable *ncomps*. A shader should never assume that there are only three components per color.

Color mixing

color mix(color0, color1, a)
    color color0, color1;
    float a;

Two colors can be intermixed by calling the function **mix**() with a value of _a_ between 0 and 1. The color returned is

$$(1{-}a)*color0 + a*color1$$

Printing

Messages can be printed from a shader to a user by using **printf**().

---

printf(format, val1,...,valN)
    string format;

printf() is similar to the C function of the same name. However, the only format specifiers supported in the format string are "%f" for a **float**, "%p" for a **point**, "%c" for a **color** and "%s" for a **string**. Naturally, the types of the corresponding arguments must match the specified type. Printing occurs in an implementation-dependent manner, but usually appears on the user's console.

Further Reading

The improvements on Phong shading were developed by Jim Blinn [BLINN77]. The use of the **noise**() function can best be understood by reading Ken Perlin's paper "An Image Synthesizer" [PERLIN85].

CHAPTER 16

A Gallery of Shaders

After three chapters on the theory of writing shaders, this chapter concerns the practice. There are almost three dozen examples showing how it's done and illustrating the power of this approach to shading. The first five sections of this chapter cover a variety of basic techniques and discuss a case study: given a detailed model, how to present it in the best possible light with different shaders for different effects. Where appropriate, there is a color plate illustrating the effect of a shader. The sixth section discusses some of the other color plates, which have no shader, and we close with a look to the future.

The shaders presented here vary in a number of ways. Some are included primarily to illustrate a point or two, some show interesting ways of doing things, some show how to do some interesting new things, some are robust shaders intended for general use, and some are just for fun. Each one should help the user make the most of this new method of shading.

Standard Shaders

We begin with the shaders defined as a standard part of the RenderMan Interface. They were discussed in Chapter 11 from the user's point of view. The purpose here is twofold: to begin the discussion with some basic examples, and to give them a more formal definition. Even for implementations that do not support the shading language, the functionality of these shaders must be provided.

Constant surface

A constant surface always has the surface color Cs as declared with **RiColor**() and the surface opacity Os declared with **RiOpacity**(). It copies the surface reflectance Cs directly to the output color Ci, as though the surface were illuminated with a white ambient light of intensity 1. This change of meaning is implicit in the assignment, but the distinction between reflectance and color is worth keeping in mind.

```
/*
 * constant(): surface shader giving a constant color
 */
surface
constant()
{
    Oi = Os;
    Ci = Os * Cs;
}
```

Listing 16.1 *Constant-color surface shader*

In the constant shader, the output color Ci is scaled by the opacity of the surface Oi. There are a number of justifications for this requirement [PORTER84], but conceptually the simplest explanation is that it allows colors from behind the surface to show through (add to Ci) without overflowing the bounds of a color.

Matte surface

A matte surface exhibits only diffuse reflection, because it scatters light uniformly with no preferred direction(s). That makes the apparent brightness of such a surface independent of the direction from which it is viewed.

The first line of *matte*() calls the **faceforward**() function, which returns its first argument, a vector, unchanged except that it may be reversed in direction to "face forward" (form an acute angle) with respect to the second argument. In this case, the surface normal is made to face forward with respect to the "incident direction" **I**. If a two-sided surface is viewed from its back side, as defined and discussed in Chapter 7, the surface

```
/*
 * matte(): simple diffusely-reflecting surface
 */
surface
matte(
        float  Ka    = 1,
               Kd    = 1 )
{
        point Nf = faceforward(normalize(N), I);

        Oi = Os;
        Ci = Os * Cs * ( Ka*ambient() + Kd*diffuse(Nf) ) ;
}
```

Listing 16.2 *Matte surface shader*

normal faces away from the incident direction and must be re-versed if shading calculations involving it are to be correct.

The incident direction **I** (the global variable *I*) may be thought of as the direction of view. In many cases the viewing direction is from the camera, but not always, which is why *I* and camera location *E* are distinct. In a ray tracer, for example, the "viewing direction" might be from a highly specular surface that is "viewing" another surface for purposes of reflection. *No shader should assume that I and E are related*, and the worst example of that error is to use (*P–E*) instead of *I*.

The last line of *matte*() sets reflected color *Ci* to the product of opacity *Os*, surface color *Cs*, and a weighted sum of the functions **ambient**() and **diffuse**(). The former function calculates the total color of all ambient light sources, and the latter calculates the light striking the surface at point *P*, with a falloff due to the orientation *Nf*, passed as its argument. Note that while a vector other than *N* may be passed to **diffuse**(), it always assumes that *P* is the point being illuminated. The values returned by **ambient**() and **diffuse**() are light values; these are scaled by the ambient and diffuse coefficient instance variables *Ka* and *Kd*, then multiplied by the surface reflectance *Cs* and opacity *Os* to get the light emerging from the surface due to reflection.

diffuse() demonstrates the need for *Nf* to point correctly. Since **diffuse**() believes whatever vector is passed to it, if the normal

points in the wrong direction it will calculate the diffuse reflection on the wrong side of the surface!

Metal surface

The next step up in realism is to include specular reflections
from the surface. In fact, the only difference between *matte*()
and the *metal*() surface shader is that the latter substitutes a
specular reflection for the former's diffuse component.

```
/*
 * metal(): give a surface a metallic appearance
 */
surface
metal (
        float  Ka        = 1,
               Ks        = 1,
               roughness = .25)
{
        point Nf = faceforward(normalize(N), I) ;

        Oi = Os;
        Ci = Os * Cs * ( Ka*ambient() + Ks*specular(Nf,-I,roughness) );
}
```

Listing 16.3 *Surface shader giving a metallic appearance*

As outlined in the previous chapter, the **specular**() function
implements a surface reflection that is not diffuse (evenly scattered in all directions), but is rather concentrated around the
mirror direction. The instance variable *roughness* of *metal*() is
passed to **specular**() to control the concentration of the specular highlight, a high *roughness* value giving a more diffuse reflection.

Plastic surface

The plastic surface shader is a combination of *matte*() and *metal*(), with the addition of a separate color for the specular highlight. This shader serves a model of plastic as a solid medium
with microscopic colored particles suspended within it. The
specular highlight is assumed to be reflected directly off the
surface, and the surface color is assumed to be due to light en-

tering the medium, reflecting off the suspended particles, and re-emerging. This model explains why the color of the specular reflection is different from the surface; it also explains why so many early high-quality computer graphic images looked like plastic: their specular reflections were white, unlike the diffuse reflections [COOK81].

```
/*
 * plastic(): give the appearance of a plastic surface
 */
surface
plastic(
        float   Ks              = .5,
                Kd              = .5,
                Ka              = 1,
                roughness       = .1;
        color specularcolor     = 1 )
{
        point Nf = faceforward(normalize(N), I );
        point V = normalize(-I);

        Oi = Os;
        Ci = Os * ( Cs * (Ka*ambient() + Kd*diffuse(Nf)) +
                specularcolor * Ks * specular(Nf,V,roughness) );
}
```

Listing 16.4 *Surface shader for a plastic appearance*

Ambient light

An ambient light source supplies light of the same color and intensity to all points on all surfaces. As a result, it is about as simple as the *constant()* surface shader. All it does is multiply its instance variables, *lightcolor* times *intensity*. The result is placed in global variable *Cl*, which is the output of all light sources.

It is not strictly necessary that *lightcolor* and *intensity* be separate instance variables. The color could just a easily be scaled by the intensity by the application before instancing the shader. RenderMan keeps the two separate in honor of the notion that the components of a color are in the range [0,1].

```
/*
 * ambientlight(): non-directional ambient light shader
 */
light
ambientlight(
        float   intensity = 1;
        color lightcolor= 1 )
{
        Cl = intensity * lightcolor;
}
```

Listing 16.5 *Ambient light source shader*

Distant light

Unlike an ambient source, a distant source casts its light in only the direction defined by its instance variables *to* and *from*. The vector defined by the difference of points (*to–from*) is used in a **solar** statement to restrict the emission to that direction. Otherwise, the output light is the same as in **ambient()**.

```
/*
 * distantlight(): provide the behavior of a quasi-solar light source
 */
light
distantlight(
        float   intensity     = 1 ;
        color lightcolor    = 1 ;
        point from  = point "camera" (0,0,0),
              to    = point "camera" (0,0,1) )
{
        solar( to - from, 0.0 )
                Cl = intensity * lightcolor;
}
```

Listing 16.6 *Distant light source shader*

to and *from* are defined in shader space. That is, they are in the current coordinate system at the time the shader was instanced. This is in contrast to the case where they were defined in an explicit space. For example, the shader might be declared as

```
          light
          distantlight(
                  float     intensity       = 1 ;
                  color     lightcolor      = 1 ;
                  point     from     = point "camera" (0,0,0) ;
                            to       = point "camera" (0,0,1) )
```

This light would invariably point along the positive z axis of camera space, regardless of the configuration of the scene or camera. The same would be true of any other named space in the declaration. For example, one could arrange a "traveling" camera in animation simply by naming the appropriate space. The lesson here is that a distant light source instanced with explicit position and direction is treated like any other object.

Point light

A point light source is the converse of a distant light. It radiates light in *all* directions, but from a single location. It has a *from* instance variable, but no *to*.

```
/*
 * pointlight(): provide a light with position but no orientation
 */
light
pointlight(
        float   intensity     = 1;
        color   lightcolor    = 1;
        point   from          = point "camera" (0,0,0) )      /* light position */
{
        illuminate( from )
                Cl = intensity * lightcolor / L.L;
}
```

Listing 16.7 *Point light shader*

from is used in an **illuminate** statement. Inside, the output calculation is as it was in *distantlight*(), but the color is divided by $L.L$. Within **illuminate** (the only place it is defined), L is a vector from the position of the light source to the surface point being illuminated. Its length is therefore the distance from the point source to the surface point, so the dot product $L.L$ gives the square of the distance, which is exactly the quantity required to implement a square-law falloff of light intensity with distance from the source.

Spotlight

The *spotlight()* shader is shown in Listing 16.8. It also uses the **illuminate** construct, but it supplies not just the spotlight position, but also a cone of illumination. The latter is specified as a direction, **A**, and a width, specified in radians by the *coneangle* instance variable.

```
/*
 * spotlight(): cast a fuzzy cone of light
 */
light
spotlight(
        float   intensity      = 1;
        color lightcolor     = 1;
        point from            = point "camera" (0,0,0),      /* light position     */
              to              = point "camera" (0,0,1);      /* light direction   */
        float   coneangle          = radians(30),
                conedeltaangle     = radians(5),
                beamdistribution   = 2 )
{
        uniform point     A = (to - from) / length(to - from);
        uniform float     cosoutside= cos(coneangle),
                          cosinside = cos(coneangle-conedeltaangle);
        float   atten,
                cosangle;

        illuminate( from, A, coneangle ) {
                cosangle = L.A / length(L);
                atten = pow(cosangle, beamdistribution) / (L.L);
                atten *= smoothstep( cosoutside, cosinside, cosangle );
                Cl = atten * intensity * lightcolor;
        }
}
```

Listing 16.8 *Spotlight shader*

spotlight() begins by calculating the vector *A*, its direction, as the difference of points *to* and *from*. The vector is divided by its own **length**() to ensure that it is 1 unit in length. *A* is a **uniform** variable, the first example of one such we have seen;

since its value depends only on *from* and *to*, which are also **uniform**, it can be calculated once when the shader is instanced and used every time the shader is called.

Within the **illuminate** block, the spotlight uses the illumination vector $\underline{L}$ to calculate the square-law falloff with distance from the light. This time, though, $\underline{L}$ is also used to determine the angle between the direction to the surface point and the cone center. Since the dot product of two vectors **A** and **B** with angle *theta* between them is $\mathbf{A}.\mathbf{B} = |\mathbf{A}||\mathbf{B}|\cos(theta)$, the cosine *cosangle* of the angle between $\underline{L}$ and the cone direction vector *A* is given by $A.\underline{L}/|A||\underline{L}|$. *A* is set in the beginning to length 1, so the division is only by the length of $\underline{L}$.

The falloff from the cone center is based on this cosine; it is raised to the power *beamdistribution*, and the square-law falloff is brought in by dividing by $\underline{L}.\underline{L}$. Finally, the smooth barndoor falloff is provided by calling **smoothstep**(). If *cosangle* is less than **cos**(*coneangle–conedeltaangle*) — the surface point lies well inside the cone — the falloff is 1 and the attenuation is unaffected. If greater than **cos**(*coneangle*) — the point is outside the cone — the attenuation and the illumination go to 0. In between there is a smooth falloff. Note that **smoothstep**() still works correctly even if its second argument (nominally *max*) is less than its first (*min*).

Depth-cue volume

A depth-cue volume shader, normally used by **RiAtmosphere**(), linearly adds a specific color *background* to $\underline{Ci}$ according to the distance between the surface and the eye. The color added is 0 if the surface is less than *mindistance* away. The *background* color eliminates the surface color entirely for points farther than *maxdistance*. In between, the two colors are mixed.

The **mix**() function implements a linear interpolation between its first and second parameters based on its third parameter, which should be between 0 and 1. This mix ratio is calculated in the call to **clamp**(), which is here used to determine the relative distance of surface point $\underline{P}$ (which produced $\underline{Ci}$) between *mindistance* and *maxdistance*. The **depth**() function gives the distance of $\underline{P}$ from the camera. It is equivalent to

```
/*
 * depthcue(): darken objects according to their depth. Mindistance and
 *     maxdistance cover the range between clipping planes.
 */
volume
depthcue(
        float   mindistance  = 0,
                maxdistance  = 1;
        color background    = 0 )
{
        float d = clamp( (depth(P) - mindistance) / (maxdistance - mindistance),
                        0, 1 );
        Ci = mix( Ci, background, d );
}
```

Listing 16.9 *Depth-cue volume shader*

length($\underline{P}$–$\underline{E}$). In this case we may assume that the view is from the camera under the assumption that this shader will be used for atmosphere. **length**($\underline{I}$) could be used otherwise.

Fog volume

A fog shader is a somewhat more realistic function for atmospheric absorption. It assumes that the attenuation of the surface color in the fog is never complete, as it is in the depth-cue shader, but only asymptotically approaches complete attenuation.

```
/*
 * fog(): introduce depth-based fog
 */
volume
fog (
        float   distance    = 1;
        color background = 0 )
{
        float d = 1 - exp( -length(I)/distance );
        Ci = mix( Ci, background, d );
}
```

Listing 16.10 *Fog volume shader*

Instead of linearly interpolating the distance to the surface between two arbitrary distances, *fog()* takes

$$1-e^{-r}$$

where r is a relative distance, taken as the ratio between the actual distance to the surface and the distance passed in instance variable *distance*. The latter specifies the distance at which the relative amount of fog is $(1-1/e)$.

This concludes the discussion of the built-in shaders. Their functionality is guaranteed to be available by the definition of RenderMan. In the remainder of the chapter we present original shaders. The capability to write them is only available in implementations supporting the RenderMan Shading Language.

Procedural Texturing

Since the RenderMan Shading Language is a full-featured programming language, one of the simplest techniques it allows is **procedural texturing**, by which textures are generated on the fly based on object geometry. A procedural texture can be a function of surface parameters. More important, though, it can also be defined in terms of points in three-dimensional space. For example, if the color of a marble material can be defined and computed for any point in three-dimensional space, the procedure that computes it can be used as a procedural texture for *surfaces* in three-dimensional space [PEACHEY85]. This offers the possibility of an interplay between the surface of the object and the texture that makes the object appear to be carved out of a solid material.

Since a three-dimensional space is potentially huge, a procedural texture can also represent information that, if stored explicitly as a texture, would require prohibitively large amounts of storage—it's one thing to store two dimensions of texture, quite another to store three or four. A procedural texture can also be given parameters to vary its appearance in subtle ways that would be difficult to duplicate with a fixed texture.

Object space functions

We begin with some simple shaders for setting surface color and opacity as functions of surface and object-space coordinates.

show_st surface

The surface shader *show_st()*, shown in Listing 16.11, shows just how simple a shader can be. For each point on a surface, it sets red and green in the output color to the texture coordinates at that point. Red and green will be set regardless of the color space defined by **RiColorSamples()**, since the color is cast with "rgb". (This is actually redundant, since "rgb" would have been assumed in the absence of an explicit cast.) The shader also sets the surface opacity to 1 (completely opaque), ignoring that set by **RiOpacity()**. Like color Cs, Os is only an advisory value and may be ignored by any shader.

Since color channel values normally lie in the range [0,1], and so do texture coordinates, this function is reasonable: under the default texture coordinate space, the upper left ($s=0,t=0$) corner of a surface in s,t space will be black, the upper right red, the lower right yellow and the lower left green. If texture space is changed by **RiTextureCoordinates()** or vertex binding so that texture coordinates are not the defaults, the results will be different. The parametric coordinates u and v might seem to be a better choice to use, but they are always fixed over a surface; if the user wants to redistribute the colors over a set of adjoining surfaces, only texture coordinates will do.

```
/*
 * show_st(): color surface point according to its s,t coordinates.
 */

surface
show_st()
{
        Ci = color "rgb" (s, t, 0);
        Oi = 1;
}
```

Listing 16.11 *Shader mapping texture-space coordinates to colors*

Plate 1 shows the result of applying *show_st()* to a light bulb. It reveals that the globe of the light bulb consists of a hemisphere and four patches. This shader is useful during the debugging process for displaying the boundaries of surfaces.

checkerboard surface

The shader *checks()* in Listing 16.12 shows how to use texture space to provide a patterned surface, in this case a checkerboard.

```
/*
 * checker(): surface shader for applying a checkerboard pattern.
 */
surface
checker(
        float  Kd          = .5,
               Ka          = .1,
               frequency   = 10;
        color blackcolor   = color (0,0,0) )
{
        float  smod = mod(s*frequency,1),
               tmod = mod(t*frequency,1);

        if(smod < 0.5) {
           if(tmod < 0.5)
                Ci = Cs;
           else
                Ci = blackcolor;
        } else {
           if(tmod < 0.5)
                Ci = blackcolor;
           else
                Ci = Cs;
        }

        Oi = Os;
        Ci = Oi*Ci*(
                Ka*ambient() +
                Kd*diffuse(faceforward(normalize(N),I)) );
}
```

Listing 16.12 *Surface shader providing checkerboard pattern*

The *frequency* instance variable of *checks()* states how many times the checkerboard pattern is to repeat within a single

Figure 16.1 *Checkered light bulb*

unit interval of *s* and *t*. Therefore, when the texture coordinates of a point are multiplied by *frequency*, the fractional part of the result gives the "phase" of the cycle of that point. If *smod* and *tmod* are both less than or both greater than 0.5 (*s* and *t* are both in the first half or both in the last half of a cycle), the surface color *Cs* is used to shade the point, otherwise the instance variable *blackcolor* determines the color.

Figure 16.1 shows the result of applying *checks()* to a light bulb. The revealing thing about this image is that the checks are not all square; on the hemisphere at the top of the bulb they are especially elongated, although they bunch together more at the top. This is because 1 unit of *s* (10 check cycles) covers the entire circumference of the sphere, while 1 unit of *t* providing the same number of cycles only goes from the equator to the pole.

Figure 16.1 is a graphic illustration of the fact that texture space is not uniform in world space. Actually, it is difficult to imagine how it could be otherwise over a curved surface like this one. For example, the length of a unit of *s* space goes to 0 at the poles of a sphere. In many cases there are ways of linearizing parameter space again, and it can help to redistribute texture space with **RiTextureCoordinates**(), but it is a recurrent and important problem. Often the solution is to use world space directly, as in the next shader.

show_xyz surface

The third simple example of a mapping from surface position to output color is shown in Listing 16.13. The *show_xyz*() surface shader maps points within a bounding box, given by its instance variables, into red, green and blue values in the range [0,1].

```
/*
 * show_xyz(): Color a surface point according to its xyz coordinates
 *      within a bounding box.
 */

surface
show_xyz(
        float   xmin  = -1,
                ymin  = -1,
                zmin  = -1,
                xmax  =  1,
                ymax  =  1,
                zmax  =  1 )
{
        uniform point scale, zero;
        point objP, cubeP;

        /* Check for zero scale components. */
        if(xmax==xmin || ymax==ymin || zmax==zmin) {
                printf( "bad bounding box %f %f %f %f %f %f in show_xyz()",
                        xmin, xmax, ymin, ymax, zmin, zmax );
        } else {
                scale = point (1/(xmax-xmin), 1/(ymax-ymin), 1/(zmax-zmin));
                zero = point (xmin, ymin, zmin);

                objP = transform("shader", P);
                cubeP = (objP - zero) * scale;
                Ci = color (xcomp(cubeP), ycomp(cubeP), zcomp(cubeP));
        }
}
```

Listing 16.13 *Shader mapping shader-space coordinates to colors*

show_xyz() works in "shader" space, the coordinate space in which the shader is instanced. The space in which a shader operates is important to the coherence of the shading. Using a coordinate space shared by all the surfaces of an object ensures that adjacent points on two different surfaces in the image will be colored similarly. If, by contrast, the object space of each object were used instead, there would be no such guarantee possible, and if world space were used, objects' appearances would change as they moved in animation. Using coordinates in a physical space may also lend a uniformity of appearance difficult to achieve using parametric coordinates.

screen surface

A slightly more complex use of texture coordinates is shown in the *screen()* shader of Listing 16.14. This shader is a modification of the plastic surface shader that provides ambient, diffuse and specular reflections. The difference is in opacity. A regular grid is laid over the surface in *s,t* space, and points that lie in the middle of grid squares (that are more than a certain distance from the grid lines) are shaded with opacity of 0, making them transparent. *That is all the shader has to worry about.* The renderer takes care of displaying surfaces behind the transparent portions of the surface.

The *frequency* instance variable controls how many grid lines there are per unit in *s* and *t*; the default 20 produces 20 grid lines per surface under the default texture space. The *density* parameter controls the portion of the surface that is opaque. The default .25 means that the "wires" will cover 25% of the texture space horizontally and 25% vertically.

In Plate 3, the teapot at the bottom shows the effect of using the *screen()* shader.

Anti-aliasing thresholds

The conditional in *screen()* is theoretically sound, but it is an either-or test, which can sometimes lead to aliasing problems arising from the hard edge it produces. A useful technique for eliminating this hazard is to put a "fuzzy" edge onto the edges of the screen using the **smoothstep()** function. If *fuzz* is an in-

```
/*
 * screen(): surface shader for giving "wireframe" appearance. The method is
 *      to render the surface opaque within a small distance of a grid in s,t
 *      space. The grid is derived from a modulus function.
 */
surface
screen(
        float   Ks          = .5,
                Kd          = .5,
                Ka          = .1,
                roughness   = .1,
                density     = .25,
                frequency   = 20;
        color specularcolor = color (1,1,1) )
{

        varying point Nf = faceforward( normalize(N), I );

        if( mod(s*frequency,1) < density || mod(t*frequency,1) < density)
                Oi = 1.0;
        else
                Oi = 0.0;

        Ci = Oi * (  Cs * ( Ka*ambient() + Kd*diffuse(Nf) ) +
                        specularcolor*Ks*specular(Nf,normalize(-I),roughness)) ;
}
```

Listing 16.14 *Shader outlining an object with metallic wire mesh*

stance variable giving the width in texture space of a transition between points which are on the screen and those off the screen, then it can be used to replace the conditional statement above with

$$
\begin{aligned}
Oi = 1 - \textbf{smoothstep}(\ &density-fuzz/2, \\
&density+fuzz/2, \\
&\textbf{mod}(s*frequency,1)) \\
*\textbf{smoothstep}(\ &density-fuzz/2, \\
&density+fuzz/2, \\
&\textbf{mod}(t*frequency, 1));
\end{aligned}
$$

The **smoothstep()** function defines a range with its first two parameters. It returns 0 if its third argument is outside the range from below (i.e., if the surface point is completely inside the screen), 1 if outside above (completely outside the screen), and ramps smoothly in between. The effect here is to blur the edges of the screen by varying the surface's transparency. **smoothstep()** is a very useful tool for reducing aliasing.

Noise functions

A very useful class of procedural textures uses the shading language's **noise**() function, operating on points in a common coordinate space. The uses of noise in procedural texturing are discussed in Ken Perlin's paper "An Image Synthesizer" [PERLIN85].

wood surface

The *wood*() shader shown in Listing 16.15 shows how to use the **noise**() function to give a surface a wood-grain appearance. It operates in object space, as if each surface were separately carved out of wood and assembled by the modelling transformation.

The basic idea is that a tree consists of concentric rings that can be modeled by cylinders warped with noise. In this case, the cylinders are centered on the x axis. The warp depends on both the angle about the axis (*spoke*) of a point and the point's distance from the axis (r). After perturbation, r is mapped into the range [0,1], then passed through the **smoothstep**() function twice. Multiplying the pairs of **smoothstep**()s shown here has the effect of creating a function that rises smoothly to one between 0 and 0.8, then falls sharply back to zero between 0.83 and 0.86.

r is then used to select between two colors of wood, and also, interestingly, to control the shininess of the surface. This feature simulates the characteristic of real wood that the dark parts absorb less finish and so appear shinier.

The small elephant in Plate 4 shows the *wood*() shader in action. Close inspection confirms the aforementioned (subtle) variation in shininess. The difference between using a procedural three-dimensional wood texture and a two-dimensional texture map is the difference between carving an object out of wood and wrapping a picture of wood around the object.

dented

The *dented*() shader in Listing 16.16 uses fractal noise to perturb a surface. The loop sums the output of **noise**() over six octaves. The sequence of values passed to **noise**() are doubled

```
/*
 * wood(): calculate a solid wood texture using noise()
 */
surface
wood(
        float   ringscale     = 10;
        color   lightwood     = color (0.3, 0.12, 0.03),
                darkwood      = color (0.05, 0.01, 0.005);
        float   Ka            = 0.2,
                Kd            = 0.4,
                Ks            = 0.6,
                roughness     = 0.1 )
{
    point NN, V;
    point PP;
    float y, z, r;
    /*
     * Compute the forward-facing normal NN and the vector
     * toward the ray origin V, both normalized.
     * These vectors are used by "specular" and "diffuse". */
    NN = faceforward(normalize(N),I);
    V = -normalize(I);

    /* put point in shader space and perturb it to add irregularity */
    PP = transform("shader", P);
    PP += noise(PP);

    /* compute radial distance r from PP to axis of "tree" */
    y = ycomp(PP);
    z = zcomp(PP);
    r = sqrt(y*y + z*z);

    /* map radial distance r into ring position [0,1] */
    r *= ringscale;
    r += abs(noise(r));
    r -= floor(r);        /* == mod(r,1) */

    /* use ring position r to select wood color */
    r = smoothstep(0, 0.8, r) - smoothstep(0.83, 1.0, r));
    Ci = mix(lightwood, darkwood, r);

    /* shade using r to vary shininess */
    Oi = Os;
    Ci = Oi * Ci * (Ka * ambient() + Kd * diffuse(NN))
            + (0.3*r + 0.7) * Ks * specular(NN, V, roughness);
}
```

Listing 16.15 *Surface shader providing wood-grain texture*

(using *size*) each time through the loop to obtain successively higher-frequency noise. The return value is also scaled by *size*, effectively creating a 1/f noise function. The resulting displacement is exaggerated by taking it to the third power. The single instance variable *Km* controls the absolute amount of indentation. Note that *dented*() only resets the surface normal $\underline{N}$, not position $\underline{P}$, and that **calculatenormal**() works fine nonetheless.

```
/*
 * dented(): Create a worn surface.
 */
displacement
dented (
        float   Km    = 1.0 )
{
        float   size          = 1.0,
                magnitude  = 0.0,
                i;
        point P2;

        P2 = transform("shader", P);
        for (i = 0; i < 6.0; i += 1.0) {
                /* Calculate a simple fractal 1/f noise function */
                magnitude += abs(.5 - noise(P2 * size)) / size;
                size *= 2.0;
        }
        P2 = P - normalize(N) * (magnitude * magnitude * magnitude) * Km;
        N = calculatenormal(P2);
}
```

Listing 16.16 *Displacement shader to dent a surface*

The surface of the middle elephant in Plate 4 was bumped with *dented*(), then shaded using the standard *metal*() shader.

eroded

The shader *eroded*(), shown in Listing 16.17, does a similar job, but in the context of a surface shader. It also uses a noise function to calculate a disturbance on the surface, but it also uses **smoothstep**() to threshold the opacity of the surface according to the perturbation: if the perturbation *magnitude* is less than .0001, the surface is taken to be transparent (opacity =

0); if greater than .003, it is opaque (opacity = 1). In between, the opacity will be smoothly graded between 0 and 1.

Once the opacity has been calculated, the surface is shaded using the plastic surface algorithm and instance variables *Ka*, *Kd* and *Ks*.

```
/*
 * eroded(): Simulate a metallic surface eaten away with acid
 */
surface
eroded(
        float   Ks              = .4,
                Ka              = .1,
                Km              = 0.3,
                roughness       = .25 )
{
        float   size            = 4.0,
                magnitude       = 0.0,
                i;
        point Nf,
              W = transform("object", P);
        point x=(1,0,0);

        for (i = 0; i < 6.0; i += 1.0) {
                /* Calculate a simple fractal 1/f noise function */
                magnitude += 4.0 * abs(.5 - noise( W*size )) / size;
                size *= 2.0;
        }

        /* sharpen peaks */
        magnitude = magnitude * magnitude * magnitude * Km;

        N = calculatenormal( P-magnitude*normalize(N) );

        Nf = faceforward( normalize(N), I ) ;
        point V = normalize(-I);
        Oi = smoothstep(0.0001, 0.003, magnitude);
        Ci = Oi * Cs * (Ka*ambient() + Ks*specular(Nf,V,roughness) ) ;
}
```

Listing 16.17 *Surface shader eroding the surface of an object*

In Plate 3, the teapot at right was rendered using *eroded()*. As with *screen()*, other surfaces show through where the opacity is not 1, without any intervention by the shader.

granite surface

Listing 16.18 shows the shader *granite()*, which uses another six octaves of 1/f noise to calculate a diffuse granite-like surface.

```
/*
 * granite(): Provide a diffuse granite-like surface texture.
 */
surface
granite(
        float   Kd    = .8,
                Ka    = .2 )
{
        float sum = 0;
        float i, freq = 1.0;

        for (i = 0; i < 6; i = i + 1) {
                sum = sum + abs(.5 - noise( 4 * freq * I))/freq ;
                freq *= 2;
        }
        Ci = Cs * sum * (Ka + Kd * diffuse(faceforward( normalize(N), I )) ) ;
}
```

Listing 16.18 *Surface shader for granite-like surface*

blue_marble surface

The final noise-based shader lends a particularly delicate marble-like appearance to a surface. *blue_marble()* is shown in Listing 16.19.

blue_marble() is based on the observation [PERLIN85] that the effect of turbulence can be modeled by several octaves of noise whose magnitude decreases with frequency ("1/f noise"). The shader calculates such a turbulence function, then uses the resulting value, between .75 and 1, in a spline between several shades of blue representing different colors of marble.

The blue teapot in Plate 3 and the rearmost elephant in Plate 4 were both shaded with *blue_marble()*.

```
/*
 * blue_marble(): a marble stone texture in shades of blue
 */

surface
blue_marble(
        float   Ks    = .4,
                Kd    = .6,
                Ka    = .1,
                roughness = .1,
                txtscale = 1;
        color specularcolor = 1)
{

        point PP;            /* scaled point in shader space */
        float csp;           /* color spline parameter */
        point Nf;            /* forward-facing normal */
        float pixelsize, twice, scale, weight, turbulence;

        /* Obtain a forward-facing normal for lighting calculations. */
        Nf = faceforward(normalize(N), I);

        /*
         * Compute "turbulence" a la [PERLIN85]. Turbulence is a sum of
         * "noise" components with a "fractal" 1/f power spectrum. It gives the
         * visual impression of turbulent fluid flow (for example, as in the
         * formation of blue_marble from molten color splines!). Use the
         * surface element area in texture space to control the number of
         * noise components so that the frequency content is appropriate
         * to the scale. This prevents aliasing of the texture.
         */
        PP = transform("shader", P) * txtscale;
        pixelsize = sqrt(area(PP));
        twice = 2 * pixelsize;
        turbulence = 0;
        for (scale = 1; scale > twice; scale /= 2)
                turbulence += scale * noise(PP/scale);

        /* Gradual fade out of highest-frequency component near limit */
        if (scale > pixelsize) {
                weight = (scale / pixelsize) - 1;
                weight = clamp(weight, 0, 1);
                turbulence += weight * scale * noise(PP/scale);
        }

        /*
         * Magnify the upper part of the turbulence range 0.75:1
         * to fill the range 0:1 and use it as the parameter of
         * a color spline through various shades of blue.
         */
        csp = clamp(4 * turbulence - 3, 0, 1);
```

```
Ci = color spline(csp,
        color (0.25, 0.25, 0.35),      /* pale blue            */
        color (0.25, 0.25, 0.35),      /* pale blue            */
        color (0.20, 0.20, 0.30),      /* medium blue          */
        color (0.20, 0.20, 0.30),      /* medium blue          */
        color (0.20, 0.20, 0.30),      /* medium blue          */
        color (0.25, 0.25, 0.35),      /* pale blue            */
        color (0.25, 0.25, 0.35),      /* pale blue            */
        color (0.15, 0.15, 0.26),      /* medium dark blue     */
        color (0.15, 0.15, 0.26),      /* medium dark blue     */
        color (0.10, 0.10, 0.20),      /* dark blue            */
        color (0.10, 0.10, 0.20),      /* dark blue            */
        color (0.25, 0.25, 0.35),      /* pale blue            */
        color (0.10, 0.10, 0.20)       /* dark blue            */
        );

    /* Multiply this color by the diffusely reflected light. */
    Ci *= Ka*ambient() + Kd*diffuse(Nf);

    /* Adjust for opacity. */
    Oi = Os;
    Ci = Ci * Oi;

    /* Add in specular highlights. */
    Ci += specularcolor * Ks * specular(Nf,normalize(-I),roughness);
}
```

Listing 16.19 *Blue marble surface shader*

Other functions

The shaders *windowhighlight*() and *windowlight*(), shown in Listings 16.20 and 16.21, were developed for the film *Tin Toy*. They illustrate the kinds of special-purpose effects for which the shading language is suitable because it encourages writing special shaders for special jobs. They form a matched pair.

The eponymous hero of *Tin Toy* is a small, very shiny windup toy. The film takes place in a room lit by a large, paned picture window that casts light in rectangular patches.

windowhighlight surface

One would expect the light from the window to produce a patchy highlight on the surface of a very shiny object like the toy, and that is what *windowhighlight*() provides.

```
/*
 * windowhighlight(): Give a surface a window-shaped specular highlight.
 */
surface
windowhighlight(
        point center= point "world" (0, 0, -4),       /* center of the window */
              in    = point "world" (0, 0, 1),        /* normal to the wall    */
              up    = point "world" (0, 1, 0);        /* 'up' on the wall      */
        color specularcolor =1;
        float Ka        = .3,
              Kd        = .5,
              xorder     = 2,   /* number of panes horizontally           */
              yorder     = 3,   /* number of panes vertically             */
              panewidth  = 6,   /* horizontal size of a pane              */
              paneheight = 6,   /* vertical size of a pane                */
              framewidth = 1,   /* sash width between panes               */
              fuzz       = .2;) /* transition region between pane and sash */
{
    uniform
    point   in2,            /* normalized in                             */
            right,          /* unit vector perpendicular to in2 and up2  */
            up2,            /* normalized up perpendicular to in         */
            corner;         /* location of lower left corner of window   */
    point   path,           /* incident vector I reflected about normal  N  */
            PtoC,           /* vector from surface point to window corner */
            PtoF;           /* vector from surface point to wall    along path */
    float   offset, modulus, yfract, xfract;
    point   Nf = faceforward( normalize(N), I );

    /* Set up uniform variables as described above */
    in2 = normalize(in);
    right = up ^ in2;
    up2 = normalize(in2^right);
    right= up2 ^ in2;
    corner = center - right*xorder*panewidth/2 -
                    up2*yorder*paneheight/2;

    path = reflect(I, normalize(Nf));      /* trace source of highlight       */
    PtoC = corner - Ps;

    if (path.PtoC <= 0) {                   /* outside the room                */
        xfract = yfract = 0;
    } else {

        /*
         * Make PtoF be a vector from the surface point to the wall
         *     by adjusting the length of the reflected vector path.
         */
        PtoF = path * (PtoC.in2)/(path.in2);
```

```
   /*
    * Calculate the vector from the corner to the intersection point, and
    *      project it onto up2. This length is the vertical offset of the
    *       intersection point within the window.
    */
   offset = (PtoF - PtoC).up2;
   modulus = mod(offset, paneheight);
   if( offset > 0 && offset/paneheight < yorder ) { /* inside the window */
       if( modulus > (paneheight/2))        /* symmetry about pane center  */
           modulus = paneheight - modulus;
       yfract = smoothstep(                 /* fuzz at the edge of a pane        */
           (framewidth/2) - (fuzz/2),
           (framewidth/2) + (fuzz/2),
           modulus);
   } else {
       yfract = 0;
   }

   /* Repeat the process for horizontal offset */
   offset = (PtoF - PtoC).right;
   modulus = mod(offset, panewidth);
   if( offset > 0 && offset/panewidth < xorder ) {
       if( modulus > (panewidth/2))
           modulus = panewidth - modulus;
       xfract = smoothstep(
           (framewidth/2) - (fuzz/2),
           (framewidth/2) + (fuzz/2),
           modulus);
   } else {
       xfract = 0;
   }
   }
   /* specular calculation using the highlight */
   Ci = Cs * (Kd*diffuse(Nf) + Ka*ambient())
           + yfract*xfract*specularcolor ;
}
```

Listing 16.20 *Surface shader providing a paned-window highlight*

As illustrated in Figure 16.2, the *modus operandi* of *windowhighlight*() is to follow a ray of sunlight from the surface point back to the wall with the window. The center of the window is given in the instance variable *center, in* points perpendicular to the wall, and *up* is parallel to the wall in the vertical direction. The horizontal and vertical distance of the backprojected point relative to the lower left *corner* of the window determines whether the point hits a pane or the frame in between panes, or falls outside the window altogether. In the first case,

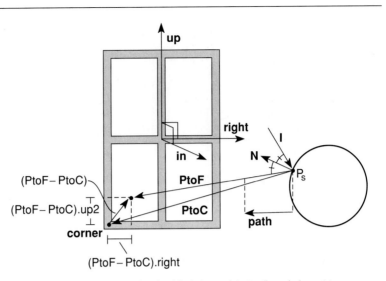

Figure 16.2 *Operation of windowhighlight(); path is I reflected about N.*

the highlight is *specularcolor*, in the latter, dark. The **smooth-step**() function is used to provide a fuzzy boundary between light and dark regions.

windowhighlight() shows the power of the dot product and cross product operators in the shading language. A few cross products are sufficient to set up the orthogonal vectors *in2*, *right* and *up2*, which completely describe the window's location and orientation. Thanks to the definition of cross product, they are correct even if the input vectors *in* and *up* are not originally orthogonal.

The dot product operator is used to project the reflected ray *PtoF* onto the window wall, then to project the intersection point onto *right* and *up2*. The latter projections completely describe the ray's relationship to the panes of the window.

windowlight

windowlight() operates in a very similar fashion. Figure 16.3 shows the differences between *windowlight*() and *windowhigh-*

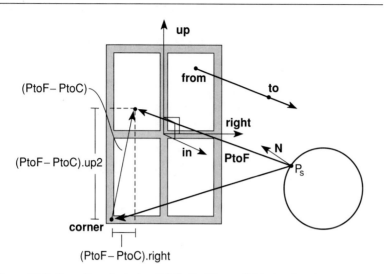

Figure 16.3 *Operation of windowlight(); PtoF is parallel to (to–from).*

light(). Rather than tracing along the reflected ray from the surface point *Ps*, a path parallel to (*to-from*) is traced from *Ps*.

Like *windowhighlight()*, *windowlight()* takes advantage of the dot product and cross product operators in performing its projection to the windowed wall.

Simple Tricks

Beyond supporting the development of shaders for special purposes, the shading language encourages finding "tricks" to make modeling and rendering easier or the resulting appearance more interesting. In that spirit, shading can often be used to add information to relatively crude geometry, giving it a complexity of appearance far greater than that of the actual model. The fact that shaders are often independent of the underlying surface means that one shader can serve across many different models with no more effort than it takes to call **Ri-Surface()**. The speed and ease with which useful shaders can be developed also adds an element of fun at the same time.

```
/*
 * windowlight(): Cast patches of light as through a paned window.
 */
light
windowlight(
        point   from        = point "world" ( 0, 0, -20),
                to          = point "world" (0, 0, 0),
                center      = point "world" (0, 0, -4),
                in          = point "world" (0, 0, 1),
                up          = point "world" (0, 1, 0);
        color   lightcolor  = color (1, .9, .6),
                darkcolor   = color (.05, .2, .1);
        float   intensity   = 1,
                xorder      = 2,  /* number of panes horizontally           */
                yorder      = 3,  /* number of panes vertically             */
                panewidth   = 6,  /* horizontal size of a pane              */
                paneheight  = 6,  /* vertical size of a pane                */
                framewidth  = 1,  /* sash width between panes               */
                fuzz        = .2;) /* transition region between pane and sash */
{
    uniform
      point   in2,          /* normalized in                           */
              right,        /* unit vector perpendicular to in2 and up2 */
              up2,          /* normalized up perpendicular to in       */
              corner,       /* location of lower left corner of window  */
              path;         /* direction of sunlight travel            */
      point   PtoC,         /* vector from surface point to window corner */
              PtoF;         /* vector from surface point to wall  along path */
    float offset, modulus, yfract, xfract;
    point Nf = faceforward( N, I );

    /* Initialize the uniform variables */
    path = (from - to);
    in2 = faceforward(normalize(in), path);
    right = up ^ in2;
    up2 = normalize(in2 ^ right);
    right = up2 ^ in2;
    corner = center - right*xorder*panewidth/2 -
                    up2*yorder*paneheight/2;

    solar( -path, 0.0 ) {

        PtoC = corner - Ps;
        if (path.PtoC <= 0) {                    /* outdoors => full illumination */
            xfract = yfract = 1;
        } else {

            /*
             * Make PtoF be a vector from the surface point to the wall
```

```
    *      by adjusting the length of the reflected vector path.
    */
      PtoF = path * (PtoC.in2)/(path.in2);

    /*
    * Calculate the vector from the corner to the intersection point, and
    *      project it onto up2. This length is the vertical offset of the
    *       intersection point within the window.
    */
      offset = (PtoF - PtoC).up2;
      modulus = mod(offset, paneheight);
      if( offset > 0 && offset/paneheight < yorder ) { /* inside window */
          if( modulus > (paneheight/2))
              modulus = paneheight - modulus;          /* symmetry in pane */
          yfract = smoothstep(                         /* include sash fuzz */
              (framewidth/2) - (fuzz/2),
              (framewidth/2) + (fuzz/2),
              modulus);
      } else {
          yfract = 0;
      }

    /* Repeat for horizontal offset */
      offset = (PtoF - PtoC).right;
      modulus = mod(offset, panewidth);
      if( offset > 0 && offset/panewidth < xorder ) {
          if( modulus > (panewidth/2))
              modulus = panewidth - modulus;
          xfract = smoothstep(
              (framewidth/2) - (fuzz/2),
              (framewidth/2) + (fuzz/2),
              modulus);
      } else {
          xfract = 0;
      }
    }
      Cl = intensity * mix( darkcolor, lightcolor, yfract*xfract);
  }
}
```

Listing 16.21 *Light shader simulating sunlight through a window*

easysurface

A simple yet useful surface shader is shown in Listing 16.22.
easysurface() is a surface shader that gives objects a color with
information content even without any light sources declared
in the scene. Up to now, the only way to view a surface with-

out any light sources has been to use the "constant" shader, but that method makes only the outline of the surface visible (as did providing only ambient lights). *easysurface()* gives each surface a uniform color, but varies the intensity with the orientation of the surface, dropping it to 0 as the surface faces away from the camera. The effect is as if a distant light had been placed at the origin of camera space.

```
/*
 * easysurface(): orientation-sensitive surface shading without a light source
 */
surface
easysurface(
        float   Kd      = .8,
                Ka      = .2,
                falloff = 2.0 )
{
        float diffuse ;

        diffuse = I.N / (I.I * N.N);
        diffuse = pow(diffuse, falloff);

        Ci = Cs * (Ka + Kd * diffuse ) ;
}
```

Listing 16.22 *Surface shader for use without a light source*

edge-rounding displacement

The *round()* displacement shader shown in Listing 16.23 can be used to ease the hard-edged appearance of some adjoining surfaces by beveling the joint. It works by displacing the surface of a bilinear patch according to the distance from the edge of the surface. It puts a nice round edge on the joint if two patches meet at a 90 degree angle.

round() works as follows: call the joint between the displaced and undisplaced surface the *inflection edge*. For surfaces joined at a 90 degree angle, which we assume here, there is an inflection edge exactly *radius* distant from each surface edge. A surface point needs to be displaced if it is beyond an inflection edge (it is less than *radius* in distance from some edge).

```
/*
 * round(): displace the edge of a bilinear patch so that, if it is placed next to
 *  another patch at a right angle, the edge will be rounded.
 */

displacement
round(
        float   radius = .10 )
{
        float   uu,    /* distance in u to the nearest "vertical" edge          */
                vv,    /* distance in v to the nearest "horizontal" edge        */
                lu,    /* "real" distance to the nearest "vertical" edge        */
                lv;    /* "real" distance to the nearest "horizontal" edge      */
        point   center,     /* point toward which the surface is displaced      */
                dpdu,       /* dPdu pointed toward patch center line            */
                dpdv;       /* dPdv pointed toward patch center line            */

        /* Find the distance in parameter space from the nearest edge in
           u and in v, and the directions away from those edges. */
        if (u < .5) {
                uu = u;
                dpdu = dPdu;
        } else {
                uu = 1 - u;
                dpdu = -dPdu;
        }
        if (v < .5) {
                vv = v;
                dpdv = dPdv;
        } else {
                vv = 1 - v;
                dpdv = -dPdv;
        }

        /* Find the distances from the edges in the current space. */
        lu = length(dPdu*uu);
        lv = length(dPdv*vv);

        if (lu < radius || lv < radius) {    /* only if within radius of an edge...   */
                /*
                 * Find the point towards which the surface  point will be
                 * moved. This center is on the center line of a cylinder, if we
                 * are not near the corner of the patch, or is the center of a
                 * sphere, if we are. We move 'center' to the nearest inflection
                 * edge along u and/or v.
                 */
                center = point(0,0,0);
                if (lu < radius)
                        center = (radius-lu)*normalize(dpdu);
                if (lv < radius)
                        center += (radius-lv)*normalize(dpdv);
```

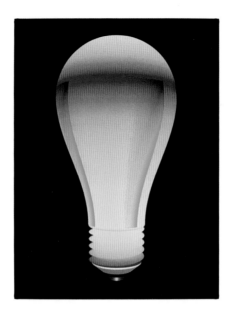

PLATE 1 *Shader show_st() (see Listing 16.11) applied to a light bulb*

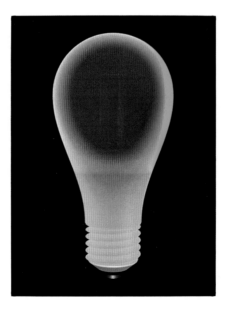

PLATE 2 *Shader show_xyz() (see Listing 16.13) applied to a light bulb*

PLATE 3 *Feature spread for* Dr. Dobb's Journal *executed using shader screen()
(Listing 16.14) on the teapot at bottom, eroded() (Listing 16.17) at right, and
blue_marble() (Listing 16.19) on the teapot in the middle*

PLATE 4 *Use of shaders wood() (Listing 16.15) on the near elephant, dented()
(Listing 16.16) on the middle, blue_marble() (Listing 16.19) on the far elephant, granite() (Listing 16.18) on the pedestal, and the shadowed spotlight
shadowspot() (Listing 16.33) as two of the light sources*

PLATE 5 *Frame from the film* Tin Toy *showing a window-shaped highlight on the surface rendered using the* windowhighlight() *shader (Listing 16.20)*

PLATE 6 *Another frame from* Tin Toy *showing solar light cast by a window using the* windowlight() *shader (Listing 16.21)*

PLATE 7 *A light bulb rendered using the RenderMan Interface*

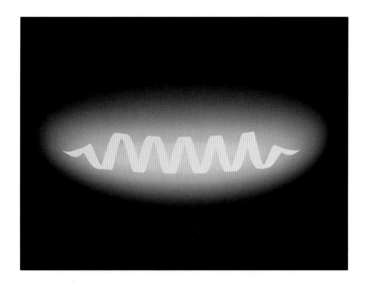

PLATE 8 *Close-up of the light bulb filament, showing the effect of using shaders filament() (Listing 16.25), glow() (Listing 16.26) and droop() (Listing 16.27)*

PLATE 9 *Close-up of light bulb base, produced from a cylinder using the threads() displacement shader (Listing 16.24)*

PLATE 10 *A light source mimicking a slide projector in slideprojector() (Listing 16.28)*

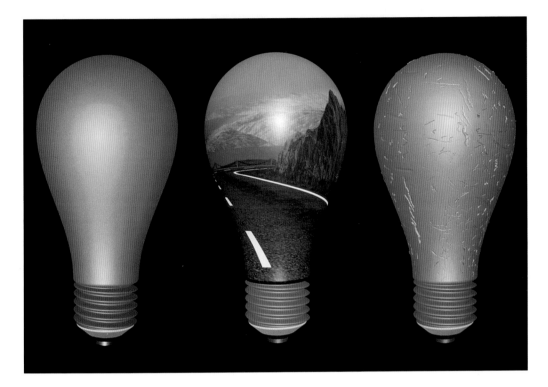

PLATE 11 *Three light bulbs rendered as: copper using the metal() shader (Listing 16.3) at left, textured plastic with txtplastic() (Listing 16.29) in middle, and a pitted metal surface displaced with pits() (Listing 16.30) at right*

PLATE 12 *Close-up of a single bowling pin from the cover, shaded using pin_color() (Listing 16.31)*

PLATE 13 *Textures used on the bowling pin, facing page; at lower right, the texture used to gouge the surface*

PLATE 14 *Six views of a room environment used to create a reflection map*

PLATE 15 *Room view including a teapot shaded with shader shiny() (Listing 16.34) using the reflection map from PLATE 14*

PLATE 16 *Pencils rendered using a variety of shaders*

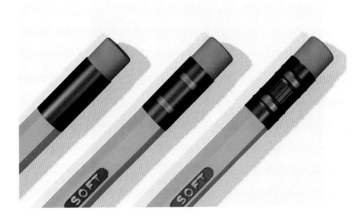

PLATE 17 *Three pencils. Each pencil uses rubber() (Listing 16.38) for the eraser, emboss() (Listing 16.36) to displace the label, and sdixon() (Listing 16.37) to color the label. On the pencil at left, the ferrule was given a flat color, in the middle a texture was used, and on the right, dferrule() (Listing 16.35) was used to provide the ridges.*

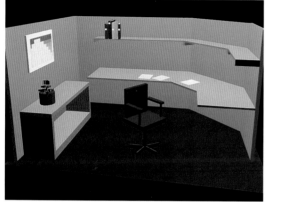

PLATE 18 *Before and after RenderMan*

PLATE 19 *Gears modeled by AutoCAD and rendered with RenderMan*

PLATE 20 *Guitar modeled by CADKEY and rendered with RenderMan using a reflection map*

PLATE 21 *Cover for "MacWorld" magazine, modeled by TASC and rendered using RenderMan*

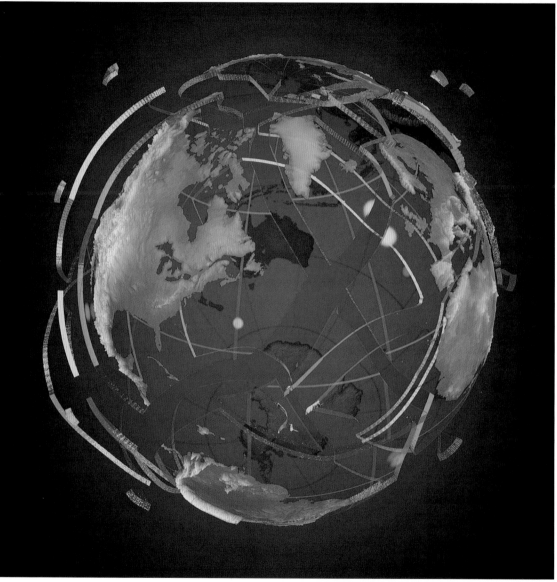

PLATE 22 *Exploding globe for* National Geographic

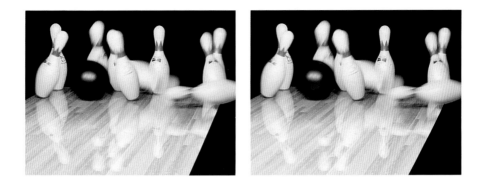

PLATE 23 *Stereo pair of cover image*

PLATE 24 *Stereo pair of Luxo Jr.*

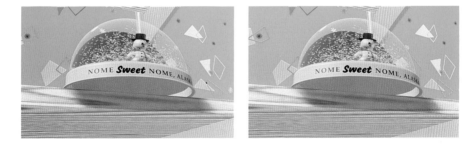

PLATE 25 *Stereo pair from* Knickknack

The plates above are stereo pairs, which can be viewed directly. Place the book 10 inches from the eyes, and relax the eyes as if staring into the distance. It may help to place a vertical divider extending from between the stereo images to the tip of the reader's nose.

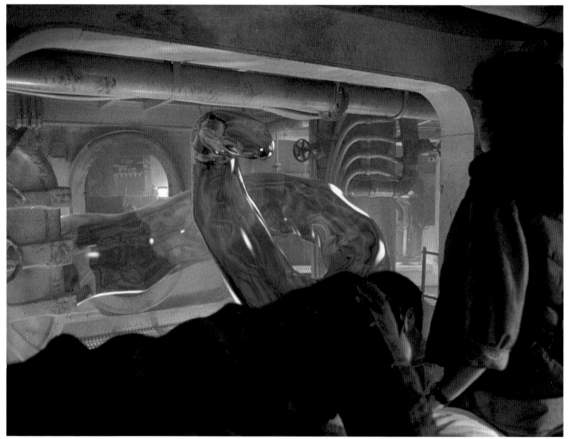

PLATE 26 *Frame from* The Abyss, *depicting a creature made of seawater*

```
        /* Move center perpendicular to the surface */
        center += P - radius*normalize(N);
        /* Make P be distance 'radius' along the line from 'center' to P */
        P = center + radius*normalize( P-center );
    }
    N = calculatenormal(P);
}
```

Listing 16.23 *Displacement shader for bevelling perpendicular bilinear patches*

Exactly *radius* beneath the inflection edge runs the center of a cylinder around which beveled points need to be wrapped. Two surfaces adjoining at a 90° angle will have coincident cylinder centers, so the cylinder points will join smoothly.

The shader wraps the surface around the cylinder by projecting points on the surface toward the center line until they are *radius* away. Figure 16.4 illustrates. The point on the center line (*center*) to project toward is found for each surface point by moving *P* perpendicularly to the nearest inflection edge (using *dPdu*, *−dPdu*, *dPdv* or *−dPdv* as appropriate), then dropping *radius* in distance below the surface along the surface normal.

The results of using *round()* are shown in Figure 16.5. This shader is less generally useful than many of the shaders in this chapter. It is included here largely to demonstrate this particular possibility for a displacement shader. It would be fairly

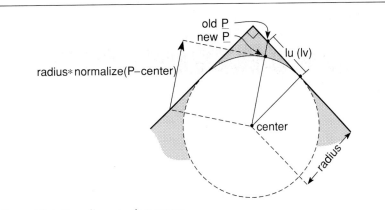

Figure 16.4 *Rounding a surface corner*

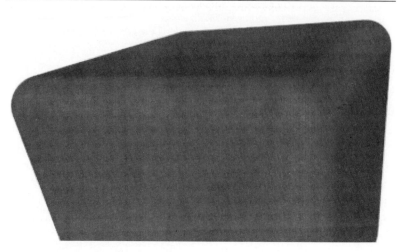

Figure 16.5 *round() applied to a cube*

straightforward to extend it to work for non-perpendicular joints and other widths and shapes of joint. Any geometric information about adjoining surfaces and their angles would, of course, have to be provided in instance variables.

threads displacement

The following four shaders were written for the light bulb seen in Plate 7. The first, *threads()*, is a displacement shader that turns a cylinder into a threaded base for a light bulb. It takes four instance variables: *frequency* controls how many threads appear per unit of texture parameter *t*; *amplitude* gives the maximum displacement; *phase* "turns" the threads; *offset* provides a base displacement; and *dampzone* provides damping at the ends so the cylinder still presents a circular opening.

The first line of *threads()* calculates a displacement from the surface as a phased sinusoid. *t* is used for the modulation lengthwise along the cylinder, and *s* provides a phase factor so that the threads really do spiral. Normally the modulation is centered around the actual surface, but *offset* may be used to modify that.

```
/*
 * threads(): wrap threads around a cylinder
 */
displacement
threads (
        float   Km          = .1,
                frequency   = 5.0,
                phase       = .0,
                offset      = .0,
                dampzone    = .05 )
{
        float magnitude;

        /* Calculate the undamped displacement */
        magnitude = (sin( PI*2*(t*frequency + s + phase))+offset) * Km;

        /* Damp the displacement to 0 at each end */
        if( t > (1-dampzone))
                magnitude *= (1.0-t) / dampzone;
        else if( t < dampzone )
                magnitude *= t / dampzone;

        /* Do the displacement */
        P += normalize(N) * magnitude;
        N = calculatenormal(P);
}
```

Listing 16.24 *Displacement shader providing light-bulb threads to cylinder*

Before perturbing the surface, the magnitude of the perturbation may be scaled down, or damped, to 0 if the point to be perturbed is near one end of the cylinder. This provides a perfectly circular interface so other round shapes like the light-bulb glass can be joined with the threads.

A close-up of the threaded cylinder is shown in Plate 9. This object dramatically illustrates the distinction between shape and shading. Specifying surface geometry with the same appearance is far more difficult than applying this shader.

filament

The second shader from the light bulb is shown in Listing 16.25. *filament()* is like a combination of *screen()* and *threads()*. It turns a cylinder into a spiral filament. As shown in Plate 8, the filament can be brought to a point by applying the same shader to two cones at the ends of the cylinder.

In *filament()*, the *frequency* and *phase* instance variables are identical to those of *threads()*. *width* specifies the fraction of the surface to be covered by the filament, and is used to threshold the distance of each point from the edge of the filament. Since the filament is self-illuminating, the output surface color is always <u>Cs</u>.

```
/*
 * filament(): map a filament-like spiral onto the surface of a cylinder.
 */
surface
filament (
        float   frequency   = 5.0,
                phase       = 0.0,
                width       = 0.3 )
{
        /* Calculate the distance of (s,t) from a spiral as a fraction [0,1] */
        float offset = mod((t*frequency + s + phase), 1.0);

        /* Threshold the fraction against the fractional filament width */
        if (offset < width) {
                Ci = Cs;
                Oi = 1.0;
        } else {
                Ci = 0.0;
                Oi = 0.0;
        }
}
```

Listing 16.25 *Surface shader to make a cylinder look like a filament*

glow surface

When the filament is rendered using only *filament()*, something seems to be missing. Its geometry is more interesting than a simple cylinder, but it is shaded as a simple constant-colored surface, whereas a real filament would be glowing. A glow can be imparted (see Plate 8) to this filament by surrounding it with a sphere shaded appropriately. The *glow()* shader shown in Listing 16.26 does the trick.

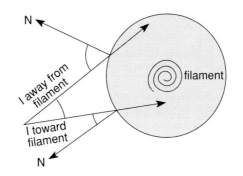

Figure 16.6 *"Directness of view" on filament corresponding to "obliqueness of view" on surrounding sphere*

A glow is brightest when looking directly at the glowing object, and falls off rapidly nearby. If the glowing object is centered inside a sphere, then closeness of view to the object corresponds to directness of view on the sphere. Figure 16.6 shows that relationship. *glow*() diminishes the opacity of the sphere (brightness of glow) according to the obliqueness of I as measured by its angle with $\underline{N}$.

```
/*
 * glow(): a shader for providing a centered "glow" in a sphere
 */
surface
glow( float  attenuation = 2 )
{
        float falloff = I.N;          /* Direct incidence has cosine closer to 1.*/

        if (falloff < 0) {            /* Back of sphere only */
                /* Normalize falloff by lengths of I and N */
                falloff = falloff * falloff / (I.I * N.N) ;
                falloff = pow(falloff, attenuation);
                Ci = Cs * falloff;
                Oi = falloff;
        } else
                Oi = 0;
}
```

Listing 16.26 *Shader mapping object-space coordinates to colors*

The obliqueness of view on the sphere corresponds to the dot product between the surface normal vector $\underline{N}$ and the incident direction $\underline{I}$. glow() takes that dot product (between 0 and 1), raises it to the power *attenuation*, and uses the result to set both the color and opacity of the sphere.

In Plate 8, the glow is oblong; this effect was achieved by scaling the sphere non-uniformly, elongating it along the length of the filament.

droop displacement

The last shader seen in the light bulb concerns the fact that the filament of a real light bulb bends with gravity. Therefore, the displacement shader *droop()* is used to provide a catenary droop to both the cylinder of the filament and the surrounding sphere. For purposes of drooping, "down" is assumed to be in negative *y* in shader space.

```
/*
 * droop(): a displacement shader for making a surface "sag" along t.
 */
#define M_E        2.7182818284590452354      /* e */

displacement
droop (
        float   Km = 0.05 )
{
        float droop, yDel;

        droop = (t-.5)*2;          /* t in [0,1] goes to droop in [-1,1] */

        yDel = -Km * ( M_E + (1/M_E) - (exp(droop)+exp(-droop)) );
        setycomp(P, ycomp(P) + yDel);
        N = calculatenormal(P);
}
```

Listing 16.27 *Displacement shader with catenary droop in y*

The surface is assumed to be supported at its extremities in *t*, which for a cylinder and sphere are the ends and poles, respectively. The translation of $\underline{P}$ is strictly in *y*, and is 0 at the ends. In between, the droop is scaled by the *Km* instance variable.

Texture Mapping

As outlined in Chapter 12, the texture mapping facilities of RenderMan provide control over a wide variety of surface attributes. However, the subject really opens up only when one begins to write shaders. This section presents mapping shaders for all occasions.

Texture

The most basic kind of map is the texture map. Since the access functions are defined as part of the shading language, they can be used in any kind of shader, but they are most useful in surface and displacement shaders, and to a lesser extent in light sources.

slide projector light

A light source shader can provide dramatic variations in lighting across a scene because it has access to surface locations and the location and direction of the light source itself. This capability meets texture mapping in the shader *slideprojector*(), shown in Listing 16.28. The slide projector is shown in action in Plate 10.

The interesting instance variable in *slideprojector*() is *fieldofview*, giving the angle over which the projector casts its image. A small field of view makes the image smaller at any distance, and makes it more difficult to aim.

The *from* and *to* instance variables give the location and direction, respectively, of the projector. The *up* variable determines the orientation of the projection. Rather than depend on instance variables to specify the location and direction of the light source, *slideprojector*() might have located the projector at the coordinate origin pointing along the z axis and let the source be positioned by the modeling transformation.

As shown in Figure 16.7, *slideprojector*() casts an **illuminate** cone that is wider than *fieldofview* by **sqrt**(2), to make it enclose the entire image. Within the **illuminate** statement, *sloc* and *tloc* essentially represent a perspective projection of the surface point relative to the light position, direction, orienta-

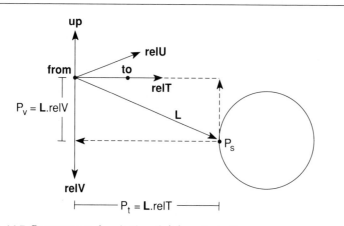

Figure 16.7 *Parameters and projection of slideprojector()*

tion and field of view. *relT*, *relU* and *relV* are mutually orthogonal vectors pointing in the light source direction and horizontally and vertically (in the *u* and *v* directions) on the slide, respectively. Given the vector $\underline{L}$ from the location of the projector to the surface point $\underline{Ps}$, the dot product $\underline{L}.relU$ projects $\underline{Ps}$ along the *u* direction, and $\underline{L}.relV$ the *v* direction. *Pt* is the dot product $\underline{L}.relT$, which represents the distance of the surface point along the projection direction. *Pt* is used to provide the perspective by scaling the projected horizontal and vertical distances $\underline{L}.relU$ and $\underline{L}.relV$.

The −1 to +1 range of values of *sloc* and *tloc* is mapped into the range [0,1] for indexing the texture. All textures in the shading language are indexed in this range regardless of their resolution. Some $\underline{Ps}$ may yield *sloc* and *tloc* outside the interval [-1,1], and therefore index the texture outside [0,1], but the **texture()** function will handle them correctly by returning black.

The texture map is accessed by calling the function **texture()**, passing it the texture map name which was passed to the shader in the *slidename* **string** instance variable. **texture()** also takes the floating-point coordinates indexing the map and returns a **color**, the color of the texture at that point, filtered to eliminate aliasing.

```
/*
 * slideprojector(): Cast a texture map into a scene as a light source
 */
light
slideprojector(
        float   fieldofview=PI/32;
        point   from        = (8, -4, 10),
                to          = (0,0,0),
                up          = point "eye" (0,1,0);
        string  slidename   = "",
                shadowname = "" )
{
        uniform point     relT,  /* normalized direction vector              */
                          relU,  /* "vertical" perspective of surface point  */
                          relV;  /* "horizontal" perspective of surface point */
        uniform float spread = 1/tan(fieldofview/2);        /* spread of "beam"  */
        float   Pt,                     /* projection of Ps on relT (distance of
                                           surface point along light direction) */
                Pu,                     /* projection of Ps on relU             */
                Pv,                     /* projection of Ps on relU             */
                sloc, tloc;             /* perspected surface point             */

        /* Initialize uniform variables for perspective */
        relT = normalize(to - from);
        relU = relT ^ up;
        relV = normalize(relT ^ relU);
        relU = relV^relT;

        illuminate(from, relT, atan(sqrt(2)/spread)) {
                L =  Ps - from;      /* direction of light source from surf. point  */
                Pt = L.relT;         /* coordinates of Ps along relT, relU, relV    */
                Pu = L.relU;
                Pv = L.relV;
                sloc = spread*Pu/Pt;        /* perspective divide                   */
                tloc = spread*Pv/Pt;
                sloc = sloc*.5 + .5;        /* correction from [-1,1] to [0,1]      */
                tloc  = tloc*.5 + .5;
                Cl = color texture(slidename, sloc,tloc);
                if( shadowname != "" )
                        Cl *= 1-shadow(shadowname, Ps);
        }
}
```

Listing 16.28 *Slide-projector light source shader*

This shader also uses a shadow map, since it would be strange
for the same point on a projected image to project onto more
than one surface. This last is indexed by surface point *Ps* and

uses a depth map to determine to what extent that surface point is obscured from a light source. **shadow**() returns a "shadow fraction" suitable for scaling the projection color, which is done here.

txtplastic surface

Listing 16.29 shows a simple surface shader using a texture map. *txtplastic*() is a revised version of the standard plastic shader. Instead of the surface color _Cs_ passed by **RiColor**(), *txtplastic*() uses a texture map to provide the surface's diffuse reflection.

```
/*
 * txtplastic(): version of plastic() shader using an optional texture map
 */
surface
txtplastic(
        float   Ks          = .5,
                Kd          = .5,
                Ka          = 1,
                roughness   = .1;
        color  specularcolor = 1;
        string mapname = "")
{
        point  Nf = faceforward( N, I );

        if( mapname != "" )
                Ci = color texture( mapname );      /* Use s and t */
        else
                Ci = Cs;
        Oi = Os;
        Ci = Os * ( Ci *
                    (Ka*ambient() + Kd*diffuse(Nf))
                 + specularcolor * Ks * specular(Nf,-I,roughness) );
}
```

Listing 16.29 *Plastic surface shader using a texture map*

Plate 11 shows three light bulbs. The upper left bulb is given a simple copper appearance using the standard *metal*() shader. The middle bulb was shaded using *txtplastic*().

Bump mapping

The third light bulb in Plate 11 provides an interesting variation on the theme of texture mapping. In the *pits()* shader, the value in the optional texture map is used to displace the surface. The fact that the surface is actually being displaced (as opposed to simply manipulating the normal) is shown in the bulb's profile. The texture used in Plate 11 is shown in Plate 13; it was also used in the bowling pins on the cover and in Plate 12.

```
/*
 * pits(): use a texture map to apply pits to a surface
 */
displacement
pits(
        float Km = 0.03;
        string marks = "" )
{
        float magnitude;

        /* Get the displacement, if any, from the texture map. */
        if(marks != "")
            magnitude = float texture(marks);            /* Use s, t */
        else
            magnitude = 0;

        /* The texture determines the size of the gouge, scaled by Km. */
        P += -Km * magnitude * normalize(N);
        N = calculatenormal(P);
}
```

Listing 16.30 *Displacement shader using a texture for pits and gouges*

Bowling pin surface

Plate 12 shows one of the bowling pins on the cover. Listing 16.31 shows the surface shader used on the bowling pins. It starts by dividing the height of the pin into different-colored areas, coloring the base gray, applying a neutral color to the body and top, and using a procedural texture for the red triangles on the neck.

pin_color() then checks the surface point against a series of bounding boxes. If the surface point is within a bounding box, a texture associated with that box is applied. The "coated plastic," "ABC circle" and "Brunswick B" labels, shown in Plate 13, are all applied this way, normalizing surface points within the bounding boxes. If the texture coordinates that come out of the normalization are outside the range [0,1] (i.e., the points lie outside the bounding box) the **texture**() function will return black (0).

Finally, the dirt and gouges, contained in the texture map "marks.txt" and shown in Plate 13, are applied to the pin. The instance variable *spin* is used to rotate this texture with respect to the labels so that each pin appears different. "marks.txt" must have been created to be cyclic so that accesses outside the range [0,1] wrap around.

```
/*
 * pin_color(): Shade a bowling pin with color, labels, and marks.
 */
#define REDCOLOR        color (0.6,0.05,0.05)   /* red band on neck */
#define CIRCLECOLOR     color (0.6,0.05,0.05)   /*... for "circle" label */
#define NEUTRALCOLOR    color (1.0,.8,.4)       /*... for body         */
#define GRAYCOLOR       color (.3,.3,.3)        /*... for base         */
#define BLUECOLOR       color (.0,.0,.9)        /*... for "Brunswick" */

/* Bounding box in texture space for "ABC Circle" label */
#define x1MIN -0.25
#define x1MAX  0.45
#define y1MIN  6.7
#define y1MAX  7.4

/* Bounding box in texture space for "Coated Plastic" label */
#define x2MIN -1.1
#define x2MAX  1.1
#define y2MIN  6.4
#define y2MAX  8.6

/* Bounding box in texture space for "Brunswick B" label */
#define x3MIN -1.3
#define x3MAX  1.3
#define y3MIN  6.0
#define y3MID  6.55
#define y3MAX  8.6

surface
pin_color(
        float   Ka          = .5,
                Kd          = .5,
                Ks          = .8,
                roughness   = .1,
```

```
          spin         = 0;
color  specularcolor = 1;
string texturename   = "marks.txt" )
{

float  strength;
point  Nf;
float  x,y,z;
color  cs ;

Nf = faceforward( normalize(N), I );
x = xcomp(transform("object",P));
y = ycomp(transform("object",P));        /* Pins are 15" tall */
z = zcomp(transform("object",P));

if (y <= 0.25) cs = GRAYCOLOR;           /* gray base       */
else if (y <= 9.5) cs = NEUTRALCOLOR;    /* neutral body    */
else if (y <= 10.5) cs = REDCOLOR;       /* red ring        */
else if (y >  12.0) cs = NEUTRALCOLOR;   /* neutral top     */
else {                        /* between ring and top, create red crown  */
        u = (u+.2)*6; u = u-floor(u);
        if (u < .5)
                if (2*u - 0 > (y-10.5)/(12.0-10.5))
                        cs = REDCOLOR;
                else
                        cs = NEUTRALCOLOR;
        else
                if (2*u - 1 + (y-10.5)/(12.0-10.5) < 1)
                        cs = REDCOLOR;
                else
                        cs = NEUTRALCOLOR;
}

if (z < 0)                               /* on the back side */
        /* Go fetch the "Coated Plastic" label. This is a single-
         * channel texture that we want to appear black. */
        cs = cs * (1 - float texture("coated.txt",
                (x-x2MIN)/(x2MAX-x2MIN),
                1.0 - (y-y2MIN)/(y2MAX-y2MIN) ));

else {                                   /* on the front side */
        /* Go fetch the "ABC circle" label. This is a single-
         * channel texture that we want to appear red. */
        strength = float texture("circle.txt",
                1.0 - (x-x1MIN)/(x1MAX-x1MIN),
                1.0 - (y-y1MIN)/(y1MAX-y1MIN));
        cs = mix(cs,CIRCLECOLOR,strength);

        /* Go fetch the "Brunswick B" label. This is a single-
         * channel texture that we want to appear red at the bottom
         * and blue at the top. */
        strength = float texture("b.txt",
```

```
                    1.0 - (x-x3MIN)/(x3MAX-x3MIN),
                    1.0 - (y-y3MIN)/(y3MAX-y3MIN));
        if (y > y3MID)
                cs = mix(cs,BLUECOLOR,strength);
        else
                cs = mix(cs,REDCOLOR,strength);
    }

    /*
     * Now for the dirt and gouges. Look up in a single channel texture
     *   for the dirt applied to the surface. Spin the texture differently for
     *   each pin so that the similarity is not apparent. This same access is
     *   made in the displacement shader to align the gouges with the dirt.
     */
    strength = 1 - float texture(texturename,s+spin,y/15.0);
    cs = cs * strength ;

    /* Now that cs has been set, perform the standard plastic shading
     * calculation */
    Oi = 1.0;
    Ci = cs * (Ka*ambient() + Kd*diffuse(Nf))
            + Ks*specularcolor*specular(Nf,normalize(-I),roughness);
}
```

Listing 16.31 *Surface shader for a bowling pin*

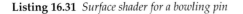

bowling pin bump map

For the greatest realism in the bowling pin, the displacement shader *gouge()* is also used. It also applies the "marks.txt" map, but uses it to displace the surface so that it really appears dented. The instance variable *spin* should be the same as for the corresponding call of *pin_color()*, to synchronize mark with dent. The variable *Km* scales the magnitude of the texture map values to provide the actual displacement. Plate 12 depicts the bowling pin.

Shadow-mapped spotlight

The next shader shows a simplified use of a shadow map. *shadowspot()*, shown in Listing 16.33, is just the standard *spotlight()* shader modified slightly to use an optional shadow map. In fact, the modification involves the addition of only three lines. An instance variable, *shadowname*, is added and set to the empty string. Just before setting *Cl*, the string is

```
/*
 * gouge(): Use a texture map to displace a surface.
 */
displacement
gouge(
        float   Km   = 0.03,
                spin = 0.0;        /* each pin gets its texture spun */
        string  texturename = "marks.txt")
{

        float   y = ycomp(transform("object",P));    /* convert to object space */

/* Use the same texture map that the surface shader uses. Spin it a different
 *  amount for each pin so that similarity is not detected.  The texture
 *  determines the size of the gouge. Multiply by the Km factor, then
 *  displace the surface point inwards by that amount. */
        P += (-Km * texture(texturename,s+spin,y/15.0)) * normalize(N);
        N = calculatenormal(P);
}
```

Listing 16.32 *Displacement shader for beating up a surface with a texture*

checked. If it is not empty (because it was set when the shader was instanced), the corresponding shadow map is used to modify the light's attenuation.

The main point here is that the value returned by **shadow**() gives the extent to which the surface point lies in shadow, a value between 0 and 1. Therefore, its return value is subtracted from 1 to get the extent to which the point is illuminated. In *shadowspot*(), *attenuation* is scaled by the latter amount.

Environment-mapped surface

Plate 15 is the result of using a reflection map. Plate 14 shows the set of images used as input to the reflection map. The shader *shiny*(), in Listing 16.34, shows how reflection maps are actually used.

shiny() is basically a standard metal shader with a few lines added to access the reflection map. After checking that a map has been passed to the shader, the vector **D** is set to the incident vector *I* reflected about surface normal *N*. Note that *Nf* is normalized, as **reflect**() expects.

```
/*
 * shadowspot(): spotlight with an optional shadow map
 */
light
shadowspot(
        float  intensity    = 1;
        color  lightcolor   = 1;
        point  from         = point 0,              /* light position */
               to           = point (0,0,1);
        float  coneangle          = radians(30),
               conedeltaangle     = radians(5);
               beamdistribution   = 2;
        string shadowfile   = "" )
{
        uniform point    A = (to - from) / length(to - from);     /* direction */
        uniform float    cosoutside= cos(coneangle),
                         cosinside = cos(coneangle-conedeltaangle);
        float  attenuation,       /* falloff from center of illumination cone    */
               cosangle;          /* cosine of angle wrt center of cone           */

        illuminate( from, A, coneangle ) {
               cosangle = L.A / length(L);       /* A is already normalized */
               attenuation = pow(cosangle, beamdistribution) / (L.L);
               attenuation *= smoothstep( cosoutside, cosinside, cosangle );
               if( shadowfile != "" )
                   attenuation *= (1.0 - shadow( shadowfile, Ps ));
               Cl = attenuation * intensity * lightcolor;
        }
}
```

Listing 16.33 *Spotlight using shadow map*

The reflected vector **D** is transformed to the world space of the scene for passing to the **environment**() function. It is critical that the map be indexed in the same space in which it was created, translations aside. Here we use "world" space under the assumption that the axes of the current world space are parallel to those that applied when the environment map was originally rendered. This is why, in Listing 12.3, the only rotations performed in setting up the environment images were those required to look at the cube faces, so that the axes of the cube were parallel to those of world space. As long as world space doesn't change, a scene that includes an environment map may be viewed with any camera.

```
surface
shiny(
        float   Ka          = .3,
                Ks          = .8,
                roughness   = .05;
        string  mapname = "" )
{
        color ev;
        point D, Nf, NI;

        Nf = faceforward(normalize(N), I);
        NI = normalize(I);

        if( mapname != "" ) {
            /* compute the environment index direction, D */
            D = reflect(NI, Nf);
            /* convert D to environment space. */
            D = transform("world", point "world" (0,0,0) + D);
            ev = environment(mapname, D);
        } else
            ev = 0;

        Oi = Os;
        Ci = Oi * (Ka * ambient() +
                Ks * (ev + specular(Nf, -NI, roughness)));
}
```

Listing 16.34 *Metal shader with optional environment map*

A Case Study: One Perfect Pencil

This section illustrates the results of an attempt to render a particular object with the greatest realism. The pencil in Plates 16 and 17 used CSG for modeling, plus a variety of displacement and surface shaders. The middle pencil in plate 16 attempts to hew as close to reality as possible, while the outer two substitute other shaders to amusing effect. The most interesting of the shaders used in the middle pencil appear below.

ferrule

The ferrule of a pencil is a ribbed cylinder. The ribs could be modeled with partial tori, but an alternative is to use the *dferrule()* displacement shader, shown in Listing 16.35.

```
/*
 * dferrule(): Deform the cylinder that models the ferrule of a pencil.
 *   The shader adds four ridges that circumscribe the cylinder and
 *   many more between the innermost ridges that are parallel to
 *   the cylinder's axis. The ridges are displaced sine waves.
 *   The ferrule is also slightly flared at the eraser end.
 */
#define UFREQ 219.911
#define VFREQ 104.72
#define R1MIN .17
#define R1MAX .23
#define R2MIN .31
#define R2MAX .37
#define R3MIN .63
#define R3MAX .69
#define R4MIN .77
#define R4MAX .83
displacement
dferrule(
        float   Km = .005 )
{
        float   magnitude = 0;

        /* Compute the distance the surface should be displaced. */
        if (v <= .02)                               /* the eraser-end flair */
                magnitude = 2*(1 - sin(78.54*v));

        if ((v >= R1MIN) && (v <= R1MAX))           /* first circular ridge */
                magnitude = 3*(1 - cos(VFREQ*(v-R1MIN)));
        else if ((v >= R2MIN) && (v <= R2MAX))      /* second circular ridge */
                magnitude = 3*(1 - cos(VFREQ*(v-R2MIN)));
        else if ((v >.37) && (v < .63))             /* the longitudinal ridges */
                magnitude = -sin(UFREQ*u) - 1;
        else if ((v >= R3MIN) && (v <= R3MAX))      /* third circular ridge */
                magnitude = 3*(1 - cos(VFREQ*(v-R3MIN)));
        else if ((v >= R4MIN) && (v <= R4MAX))      /* fourth circular ridge */
                magnitude = 3*(1 - cos(VFREQ*(v-R4MIN)));

        /* Now apply the displacement in the direction of the normal. */
        P += Km * magnitude * normalize(N);

        /* Recalculate the normal. */
        N = calculatenormal(P);
}
```

Listing 16.35 *Ferrule displacement shader for a pencil*

The displacement is different for a variety of subranges of surface parameter v, which runs from 0 to 1 along the length of

the ferrule cylinder. This usage is identical to that of t in the light bulb shaders, barring any changes to texture coordinates. Within the appropriate intervals of v, the displacement is based on sinusoids of empirically determined frequency and phase. The instance variable Km may be used to exaggerate all of the ridges.

emboss

The *emboss()* shader is a general-purpose version of the *gouge()* displacement shader of Listing 16.32. The values returned from the texture access function **texture()** lie between 0 and 1. This value is scaled by instance variable Km to yield a scalar displacement, which in turn is multiplied by the normalized surface normal vector to get a displacement vector. The surface normal is then recalculated using **calculatenormal()**.

```
/*
 * emboss(): emboss a pencil with lettering. It uses the same texture
 *     map as sdixon() to define the lettering.
 */
displacement
emboss(
        float   Km          = .05;
        string  texturename= "dixon.tx")
{
        if( texturename != "") {
                P -= Km * texture(texturename, s, t) * normalize(N);
                N = calculatenormal(P);
        }
}
```

Listing 16.36 *Displacement shader embossing a surface using a texture*

This embossing technique is really appropriate only for an anti-aliased texture, in which pixels at the edge of characters grade smoothly between 0 and 1. It works very well for any texture with that characteristic. It can be used to give ordinary mapped text a striking appearance with virtually no effort. The highlight on the surface of the "Dixon" label on the pencil shows off its embossing.

label

Once the body of the pencil is displaced by the label, it is painted by the special-purpose surface shader *sdixon()* shown in Listing 16.37. It uses a label texture map as in the embossing shader above to control the color of the surface; the texture itself is applied to the pencil as green, and the background is yellow. But the interesting point is that the texture is also used to control the specular brightness of the surface. As a result, the label appears as *metallic* green and the rest as *matte* yellow.

```
/*
 * sdixon(): Paint the body of a pencil.
 */
surface
sdixon(
        float   Ka           = 1.0,
                Kd           = 1.0,
                Ks           = 1.0,
                roughness    = .25;
        color   green        = color(0, .2, 0),
                yellow       = color(.56, .23, 0),
        string  texturename  = "dixon.tx")
{

        point Nf = faceforward(normalize(N),I);
        float ink;
        color cout;

        /* This shader uses a single-channel texture map to apply a
         *   metallic-green ink to a matte-yellow background. */

        /* Get the amount of ink from texture file. */
        ink = texture(texturename, s, t);

        /* Use ink to mix yellow and green */
        cout = mix(yellow, green, ink);

        /* Compute the output color. Notice that as ink goes from zero to
           one, the diffuse component goes to zero and the specular
           component is increased. This has the effect of transitioning
           from a matte surface to a metallic one as ink is added. */
        Oi = Os;
        Ci = Os * cout * ( Ka*ambient() + (1-ink)*Kd*diffuse(Nf) +
                                ink*Ks*specular(Nf,normalize(-I),roughness)    )

;
}
```

Listing 16.37 *Pencil-labeling surface shader*

rubber

The final subtlety in the pencil is on the rubber eraser. Rather than using a simple matte surface shader, the shader *rubber()*, shown in Listing 16.38, includes a small amount of white dust in the surface of the eraser. The amount of dust is given by the **noise()** function using scaled surface position points as input.

```
/*
 * rubber(): This shader generates a rubber surface. It is a matte shader that
 * adds in a little white dust to mimic the dust on a new eraser.
 */
surface
rubber(
        float   Ka          = 1.0,
                Kd          = 1.0,
                txtscale    = 1.5 )
{
        point Nf = faceforward(normalize(N),I),
                Ploc = transform("shader", P);  /* Move to shader space */
        color cout, white=1;

        /* Mix in some white dust. */
        cout = mix(Cs, white, .05* (noise(txtscale*Ploc)));

        /* Compute a matte surface. */
        Oi = Os;
        Ci = Os * cout * ( Ka*ambient() + Kd*diffuse(Nf) ) ;
}
```

Listing 16.38 *Rubber surface shader*

Results

Plate 17 shows what a difference in credibility can be obtained by relatively subtle improvements in the realism of shading. From left to right the ferrule goes from flat, to textured, to textured and displaced (the label and the eraser remain the same). The dust on the eraser, the rings on the ferrule and the highlights on the label are all nearly subliminal, but the right-hand pencil is much more credible than the other two.

Further Examples

The remaining color plates are included as examples of images using the RenderMan Interface. They are included to evoke some of the possibilities of RenderMan.

Enhanced CAD

Plate 18 shows a before-and-after pair depicting an open office plan created using Autodesk's AutoCAD™ modeling software. The version at top was rendered using standard shading techniques. At bottom is an image rendered from the same scene using the RenderMan Interface to provide shadows, local light sources, reflections from the floor, and a variety of textures for the wall, the floor, the pictures on the wall, the chair and even some work on the desk.

Gears

Plate 19 shows a set of gears courtesy of CADKEY. The image shows the qualitative effects of using smooth curved surfaces and an accurate model of metallic reflection.

Guitar

Plate 20 shows an electric guitar (also modeled by CADKEY). The reflections from the wall are quite subtle, but provide considerable depth to the walls. The guitar body itself is composed of polygons.

Movie camera

The movie camera in Plate 21 was modeled at The Analytical Sciences Corporation and rendered at Pixar. The "Mitchell" stamp was debossed using a displacement shader.

Exploding globe

Plate 22 is an image produced for *National Geographic*, a depiction of a fragile earth. This image depended on the use of partially opaque materials and accurate textures.

RenderMan in the Movies

The last three plates show frames from computer animation created using RenderMan. Plate 24 is from *Luxo Jr. in "Light Entertainment,"* an 1989 film from Pixar, showing the dramatic effect of proper motion blur. Plate 25 appears in *Knickknack*, another 1989 Pixar film. The snowflakes are individual bicubic patches. Both the patterned wallpaper and the wood shelf are shaded using procedural textures.

Finally, Plate 26 shows a special-effects shot from the 1989 James Cameron film *The Abyss*, executed by the Computer Graphics Group at Industrial Light and Magic. The scene concerns a creature, a pseudopod formed from seawater. The transparent creature reflects and refracts its environment as it snakes through an underwater drilling platform. It was modeled using thousands of bicubic patches and rendered with a variety of special-purpose shaders to provide reflection and refraction.

This scene would have been nearly impossible to execute with any other technology. The fact that a synthetic image can share the frame with live actors and sets, yet appear perfectly natural, is a high-water mark for computer-generated imagery.

The Future

The RenderMan Interface as a whole frees the modeling world from concerns about rendering by providing a consistent way to access a variety of renderers. In a similar way, the RenderMan Shading Language frees new and novel techniques of shading from concerns either of the models involved or the rendering system in which they will be applied. The fact that shaders and textures can be used in many different renderers, in conjunction with a panoply of modeling systems, provides a powerful impetus for the development of whole collections of innovative and interesting shading tools.

The shaders in this chapter only evoke the possibilities. Just as modeling systems provide special constructs for different domains of modeling, the shading realm should see development aimed at rendering specific kinds of scenes. For example, one might hope to see catalogs of shaders and textures for use in rendering architects' models both realistically and with the appearance of more traditional architectural "renderings." Whereas any specificity designed into a particular modeler is good for that program only, the generality of the shading language makes one shader valid in a variety of contexts. With RenderMan providing the ground for the technology, the shading language should open the door to a whole world of dramatic improvements in the quality of synthetic imagery.

Summary of RenderMan Program Structure

Order of Transformations

Transformations are applied to the points in a scene in the reverse order from which they were called.

Given:

G = Points to be transformed
M = Object transformations
C = Camera positioning matrix
P = Perspective matrix
S = Screen transformation matrix
I = Identity
T = Current transformation matrix

The illustration below shows how these matrices are applied. Applicable notes appear on the next page.

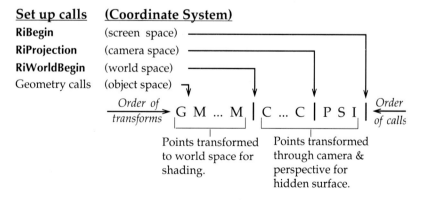

Set up calls   (Coordinate System)

RiBegin   (screen space)
RiProjection   (camera space)
RiWorldBegin   (world space)
Geometry calls   (object space)

$$\xrightarrow[transforms]{Order\ of} \underbrace{G\ M\ ...\ M}\ \Big|\ \underbrace{C\ ...\ C}\ \Big|\ P\ S\ I\ \Big|\ \xleftarrow[of\ calls]{Order}$$

Points transformed to world space for shading.

Points transformed through camera & perspective for hidden surface.

1. At **RiBegin** the current transformation T is set to identity.

2. Subsequent transformation calls S apply to T. This allows for skewed planes when off-center projections are required. Very few people will ever use this.

3. When **RiProjection** is called, the perspective transformation is multiplied times T and T is then saved as the projection to the screen. T is then set to identity.

4. Subsequent transformation calls C...C are used to position the camera.

5. At **RiWorldBegin** the world-to-camera matrix is set to T, and then T is set to identity.

6. Subsequent transformation calls M...M position objects in world space.

The above transformation pipeline transforms objects into screen space. The next step, not illustrated above, is to take part of the image plane and map it onto the raster.

Begin-End pairs always cause the transformation to be pushed or popped.

RenderMan Program Structure

The following table summarizes the structure and scoping rules of a RenderMan program. The following notes apply:

1. **ObjectBegin-End** may happen at any time. If defined within a **FrameBegin-End** or **WorldBegin-End** then it will disappear after the corresponding **End**.

2. Within **FrameBegin-End** there may be multiple **WorldBegin-Ends** with different display options. This can be used to create shadows and environment maps.

3. **WorldBegin-End** cannot be nested.

4. **AttributeBegin-End** and **TransformBegin-End** may be nested within themselves or each other, and may occur anywhere including around a **WorldBegin-End** block to help reset matrices.

5. Note that **RiProjection** should be called somewhere between **RiBegin** and **RiWorldBegin**. This call freezes the screen mapping, sets up the perspective transformation, and sets the current transformation matrix to identity.

Summary of RenderMan Program Structure		
Scoping	**Scoping Rules**	**Typical Calls In Block**
RiBegin	Everything must occur between **RiBegin-End**. Current transform set to identity.	Permanent options for hiders and display. Permanent attributes, light sources and retained objects. *No* Geometry (except in retained objects).
RiFrameBegin	Pushes options, attributes and transformations.	Camera transform setup. Options. Attributes constant for frame. **RiMake...** calls. *No* Geometry (except in retained objects).
RiWorldBegin	Camera projection frozen. Current transform set to identity. Pushes attributes and transformations.	Lights and attributes. *No* Options.
RiAttributeBegin	Pushes attributes and transformations. May be nested in or around other **Begin-End** pairs.	Attributes, transformations and geometry. *No* Options.
RiAttibuteEnd	Pops attributes and transformations. Turns off, but does not delete, lights.	
RiTransformBegin	Pushes transformations. May be nested in or around other **Begin-End** pairs.	Attributes, transformations and geometry. *No* Options.
RiTransformEnd	Pops transformations.	
RiWorldEnd	Pops attributes and transformations. Deletes enclosed lights and retained objects. Finish frame.	
RiFrameEnd	Pops options, attributes & transformations. Deletes enclosed lights and retained objects.	*No* Geometry.
RiEnd	Shutdown	

Constructing Basis Matrices for Bicubic Surfaces

Introduction

The basis matrices used to specify surfaces in the RenderMan Interface provide a variety of useful surface types, but their generality is limited by the fact that the matrices themselves are predefined, and therefore constant. Learning to construct basis matrices is well worth the effort, because it provides access to several much more flexible classes of surfaces. This appendix provides the information needed to construct these matrices and shows examples of them applied to surfaces.

This information, and the characterization of a wide variety of uniform bicubic splines in terms of basis matrices, is due to an unpublished paper by Tom Duff [DUFF83]. His work there is truly insightful and powerful, adding significantly to the generality of the basis matrix formulation.

Interpolating vs. approximating

We have already seen in Chapter 6 the distinction between interpolating and approximating surfaces: interpolating splines like the Catmull-Rom and Hermite splines guarantee that a curve or surface will pass through its control points. An approximating spline like the B-spline is influenced by its control hull, but does not in general pass through any of the points. The Bézier splines represent a compromise between the two: they interpolate some points of the control hull, but not others.

Each type of spline is useful in its place: an interpolating spline is most likely to be used where a surface is fit to a set of points, but an approximating spline is more useful for interactive design where the smoothness of the surface is of greatest importance.

Tension and bias

Even restricting the interpretation of control points in a surface to approximation or interpolation, there is still plenty of freedom. A given set of control points can be interpolated into many different surfaces, for example. The classes of splines discussed here differ in how they incorporate characteristics of bias and tension into their resulting splines.

Tension refers to the "gravity" of a spline, the attraction of the control points for the curve or surface. A very tense spline looks more like its control hull than an untense spline. Figure B.1 shows a spline under different tensions.

Bias refers to the symmetry of the spline near a control point. The concept is best illustrated with a figure, specifically Figure B.2. More formally, bias expresses the relative strengths of the two derivatives on either side of a knot. A highly biased curve will be flatter on one side of a knot than on the other.

The spline types discussed in this chapter vary in their attention to tension and bias as well as their interpolating or approximating qualities. Tension and bias are expressed in the basis matrix using algorithms set out both mathematically and with C procedures. The resulting basis matrices are suitable for passing to **RiBasis**() to produce surfaces. The ubasis and vbasis matrices may be different.

The first section presents the tensed Cardinal splines. The second section introduces tension into B-splines. The third section presents a biased interpolating spline, and the fourth discusses basis matrix construction for the well-known Beta splines, a class of approximating spline which incorporates both bias and tension.

In the spirit of RenderMan in general, we minimize the theory here, emphasizing methods and results.

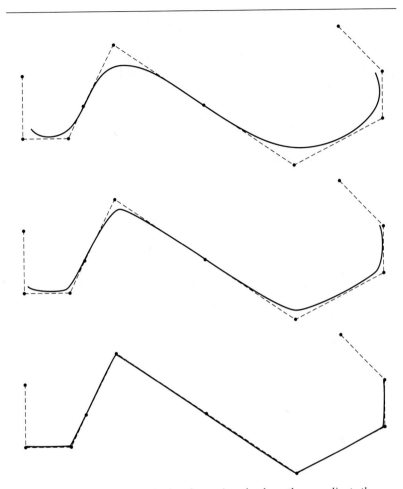

Figure B.1 *Tensed spline; the higher the tension, the closer the curve lies to the control points*

Protocol

The **RtBasis** basis matrices defined below are passed to **RiBasis()** just as the predefined matrices were in Chapter 6. In all cases, the corresponding step parameter should be 1. An $N \times M$ grid of control points, if used to create an unwrapped patch mesh, will create $(N-3)(M-3)$ patches; if wrapped, the grid will create $N \times M$ patches.

A Tensed Interpolating Spline

The Cardinal splines are a generalization of Catmull-Rom splines, introducing a tension parameter. If t represents tension in the range [0,1], the basis matrix for a Cardinal spline is given by

$$
\begin{bmatrix}
-t & 2-t & t-2 & t \\
2t & t-3 & 3-2t & -t \\
-t & 0 & t & 0 \\
0 & 1 & 0 & 0
\end{bmatrix}
$$

Listing B.1 gives a routine that generates a Cardinal spline basis matrix, given *tension*.

```
/* GetCardinalBasis(): return, in 'm', a Cardinal spline basis
        matrix from tension parameter 'tension'. */

GetCardinalBasis( tension, m )
double tension;
RtBasis m;
{
        m[0][0] = -tension;
        m[0][1] = 2 - tension;
        m[0][2] = tension - 2;
        m[0][3] = tension;

        m[1][0] = 2*tension;
        m[1][1] = tension - 3;
        m[1][2] = 3 - 2*tension;
        m[1][3] = -tension;

        m[2][0] = -tension;
        m[2][1] = 0;
        m[2][2] = tension;
        m[2][3] = 0;

        m[3][0] = 0;
        m[3][1] = 1;
        m[3][2] = 0;
        m[3][3] = 0;
}
```

Listing B.1 *Cardinal spline basis matrix*

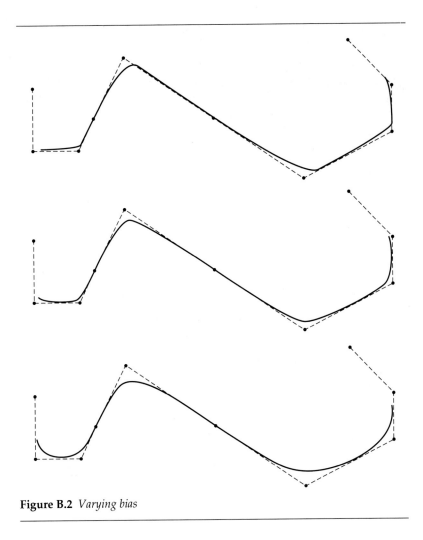

Figure B.2 *Varying bias*

Figure B.3 shows the effect of varying tension from 0 to 2, although negative tension values are allowed. A Cardinal spline with tension = 0.5 is a Catmull-Rom spline.

A Tensed Approximating Spline

Like Catmull-Rom splines, the B-spline can be generalized to include tension. Again, if t is tension, the basis matrix for a

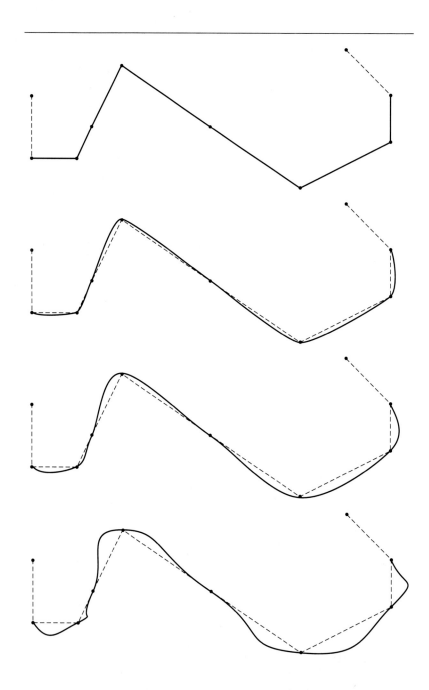

Figure B.3 *Cardinal spline with tension varying from 0 (at top) to 0.5, 1 and 2*

tensed B-spline is

$$\frac{1}{6} \begin{bmatrix} -t & 12-9t & 9t-12 & t \\ 3t & 12t-18 & 18-15t & 0 \\ -3t & 0 & 3t & 0 \\ t & 6-2t & t & 0 \end{bmatrix}$$

The routine *GetTensedBSplineBasis()* creates such a matrix, given *tension*, which should normally lies in the range [0,1].

/* GetTensedBSplineBasis(): *produce a RenderMan basis matrix for a B-spline with tension* */

```
GetTensedBSplineBasis( tension, m )
double tension;
RtBasis m;
{
    double sixth = 1.0/6.0
    m[0][0] = sixth*(-tension);
    m[0][1] = sixth*(12 - 9*tension);
    m[0][2] = sixth*(9*tension - 12);
    m[0][3] = sixth*tension;

    m[1][0] = sixth*(3*tension);
    m[1][1] = sixth*(12*tension - 18);
    m[1][2] = sixth*(18 - 15*tension);
    m[1][3] = 0;

    m[2][0] = sixth*(-3*tension);
    m[2][1] = 0;
    m[2][2] = sixth*3*tension);
    m[2][3] = 0;

    m[3][0] = sixth*tension;
    m[3][1] = sixth*(6-2*tension);
    m[3][2] = sixth*tension;
    m[3][3] = 0;
}
```

Listing B.2 *Creating a tensed B-spline basis matrix*

Figure B.4 shows a B-spline with *tension* varying from 0 to 2.

If *tension* = 1, the basis matrix from this routine yields **RiB-SplineBasis**. Note that *tension* has an unusual sense here:

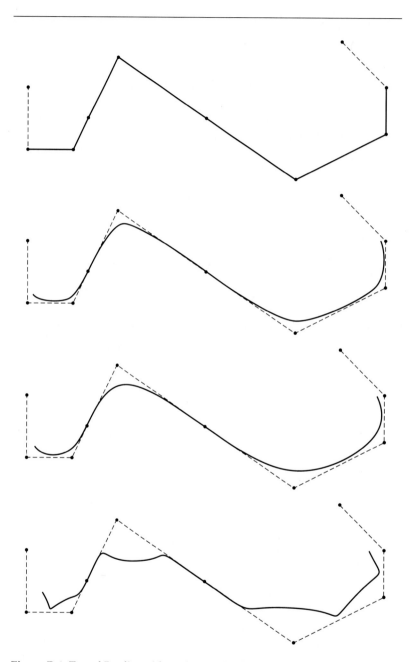

Figure B.4 *Tensed B-spline with tension varying from 0.01 (at top) to 0.7, 1, and 2*

when it is 0, the curve is maximally tense (it coincides with the control hull).

A Biased, Tensed Interpolating Spline

The last basis matrix presented here yields an interpolating spline with both bias b and tension t. Dubbed by Tom Duff the Tau spline, its basis matrix is:

$$\begin{bmatrix} (b-1)t & 2-bt & (1-b)t-2 & bt \\ 2(1-b)t & (3b-1)t-3 & 3-t & -bt \\ (b-1)t & (1-2b)t & bt & 0 \\ 0 & 1 & 0 & 0 \end{bmatrix}$$

GetTauBasis() in Listing B.3 produces a RenderMan basis matrix according to this formulation, taking both *bias* and *tension* parameters.

```
/* GetTauBasis(): produce a basis matrix for an interpolating spline with
both bias and tension */
GetTauBasis( bias, tension, m )
double bias, tension;
RtBasis m;
{
     m[0][0] = tension * (bias-1.);
     m[0][1] = 2. - tension*bias;
     m[0][2] = tension * (1.-bias) - 2.;
     m[0][3] = tension *  bias;

     m[1][0] = tension *  2.*(1.-bias);
     m[1][1] = tension * (3.*bias - 1.) - 3.;
     m[1][2] =  3. - tension;
     m[1][3] = -tension *  bias;

     m[2][0] =  tension * (bias - 1.);
     m[2][1] =  tension * (1. - 2.*bias);
     m[2][2] =  tension *  bias;
     m[2][3] = 0.;

     m[3][0] = 0.;
     m[3][1] = 1.;
     m[3][2] = 0.;
     m[3][3] = 0.;
}
```

Listing B.3 *Creating a basis matrix for a Tau spline*

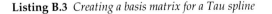

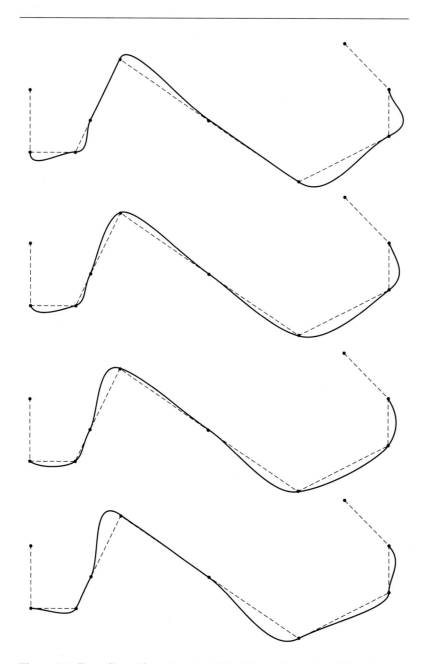

Figure B.5 *Tau spline with tension=1 and bias of (top to bottom) 0, 0.33, 0.67, 1.0*

Appendix B: Constructing Basis Matrices for Bicubic Surfaces

The Cardinal spline seen previously is equivalent to this spline with bias = 0.5. Figure B.5 shows curves generated with a basis matrix from *GetTauBasis*(). Again, *tension* and *bias* are not restricted to the range [0,1], but become more difficult to control outside.

A Biased, Tensed Approximating Spline

Beta-splines are an approximating spline with both bias and tension developed by Brian Barsky [BARSKY81]. For bias b and tension t, the Beta-spline basis matrix is

$$\frac{1}{t+2b^3+4b^2+4b+2} \begin{bmatrix} -2b^3 & 2(t+b^3+b^2+b) & -2(t+b^2+b+1) & 2 \\ 6b^3 & -3(t+2b^3+2b^2) & 3t+6b^2 & 0 \\ -6b^3 & 6(b^3-b) & 6b & 0 \\ 2b^3 & t+4b^2+4b & 2 & 0 \end{bmatrix}$$

A Beta-spline basis matrix is produced by *GetBetaSplineBasis*(), in Listing B.4.

```
GetBetaSplineBasis( bias, tension, m )
double bias, tension;
RtBasis m;

{
        double bias2, bias3, d;

        bias2 = bias*bias;
        bias3 = bias*bias2;
        d = 1/( tension + 2*bias3 + 4*bias2 + 4*bias + 2);

        m[0][0] = -d*2*bias3;
        m[0][1] =  d*2*( tension + bias3 + bias2 + bias );
        m[0][2] = -d*2*( tension + bias2 + bias + 1 );
        m[0][3] =  d*2;

        m[1][0] =  d*6*bias3;
        m[1][1] = -d*3*( tension + 2*bias3 + 2*bias2 );
        m[1][2] =  d*3*( tension + 2*bias2 );
        m[1][3] =  0;

        m[2][0] = -d*6*bias3;
        m[2][1] =  d*6*( bias3 - bias );
        m[2][2] =  d*6*bias;
        m[2][3] =  0;
```

```
    m[3][0] = d*2*bias3;
    m[3][1] = d*(tension + 4*( bias2 + bias ));
    m[3][2] = d*2;
    m[3][3] = 0;
}
```

Listing B.4 *Creating a Beta-spline basis matrix*

The previous B-spline with *tension$_B$* is equivalent to a Beta spline with a bias of *bias$_b$* = 1 and a tension of *tension$_b$* = 12(1–*tension$_B$*)/*tension$_B$*. The tension of a Beta-spline varies from 0 to infinity, whereas that of the tensed B-spline varies from 0 to 1. Figure B.1 was of a Beta spline with *bias* of 1 and *tension* varying between 0 at the top, 10 in the middle and 100 at the bottom. Figure B.2 showed a Beta spline with fixed tension of 10 and bias, from top to bottom, of 0, 1, and 2.

Further Reading

An excellent reference on the mathematics of curve and surface specification is *An Introduction to Splines for use in Computer Graphics and Geometric Modeling* [BARTELS87]. A slightly more accessible treatment is the book by Gerald Farin [FARIN88].

The ri.h Header File

```
/*_____
**
** Copyright (c) 1988 Pixar.  All rights reserved.
**
**_____
*/

/*
 *     RenderMan Interface Standard Include File
 *
 *     Pre-ANSI (aka K&R) C version
 */

        /* Definitions of Abstract Types used in RI */

typedef short       RtBoolean;
typedef long        RtInt;
typedef float       RtFloat;

typedef char        *RtToken;

typedef RtFloat     RtColor[3];
typedef RtFloat     RtPoint[3];
typedef RtFloat     RtMatrix[4][4];
typedef RtFloat     RtBasis[4][4];
typedef RtFloat     RtBound[6];
typedef char        *RtString;

typedef char        *RtPointer;
typedef int         RtVoid;
typedef double      (*RtFloatFunc)();
typedef RtVoid      (*RtFunc)();

typedef RtPointer   RtObjectHandle;
typedef RtPointer   RtLightHandle;
```

/* Extern Declarations for Predefined RI Data Structures */

```
#define RI_FALSE        0
#define RI_TRUE         (! RI_FALSE)
#define RI_INFINITY     1.0e38
#define RI_EPSILON      1.0e-10
#define RI_NULL         ((RtToken)0)

extern RtToken    RI_FRAMEBUFFER, RI_FILE;
extern RtToken    RI_RGB, RI_RGBA, RI_RGBZ, RI_RGBAZ, RI_A, RI_Z, RI_AZ;
extern RtToken    RI_MERGE, RI_ORIGIN;
extern RtToken    RI_PERSPECTIVE, RI_ORTHOGRAPHIC;
extern RtToken    RI_HIDDEN, RI_PAINT;
extern RtToken    RI_CONSTANT, RI_SMOOTH;
extern RtToken    RI_FLATNESS, RI_FOV;

extern RtToken    RI_AMBIENTLIGHT, RI_POINTLIGHT,
                  RI_DISTANTLIGHT, RI_SPOTLIGHT;
extern RtToken    RI_INTENSITY, RI_LIGHTCOLOR, RI_FROM, RI_TO,
                  RI_CONEANGLE, RI_CONEDELTAANGLE,
                  RI_BEAMDISTRIBUTION;
extern RtToken    RI_MATTE, RI_METAL, RI_PLASTIC;
extern RtToken    RI_KA, RI_KD, RI_KS, RI_ROUGHNESS,
                  RI_SPECULARCOLOR;
extern RtToken    RI_DEPTHCUE, RI_FOG;
extern RtToken    RI_MINDISTANCE, RI_MAXDISTANCE,
                  RI_BACKGROUND, RI_DISTANCE;

extern RtToken    RI_RASTER, RI_SCREEN, RI_CAMERA, RI_WORLD,
                  RI_OBJECT;
extern RtToken    RI_INSIDE, RI_OUTSIDE, RI_LH, RI_RH;
extern RtToken    RI_P, RI_PZ, RI_PW, RI_N, RI_NP, RI_CS, RI_OS,
                  RI_S, RI_T, RI_ST;
extern RtToken    RI_BILINEAR, RI_BICUBIC;
extern RtToken    RI_PRIMITIVE, RI_INTERSECTION, RI_UNION,
                  RI_DIFFERENCE;
extern RtToken    RI_WRAP, RI_NOWRAP, RI_PERIODIC, RI_CLAMP,
                  RI_BLACK;
extern RtToken    RI_IGNORE, RI_PRINT, RI_ABORT, RI_HANDLER;

extern RtBasis    RiBezierBasis, RiBSplineBasis, RiCatmullRomBasis,
                  RiHermiteBasis, RiPowerBasis;

#define RI_BEZIERSTEP          ((RtInt)3)
#define RI_BSPLINESTEP         ((RtInt)1)
#define RI_CATMULLROMSTEP      ((RtInt)1)
#define RI_HERMITESTEP         ((RtInt)2)
#define RI_POWERSTEP           ((RtInt)4)

extern RtInt      RiLastError;
```

/ Declarations of All of the RenderMan Interface Subroutines */*

extern **RtToken**   **RiDeclare**();

extern **RtVoid**   **RiBegin**(), **RiEnd**(),
    RiFrameBegin(), **RiFrameEnd**(),
    RiWorldBegin(), **RiWorldEnd**();

extern **RtVoid**   **RiFormat**(), **RiFrameAspectRatio**(), **RiScreenWindow**(),
    RiCropWindow(), **RiProjection**(), **RiProjectionV**(),
    RiClipping(), **RiDepthOfField**(), **RiShutter**();

extern **RtVoid**   **RiPixelVariance**(), **RiPixelSamples**(), **RiPixelFilter**(),
    RiExposure(), **RiImager**(), **RiImagerV**(),
    RiQuantize(), **RiDisplay**(), **RiDisplayV**();
extern **RtFloat**   **RiGaussianFilter**(), **RiBoxFilter**(),
    RiTriangleFilter(), **RiCatmullRomFilter**(), **RiSincFilter**();

extern **RtVoid**   **RiHider**(), **RiHiderV**(),
    RiColorSamples(), **RiRelativeDetail**(),
    RiOption(), **RiOptionV**();

extern **RtVoid**   **RiAttributeBegin**(), **RiAttributeEnd**(),
    RiColor(), **RiOpacity**(), **RiTextureCoordinates**();

extern **RtLightHandle RiLightSource**(), **RiLightSourceV**(),
    RiAreaLightSource(), **RiAreaLightSourceV**();
extern **RtVoid**   **RiIlluminate**(),
    RiSurface(), **RiSurfaceV**(),
    RiAtmosphere(), **RiAtmosphereV**(),
    RiInterior(), **RiInteriorV**(), **RiExterior**(), **RiExteriorV**(),
    RiShadingRate(), **RiShadingInterpolation**(), **RiMatte**();

extern **RtVoid**   **RiBound**(), **RiDetail**(), **RiDetailRange**(),
    RiGeometricApproximation(),
    RiOrientation(), **RiReverseOrientation**(), **RiSides**();

extern **RtVoid**   **RiIdentity**(), **RiTransform**(), **RiConcatTransform**(),
    RiPerspective(),
    RiTranslate(), **RiRotate**(), **RiScale**(), **RiSkew**(),
    RiDeformation(), **RiDeformationV**(),
    RiDisplacement(), **RiDisplacementV**(),
    RiCoordinateSystem();
extern **RtPoint**   *****RiTransformPoints**();
extern **RtVoid**   **RiTransformBegin**(), **RiTransformEnd**();

extern **RtVoid**   **RiAttribute**(), **RiAttributeV**();

extern **RtVoid**   **RiPolygon**(), **RiPolygonV**(),

RiGeneralPolygon(), RiGeneralPolygonV(),
RiPointsPolygons(), RiPointsPolygonsV(),
RiPointsGeneralPolygons(), RiPointsGeneralPolygonsV(),
RiBasis(),
RiPatch(), RiPatchV(), RiPatchMesh(), RiPatchMeshV(),
RiNuPatch(), RiNuPatchV(), RiTrimCurve();

extern **RtVoid**   **RiSphere**(), **RiSphereV**(), **RiCone**(), **RiConeV**(),
RiCylinder(), **RiCylinderV**(),
RiHyperboloid(), **RiHyperboloidV**(),
RiParaboloid(), **RiParaboloidV**(), **RiDisk**(), **RiDiskV**(),
RiTorus(), **RiTorusV**(),
RiProcedural(), **RiGeometry**(), **RiGeometryV**();

extern **RtVoid**   **RiSolidBegin**(), **RiSolidEnd**() ;
extern **RtObjectHandle**   **RiObjectBegin**();
extern **RtVoid**   **RiObjectEnd**(), **RiObjectInstance**(),
RiMotionBegin(), **RiMotionBeginV**(), **RiMotionEnd**() ;

extern **RtVoid**   **RiMakeTexture**(), **RiMakeTextureV**(),
RiMakeBump(), **RiMakeBumpV**(),
RiMakeLatLongEnvironment(),
RiMakeLatLongEnvironmentV(),
RiMakeCubeFaceEnvironment(),
RiMakeCubeFaceEnvironmentV(),
RiMakeShadow(), **RiMakeShadowV**();

extern **RtVoid**   **RiErrorHandler**();
extern **RtVoid**   **RiErrorIgnore**(), **RiErrorPrint**(), **RiErrorAbort**();

List of RenderMan Functions

RenderMan Interface Routines

In the following declarations, *parameterlist* represents an optional list of parameters to the routine arranged in token-value pairs and terminated with the special token RI_NULL. These are discussed on page 39.

RtLightHandle RiAreaLightSource(name, *parameterlist*)   225
    char *name;

RiAtmosphere(name, *parameterlist*)   235
    char *name;

RiAttribute(name, *parameterlist*)   46
    char *name;

RiAttributeBegin()   50

RiAttributeEnd()   50

RiBasis(ubasis, ustep, vbasis, vstep)   93
    RtBasis ubasis, vbasis;
    RtInt ustep, vstep;
    typedef **RtFloat RtBasis**[4][4];
    RtBasis RiHermiteBasis,
           RiCatmullRomBasis,
           RiBezierBasis,
           RiBSplineBasis;

RiBegin(name)   48
    RtToken name;

RiBound(bound)   125
    RtBound bound;

RenderMan Shading Language Routines

The following list of routines in the RenderMan Shading Language does not include the math functions listed in Table 15.1 on page 312.

In a few of the following declarations, *textcoords* represents an optional list of texture coordinates in a texture map as discussed on page 320.

A *parameterlist* argument represents an optional list of parameters arranged token-value pairs. These are *not* terminated with an RI_NULL token.

Glossary of Technical Terms

Terms in SMALL CAPS are defined elsewhere in the Glossary. The page numbers in parentheses indicate where the term is defined or first used.

AGGREGATE OBJECT. An OBJECT composed of many primitives. (Contrast to a PRIMITIVE OBJECT, which consists of a single primitive). (107)

ALIASING. A reduction in image quality caused by representing an image as an array of discrete pixel values. Details that are too small to be resolved can cause large, inappropriate fluctuations in pixel values unless *anti-aliasing* steps are taken. (10, 174)

ALPHA. A common name for opacity information calculated and stored for each pixel in a FRAME. (156, 174)

ALTERNATIVE REPRESENTATIONS. A set of different models for the same object that may be chosen or combined depending on its LEVEL OF DETAIL in the image. (196)

AMBIENT LIGHT SOURCE. A light source that distributes light uniformly in all directions from no specified location. All objects are illuminated equally regardless of their location and orientation. (215)

AMBIENT REFLECTION. The surface reflection of AMBIENT LIGHT SOURCES. (229)

ANAMORPHIC IMAGE. An image that has been intentionally distorted in such a way that it only looks right when viewed with a certain device, or from a certain viewpoint. (161)

ANIMATION. A sequence of images that, when shown in rapid succession, produces the illusion of a moving image. (33)

APERTURE. The size of an opening used to admit light into a VIEWING DEVICE. The aperture, as well as the FOCAL LENGTH of the lens affect the DEPTH OF FIELD characteristics of the viewing device. (5, 8)

APPROXIMATING SPLINE. A spline that produces a smooth curve from its CONTROL POINTS without necessarily passing through any of them. (90)

APPROXIMATION (OF SURFACE PRIMITIVES). *See* GEOMETRIC APPROXIMATION.

AREA LIGHT SOURCE. A light source whose light emanates from a finite surface area as opposed to a single point. The shape of the area light source is specified much like an OBJECT; in terms of surface primitives. (224)

ATMOSPHERE. Air, dust, gasses, fog, etc. surrounding a surface that can affect the properties of light passing toward the viewer. (2)

ATMOSPHERIC EFFECTS. Effects such as smoke or fog simulating the influence of ATMOSPHERE on light reflected from an object. (3)

ATTRIBUTES. Part of the GRAPHICS ENVIRONMENT concerned with characteristics of individual objects and surfaces. Examples would be object color, and the CURRENT TRANSFORMATION in effect when an object is created. (44)

ATTRIBUTE BLOCK. A sequence of RenderMan routine calls bracketed by **RiAttributeBegin**() and **RiAttributeEnd**(). ATTRIBUTES declared within the block affect only those objects created after the declaration but before the end of the block. At the end of the block, all attributes' settings return to those in effect at the start of the block. Attribute blocks can be nested. (47)

B-SPLINE. A particularly smooth class of APPROXIMATING SPLINE. *See also illustration on page 91.* (91)

B-SPLINE PATCH. A type of BICUBIC PATCH formed using B-SPLINE curves. (90)

BASIS MATRIX. A matrix that determines how a GEOMETRY MATRIX of CONTROL POINTS are to be interpreted when generating a BICUBIC PATCH. (92)

BÉZIER PATCH. A type of BICUBIC PATCH formed using BÉZIER SPLINE curves. (90)

BÉZIER SPLINES. A class of cubic SPLINE whose first and last CONTROL POINTS are endpoints of the spline. The first two control points determine a tangent vector at the first endpoint. The last two control points determine the tangent vector at the second endpoint. (90)

BICUBIC PATCH. A four-edged PRIMITIVE SURFACE specified by cubic SPLINES. It is described using a set of sixteen CONTROL POINTS arranged in a 4 x 4 GEOMETRY MATRIX. (87)

BILINEAR PATCH. A quadrilateral with straight edges formed by four vertices (not necessarily co-planar) in three-dimensional space. The position of any point on the bilinear patch is determined using bilinear INTERPOLATION between the vertices. (86)

BLOCK. A sequence of RenderMan routine calls bracketed by special **Ri...Begin**() and **Ri...End**() routines. Blocks are used to denote MODES of the RenderMan Interface and to save and restore elements of the GRAPHICS ENVIRONMENT. (47)

BOUNDARY. The outer extent of a polygon or other primitive determined by the VERTICES of the polygon and the EDGES that connect them; also, in CONSTRUCTIVE SOLID GEOMETRY (CSG), the surfaces lying between the inside and outside of a solid object. (69)

BOUNDARY REPRESENTATION. The description of a SOLID by specifying the set of adjoining SURFACES enclosing it. (126)

BOUNDING BOX. The rectilinear box that barely contains a set of geometric objects It is specified in the current coordinate system by giving its minima and maxima in x, y, and z. (124, 195)

BUMP MAP. An image used to control local changes in the surface ORIENTATION when shading a surface. This can provide subtle ''bumpiness'' effects on an otherwise flat surface. (257, 258, 320)

CALL-BY-VALUE. A method of passing parameters to a procedure that guarantees that the function cannot alter any of the variables passed to it as arguments. Specifically, the *value* of the variable is passed, and any changes affect only a *copy* of the variable, not the variable itself. (24)

CAMERA SPACE. A COORDINATE SYSTEM with its origin at the camera VIEWPOINT and positive *z* axis pointed along the direction of view. (52, 123)

CAPABILITIES (OF A RENDERER). Features and characteristics associated with a particular renderer, and not subject to user control. (44)

CATMULL-ROM PATCH. A BICUBIC PATCH formed using CATMULL-ROM SPLINES. (90)

CATMULL-ROM SPLINE. A class of cubic SPLINE that INTERPOLATES all its CONTROL POINTS but its two end points. At each interior point, the surrounding control points are used to control the spline's tangent. (91)

CHANNEL. A single component of a PIXEL. Red, green, blue and ALPHA are all examples of components. (320)

CHILDREN. For a given element in a HIERARCHICAL MODEL, those elements in the next level down that are associated with it. For example, a "foot" object might include five "toes" as children. (109)

CLIPPING PLANE. A plane in WORLD SPACE parallel to the IMAGE PLANE, used to delimit the parts of a scene to be rendered. Only the objects in the region between *near* and *far clipping planes* will be rendered. (145)

CLOSED OBJECT. An OBJECT whose surfaces can be seen only from one side (the "outside" of the object), when it is colored opaque. (118)

COMPOSITE SOLID. In CONSTRUCTIVE SOLID GEOMETRY, a SOLID formed from PRIMITIVE SOLIDS and other composite solids. (126)

CONCAVE POLYGON. A POLYGON with the property that a line can be found that passes through more that two EDGES. Equivalently, the sum of its interior angles is greater than 360 degrees. *See also Figure 5.1.* (69)

CONE. A QUADRIC SURFACE created by sweeping a line segment with one end point on the axis of rotation. (60)

CONSTRUCTIVE SOLID GEOMETRY (CSG). A method of OBJECT DESCRIPTION in which objects can be used to modify the shape of other objects. For example, a cylinder can be subtracted from a sphere to describe a finger hole of a bowling ball. (110, 125)

CONTROL HULL. *See* GEOMETRY MATRIX *and Figure 6.2.* (87)

CONTROL POINTS. The set of points used to specify the geometry of a SPLINE or PATCH. Cubic splines require four control points. BILINEAR PATCHES require four control points (the vertices) and BICUBIC PATCHES sixteen. (87)

CONVEX POLYGON. A POLYGON whose interior angles (on the inside of the polygon) sum to 360 degrees. Equivalently, there is no line that passes through more than two edges of a convex polygon. *See also Figure 5.1.* (69)

COORDINATE SYSTEM. A set of orthogonal *axes* that meet at an *origin*. A coordinate system provides a mapping between points in space and points on the axes. The location of any point can be specified by its *coordinates* relative to the origin. (22, 111)

CROP WINDOW. A subwindow of the FRAME specified by **RiCropWindow**(). Pixels outside the crop window will not be RENDERED. (162)

CURRENT INSTANCE (OF A SHADER). A SHADER and the parameters currently in effect for it that are part of the GRAPHICS ENVIRONMENT and attached to any object as it is declared. (212)

CURRENT LEVEL OF DETAIL. The LEVEL OF DETAIL set by the last call to **RiDetail**() (subject to restorals of the GRAPHICS ENVIRONMENT). (195)

CURRENT TRANSFORMATION. A transformation incorporating the sequence of global TRANSFORMATIONS invoked so far. Part of the GRAPHICS ENVIRONMENT. (44, 53, 110)

CYLINDER. A QUADRIC SURFACE created by sweeping a line segment that is parallel to the axis of rotation. (60)

DECAL. *See* TEXTURE MAP. (240)

DEPTH CUE. A visual cue providing information about the relative distance to the camera of different surfaces, (e.g., DEPTH OF FIELD effects) (4)

DEPTH OF FIELD. The range of depth over which some objects appear sharply focused. (5, 8, 185)

DEFAULT VALUES. Values in effect unless changed by the user. (23)

DEFORMATION. A nonlinear TRANSFORMATION applied to an object or series of objects effectively bending or warping the COORDINATE SYSTEM. It is concatenated to the CURRENT TRANSFORMATION. (278)

DIFFERENCE (SET). That set containing all the elements of one set that are *not* contained in another. (126)

DIFFUSE REFLECTION. The reflection caused by a surface SCATTERING light equally in all directions. The intensity of the reflection is proportional to the area the surface presents to the light source. (3, 230)

DIRECTIONAL LIGHT SOURCE. *See* DISTANT LIGHT SOURCE. (305)

DISPLACEMENT SHADER. A SHADER that specifies local changes in position of points on a surface. (118, 259, 279)

DISTANT LIGHT SOURCE. A light source that is treated as if it were an infinite distance from the scene and so casts light in only one direction. The ORIENTATION of a surface is relevant to how it reflects the light, but not its distance (from the light source) or location. (221)

DISPLAY (MONITOR). A cathode-ray tube monitor used to display a computer generated image. (9)

DITHERING. A technique used to reduce the effects of QUANTIZATION by adding a "random" amount of noise to pixel values before quantization. (184)

EDGE. Where two SURFACE PRIMITIVES meet, or where a surface primitive ends. In the RenderMan Interface, edges are implicit in the vertices of the polygon. (69)

ENVIRONMENT. The visual surroundings of an object, often seen in reflections from the surface of the object. (6)

ENVIRONMENT MAP. An image depicting a scene from a viewpoint inside one of its objects. Its most common use is as a

REFLECTION MAP simulating the effect of a surface reflecting the objects around it. (230, 257, 261)

EVALUATION WINDOW. A set of four adjacent CONTROL POINTS used when traversing a series of cubic SPLINES. In the RenderMan Interface a set of 16 adjacent points used to create a single PATCH while generating a PATCH MESH. (95)

EXPOSURE. A step in the pixel production process of RENDERING in which pixel values are passed through a function that compensates for the non-linear response to light of DISPLAY MONITORS and the human visual system. (179)

EXTERIOR VOLUME SHADER. A SHADER that calculates the effect on light passing through the space around an object. (278)

F-STOP. The ratio of FOCAL LENGTH to APERTURE. The f-stop of a camera determines its DEPTH OF FIELD. (185)

FALSE CONTOURS. Regions of abrupt changes in pixel values in an image caused by problems with QUANTIZATION. *See also Figure 9.2.* (10)

FALLOFF (WITH ANGLE F) In a SPOTLIGHT, the decay in intensity of light with the angle from the center of its beam. *See also Figure 11.5.* (222)

FIELD OF VIEW. The angle at the viewpoint specifying the part of the scene viewable by the VIRTUAL CAMERA in the direction it points. *See also, equation and figure on page 148.* (4, 141, 147, 148)

FILTER FUNCTION. A function for weighting the contribution to an output PIXEL value of different parts of the scene as projected near the pixel. When SUPERSAMPLING, the filter function determines the contribution of each SAMPLE in or near a pixel to the overall pixel value. Specifically it gives the relative sample weights as a function of x and y displacement from the center of the pixel. *See also Figure 9.2.* (176)

FILTERING. Calculating a single pixel value from multiple SAMPLES taken in the neighborhood of a pixel. (9, 174, 176)

FLAT SHADING. A form of SHADING in which each surface has the same color at all points, causing an abrupt color change at the edge between one surface and another. (71)

FOCAL DISTANCE. The distance in front of a camera at which objects appear most in focus. (185)

FOCAL LENGTH. The distance between the center of a lens and its FOCAL POINT. (146, 185)

FOCAL POINT. The point at which rays of light converge after passing through a lens. In the RenderMan Interface, the focal point is also the location of the VIRTUAL CAMERA. (146)

FRAME. A rectangle of pixels representing a SCREEN WINDOW. (137, 160)

FRAME BLOCK. A BLOCK of code in a RenderMan program bracketed by **RiFrameBegin**() and **RiFrameEnd**() statements, used to generate successive frames of an ANIMATION. **RiFrameBegin**() and **RiFrameEnd**() save and restore OPTIONS so that they may by changed between frames. (50)

FRAME ASPECT RATIO. The ratio of width to height of a FRAME, equal to the IMAGE ASPECT RATIO unless set explicitly by a call to **RiFrameAspectRatio**(). (159)

GEOMETRIC APPROXIMATION. Substituting more easily rendered PRIMITIVE SURFACE types for the primitives used to describe a scene. (171)

GEOMETRIC NORMAL (VECTOR). The SURFACE NORMAL at a point on a surface as defined by the surface geometry at that point, (as opposed to the SHADING NORMAL, which can be set explicitly by the user for the purposes of SHADING calculations). (226, 293)

GEOMETRIC TRANSFORMATION. A change in the geometric configuration of a scene such as ROTATION or TRANSLATION (change in location). A transformation can be applied to individual objects, or globally to the entire scene. (21)

GEOMETRY MATRIX. A 4 x 4 matrix of CONTROL POINTS describing the geometry of a BICUBIC PATCH. (87)

GLOBAL VARIABLE. In the RenderMan Shading Language, a variable whose value is set automatically when a SHADER is called. In this book, global variables are indicated by underlining the variable name (as in $\underline{N}$ or $\underline{Ci}$).(284)

GOURAUD SHADING. A SHADING technique in which the surface shade is calculated at surface vertices, and interpolated for points in the interior. (214)

GRANULARITY. The density with which a viewing surface is divided into physical sensors (such as pixels in an image, photoreceptors in the eye, or the grains of emulsion in film). (4)

GRAPHICS ENVIRONMENT. The content of variables and values maintained by the interface, including image parameters, the CURRENT TRANSFORMATION, color, surface appearance specification, light sources, etc. Any object added to the scene adopts any relevant part of the graphics environment in effect when it was created. (23, 44)

GRAPHICS STATE. *See* GRAPHICS ENVIRONMENT. (44)

HEIGHT FIELD. A convenient way to specify a simple PATCH or MESH by giving only the height of each point above a plane (with the x and y coordinates implicit). (246)

HERMITE PATCH. A BICUBIC PATCH defined by HERMITE SPLINES. (90)

HERMITE SPLINE. A cubic SPLINE that interpolates its first and third CONTROL POINTS, using the other two to specify the spline's tangent at the end points. (91)

HIDDEN SURFACE ELIMINATION. A step in the RENDERING process that determines what parts of the scene cannot be seen by the viewer so they can be disregarded when computing the image. (6)

HIDER. The process used during RENDERING for HIDDEN SURFACE ELIMINATION. (54)

HIERARCHICAL MODEL. An organizational model useful for OBJECT DESCRIPTION that divides a system into levels of abstraction. (108)

HIGHLIGHT. The effect of mirrorlike SPECULAR REFLECTIONS. (226)

HOLD-OUT MATTE. An image specifying regions to be cut out of another image. The resulting "holes" are rendered black and transparent and can be used for merging with other images. (216)

HOMOGENEOUS COORDINATES. A formulation of three-dimensional points as a vector of four scalar values. (88)

HYPERBOLOID. A QUADRIC SURFACE created by sweeping an arbitrary line segment about an axis of rotation. (60)

IMAGE. A two-dimensional PROJECTION of a three-dimensional scene as represented in an array of PIXELS. (4). In formal RenderMan terminology, the actual set of pixels (either in a frame buffer or in a file) designated by **RiDisplay**() to contain the results of RENDERING. (159)

IMAGE ASPECT RATIO. The ratio of width to the height of a displayed image, a function of the PIXEL ASPECT RATIO and the RESOLUTION of the display. (157)

IMAGE PLANE. The two dimensional plane upon which a scene is projected. The SCREEN WINDOW is a rectilinear subregion of this plane. (141, 146)

IMAGER. A SHADER that operates on pixel values. An imager would be used, for example, to convert RGB values to another format such as YIQ. (280)

IMAGING. A step in the pixel production process of RENDERING that passes pixel values through a SHADER. In RenderMan this shader, the IMAGER, can be written by the user in the RenderMan Shading Language. (181)

INCIDENT CONE. The cone within which light sources might contribute to a reflection in a particular direction. *See also Figure 14.2.* (302)

INCIDENT VECTOR. The vector representing the direction from the viewpoint to a point on a surface. It is generally represented as the vector **I**, and in the RenderMan Shading Language, by the global variable I. (226)

INSTANCE (OF A SHADER). A SHADER invoked with a particular set of parameters. Several instances of the same shader can be in use on different objects. (211)

INSTANCE (OF AN OBJECT). A copy of a previously described object. For example, a "bowling pin" geometry can be specified, and several *instances* of the bowling pin created in a scene, each with different color and other attributes. (31, 33, 110, 133)

INSTANCE VARIABLES (OF A SHADER). The parameters to a SHADER that distinguish one INSTANCE from another. (212)

INTERIOR VOLUME SHADER. A SHADER that calculates the effect on light as it passes through a VOLUME of material inside some object. (278)

INTERNAL REPRESENTATION. The model of a "scene" constructed within a computer, as opposed to a physical scene assembled in the real world. (5)

INTERPOLATING SPLINE. A SPLINE that passes through its CONTROL POINTS. The spline is said to *interpolate* those control points that it passes through. (90)

INTERPOLATION. Calculating values or locations of intermediate points as a smoothly varying function between end points. (74, 90)

INTERSECTION (SET). That set containing only those elements in common between two or more sets. (126)

JAGGIES. A form of ALIASING seen as the undesirable "stairstep" effect on object edges in an image. (10, 174)

JITTERING. A technique for reducing the effects of ALIASING by randomly displacing samples from a uniform distribution. (175)

LEAF. In a HIERARCHICAL MODEL, a child with no CHILDREN of its own, indicating the lowest level of abstraction. (109)

LEFT-HANDED (ROTATION). Turning an object about an axis in such a way that if a person's left thumb points along the axis of rotation, the other fingers curl in the direction of rotation. *See also Figure 2.1.* (21, 119)

LENS. A transparent surface shaped to bend light rays to focus an IMAGE on a VIEWING SURFACE. (4)

LEVEL OF DETAIL. The degree to which the surface details of an object are available for scrutiny by the viewer, measured simply as the size of the object (in pixels) on the display screen. (194, 195)

LIGHT. The source of visual information about objects in the world The computer graphics model of light assumes that it travels in a straight line, can be bent, absorbed, or reflected from a SURFACE, and that it has properties, such as color, intensity and direction, which can be altered by such an interaction. (2)

LIGHT SOURCE SHADER. A SHADER that calculates the intensity and color of light sent by a light source to a point on a surface. (210, 216, 278)

LOCAL COORDINATE SYSTEM. A COORDINATE SYSTEM that defines the origin and axis to be used in defining objects in a scene. GEOMETRIC TRANSFORMATIONS are defined relative to, and modify, the local coordinate system. (110)

LOOP. In TRIM CURVES, a series of non-uniform, rational B-splines (NURBs) in two dimensions. In polygons, a sequence of vertices. (249)

MAIN BLOCK. A BLOCK of RenderMan routine calls bracketed by **RiBegin**() and **RiEnd**() statements. All RenderMan programs include a main block. (48)

MATTE OBJECT. An object or set of objects used to cut out "holes" in an image. The objects are not shaded, but rather form black transparent areas in the image for later merging with other images. This the three-dimensional equivalent of what is traditionally called a HOLD-OUT MATTE. (216)

MESH. A two dimensional array of connected BICUBIC PATCHES defining a surface. (94)

MIRROR DIRECTION. The direction a light ray would follow after being reflected from a perfect mirror. Specifically, the light source direction reflected about the SURFACE NORMAL. (3, 230)

MIRROR REFLECTION. Light that leaves a surface only along the MIRROR DIRECTION. (3)

MODES (OF OPERATION). States of a RenderMan program, as denoted by BLOCKS with different rules and functions. For example, inside a WORLD BLOCK, options cannot be changed, but primitives can be declared and attributes set. Inside the MAIN BLOCK, but outside the world block options can be set, but primitives cannot be declared. (47)

MOTION BLOCK. A sequence of RenderMan routine calls bracketed by **RiMotionBegin**() and **RiMotionEnd**() calls, specifying how the parameters of a procedure vary over a period of time. Motion blocks are not nestable. (188)

MOTION BLUR. A blurring or "smearing" of objects seen in a photograph of a moving object. It produces a sense of motion in an image and smooths the visual transition between frames of an ANIMATION. (5, 186)

NESTED BLOCK. A BLOCK containing another block of the same type. Certain types of blocks (e.g., the MAIN BLOCK and WORLD BLOCK) cannot be nested. Nestable blocks must observe strict nesting: every block must end before the end of any block containing it. (27, 48)

NODE. In a HIERARCHICAL MODEL, an element of the hierarchy with CHILDREN of its own. (109)

NON-PLANAR POLYGON. A POLYGON in which the vertices do not lie in a plane. (69)

NORMAL (VECTOR). The vector perpendicular to a line, plane or surface at a given point. (73)

NURB. A Non-uniform rational B-spline. A general class of PARAMETRIC SURFACE supported by the RenderMan Interface. *See also* TRIM CURVES. (83, 185)

OBJECT. A set of SURFACES grouped together and treated as a single entity for purposes of shading, motion, duplication or assembling other objects. (2, 107)

OBJECT DESCRIPTION. The process of specifying the geometry of an OBJECT. (31)

OBJECT DESCRIPTION BY INSTANCE. Describing an object as an INSTANCE of a specified object geometry. (31, 33)

OBJECT DESCRIPTION BY PROCEDURE. A description of an object as a procedure to be called to create the object during RENDERING. (33)

OBJECT HANDLE. A tag returned by **RiObjectBegin**() by which a RETAINED MODEL can be INSTANCED. (133)

OBJECT SPACE. The COORDINATE SYSTEM defined when working with a particular object. (52, 111, 123)

ONE-SIDED SURFACE. A surface that is only visible when it "faces toward" the viewer. (119)

OPEN OBJECT. An OBJECT some surfaces of which can be viewed on both sides, e.g., a hemisphere. (118)

OPTICAL SYSTEM. The parts of a VIEWING DEVICE for focusing light rays on the VIEWING SURFACE (e.g., the LENS or PIN-HOLE). (4)

OPTIONS. Elements of the GRAPHICS ENVIRONMENT concerned with characteristics of the entire image. Examples would be image resolution or viewing parameters such as camera location and field of view. (44, 45)

ORIENTATION (OF A SURFACE). The angle of a surface at a given point relative to the viewer, affecting the light being reflected at that point. Often (e.g., on the surface of an orange) this orientation can change from point to point causing interesting effects in the reflected light. (6)

ORTHOGRAPHIC PROJECTION. A PROJECTION in which distance from the viewer does not affect how large an object appears, much like the effect of an infinitely long telephoto lens. (8)

PARABOLOID. A QUADRIC SURFACE created by sweeping a parabola about its axis of symmetry. (60)

PARAMETER LIST. A series of arguments to a RenderMan function in TOKEN-VALUE PAIRS, terminated by the special token RI_NULL. (39)

PARAMETER SPACE. A two-dimensional COORDINATE SYSTEM mapped onto a surface. In the RenderMan Interface, coordinates in parameter space are expressed as u and v, and range from 0 to 1 in both directions for most primitives. (245)

PARAMETRIC SURFACE. A type of PRIMITIVE SURFACE defined as a polynomial blend of CONTROL POINTS (a PATCH or a MESH). (86, 59)

PATCH. A curved surface with four vertices and four edges that can be mathematically defined in terms of 16 CONTROL POINTS. (86)

PARENT. For a given element in a HIERARCHICAL MODEL the element at the next level up with which it is associated. For example the "toes" of a "foot" object would share the same parent. (109)

PERSPECTIVE PROJECTION. The PROJECTION of a three-dimensional scene onto a two-dimensional plane in which objects near the viewer appear larger than objects of similar size that are farther away. (8)

PHONG INTERPOLATION. The method of generating a SURFACE NORMAL vector at each point on a POLYGON by INTERPOLATING between normals that are provided at the polygon VERTICES. (74)

PHONG SHADING. A SHADING technique in which each point on a surface is shaded by using SURFACE NORMALS computed with PHONG INTERPOLATION. (74)

PINHOLE. A small hole in an opaque surface allowing only certain light rays to pass through. Its effect is similar to a LENS, focusing an image on a VIEWING SURFACE. (4)

PIXEL. A "picture element" of a viewing screen. A rectangular screen is composed of thousands of pixels, each representing the color of an image at a given point on the screen. The *pixel value* calculated and stored for each pixel typically consists of several CHANNELS such as the red, green, and blue components of its color, and/or opacity or coverage information. *See also* PROJECT. (8, 172)

PIXEL ASPECT RATIO. The ratio of the width to height of a physical pixel in a display device. (156)

PLANAR (POLYGON). A POLYGON in which all vertices lie in the same plane in three-dimensional space. (69)

POINT LIGHT SOURCE. A light source that distributes light evenly in all directions from a specified point. The intensity of its light arriving at a surface diminishes with the square of the distance from the point to the surface. (221)

POINTS-POLYGON FORM. A way of specifying a set of polygons (e.g., when defining a polyhedron) in terms of a previously defined set of points. In other words, each vertex is defined only once, and used many times (by all the polygons that share it). (79)

POLYGON. A simple type of PRIMITIVE SURFACE composed of three or more VERTICES connected by straight EDGES. (59)

POLYHEDRON. A three-dimensional object with POLYGONal faces. (69)

PRIMITIVE OBJECT. An OBJECT consisting of a single PRIMITIVE SURFACE. (107)

PRIMITIVE SOLID. In CONSTRUCTIVE SOLID GEOMETRY (CSG), a
SOLID defined entirely by PRIMITIVE SURFACES. (126)

PRIMITIVE SURFACE. A geometric element from which complex surfaces can be specified. There are three kinds of
primitive surfaces in RenderMan: QUADRIC SURFACES,
POLYGONS and PARAMETRIC SURFACES. (59)

PROCEDURAL MODEL. A specification of an object geometry in
terms of a procedure. *See also* OBJECT DESCRIPTION BY PRO-
CEDURE. (94, 201)

PROCEDURAL OBJECT DESCRIPTION. *See* OBJECT DESCRIPTION BY
PROCEDURE. (33)

PROJECT. In computer graphics, to cast a three-dimensional
scene onto a two-dimensional plane. Each point in the
scene is mapped to a corresponding point on the plane.
Those surfaces not obscured by other surfaces form the resulting PROJECTION. The IMAGE is formed from this projection by taking (color) SAMPLES at regular intervals and generating PIXEL values accordingly. This is our model of vi-
sion, which captures light rays from a three-dimensional
scene on the retina of the eye or the film of a camera.
(4, 146)

PROJECTION. A two-dimensional representation of a three-dimensional scene, obtained by mapping points on visible
surfaces in the scene to corresponding points on a plane.
See also PROJECT.

QUADRIC SURFACE. A type of PRIMITIVE SURFACE definable by
quadratic equations. Examples are spheres and cones. All
RenderMan quadric surfaces are SURFACES OF REVOLU-
TION. (59)

QUANTIZATION. Reducing an arbitrarily precise SAMPLE value
to one of a number of discrete values. For example, while
pixel values of an image as computed may be arbitrarily
precise, digital DISPLAYS can display pixels at only a finite
number of discrete levels. (10, 173)

RADIOSITY. A SHADING technique that computes the light arriving at a surface by analyzing the distribution of light energy in a scene. (304)

RASTER. The arrangement of PIXELS in a DISPLAY MONITOR as
a two-dimensional *array* or *grid* of pixels. (9, 172)

RASTER SPACE. The COORDINATE SYSTEM of the rendered image used when displaying the image on a monitor. Its origin is the top left corner of the top left pixel, and each pixel has a non-negative integer location. (53, 122)

RAY TRACING. A RENDERING algorithm that computes the color of a pixel by casting an imaginary ray back into the scene from the viewpoint, until it hits an object, and then recursively casting rays toward light sources and other objects. (260)

REFINEMENT PROCEDURE. The procedure used in a PROCEDURAL MODEL to specify a portion of an object in more detail. (201)

REFLECTION MAP. An image mapped onto a surface to simulate the mirror-like reflections of other objects. (257, 261, 320).

REFRACTION. The change of direction of light as it passes through a transparent SURFACE. (3)

RELATIVE INDEX OF REFRACTION. A measure of how much a light ray will be REFRACTED when passing through the surface between two materials. (328).

RENDERING. The process of generating a synthetic image of a scene given a precise description of the geometry and other characteristics of the scene. (5, 11, 137)

RESOLUTION. The degree of GRANULARITY of a DISPLAY MONITOR specified by the number of rows and columns of PIXELS in the display. (9)

RETAINED MODEL. A geometric description of an object that may be used to make INSTANCES of the object. (133)

ROOT. In a HIERARCHICAL MODEL, the highest level of abstraction. In RenderMan, the scene itself. (109)

ROTATION. A transformation turning an object around an axis. (21)

ROUGHNESS. The property of a surface causing SCATTERING of light as it reflects off of it. A surface from which most outbound rays leave near the MIRROR DIRECTION will appear shiny; one with a great deal of scatter will appear rough. (7)

SAMPLE. A measurement or snapshot of a particular property at a specific point in time or space. For example, a PIXEL can represent a *sample* of color at a point in space, as projected onto a two-dimensional surface. (9, 173)

SAMPLING. The process of determining a SAMPLE or series of samples over a given region of time or space. For example, determining a color value (the sample) to represent the color of a projected image at a point in the IMAGE PLANE. (174)

SCALING. A transformation changing the size of an object in the x, y or z directions. (113)

SCATTERING. The dispersal of light in many directions upon being reflected from a point on a surface. (3)

SCENE DESCRIPTION. The process of specifying a scene to be RENDERED in terms of objects, light sources and viewing devices. (12, 59)

SCREEN SPACE. A unitless, device-independent two-dimensional COORDINATE SYSTEM on the IMAGE PLANE after PROJECTION. (53, 122)

SCREEN WINDOW. The two-dimensional rectangular region of the IMAGE PLANE that contains the PROJECTION of a scene to be rendered. (137, 141, 146)

SHADER. A part of the RENDERING program that calculates the appearance of visible surfaces in the scene. In RenderMan, a procedure written in the RenderMan Shading Language and used to compute a value or set of values (e.g., the color of a surface) needed during rendering. (117, 210, 211, 273)

SHADING. The part of RENDERING concerned with the appearance of each surface as seen in the output image. (209, 239)

SHADING LANGUAGE. A language employed to write SHADERS. (12)

SHADING NORMAL. A SURFACE NORMAL used for the purpose of SHADING calculations. (It may differ from the actual GEOMETRIC NORMAL in order to simplify shading calculations, or to achieve special shading effects). It is generally represented by the vector **N**, and in the RenderMan Shading Language, by the global variable $\underline{N}$.

SHADING PIPELINE. The three basic parts of the SHADING process: *illumination* (characterizing sources of light), *reflection* (determining local surface characteristics affecting the color and direction of light) and *atmospheric effects*. (209)

SHADING RATE. An ATTRIBUTE of a surface that determines how often its appearance must be calculated during SHADING. In RenderMan this is specified as an area, in pixels. (214)

SHADOW MAP. An image used by a light source to determine information for determining whether a point on a surface falls within a shadow cast by another surface. (257, 268, 320)

SHAPE. The geometry of an object or set of objects as specified by surface primitives. (209, 239)

SIBLINGS. In a hierarchical model, two or more CHILDREN with the same PARENT. (109)

SKEW. To slant an object at an angle. *See also illustration on page 113.* (113)

SOLID. A set of points in three-dimensional space with a surface unambiguously separating points in the set from those not in the set. (126)

SPECULAR (REFLECTION). Reflected light concentrated near, but not confined to the MIRROR DIRECTION. A specular reflection is brightest when seen from viewpoints along or near the mirror direction, and becomes dimmer away from that direction. (3, 230)

SPHERE. A QUADRIC SURFACE created by sweeping a circle about an axis that bisects it. (60)

SPLINE. A curve mathematically defined as a polynomial blend of a set of CONTROL POINTS. The splines used in RenderMan are based on *cubic splines*, which are specified using cubic polynomials over four control points. There are four kinds of cubic splines named in RenderMan: BÉZIER, B-SPLINE, CATMULL-ROM, and HERMITE, each differing in the way the control points are interpreted. (90)

SPOTLIGHT. A light source with a specified location and direction. Its light is distributed as a cone-shaped beam, whose intensity falls off with the angle from the center of the cone. (222)

STACKED (GEOMETRIC TRANSFORMATIONS). TRANSFORMATIONS that are performed in the reverse order in which they are declared. In RenderMan, the CURRENT TRANSFORMATION is a stack. (27)

SUBDIVISION (OF POLYGONS). The process of dividing POLYGONS into smaller polygons to compensate for the problems inherent in FLAT SHADING. (71)

SUPERSAMPLING. A technique to reduce ALIASING by taking several SAMPLES of a scene for each pixel and FILTERING the resulting values to obtain the pixel value. (174)

SUPPORT (OF A FILTER FUNCTION). The "width" of a FILTER FUNCTION; i.e., the area around a pixel center outside of which a SAMPLE will be given 0 weight. (176)

SURFACE. The set of points in space where LIGHT interacts with an OBJECT. In computer graphics this is generally modeled as a set of simpler surface shapes that can be mathematically described. (2)

SURFACE ELEMENT. A piece of a SURFACE small enough to require only a single color value, either because it is very small or because its shading varies slowly. (295, 326)

SURFACE NORMAL. The vector, usually denoted by $\mathbf{N}$, perpendicular to a surface at a given point. (226)

SURFACE OF REVOLUTION. A surface created by sweeping a curve about an axis. (60)

SURFACE SHADER. A SHADER that calculates the color of light reflecting from a point on a surface in a particular direction. (215, 225)

SWEEP ANGLE. The angular extent (often 360°) to which a curve is swept about its axis of rotation to create a SURFACE OF REVOLUTION. (60)

TEMPORAL ALIASING. The undesirable "strobing" effect in an animated sequence caused by abrupt changes in a scene between frames. Temporal aliasing can be eased by MOTION BLUR to help the eye make a smooth transition between frames of a moving object. (186)

TEMPORAL SAMPLE. A SAMPLE of a scene's configuration at a given moment in time. (186)

TENSION. The tightess with which a cubic SPLINE or a PATCH follows its CONTROL POINTS. (92)

TENSOR PRODUCT. The mathematical function used to generate a curved surface from two orthogonal sets of splines. (92)

TEXTURE. The properties of a surface that affect the local color or appearance at different points on the surface. For example, a "wood" texture causes the color of the surface to be darker or lighter from point to point simulating wood grain. (6)

TEXTURE COORDINATES. The coordinates of a point on a surface given in terms of a two-dimensional COORDINATE SYSTEM mapped onto the surface. *See Figures 12.1 and 12.2. See also* PARAMETER SPACE. (240)

TEXTURE MAP. An image that, when mapped onto a surface, specifies its TEXTURE. (13, 319)

TEXTURE MAPPING. Mapping a previously computed image onto the surface of an object. The image is referred to as a TEXTURE MAP. (240)

TOKEN-VALUE PAIR. A common construct in the RenderMan Interface, used to specify optional arguments to a procedure, consisting of a token (a specific string of characters) followed by the desired value. (19, 39)

TORUS. A QUADRIC SURFACE created by sweeping a circle about an axis that does not intersect the circle. (60)

TRANSFORMATION. A function applied to the points in a COORDINATE SYSTEM to redefine their coordinates. This is usually used to convert between coordinate systems or for ROTATION, TRANSLATION, SCALING, etc. (21)

TRANSFORMATION BLOCK. A sequence of RenderMan routine calls bracketed by calls to **RiTransformBegin**() and **RiTransformEnd**(), which save and restore the CURRENT TRANSFORMATION. Transformations invoked within the block affect only those objects created after the transformation and before the end of the block. Transformation blocks can be nested. (47)

TRANSFORMATION MATRIX. A 4 x 4 matrix used to specify a TRANSFORMATION between COORDINATE SYSTEMS. (115)

TRANSFORMATION SHADER. A SHADER that recalculates the point coordinates in a COORDINATE SYSTEM. The transformation shader is concatenated onto the CURRENT TRANSFORMATION. (279)

TRANSLATION. A TRANSFORMATION changing the location of an object. (21)

TRANSPARENT. The property of a surface allowing light to pass through it. (3)

TRIM CURVE. A surface defined by a set of LOOPS defined in the parameter space of a NURB. Each loop limits the surface to just the points inside or outside the loop. The total surface consists of the collection of these points after all loops are applied. (103, 249)

u DIRECTION. In the direction of the u axis in the PARAMETER SPACE of a surface. (92)

UNIFORM (INSTANCE VARIABLES). The parameters of a SHADER that have the same value for all points of the surface to which the shader is attached (212, 242)

UNION (SET). That set containing all the elements of two or more sets. (126)

VARIANCE. A statistical measure of the accuracy of a SUPER-SAMPLED pixel value. RenderMan allows a tolerance to be set to guarantee an acceptable level of variance. (179)

VARYING (INSTANCE VARIABLES). Those parameters of a SHADER with values that may change from point to point on a surface. For example, a geometric description of a surface may define a variable *temp* that varies from point to point on the surface, and a shader may use *temp* as one of its parameters. (212, 242)

v DIRECTION. In the direction of the v axis in the PARAMETER SPACE of a bicubic surface. (92)

VERTEX. A point where two or more EDGES meet, specified by the x, y and z coordinates of its location. (19)

VIEWER. A person or device receiving and interpreting light reflected from a scene. In a simplified model of optics, the viewer is represented by a VIEWING DEVICE. (2)

VIEWING DEVICE. In a simplified model of computer graphics, the device used to view a scene, usually an abstract eye or a VIRTUAL CAMERA model (4).

VIEWING DIRECTION. The direction the viewer is pointed within the scene. (141)

VIEWING LOCATION. The location of the viewer relative to the scene. (141)

VIEWING SURFACE. The part of a VIEWING DEVICE where the image actually forms, e.g., the retina of the eye, or the film in a camera. (4)

VIEWING TRANSFORMATION. The TRANSFORMATION that transforms points from WORLD SPACE to CAMERA SPACE. (142)

VIEWPOINT. The VIEWING LOCATION.

VIRTUAL CAMERA. The imagined device with position, orientation and other characteristics that project the scene into two dimensions to form an image. (137, 141)

VOLUME. A region of space filled with a material, e.g., air, fog or jello. (Contrast to a SURFACE, which surrounds the volume). (233)

VOLUME SHADER. A SHADER that calculates the color and intensity of light as it passes through a VOLUME. (210, 234, 278)

WORLD BLOCK. A BLOCK of RenderMan routine calls bracketed by **RiWorldBegin**() and **RiWorldEnd**() statements. Outside of the world block geometric SURFACE PRIMITIVES cannot be declared. Inside, global OPTIONS cannot be set. Upon **RiWorldEnd**() the scene is rendered and the scene data cleared. World blocks cannot be nested. (49)

WORLD SPACE. A COORDINATE SYSTEM used for SCENE DESCRIPTION, i.e., placement and orientation of the defined objects in space. (52, 123)

Bibliography

BARSKY81   Barsky, Brian. "The Beta-spline: A Local Representation Based on Shape Parameters and Fundamental Geometric Measures." Ph.D. dissertation, University of Utah, Salt Lake City, December 1981.

BARTELS87   Bartels, Richard H.; Beatty, John C.; and Barsky, Brian A. *An Introduction to Splines for use in Computer Graphics and Geometric Modeling.* Morgan Kaufmann, Los Altos, CA, 1987.

BEATTY82   Beatty, John C.,and Booth, Kellogg S. "Tutorial: Computer Graphics." *IEEE Computer Society* (1982). 2d ed.

BLINN76   Blinn, James F., and Newell, Martin E. "Texture and Reflection in Computer Generated Images." *Communications of the ACM* 19(10) (Oct. 1976): 542-547.

BLINN77   Blinn, J.F. "Models of Light Reflection for Computer Synthesized Pictures." *Computer Graphics* 11(2) (1977): 192-198.

BLINN78   Blinn, J.F. "Simulation of Wrinkled Surfaces." *Computer Graphics* 12(3) (Aug. 1978): 286-292.

CARP82   Carpenter, L.; Fournier, A.; and Fussell, D. "Computer Rendering of Stochastic Models." *Communications of the ACM* 25(8) (June 1982): 371-384.

CATMULL74   Catmull, Ed. "A Subdivision Algorithm for Computer Display of Curved Surfaces." Ph.D.

dissertation, University of Utah, December 1974.

COOK81   Cook, Robert L., and Torrance, Kenneth. "A Reflectance Model for Computer Graphics." *Computer Graphics* 15(3) (July 1981): 307-315.

COOK84   Cook, Robert L. "Shade Trees." *Computer Graphics* 18(3):223-231.

COOK86   Cook, Robert L. "Stochastic Sampling in Computer Graphics." *ACM Transactions on Graphics* 5(1) (Jan. 1986): 51-72.

CROW77   Crow, Franklin C. "The Aliasing Problem in Computer-Generated Shaded Images." *Communications of the ACM* 20(11) (Nov. 1977): 799-805.

DEROSE88 DeRose, Tony D., and Barsky, Brian A. "Geometric Continuity, Shape Parameters, and Geometric Constructions for Catmull-Rom Splines." *ACM Transactions on Graphics* 7(1) (Jan. 1988): 1.

DIPPE85   Dippe, Mark A. Z., and Wold, Erling. "Antialiasing through Stochastic Sampling." *Computer Graphics* 19(3) (1985): 69-78.

DUFF83   Duff, Tom. "Families of Local Matrix Splines." Technical Memo #104, Lucasfilm Ltd. 1983.

DUFF85   Duff, Tom. "Compositing 3-D Rendered Images." *Computer Graphics* 19(3) (1985): 41-44.

FARIN88   Farin, Gerald. *Curves and Surfaces for Computer Aided Geometric Design.* San Diego: Academic Press, 1988.

FAUX80   Faux, I.D., and Pratt, M.J. *Computational Geometry for Design and Manufacture.* Chichester, West Sussex, England: Ellis Horwood Limited, 1980.

FEIBUSH80 Feibush, Eliot A.; Levoy, Marc; and Cook, Robert L. "Synthetic Texturing Using Digital Filters." *Computer Graphics* 14(3) (July 1980): 294-301.

FOLEY82   Foley, James D., and Van Dam, Andries. *Fundamentals of Interactive Computer Graphics.* Addison-Wesley, 1982.

GORAL84   Goral, Cindy M.; Torrance, Kenneth E.; Greenberg, Donald P.; and Battaile, Bennett. "Modeling the Interaction of Light Between Diffuse Surfaces." *Computer Graphics* 18(3):213-222.

GREENE86   Greene, Ned. "Environment Mapping and Other Applications of World Projections." *IEEE Computer Graphics and Applications* 6(11) (Nov. 1986): 108-114.

HALL89   Hall, Roy. *Illumination and Color in Computer Generated Imagery*, New York: Springer-Verlag, 1989.

HECKB84   Heckbert, Paul. "Survey of Texture Mapping." *IEEE Computer Graphics and Applications* 6(11) (Nov. 1986): 56-67.

MANDEL83   Mandelbrot, Benoit B. *The Fractal Geometry of Nature*. Freeman, 1983.

NEWMAN79   Newman, William M., and Sproull, Robert F. *Principles of Interactive Computer Graphics*. McGraw-Hill, 1979.

OPPEN75   Oppenheim, Alan V., and Schafer, Ronald W. *Digital Signal Processing*. Englewood Cliffs: Prentice-Hall, 1975.

PEACHEY85 Peachey, Darwyn. "Solid Texturing of Complex Surface." *Computer Graphics* 19(3) (1985): 279-286.

PERLIN85   Perlin, Ken. "An Image Synthesizer." *Computer Graphics* 19(3) (1985): 287-296.

PORTER84   Porter, Tom, and Duff, Tom. "Compositing Digital Images." *Computer Graphics* 18(3) (July 1983): 253-259.

PRATT78   Pratt, William K. *Digital Image Processing*, New York: Wiley, 1978.

REEVES87   Reeves, William T.; Salesin, David H.; and Cook, Robert L. "Rendering Antialiased Shadows with Depth Maps." *Computer Graphics* 21(4) (1987): 283-291.

ROGERS85   Rogers, David F. *Procedural Elements for Computer Graphics*, McGraw-Hill, 1985.

TILLER83   Tiller, Wayne. "Rational B-Splines for Curve and Surface Representation." *Computer Graphics and Applications* 3(6) (Sept. 1983). IEEE Computer Society, pub.

WHITTED80   Whitted, Turner. "An Improved Illumination Model for Shaded Display." *Communications of the ACM* 6(23) (June 1980): 343-349.

WILLIAMS83 Williams, Lance. "Pyramidal Parametrics." *Computer Graphics* 17(3) (July 1983): 1-11.

Index

. operator (shading language), 299, 359
^ operator (shading language), 299–300, 359

A

abs() function, 312
absorption, 2–3
The Abyss, 387
acos() function, 312
aggregate objects, 31–33, 107–108
AimZ() program, 142–143, 144
aliasing
    defined, 174
    filtering and, 10, 173, 174–175
    jittering and, 175
    literature on, 191
    point sampling and, 173, 174
    reducing, 348–349
    See also motion blur
alpha
    storing in pixels, 156, 173–174
    See also opacity
ambient() function
    declaration of, 315
    illuminance construct and, 303–304
ambient light sources, 218–219, 303–304, 315
ambient light source shader, 218–219
    definition of, 337–338
ambient reflection, 228, 229, 230
analog signal processing, textbooks on, 191
anamorphic wide-screen movie formats, image distortion of, 161
animation
    defined, 33
    examples, 387

simple program, 33–34
    See also frames
anti-aliasing. *See* aliasing
aperture, 5, 8
approximating curved surfaces, 193
    determining quality of approximation, 171–172
    See also parametric surfaces; programs, for surface of revolution generation; quadric surfaces
area() function, declaration of, 327
area light sources, 224–225
area light source shader, 224–225, 307–308
arithmetic, on special data types, 298
array data type, 41
asin() function, 312
aspect ratios
    frame aspect ratio, 153, 158–159, 166
        default, 166
        enforced, 161–163
    image aspect ratio, 157–159
    as option, 45–46
    pixel aspect ratio,
        default, 156, 166
        specifying, 139, 156–157, 166
atan() function, 312
atmosphere shaders. *See* volume (atmosphere) shaders
atmospheric effects
    natural images and, 3–4, 233
    rendered images and, 7, 210, 233–236
    See also volume (atmosphere) shaders
attribute blocks
    aggregate objects and, 108
    defined, 47

checkerboard surface shader, definition of, 345–346

children (hierarchical), defined, 109

Ci (global variable), 292, 296

CIE XYZ color representation, 289

Cl (global variable), 292, 296

clamp() function, 312

clamping, defined, 183

clearing
    current transformation, 116–117, 143
    viewing transformation, 143

clipping planes, 145–146

clockwise order, vertex specification in, 19

closed objects, defined, 118

clouds surface shader, 282–285

coherence, of surfaces, 59

color
    as attribute, 46
    constant, 18, 215, 232, 334, 362–363
    current color, 44, 213
    default, 22
    global variable for, 292, 294
    light and, 2–3
    nonlinear encoding of, 179–180
    quantization of, 173, 182–184
        transforming before, 181
    of reflections, 226–227
    representation of, 8–9, 42–43, 156, 173,
        226–227, 244, 289
        default, 43
    shading and, 6
    specifying, 22–23, 42–43, 213, 227, 343–349
    See also pixels

ColorCube() program, 29–32, 33

color data type, 281, 284, 289
    arithmetic on, 298
    comparison of, 299
    cross product of, 299–300
    dot product of, 299

coloring, images, 22–23

coloring functions
    accessing color components, 330–331
    color mixing, 331
    shading, coloring and lighting functions,
        315–319

color separations, 181

color space
    monochromatic, 43
    multi-channel, 42–43

commutative object declaration, 27

comp() function, declaration of, 330–331

composite objects. *See* aggregate objects

composite solid objects. *See* Constructive Solid
    Geometry (CSG)

compound objects. *See* aggregate objects

computer-aided design (CAD), enhanced,
    RenderMan and, 386

computer graphics. *See* graphics (computer)

concave polygons, 69–70

cones
    declaring, 62–63
    defined, 60
    parameter space of, 246–247
    as special case of hyperboloids, 63–64

constant shading, 215

constant surface shader
    alternate, 362–363
    definition of, 334
    invoking, 18, 232
    purpose of, 232

Constructive Solid Geometry (CSG), 125–133
    declaring composite solid objects, 128–133
        difference operation, 126, 130–132
        intersection operation, 126, 128–130
        shading, 132–133
        union operation, 126, 130
    declaring solid objects, 126–127
    defined, 14, 110, 125–126
    programs,
        bowling ball generation, 131
        solid partial sphere and cylinder
            generation, 128–129
        solid surface of revolution generation,
            127

continue construct (shading language), 301

contrast, 173, 184

control constructs (shading language), 285,
    300–301

control hull. *See* geometry matrix; geometry
    vector

control points. *See* geometry matrix; geometry
    vector

convex polygons, 69–70

Cook, Rob, 237, 271, 285

coordinate systems, 52–53, 122–124
    axes of, as a three-dimensional cursor, 111
    conversion function, 329
    default system, 119
        for shading language, 291
    geometric transformations and, 122
    handedness of,

functions
- filter functions, 176–178
- in shading language,
    - color functions, 330–331
    - defining, 287–288
    - geometric functions, 325–330
    - map access functions, 319–324
    - mathematical functions, 311–314
    - print function, 332
    - shading, coloring and lighting functions, 315–319
    - *See also* **noise**() function; procedures; programs; shaders

G

Gaussian filter function, 176–178
general linear transformations, 115–116
geodesic dome program, 198–199, 200
geometric data, passing across the interface, 18
geometric functions, 325–330
- coordinate system conversion, 329
- differential surface area, 327
- distance between points, 327
- listed, 325
- point components, 326
- proportional reflection and refraction, 328–329
- refraction, 328
- relative depth, 329–330
- surface normal calculation, 330
- surface normal flipping, 328
- vector length, 326–327
- vector normalization, 327
geometric normal vector, global variable for, 293
geometric primitives. *See* primitive object types
geometric transformation environment
- bounding boxes, 124–125
- coordinate systems,
    - handedness of, 119–122
    - local coordinate systems, 109–110
    - named coordinate systems, 122–124
    - naming coordinate systems, 123
    - transforming an object's coordinate space into the current space, 123–124
- current transformation, 53, 109, 110–112
    - clearing, 116–117
    - marking as viewing transformation, 140–141
    - replacing, 117
- in- and out-facing surfaces, 118–119
- orientation, 119–122

See also geometric transformations; graphics environment
geometric transformations
- accumulating, 26–27
    - eliminating confusion arising from, 27–29
- data type for, 41
- defined, 21
- general linear transformations, 115–116
- general nonlinear transformations, 117–118
- interaction of, 23
- order of performing, 22, 140–141
- perspective transformations, 113–115
- rotation, 21–22, 26–27, 112
- scaling, 113
- skew transformations, 113
- stacking, 27–29
- translation, 21, 22, 112
- for viewing transformations, 142
- *See also* geometric transformation environment; transformation blocks
geometry. *See* Constructive Solid Geometry (CSG)
geometry matrix (control hull)
- for bicubic patches, 87, 88, 90, 92, 95
- for bicubic patch meshes, 95
geometry vector (control hull), for bicubic splines, 90
global coordinate system, mapping local coordinate systems to, 251
global variables, 284, 291–296
- listed, 292, 296
glowing surface shader, definition of, 368–370
gouged surface displacement shader
- definition of, 378, 379
- *See also* dented surface displacement shader; embossed surface displacement shader; pitted surface displacement shader
Gouraud shading, 214, 215
granite surface shader, definition of, 354
granularity, of viewing surfaces, 4
graphics (computer)
- camera models used in, 7–8
- three-dimensional, basic model of, 2
graphics environment (graphics state)
- aggregate objects and, 108
- attributes, 44, 46–47
- capabilities, 44–45
- defined, 23
- hierarchical nature of stack, 109

screen window's relationship to, 157–162, 166
size of, 146, 157
storing, 154–156, 160, 161
tilting, 152
imaging pipeline, 174, 175
incident cone, 302
incident vector, 226
inflection edge, defined, 363
initializing, graphics environment, 18
instance paradigm, defined, 31, 33
instance variables, 212, 283–284, 296–297
instancing
objects, 31, 110, 133–134
shader procedures, 211–212
integer data type, 41
integration, **illuminance** construct and, 305
intensities, ratio of, 173, 184
interior volume shaders, 235, 278
internal representation, 5
interpolation
basis of, 244–245
for bicubic patches and meshes, 245–246
for bilinear patches and meshes, 86–87, 245–246
linear, 86–87
motion blur and, 187–188
Phong interpolation, 73–75
for polygons, 248
for quadric surfaces, 246–247
shading and, 212, 215
See also variables
intersection operation (Constructive Solid Geometry), 126, 128–130

J

jaggies, 10, 174
jittering, 175

K

Knickknack, 387

L

L (global variable), 292, 296
label surface shader, definition of, 384
latitude-longitude environment map, creating, 263
leaves (hierarchical), defined, 109

left-handed coordinate systems, 119–122
left-handed rotation, 21, 112
length() function, declaration of, 326–327
lenses
depth of field of, 5
fisheye, field of view setting corresponding to, 150
as optical system, 4
telephoto, field of view setting corresponding to, 150
level of detail
calculating, 195–196
current, 195, 196
defined, 194, 195
overview of, 194
programs,
dissolving a crude model into a refined one, 200
geodesic dome, 198–199, 200
range of detail,
declaring, 197
meaning of, 197–198
smooth transition between alternatives, 199–200
relative, specifying, 196
using, 196–197
light
global variables for, 294
and natural images, 2–5
and rendered images,
calculating light travel, 5–6
exposure modeling, 179–180
hidden-surface elimination, 6, 54, 173
See also light sources; shading
light bulb shaders, 366–370, 374–375
light emission
model of, 306–307
natural images and, 2
rendered images and, 210
lighting functions, declaration of, 315–319
light source handles, 41, 216
light sources
ambient, 218–219, 303–304, 315
area, 224–225
defined, 6
distant, 20–21, 221
point, 221, 224, 339
positioning, 223–224
preparing, 20–21
rendering images without a light source, 18, 232, 362–363
surface appearance and orientation to, 73

patch and mesh parameter space, 245–248
polygon parameter space, 248
quadric surface parameter space, 246–247
surface shaders and, 242, 248
variables,
  extending the set of, 242–244
  predefined, listed, 243
  varying vs. uniform, 241–242
See also texture mapping
surface normal vector
  calculation function, 330
  defined, 73
  flat shading problem and, 73–77
  flipping function, 328
  orientation and, 119
  for parametric surfaces, 120, 258
  for polygons, 258
  for quadric surfaces, 119, 120, 258
  shading and, 226
surfaces
  attributes of, 44, 46, 47
  coherence of, 59
  controlling appearance of, key to, 248
  declaring, 53
  default appearance of, 23
  defined, 2
  inside and outside of, 119
  orientation of, 73
  sides of, specifying visible, 118–119
  variations in, visual interest and, 12
  See also parametric surfaces; polygons;
    quadric surfaces; shaders; shading
surface shaders, 225–233
  ambient reflection, 228, 229, 230
  blue-marble shader, 354–356
  bowling pin shaders, 375–378
  checkerboard shader, 345–347
  clouds shader, 282–285
  color of reflections, 226–227
  constant shader, 232, 334, 362–363
  diffuse reflection, 228, 229, 230, 231
  elements of surface shading, 226
  eroded surface shader, 352–353
  filament shader, 367–368
  functions that aid in writing, 315–319
  glow shader, 368–370
  granite shader, 354
  illuminance construct and, 302–305
  instancing, 211, 212
  invoking, 231–233
  mapping shader-space coordinates to
    colors, 347–348

mapping texture-space coordinates to
  colors, 344–345
matte shader, 22, 232, 334–336
metallic wire mesh shader, 348–349
metal shader, 232–233, 237, 336
  with environment map, 379–381
orientation-sensitive shading without a
  light source, 362–363
parameter space and, 248
pencil eraser shader, 385
pencil-labeling shader, 384
plastic shader, 233, 336–337, 348–349
  with texture map, 374
purpose of, 210, 225, 279–280
rubber shader, 385
specular reflection (mirror reflection), 226,
  228, 229, 230–231, 237
surface mapping and, 242, 244
types of reflection, 227–229
window highlight shader, 356–359
window light shader, 359–360, 361–362
wood-grain shader, 350, 351
surfaces of revolution
  approximating, 193
    determining quality of approximation,
      171–172
  types of, 60–61
  See also parametric surfaces; programs, for
    surface of revolution generation;
    quadric surfaces
SurfOR() program
  using bicubic patch mesh, 100, 101
    with wrapping, 101–103
  using hyperboloids, 64–65
    with texturing, 255–256
sweep angle, 60
  of hyperboloids, 64
synthetic camera. *See* camera (virtual)
synthetic rendering. *See* rendering

T

t (global variable), 292, 296
tan() function, 312
target raster, 166
telephoto lens, field of view setting corresponding to, 150
template, for standard programs, 54–55
temporal aliasing. *See* motion blur
tension, of curves, 92
terrain data, compact representation for, 246
TextSurfOR() program, 255–256

defined, 103, 249
two-dimensional coordinate systems, 53
two-dimensional image, transforming three-dimensional scene to a, 137, 139, 146
two-dimensional nature, of viewing surfaces, 4

U

u (global variable), 292, 296
u (direction), 92
uniform non-rational patches. *See* bicubic patches; bicubic patch meshes; bilinear patches; bilinear patch meshes
uniform variables, 212, 242, 244
    in shading language, 297, 313
union operation (Constructive Solid Geometry), 126, 130
UnitCube() program, 23–29, 30–31
unit cubes
    animating, 33–34
    defining, 24–29, 80, 81
    defining color, 29–32
    ninety-degree perspective transform on, 114–115
unit square, 123

V

v (global variable), 292, 296
v (direction), 92
variables
    extending the set of, 242–244
    predefined, 243–244
    in shading language,
        global, 284, 291–296
        instance variables, 212, 283–284, 296–297
        local, 284, 297
        uniform, 297, 313
        varying, 297, 313
    uniform, 212, 242, 244
    varying, 212, 242, 244
    See also tokens
vector data types, 41
vectorized versions of procedures, 40
vectors
    geometric normal vector, global variable for, 293
    halfway vector, 226
    incident vector, 226
    length function, 326–327
    normalization function, 327

shading normal vector, global variable for, 293
    See also surface normal vector
vertices
    defined, 19, 69
    of polygonal curved surfaces, flat shading problem and, 71–78
    specifying,
        order of, 19
        for polygons, 19, 70, 78–79
        for polyhedra, 79–80, 82–83
view
    default, 19–20, 139
    defining parameters, 21–22
        boilerplate program for, 138–141
        improved boilerplate program for, 167–169
    options, 45
    viewpoint scenes are rendered from, 141
    See also camera (virtual)
viewer
    changing the, 21–22
    defined, 2, 4
    light and, 2, 4
viewing devices, natural images and, 4
viewing direction, defined, 141
viewing location, defined, 141
viewing pyramid, 114
viewing surfaces
    natural images and, 4, 9
    rendered images and, 8–9
viewing transformation, 141–142
    clearing, 143
    marking current transformation as the, 140–141
    simple program for, 142–145
    See also current transformation
virtual camera. *See* camera (virtual)
visible sides of surfaces, specifying, 119
visual artifacts, natural images and, 4–5
visual interest
    level of detail and, 194
    sources of, 12, 274
volume, defined, 234–235
volume (atmosphere) shaders, 233–237
    default, 235
    depth-cue shader, 236, 237, 341–342
    fog shader, 236–237, 342–343
    instancing, 212
    interior/exterior, 235, 278
    purpose of, 210, 233235, 236, 278

specifying, 235
See also shading language

W

while construct (shading language), 301
white, specifying the color, 22, 227
window highlight shader, definition of,
      356–359
windowing onto a display, 161
window light shader, definition of, 359–360,
      361–362
window of evaluation. *See* evaluation window
      (bicubic patch mesh)
wire mesh surface shader, definition of, 348–349
wood-grain surface shader, definition of, 350,
      351
world, describing the, 18, 48–49
world blocks, 48–49
    nesting, 48, 109
    retained models and, 133, 134
    as root of object hierarchy, 109
    within frame blocks, 51, 133
world space, 52, 53, 116, 123
    returning local coordinate system to, 117
    texture space not uniform in, 346–347
    transforming to camera space, 141–142,
        144–145
worn surface displacement shader, definition of,
      350–352
wrapping, bicubic patch meshes, 98, 100–103

X

xcomp() function, declaration of, 326

Y

ycomp() function, declaration of, 326

Z

zcomp() function, declaration of, 326

Credits and Production Notes

Picture Credits

Mike Malione of Pixar designed the images and wrote the shaders for Plates 1, 2, 4, 10 and 11. Steve Upstill created the teapots and light bulbs of Plates 3, 7, 8, and 9. Thomas Porter modeled the bowling pin of Plate 12 as part of the cover image *Textbook Strike*, also reproduced in Plate 23. The three labels at the top and left of Plate 13 are courtesy of Brunswick Corporation and the American Bowling Congress. The texture map at the lower right is digitally painted. Darwyn Peachey of Pixar designed the room of Plate 15 and its environment maps shown in Plate 14. The couch and chair were modeled by Eben Ostby. Malcolm Blanchard of Pixar created the pencils and ferrules of Plates 16 and 17. Malcolm used a standard AutoCAD scene description courtesy of Autodesk and attached shading attributes to create Plate 18. Malcolm collaborated with CAD-KEY to produce the guitar of Plate 20. The guitar started out as wire frame data, and was converted to a solid by CADKEY SOLIDS. Kevin Bjorke of deGraf/Wahrman used AutoCAD data to produce the gears of Plate 19. Mike Malione collaborated with TASC to produce the movie projector of Plate 21.

The Pixar Animation Production Group created Plates 5, 6, 22, 24 and 25. John Lasseter, William Reeves, Eben Ostby, Flip Phillips, and Craig Good collaborated on the creation of these images. Plates 5 and 6 are taken from the 1988 film *Tin Toy*. Plate 22 is printed here courtesy of the National Geographic Society. Plate 24 is taken from the 1989 film *Luxo Jr. in "Light Entertainment,"* and Plate 25 is from the 1989 film *Knickknack*.

Plate 26 is a frame from the "pseudopod" sequence in the motion picture *The Abyss*, created by Industrial Light and Magic using Alias modeling and animation software, RenderMan rendering software and a variety of proprietary software tools. Modeling, animation and rendering was performed on Silicon Graphics workstations, and compositing was performed on Pixar Image Computers. The image is provided by Industrial Light and Magic, a division of Lucasfilm, Ltd., and is courtesy of GJP Inc. All rights reserved.

All color plates were rendered using Pixar's Photorealistic RenderMan software. Pixar color plates were collected and recorded on film by Don Conway.

Cover Image

Textbook Strike was created by Thomas Porter of Pixar. The RenderMan interface was used to describe the scene, and Pixar's Photorealistic RenderMan software computed it. Reflections, shadows, motion blur, surface texture and displacements are all incorporated.

The image includes three light sources and only twelve objects, though each carries complex shading attributes. The shading procedure for the bowling pins, for example, details the coloration of the plastic, applies three scanned color textures for the labels and a painted displacement texture for the marks and gouges. Source code for setting up both the geometry and visual attributes of the image is provided throughout the book.

Darwyn Peachey and Tony Apodaca of the RenderMan staff provided a great deal of technical guidance and programming assistance in the rendering of the image. Flip Phillips of the Animation staff provided crucial help in directing the framing and dynamics of the image.

The image was computed at a resolution of 3072 x 2304 and scanned onto film using a MacDonald Dettwiler Color Fire 240.

Production Notes

The text of this book was originally written using Microsoft Word 3.0 on a Macintosh Plus. Camera-ready copy was produced using FrameMaker software (version 1.3) on a Sun 3/50 workstation. We used Adobe's Palatino font for text, Optima for code and headings, and Helvetica for illustration labels.

The raster images generated by example programs were produced by compiling and running the examples. Other gray-scale illustrations were modeled in the Menv modeling language and fine-tuned using the modeling and animation tools of Pixar's Animation Production Group. All were rendered by the RenderMan Interface driving Pixar's PhotoRealistic RenderMan rendering software. Once rendered, all gray-scale imagery was converted to FrameMaker's Encapsulated PostScript format (EPSF) and imported into FrameMaker.

Line art was created with Adobe Illustrator 88 on a Macintosh Plus, converted into EPSF, and imported into FrameMaker. Illustrations combining line art and raster images were produced by converting the raster images into Encapsulated PostScript, then PICT format for use as an Illustrator template. High-resolution raster imagery was later substituted into the resulting EPSF file for production.

FrameMaker's PostScript output was directed to a file, transferred to floppy disks, and output on a Linotronic 300 using a 120-line screen.